2010 California Biennial

Curated by Sarah C. Bancroft

Orange County Museum of Art
Newport Beach, California

DelMonico Books • Prestel
Munich London New York

This catalog was published on the occasion of the 2010 California Biennial, organized and presented by the Orange County Museum of Art, Newport Beach, California, October 24, 2010– March 13, 2011.

The 2010 California Biennial is sponsored by

Deutsche Bank

Major support for the California Biennial catalog is provided by the Segerstrom Foundation.

Significant support for the exhibition is provided by Barbara and Victor L. Klein, with additional support from Moira and Fred Kamgar, Toby Devan Lewis, and the Nimoy Foundation.

Special thanks to the San Diego Jewish Community Foundation for additional project support.

Media support is provided by The Armory Show, X-TRA, and KPCC 89.3 Southern California Public Radio

ISBN: 978-3-7913-5119-3

Published by the
Orange County Museum of Art
850 San Clemente Drive
Newport Beach, California 92660
USA
Tel +1 949-759-1122
Fax +1 949-759-5623
www.ocma.net

In association with DelMonico Books,
an imprint of Prestel
Prestel is a member of Verlagsgruppe Random House GmbH

Prestel Verlag
Neumarkter Strasse 28
81673 Munich
Germany
Tel 49 89 242908 300
Fax 49 89 242908 335
prestel.de

Prestel Publishing Ltd.
4 Bloomsbury Place
London WC1A 2QA
United Kingdom
Tel 44 20 7323 5004
Fax 44 20 7636 8004

Prestel Publishing
900 Broadway, Suite 603
New York, NY 10003
Tel 212 995 2720
Fax 212 995 2733
sales@prestel-usa.com
prestel.com

Project manager: Anna Brouwer
Editor: Karen Jacobson
Designer: Brian Roettinger, Hand Held Heart
Principal photographer: Joshua White
Prepress and printing: Shapco, Minneapolis

Cover:
Zlatan Vukosavljevic
DuckBunny Chamber, 2010 (detail)—cat. no. 129

Inside cover:
Stanya Kahn
Still from *It's Cool, I'm Good*, 2010—cat. no. 83

4 Foreword **Dennis Szakacs**

6 Sponsor's Statement **Deutsche Bank**

8 Curator's Acknowledgments **Sarah C. Bancroft**

10 Introduction: Curating the 2010 California Biennial **Sarah C. Bancroft**

16 **David Adey**

20 **Agitprop**

24 **Gil Blank**

28 **Nate Boyce**

32 **Luke Butler**

36 **Juan Capistran**

40 **Zoe Crosher**

44 **Brian Dick**

48 **Dru Donovan**

52 **Mari Eastman**

56 **Electronic Disturbance Theater/b.a.n.g. lab**

60 **Carlee Fernandez**

64 **Finishing School**

68 **Eve Fowler**

74 **Rebecca Goldfarb**

78 **Katy Grannan**

82 **Alexandra Grant**

86 **Sherin Guirguis**

90 **Drew Heitzler**

94 **Violet Hopkins**

98 **Alex Israel**

102 **Glenna Jennings**

106 **Barry Macgregor Johnston**

110 **Vishal Jugdeo**

114 **Stanya Kahn**

118 **Andy Kolar**

122 **Jennifer Locke**

126 **Los Angeles Urban Rangers**

130 **Tom Mueske**

134 **Tucker Nichols**

138 **Camilo Ontiveros**

142 **Nikki Pressley**

146 **Andy Ralph**

150 **Will Rogan**

154 **Paul Schiek**

158 **Taravat Talepasand**

162 **Wu Tsang**

166 **Zlatan Vukosavljevic**

170 **Nina Waisman**

174 **Flora Wiegmann**

178 **Allison Wiese**

182 **Lisa Williamson**

186 **David Wilson**

190 **Patrick Wilson**

194 **John Zurier**

198 Installation Map

199 Works in the Exhibition

Foreword

The 2010 California Biennial is the fourth edition of the exhibition under my directorship of the museum. During this time the biennial has become a cornerstone of the museum's programming, supporting young and emerging artists when they need it most and providing audiences in Southern California with the opportunity to learn about the latest developments in art. Just over the last decade, the biennial exhibitions and publications, as well as the addition to our collection of works by participating artists, have provided a singular record of new art produced in one of the world's great creative centers and already serve as a major historical compendium of artistic activity statewide. We are in fact securing the future for our art and artists, and I can point to few activities as powerful or as meaningful to pursue. In little more than twenty-five years, the documentation provided by the biennials will be essential to scholars, art historians, and curators worldwide; by the end of the century it will constitute an invaluable artistic resource for future generations seeking to understand our time, our place, and our culture. This is what we are working toward, and it is this kind of clear-eyed emphasis on the long view that only museums can provide—if they are nimble and agile enough to engage with the present over a sustained period of time. Supporters of the California Biennial understand this, and our staff, members, and visitors experience it each time we present a new biennial. We are all engaged in the exhilarating and provocative process of making history now.

Curator Sarah Bancroft has done an outstanding job of organizing the 2010 California Biennial. Her research has led the biennial into several new areas, including increased representation of artists from San Diego and San Francisco. This edition of the biennial also includes far more artists without commercial gallery representation than its predecessors. I also offer my sincere thanks to adjunct curator Karen Moss for her early work with the artists' residencies for the biennial, and to Anna Brouwer, publications manager, who did an excellent job of developing and overseeing this catalog.

The Orange County Museum of Art is able to maintain a commitment to the biennial exhibitions over time thanks to the vision and support of its Board of Trustees, led by Craig Wells. We extend our deep appreciation to this dedicated group of community leaders for helping the museum sustain its focus on the art of today.

A very special thank-you goes to Deutsche Bank for its leadership and support as the presenting corporate sponsor of the California Biennial since 2004. Deutsche Bank has supported and engaged in the development of contemporary art across the globe for more than two decades, and we are proud that our museum and the biennial are part of this significant effort. We offer many thanks to Alessandra Digiusto, director of the Deutsche Bank Americas Foundation; Liz Christensen, curator of Deutsche Bank Art, DB Americas; Ana Zamora, vice president, events, Deutsche Bank Trust Company Americas; Michael J. Davis, head of Western Region, US Private Bank; and trustee Craig Wells, managing director, Deutsche Bank National Trust Company.

We are especially grateful to the Segerstrom Foundation for continuing its legacy of support for the museum's most important publications through an underwriting gift for the production of this catalog. We are indebted to Barbara and Victor L. Klein and Toby Devan Lewis for returning as key benefactors of the biennial and the work of emerging artists, and to Moira and Fred Kamgar for joining this important group of underwriters. We gratefully acknowledge the support of the Nimoy Foundation, which has continued to sponsor the artist residencies that are vital to this exhibition. For additional project support, we extend our thanks to the San Diego Jewish Community Foundation. We are also grateful to our media sponsors: The Armory Show, X-TRA, and KPCC Radio.

We offer our sincere gratitude to the lenders to the exhibition, who graciously parted with works from their collections: Art Now International, Michael Frank Black, Collection Goya Contemporary, JoAnne Colonna and James Acheson, Crowell & Moring LLP, Siri Kaur, Christopher Kronner, Scott London, the Los Angeles County Museum of Art, the Miller Meigs Collection, the Museum of Contemporary Art San Diego, Jennifer and Manfred Simchowitz, and Arnd F. Stockhausen.

California Biennial catalogs serve as permanent documents of the development of contemporary art in the state. We are delighted to be partnering with DelMonico Books·Prestel as distributor of this catalog; this collaboration will undoubtedly allow for greater visibility for the artists in the exhibition.

The entire staff of the museum has contributed to the success of the biennial, and I join curator Sarah Bancroft in thanking the curatorial staff members who have lent their considerable talents to the realization of this exhibition. I also thank exhibitions and collections manager Anna-Marie Sanchez, who ensured the safe and timely arrival of all the art, and director of operations Albert Lopez for his attention to all aspects of the installation. Director of marketing and communications Kirsten Schmidt, assistant director of marketing and communications Chivan Wang, and advertising and promotions manager Amanda Conley deserve special recognition for their tireless efforts to promote the exhibition. I am also grateful to director of education and public programs Lisa Silagyi and her team—Jenni Stenson, Kelly Bishop, and Dorothy McClelland—for their work on the education and public programs that are a key part of the biennial. Director of development Patricia Falzon and development staff Bridget Jesionowski, Kristen Sweetland, and Darcy Ruesch were integral to the fund-raising for the exhibition and the organization of special events. I likewise thank deputy director Glenn Peters for his administrative oversight and director of finance Paulette Gibson and senior accountant Kelly Smith for their attention to the exhibition.

Finally, our warmest appreciation and thanks go to all the artists in the 2010 California Biennial. The California Biennial is ultimately about the vision of the artists and their essential role in our culture. We are honored to collaborate with them and to bring their voices and unique perspectives to a broader public.

Dennis Szakacs
Director, Orange County Museum of Art

Sponsor's Statement

Deutsche Bank is proud to sponsor the 2010 California Biennial. Deutsche Bank has long been an ardent supporter of the arts and has always viewed its commitment to culture as a core value in being a responsible corporate citizen. On the walls of our offices from Frankfurt to New York to Singapore, you will find some fifty thousand works of contemporary art, one of the largest and most comprehensive corporate art collections in the world. We believe in supporting artists in the communities where we do business.

Deutsche Bank believes that promoting art and culture—through museum sponsorships, artist commissions, and economic revitalization programs for the arts—is an important way to give back to communities where the Bank does business. As a long-standing patron of new art, and an ongoing partner with the Orange County Museum of Art, Deutsche Bank is proud to once again support the California Biennial.

Michael J. Davis
Head of Western Region/US Private Bank
Deutsche Bank Private Wealth Management

Deutsche Bank 

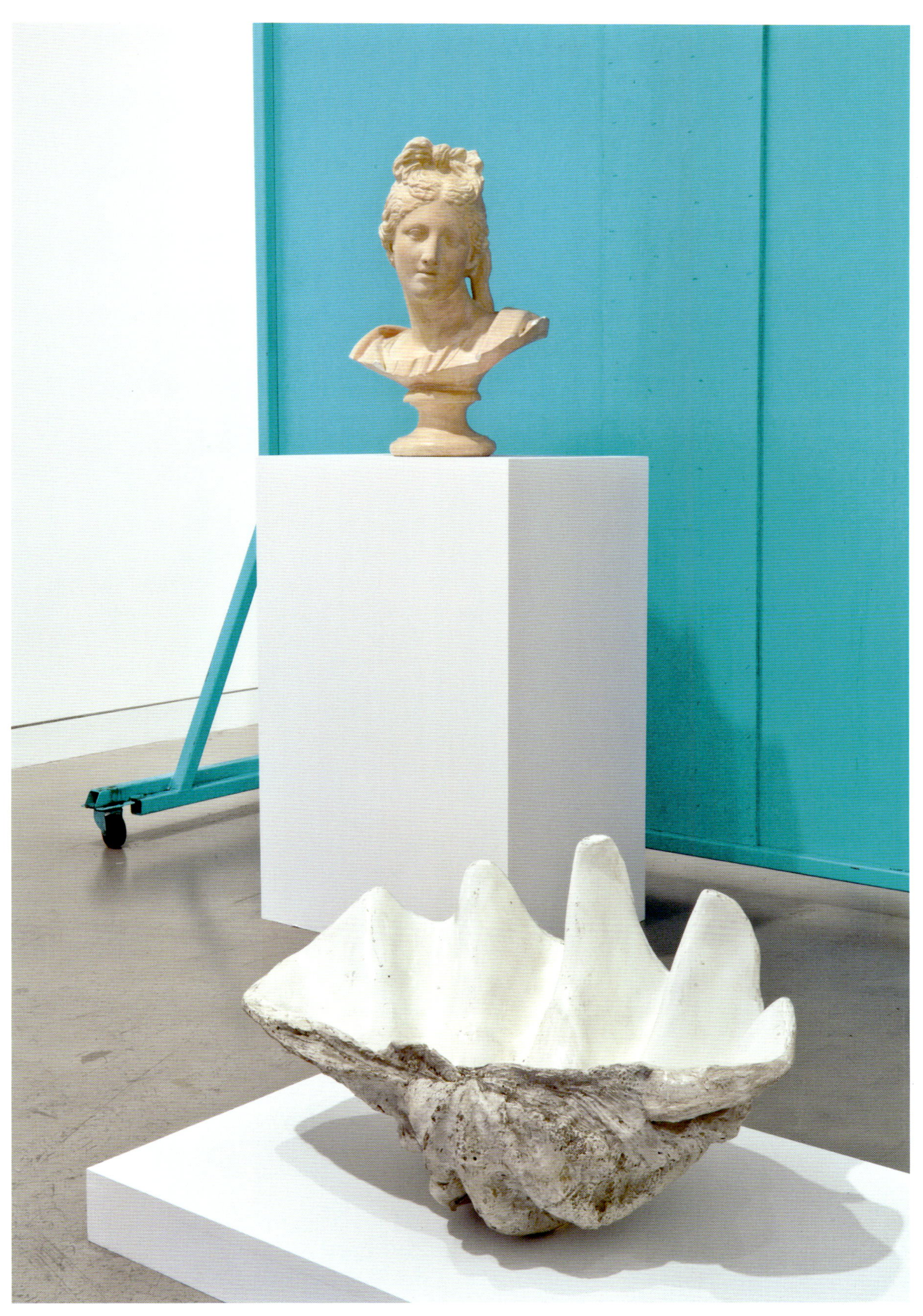

Alex Israel
Property, **2010** — cat. no. 73
Installation view with *Diana* (cat. no. 73M) and *Venus* (cat. no. 73N)

Curator's Acknowledgments

The 2010 California Biennial came to fruition with the support and assistance of numerous individuals and entities. First, I must acknowledge the artists with whom I have had the privilege and joy to work. Thank you. This biennial is foremost your exhibition, a forum for your work and ideas, and it has been my pleasure to compose it with you. To my institution, the Orange County Museum of Art, and its director, Dennis Szakacs, who gave me the freedom to develop the exhibition, as well as to its trustees, who ensure that the museum remains a vital place for presenting art, I am grateful.

Many of my colleagues and professional contacts were instrumental in bringing to my attention artists whom I might not otherwise have encountered. Indeed, there are many more individuals who generously and enthusiastically recommended artists than I could possibly list here. In San Diego, Lucia Sanroman and Michael Krichman were particularly significant sources of information and insight. In San Francisco, Tara McDowell, Julio Cesar Morales, Margaret Tedesco, and others were exceptionally helpful. In Los Angeles, suggestions poured in from innumerable sources—more than I was able to follow up on. Pilar Tompkins, Lauri Firstenberg, Aram Moshayedi, and others, thank you for your generous insights. Many vital recommendations of artists to consider came courtesy of other artists; these proved to be especially important introductions to emerging artists without gallery representation. I am grateful to Edgar Arceneaux, Gil Blank, Andrea Bowers, Jedediah Caesar, Katy Grannan, Drew Heitzler, Stanya Kahn, and many others for their suggestions. Of course, sincere thanks go to the galleries that supported in small and large ways the artists in the exhibition, in particular Thomas Solomon for support of Vishal Jugdeo's installation and Foxy Production, which provided framing for Violet Hopkins's newest cave drawing.

Within the museum, a team of curatorial associates and interns was crucial to the success of the exhibition. Curatorial associates Stacie Martinez and Fatima Manalili and former curatorial associate Glenn Bach all aided and abetted the development and realization of the biennial. The exhibition also benefited greatly from the contributions of our enthusiastic and exceptional biennial interns: Chloë Flores, Katherine Lukacher, Chris Martinez, and Grant Wahlquist.

The catalog interviews were greatly enhanced by the efforts, insights, and distinct voices and perspectives of Anna Brouwer, Chloë Flores, Katherine Lukacher, Stacie Martinez, Karen Moss, and Grant Wahlquist. The catalog itself and more aspects of the exhibition than I can list here were deftly, superbly, and professionally managed by Anna Brouwer, who has served as my biggest supporter in this process (whether she knows it or not). Karen Jacobson edited the catalog, and the numerous artist interviews within, with prowess and precision. I am most grateful for her collaboration. Catalog designer Brian Roettinger brought his exceptional vision and sensibility to the project, and his receptiveness to the artists and their work is especially appreciated. This volume was also immeasurably enriched by Joshua White's stellar photography of the artworks and installations in the exhibition.

I join Director Dennis Szakacs in thanking our exhibition sponsors, whose commitment and support are so vital to continued artistic expression and exploration, as well as the many generous lenders to the exhibition. Likewise, the combined efforts of multiple museum departments have made this biennial possible. My colleagues in marketing, education, development, registration, facilities, finance, and visitor services have my enduring and immense gratitude.

A remarkable marshaling of aesthetic, collegial, artistic, and institutional forces has contributed to the realization of the 2010 California Biennial. I express my heartfelt gratitude to the artists and my colleagues for their unwavering involvement and support, and I offer sincere apologies and thanks to anyone I have overlooked.

With the artists and all those whose combined efforts have made this exhibition a reality, I share any measure of its success.

Sarah C. Bancroft

DEAR BIENNIAL FRIEND,

ON THE NIGHT OF OCT 23rd ON THE OCCASION
OF SO MANY FINE CALIFORNIA VOICES SHARING
A BIT OF THEIR SONGS UNDER ONE ROOF, ON
THE OCCASION OF THE FULL MOON, YOU ARE
INVITED TO JOIN IN FOR A POST OPENING, GROUP
WALK FROM THE MUSEUM TO A HIDDEN DANCEHALL

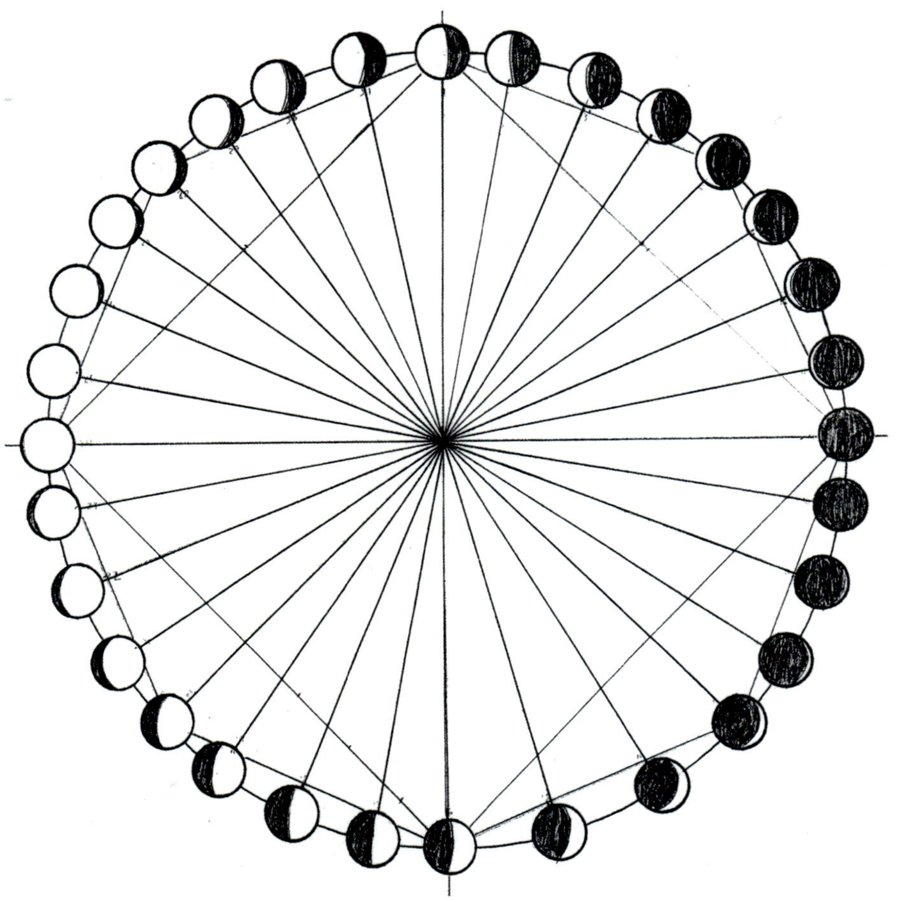

TUCKED AWAY WITHIN A FORGOTTEN STRETCH OF
WOODS FOR A MOONLIT DANCE. GRAB A SET OF
DIRECTIONS FROM DAVID WILSON'S INSTALLATION.
AT 10PM EITHER WALK ON YOUR OWN OR MEET
IN FRONT OF THE MUSEUM AND ENJOY A GROUP
PROCESSION TO THE PLACE. IT IS A 12 MIN WALK
SO LEAVE THE CARS BEHIND AND MAYBE HAVE COMFY
SHOES. LET'S SHARE A FULL MOON MOMENT ALL TOGETHER.
XOX   FOR   FUN.   XOX

David Wilson (Ribbons)
Invitation to **Walk to the Place Gathering, 2010** (back)
Courtesy of the artist

Introduction: Curating the 2010 California Biennial

Sarah C. Bancroft

Visiting the 2010 Whitney Biennial this past spring, I overheard two visitors discussing the exhibition.

> "Did you like it?"
> "No, I think it's awful!"
> "Why? Did something offend you?"
> "No, I'm just insulted by how bad the work is."

I laughed, reminded after having lived in New York for more than ten years that people approach the exhibition with equal parts excitement and low expectations. Indeed, people love to hate the Whitney Biennial. Yet we keep on going, keep on looking, and quietly we find work to enjoy amid the voices of dissent and the cacophony of criticism.

For the curator of the California Biennial, this may be somewhat disheartening. After all, what is a biennial? How and why does one choose an artist, a coherent group of artists? Can any one biennial capture the flavor and pulse of artists working across the state? Will looking at various biennials over time reveal more specific trends, focuses, and occurrences in the state, or will it simply highlight the varied interests, strengths, lacunae, or weaknesses within the curators' disparate visions? And how in the world does one begin the enormous task of *taking* the pulse of the emerging artists and trends throughout California?

As I am a relative newcomer—I moved to California in the spring of 2008 to begin work as curator at the Orange County Museum of Art—the development of the 2010 California Biennial has been a mission of discovery. Arriving with no allegiances or acquired biases, relatively ignorant of the many cliques and groups that define the larger Los Angeles art community, and with no predefined "program" to endorse, I set out quietly exploring, with an open mind. One doesn't know what the field of artists looks like until one walks through it, so I didn't discriminate across media or define in advance what I was looking for. I just got down to the task of visiting as many artists across the state as I physically could. And the whole time I kept asking myself: "So what am I going to do? What shall this biennial be?"

A group exhibition may be defined by a theme from the outset, but whereas thematic exhibitions require curators to cast artists in roles according to the scripts that we write for our exhibitions, a biennial offers the opportunity to respond to what is happening. For the 2010 California Biennial, there is no overriding theme other than the goal of capturing a compelling variety of artists and art practices across the state today. I compiled lists of artists whose work I had seen or read about or who were recommended by other artists and curatorial colleagues. The list included several hundred artists and collectives who have contributed something of note to the scene.

After researching each one, I developed a shorter list of nearly 150 artists and collectives with whom I would arrange studio visits. These studio visits informed my choices for the biennial, a selection of artists who represent the strength and diversity of practices across the state and whom I think people should be aware of, pay attention to, and watch going forward.

The studio visits were arduous and wholly satisfying. I traveled via plane, bus, subway, and bike; by car and boat; and on foot. The visits took me down dirt roads and to strip malls and campuses, urban centers and suburban neighborhoods, galleries and garages, lofts and living rooms, residency programs and cafés, independent art spaces and fabricators' shops. No visit lasted less than an hour. Some ideas, concepts, or approaches seeped out more slowly than others during these visits; some artists are quite articulate in explaining or presenting their work, and for others the artwork does most of the communicating. The artists I met with and the studios I visited extended from north of San Francisco to south of the border in Tijuana.

There came a moment in every studio visit when the artist or group would offer a sentence, a phrase, a statement that served as a summary, a catalyst, a hinge in my understanding of the work. This was a moment of clarity, when the practice was crystallized by words that I have since used to remember the artists and their work. These comments remain signposts for me, my own personal collection of ideas and statements.

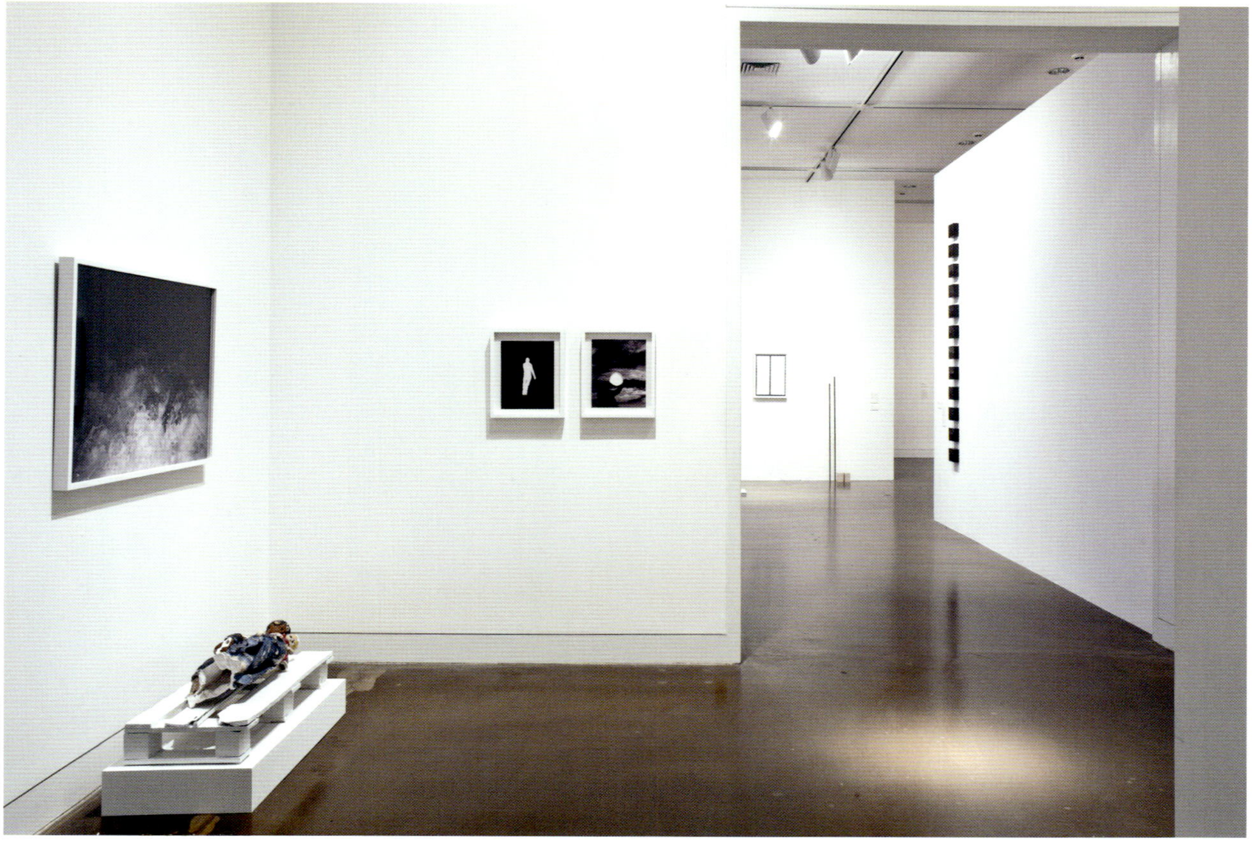

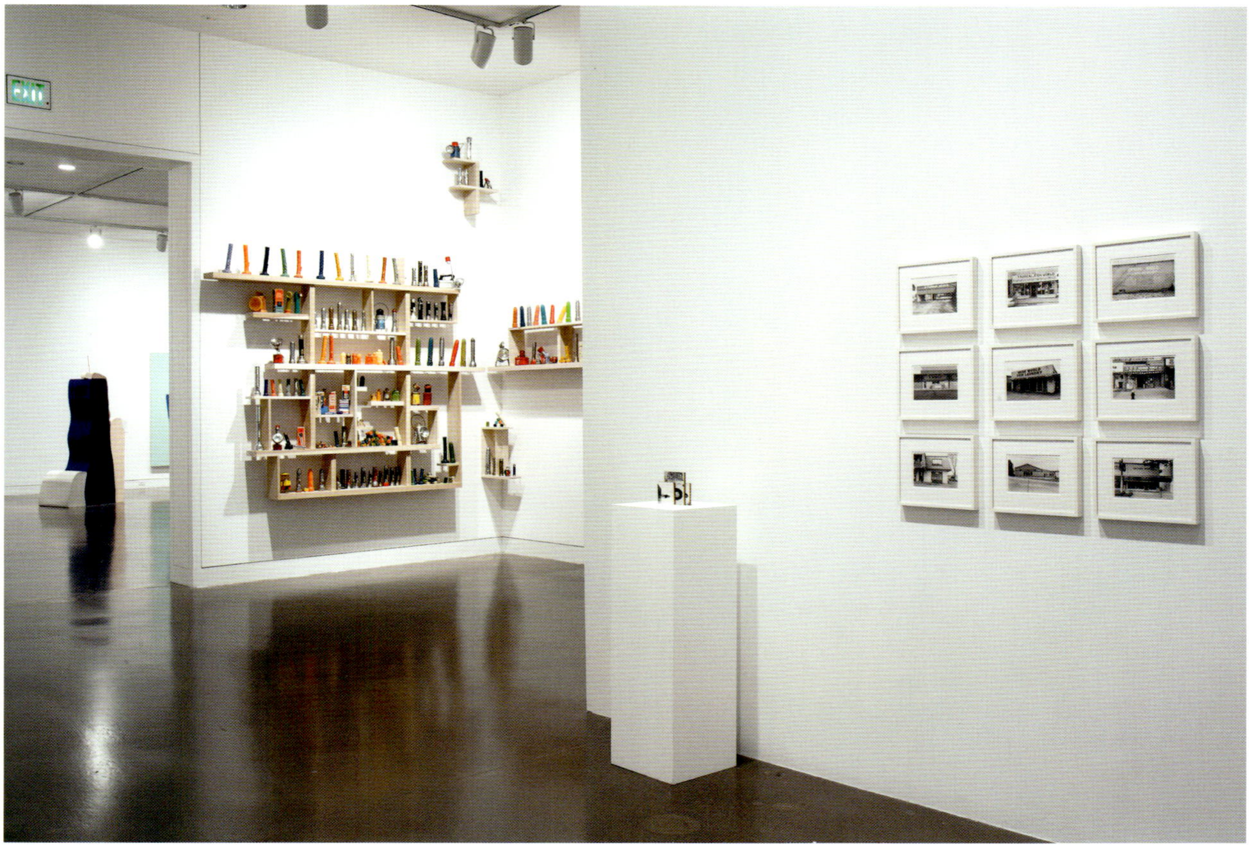

Installation views, 2010 California Biennial
Top: Paul Schiek, Lisa Williamson, Gil Blank
Bottom: Andy Kolar, Rebecca Goldfarb, Will Rogan

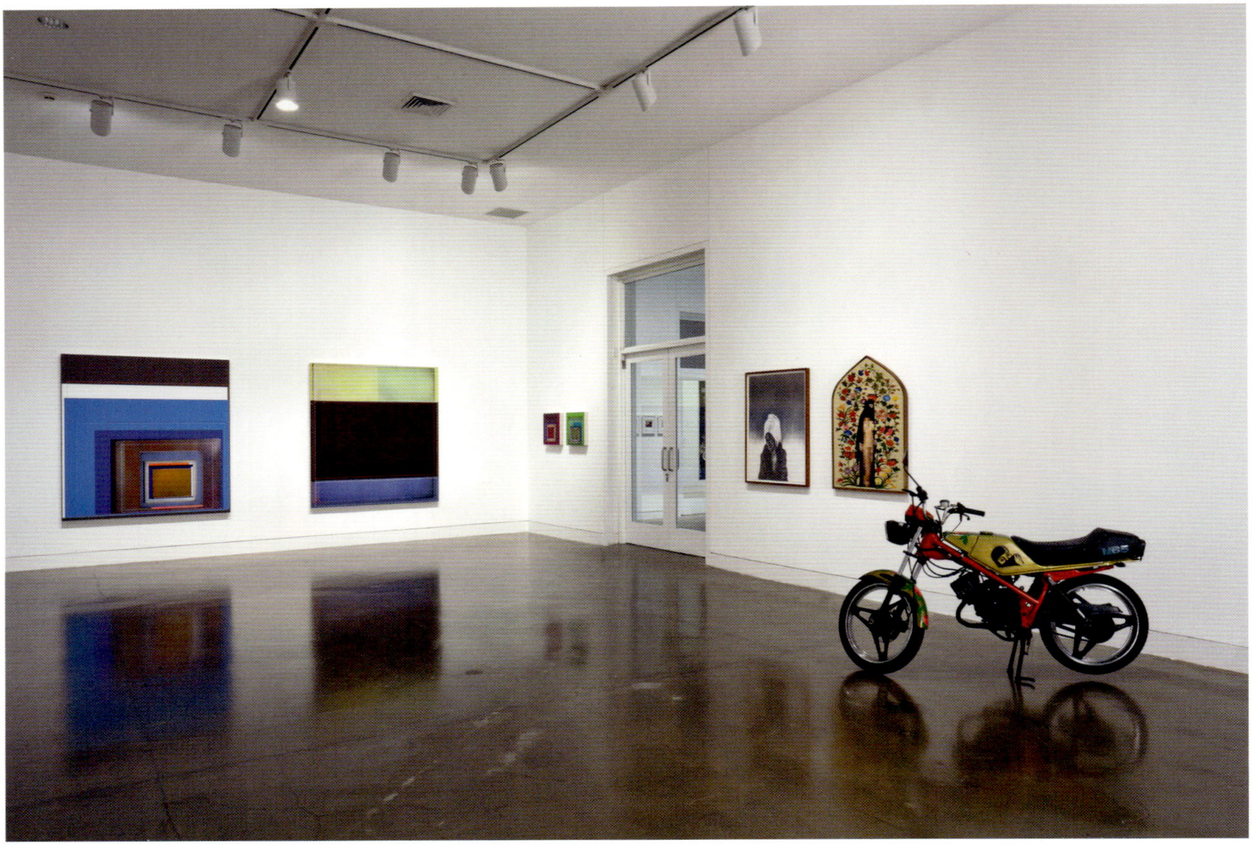

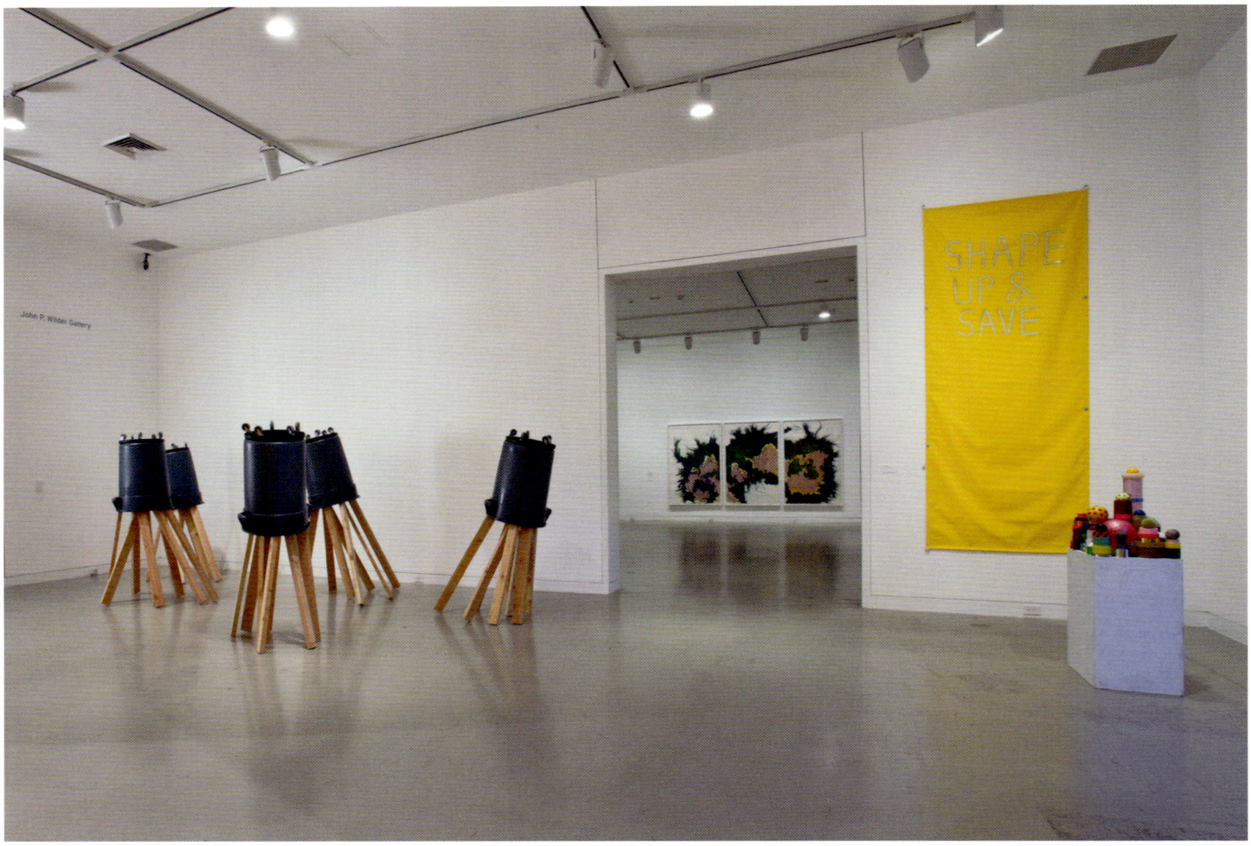

Installation views, 2010 California Biennial
Top: Patrick Wilson, Taravat Talepasand
Bottom: Andy Ralph, Sherin Guirguis, Tucker Nichols

It was immediately apparent that certain artists and collaborative groups would be included in the biennial. In other cases, the memory of the studio visit worked on me for weeks or for a couple of months before I came to a decision. In either case, the work, concept, or motivation may be unattractive; it may be disturbing or disconcert the visitor. It might push my buttons or yours. This doesn't mean that it should not be exhibited; it simply means that some viewers may not want to live with it at home. Artwork in an institution serves different purposes and can achieve different goals than work in a domestic setting. Perhaps this is why some "civilians" find museums so difficult. We curators often speak to an in crowd, people whose language we share—art historians, artists, gallerists, writers, critics, and colleagues. But we are working to bring crucial, new, or underrecognized work to a larger audience, to share, to offer something to consider. Not everything will appeal to everyone's sensibilities, politics, and desires. The goal is to keep looking and to keep the visitor looking.

What is the sum of this undertaking, of this biennial? When the final list of forty-five artists and collectives to be represented in the biennial was confirmed in May 2010, there were twenty-three living and working in greater Los Angeles and Orange County, thirteen practicing in the Bay Area, and nine from the greater San Diego area. (Since that time, an artist from San Francisco and another from San Diego have relocated to Los Angeles.) The presentation includes emerging artists (many without gallery representation), as well as a selection of established and midcareer artists who have presented discrete bodies of work in the United States and abroad with a great deal of success yet remain underrecognized in California or in Southern California at present.

The biennial artists work in an extremely diverse array of practices: painting and drawing, film and video, multimedia installation, performance and dance, photography and photographic processes, sculpture, sound- and text-based work, and more. Although they all work in California, they are an international group, and their work touches on personal, local, national, and global themes. There are a number of artists who engage with identity through explorations of religion, race, sexual orientation, nationality, or heritage. There are others for whom politics and provocation are part of their

practice. There are particular works that explore questions of individual freedom versus national interest, creative expression versus notions of legality, and thereby engage with current debates on immigration policy in the border states of California and Arizona and across the Southwest. Play and humor are also at work, alongside kitsch. Abstraction and figuration still feature prominently in painting practices across the state. Performance and audience participation, local environments and global concerns, collections and typologies, accretion and ablation, memory and nostalgia, presentation and perception, whimsy and gravity, the body and the mind, experience and knowledge, and poetry and prose are all explored and on offer.

The exhibition has been organized both to convey a sense of place—what is happening in certain regions—and to present diverse practices thematically and by media. There are galleries devoted to works on paper, to photography, and to painting. There are discrete presentations that feature Bay Area– and San Diego–based practitioners. There are spaces dedicated to work by individual artists, and there is a gallery occupied by works that address the ideas of transcendence, travel, and passage in distinct ways.

Although it would be a challenge to neatly summarize what is happening in the state or in individual regions, there are compelling trends: San Diego has a considerable number of artists practicing sculpture, a phenomenon noted during my studio visits and reflected in the biennial. While planning the layout for this exhibition, I noticed a tendency to amass collections, create typologies, and explore variations among practitioners from the Bay Area, whether through sculpture, painting, photography, or process-based work. Los Angeles is home to many rigorous practitioners of large-scale installation and conceptual work who use video, text, objects, and even taxidermy. But of course these observations do not define the practices in these geographic areas; there are no hard-and-fast rules.

To organize an exhibition is ultimately to compose the galleries using other people's work, to create a visual, sensorial, intellectual experience for the visitors. Each part of the process leading up to this point is an act of faith, a speculative undertaking. There are many works that I will not have seen in finished form until the biennial is installed. Andy Ralph, Gil Blank, Juan Capistran, Zoe Crosher, Brian Dick, Carlee Fernandez, Rebecca Goldfarb, Drew Heitzler, Alex Israel, Barry Macgregor Johnston, Vishal Jugdeo, Andy Ralph, Zlatan Vukosavljevic, Nina Waisman, Flora Wiegmann, Allison Wiese, and Lisa Williamson are all creating new work or adapting existing installations that will be fully realized just before or during the installation period. Others will make work that operates during the course of the exhibition, fully activated and realized by the biennial visitors in some way, such as Finishing School's new participatory film, *54*, which they will shoot on-site and complete in Italy during the 2011 Venice Biennale. Flora Wiegmann will dance on thirteen occasions during the run of the biennial, each time presenting a different, spontaneous performance within the galleries. This is the beauty of an exhibition that highlights artists making work contemporaneously with the organization of the exhibition and even after the doors have opened. The exhibition evolves and flexes in interesting, challenging ways; it is not easily contained, and it intentionally runs away to more interesting places than we would craft or venture to ourselves.

Organizing a biennial is a messy and joyous affair. It is an imperfect science, not lending itself to the didactic ends that thematic or monographic exhibitions may pursue. My own approach is to show, not to tell—to share the work and provide the experience rather than describe it in words. And so I have asked the artists to do the telling in individual interviews in this catalog, which speak to their practices and to the works in the exhibition. Furthermore, in a change from previous formats, this exhibition catalog will serve as a document of the exhibition—with a detailed map of the installation layout and installation shots of site-specific works therein. As a result, this publication will go to press just after the exhibition opens in order to allow the show to be photographed and the final arrangement in the galleries to be illustrated in the catalog.

A biennial is never just what you see on the walls and in the galleries, what you approach on-site, and what you read about off-site; a biennial is the accretion of the experiences and decisions leading up to and including the installation, as well as the ricocheting of experiences and ideas after that.

This essay attests to the messier stuff, to my own role in the process. Any exhibition is an excursion of discovery. So I am sharing mine with you and providing you with some tools to discover the work yourself.

California is an inimitable and variegated environment in which to work as an artist, something that I hope this biennial captures. My mission is to champion emerging artists, to celebrate a selection of more established practitioners working in the state today, and to create a rich presentation that speaks to the exhilarating work made not only in the fertile climate of Los Angeles but in Northern California and the southern reaches of the state as well. This is a focused exhibition, smaller than the last biennial yet providing a richer presentation of artists from the Bay Area and especially San Diego. I am confident that this biennial will offer audiences a unique vision of the vibrant practices and the disparate media in which California artists are working, reflecting the state's wide-ranging communities and cultural milieus, geographic locales, and artistic orientations. More than that, this exhibition is about creating a forum for the artists and the artworks and for the audience to participate in. People come to museums to see something new, to be exposed to work that they would not otherwise have the opportunity to experience, to be pushed in some way and even inspired. And so my role, my desire, is to provide an opportunity for that engagement. ∎

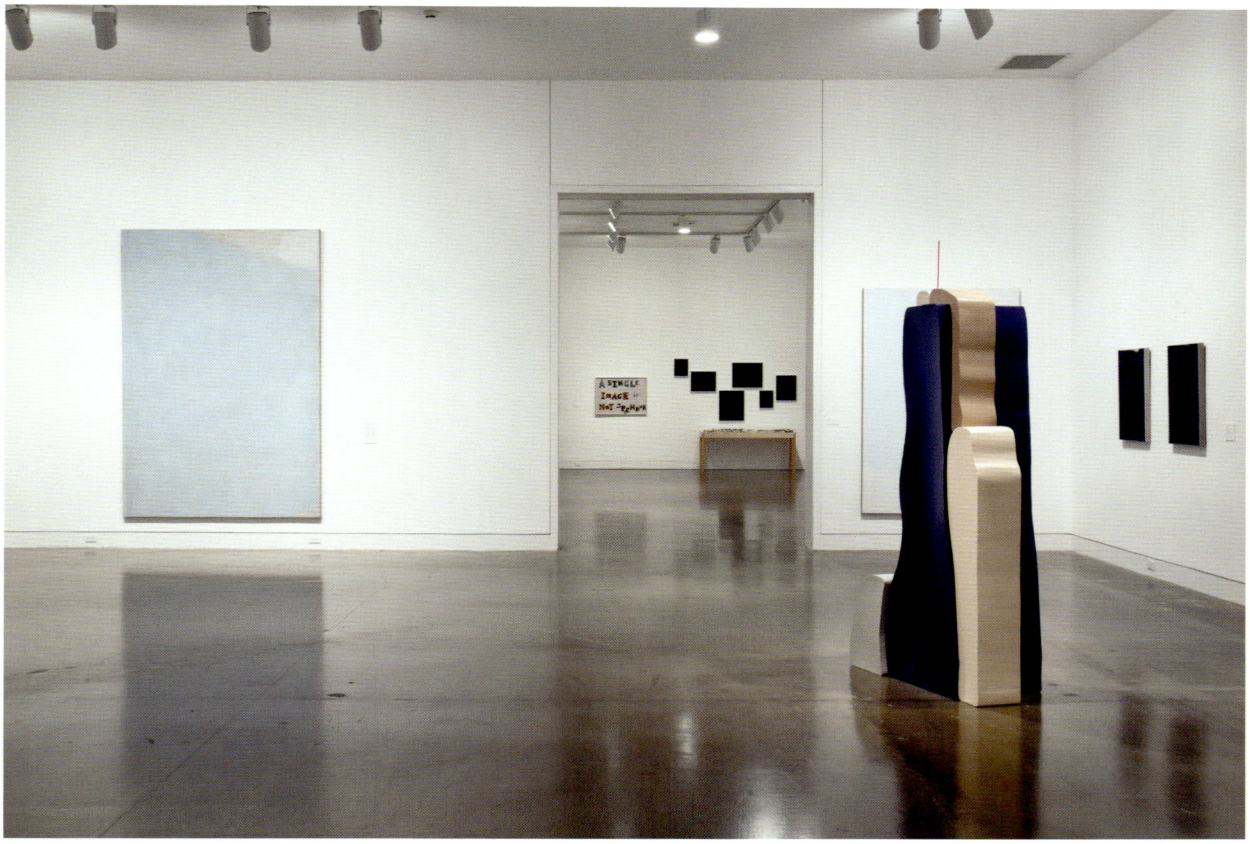

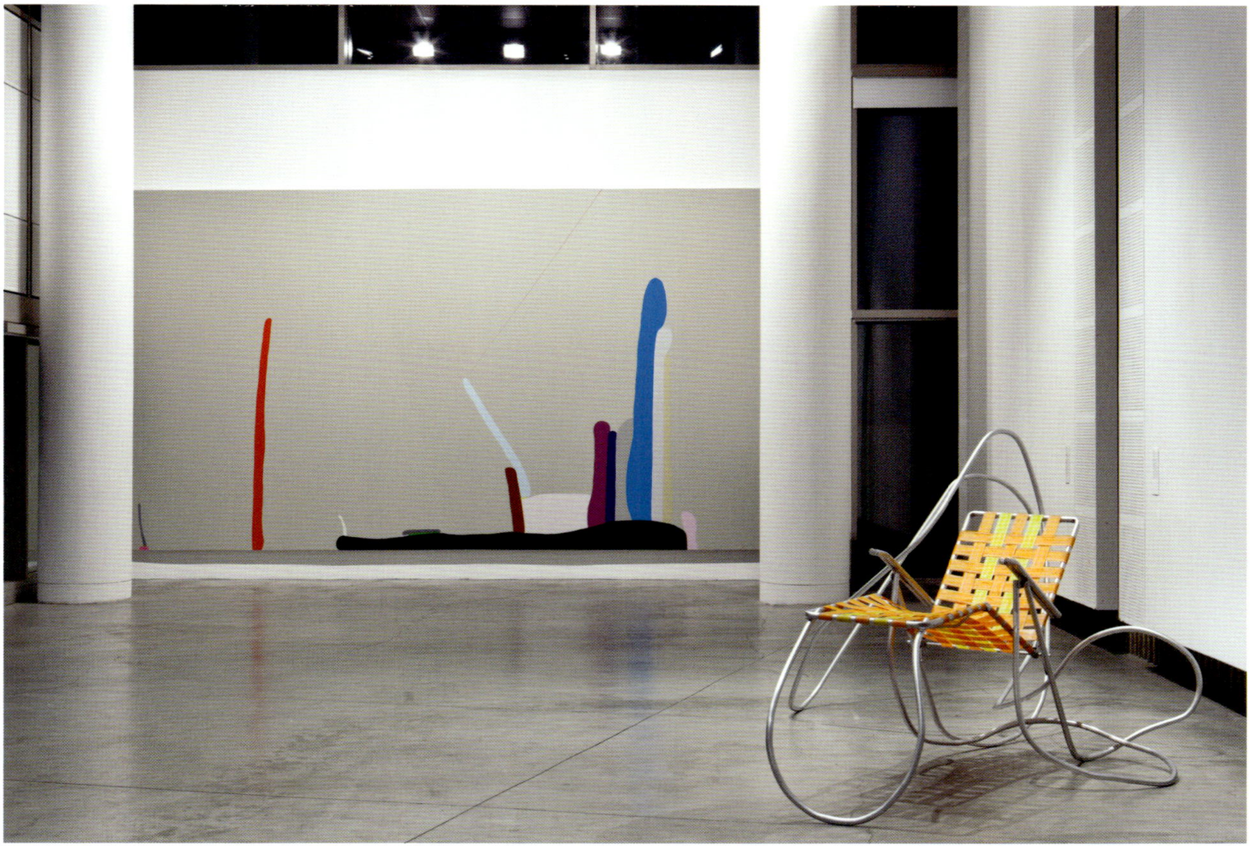

Installation views, 2010 California Biennial
Top: John Zurier, Eve Fowler, Andy Kolar, John Zurier
Bottom: Andy Kolar, Andy Ralph

David Adey

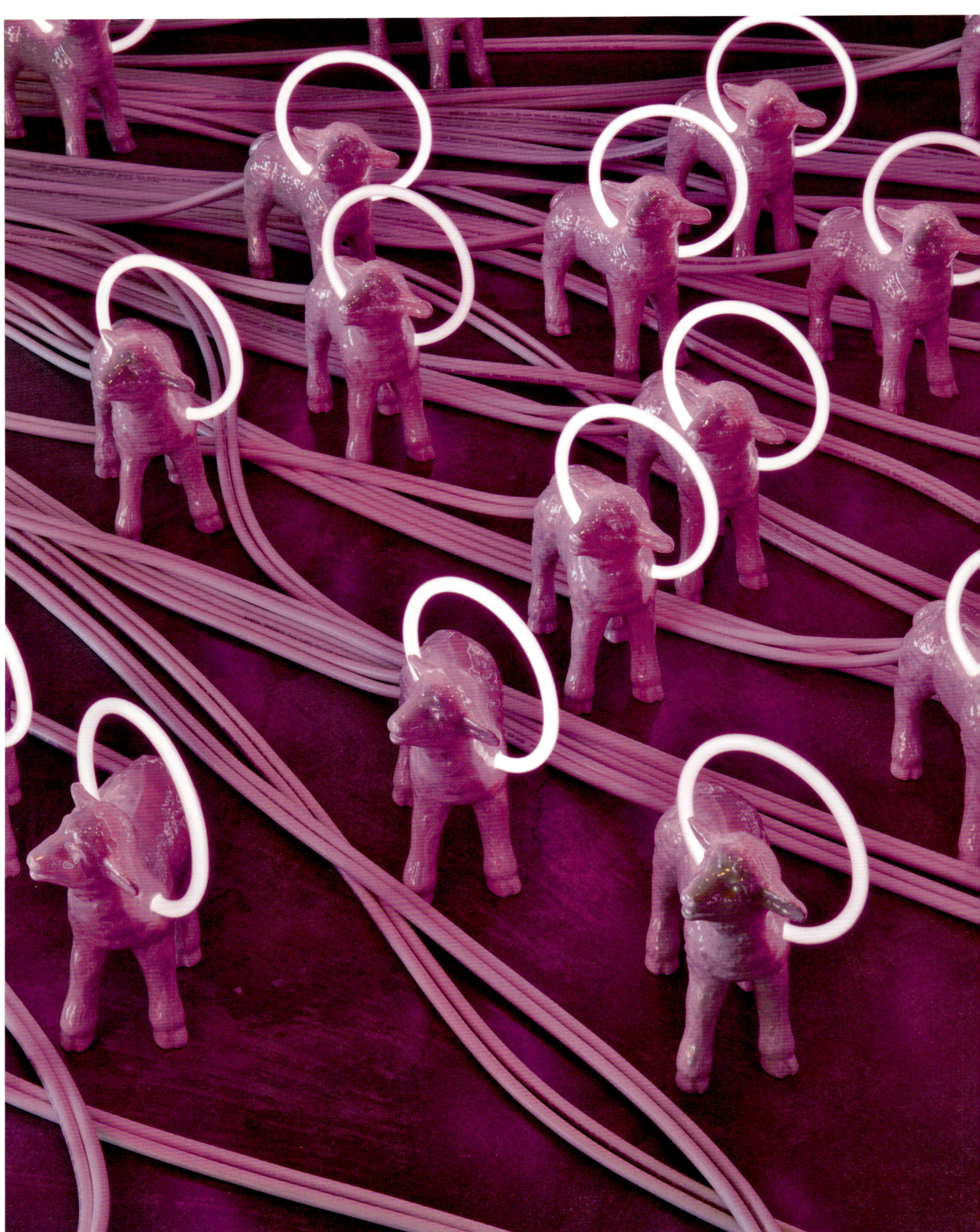

16

Interview with Sarah Bancroft

SB: You've described your artistic practice in terms of constraints. Does this idea of constraint inform your whole practice? When there are not external constraints that direct certain aspects of the work, do you create constraints for yourself?

DA: Constraints are important in all aspects of my work and inform nearly every decision I make. There are always external constraints of time, budget, space, etc., that can inform the work, but many of the concepts are rooted in a set of constraints. I guess you could say that I create the constraints, but more accurately I would say that I choose them since the idea is often a response to something that already exists, and the outcome is often a simple shift within an object's context. I'm continuing a body of work in which I've been extracting the skin from a series of fashion and celebrity images with a collection of more than three hundred craft punches. I'm using consumer images from magazine covers and advertisements and extracting only the visible skin from each image—skinning the image, in a way. The method of consumption is constrained by the availability of the craft punch stock shapes. The skin is broken down into hundreds of individual pieces and then reassembled with specimen pins on foam panels like an entomological study. I have no control over the final composition other than choosing the original image. The final result is the same image with everything but the skin removed. The titles come directly from the ad campaign or magazine cover text. Every aspect of the work is informed by these constraints, which are embedded in the concept, and the work depends upon them for its integrity. This method of working is also present in a recent sculpture titled *John Henry* (2010), in which I suspended two perpendicular rows of books between the walls of the gallery. The idea is simple, but the engineering was much more complicated and required months of experimentation and many failed attempts. When I first presented the idea to the gallery, I wasn't sure how or if it would actually work, but I was committed to the idea of embracing the process, so whatever it took to make it work would become the piece, and it would all be visible. Each row is under several thousand pounds of pressure, so the books were rendered useless, but they were unharmed. Everything that is present in the final installation is necessary for the structural integrity of the rows, including steel bracing, clamps, keystone wedges, wood shims, etc. Even the placement of the books is determined by size, which is necessary for the structure, so I really didn't make any purely aesthetic decisions, and the outcome was far different than I had initially imagined. As the process unfolded, it took on references to the folk spectacle, absurd feats of strength and the futility and poetry of the John Henry legend. I suppose I do give up a certain level of intuitive artistic freedom by working this way, but there is a different type of freedom that's gained when the outcome is uncertain.

SB: Destruction and resurrection are recurrent themes and objectives in your work. How is transmogrifying the physical presence of the objects in your work a form of reification? Or is this a more direct or subtle investigation of religion?

DA: The idea of creating something new through an object's destruction and restoration is where many of my ideas begin, but each piece is informed by the particular process and takes on its own meaning. I think there is potential for a range of implications to develop out of these processes, but personal and cultural ideas of faith, consumption, and identity are continued areas of investigation for me.

SB: Can you talk a bit about your project for the biennial and how it fits into your practice.

DA: My interest in the lamb stems from its significance as a Christian symbol as well as its place in scientific history as the first documented animal to ever be cloned. I've created several sculptures over the past ten years using the same ceramic lamb figurine, and I seem to keep returning to it. With past pieces I've duplicated hundreds of them and made larger forms from all of their broken pieces. In *The New Lamb* (2005), a larger mother sheep was created with the corresponding parts of the smaller lambs—the mouth was created from all mouth parts, legs from all leg parts, etc. With *Flock* (2010), I'm interested in the homogenization of the group. All of the lambs with their neon halos are connected to a single power source. *Pump* (2007–10) is a piece that has been retooled several times but began as a simple experiment in the destruction of a football by piercing it with drywall screws. It's then hooked up to a horse respirator for its life support. My attempt was to take the piercing process as far as it could go, to the point where the method of destruction became its source of new life.

SB: *Flock* is at once kitschy and menacing, cute and eerie, all those little lambs staring out in one direction with their neon halos. One can imagine a uniform bleating, in unison—anything but natural.

DA: What I love about kitsch is this sense of disparity between an object's intentions and reality. We see these objects as pathetic but also comforting and even horrific all at once. I wanted to see if they would reach a critical mass or some form of transformation. There isn't a leader, just uniformity and a common power source. They're all networked together and dependent upon their identity in the group for their existence. ∎

Born 1972 in Morristown, New Jersey; lives and works in San Diego. Adey is a graduate of Point Loma Nazarene University (BA, 1994) and Cranbrook Academy of Art (MFA, 2002). His work has been featured in one-person exhibitions at Luis De Jesus, Los Angeles; the Athenaeum of Music and Arts Library, La Jolla, California; and Spacecraft Gallery, San Diego. He has participated in group exhibitions at the Museum of Contemporary Art San Diego; the Torrance Art Museum, Torrance, California; the Wignall Museum of Contemporary Art, Chaffey College, Rancho Cucamonga, California; and Quint Contemporary Art, La Jolla. Adey is associate professor in the Department of Art and Design at Point Loma Nazarene University and a recipient of the 2010–11 San Diego Art Prize in the Emerging Artist category.

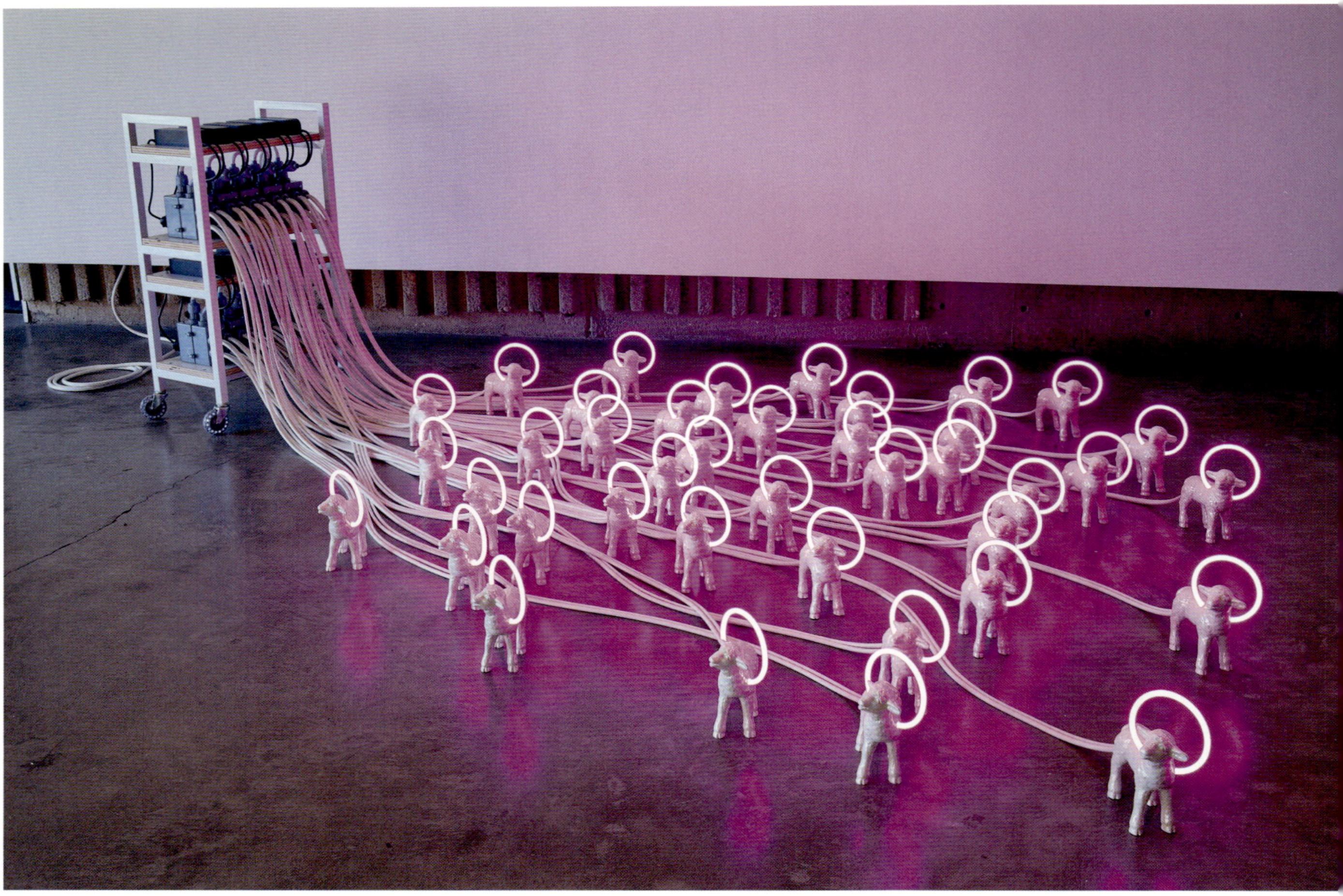

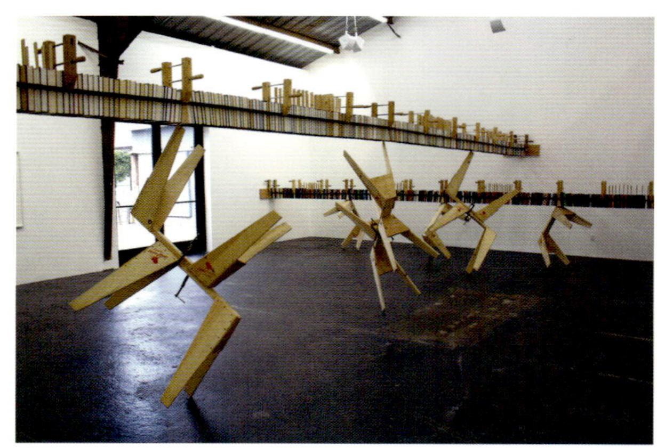

Top and previous
Flock, 2010 — cat. no. 2

John Henry, 2010
Installation view, Luis De Jesus Los Angeles, Santa Monica, California
Courtesy of the artist and Luis De Jesus Los Angeles

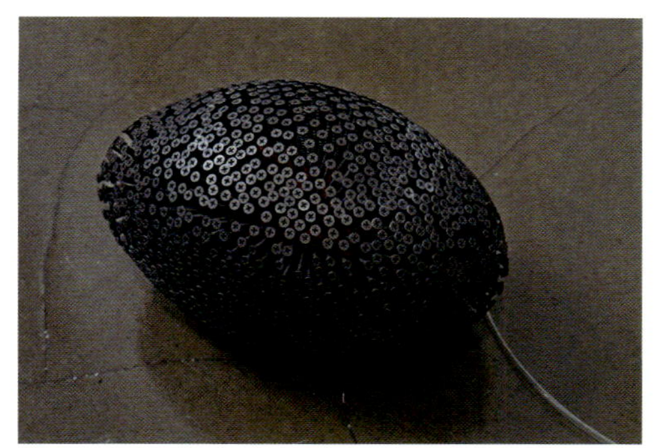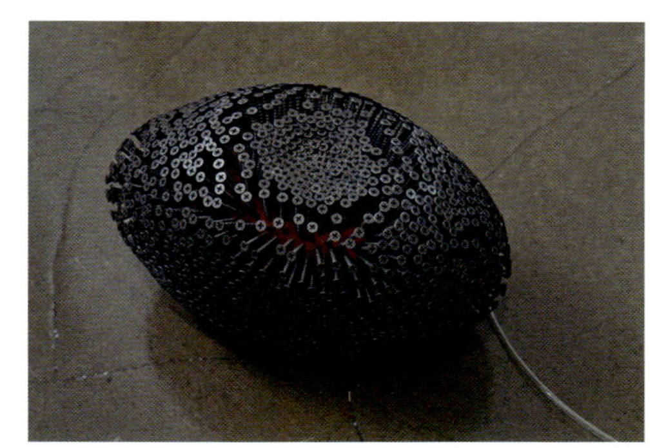

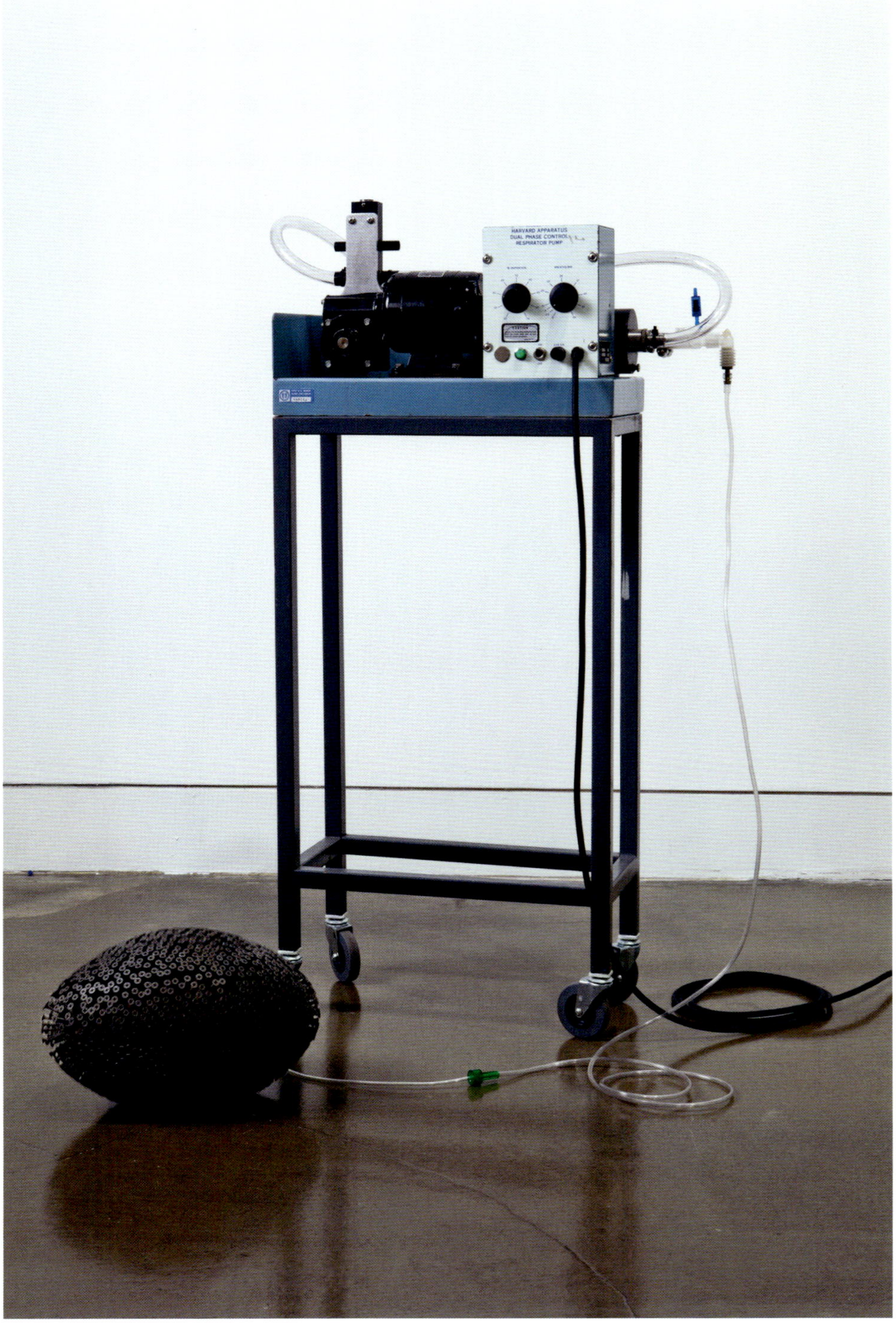

Pump, 2007–10 — cat. no. 1

Agitprop

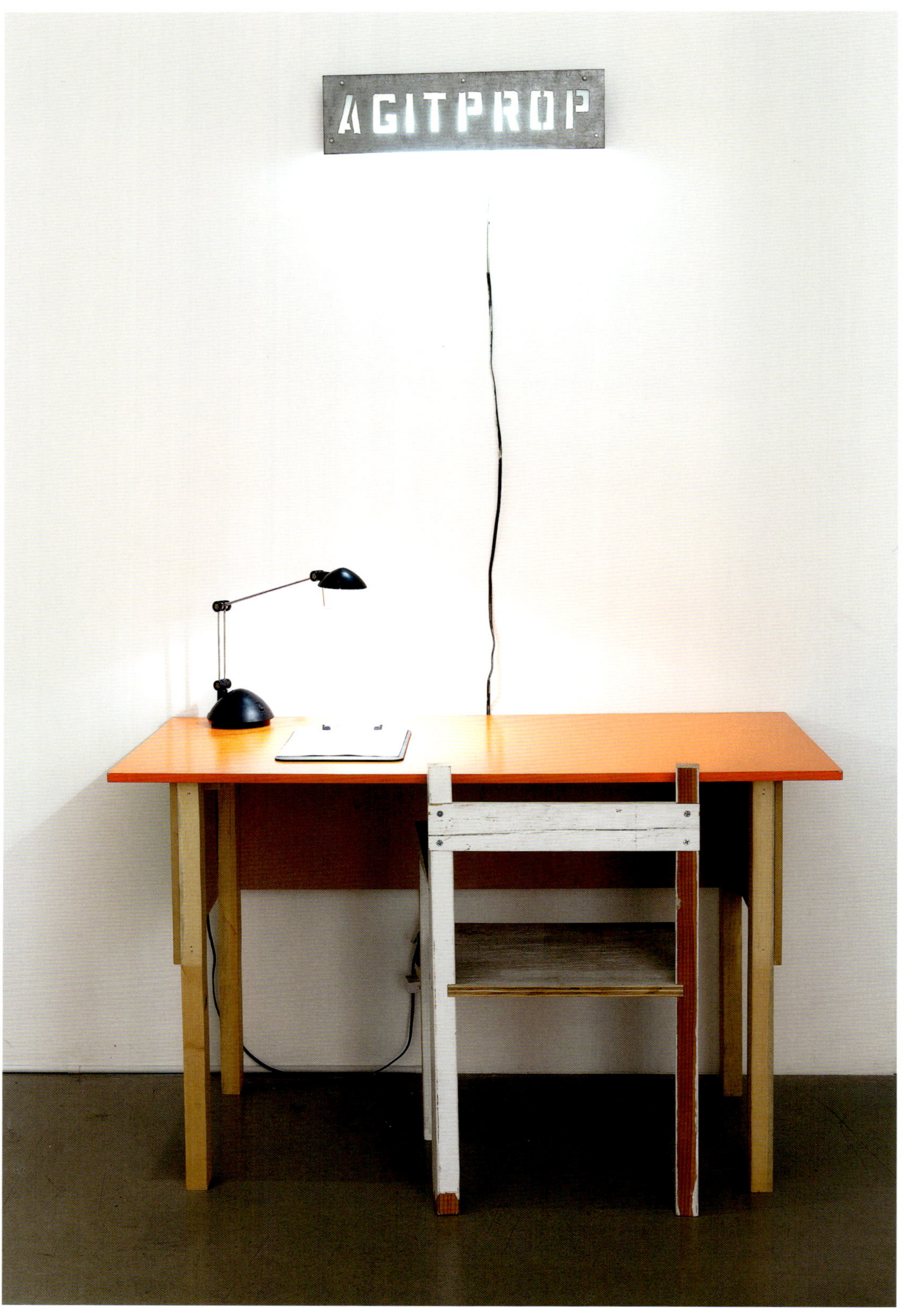

Agitprop workspace on-site at the Orange County Museum of Art
during the 2010 California Biennial

Interview with Grant Wahlquist

GW: What was the impetus behind Agitprop's formation, both in terms of global trends and the specific needs of the North Park and broader San Diego communities?

DW: The impetus behind Agitprop in many ways came out of a certain frustration with trying to create work that fits into the categories and opportunities out in the world, which tend to favor work that operates at the level of the discrete object. I had tried working in that way in the past and always felt that there was something missing. So Agitprop was a way to place an experiment out into the world. It was an experiment to see, as an artist, if I could start from scratch, from the beginning. When I began to send announcements to the press, I would simply refer to the events as "Agitprop" and then the paper would come out, and the posting would say, "Agitprop Gallery." I would send e-mails correcting them for the following event, and it would again have the word *Gallery* tacked onto the end. It was a fascinating lesson in how linguistically and ideologically embedded in specific ontological preconditions people are.

With Agitprop I wanted to embed myself into a localized set of conditions. I wanted the space to be an anchor into a neighborhood and to have to deal with the conditions of that neighborhood as I found them. This is also what is interesting about being a transplant to San Diego. It is not an art mecca. It is a bizarre and fascinating place where the developing world literally abuts the epitome of consumer culture and where the largesse of the military-industrial complex overlaps with post-hippie/surfer culture and Shamu. Meanwhile there are all of these great, urban, diverse neighborhoods that are overlooked.

GW: Agitprop is animated by some fundamental questions, one of which is "What is the limit of structure versus structurelessness?" How has this worked itself out in your practice? How do you hope to translate the idea of structurelessness into the context of the biennial?

DW: Starting with the bare minimum and working up has really made me examine each aspect of what it is that I'm doing and question if those processes could be done differently. One example of this is *Brain Trust*. It consists of concrete cubes in the shape of brain matter, which were created in an edition of one thousand. The initial idea came from examining how to fund projects and looking at how the arts in general are funded, which is usually through commercial exchange or grants that, when traced, have their fiscal origins in the corporate sector. I wanted to come up with a way to have at least some of the projects be funded by the same audiences that the projects target. I also wanted the piece to be a way for people to have some stake in what is happening with Agitprop and the projects that extend out from the space. So I sell them as stock and hope for participation, feedback, and debate.

In terms of transferring these approaches to OCMA, I think this is another aspect of the Agitprop project that has been working well so far. The flexibility of operating in this way allows for the "fieldwork" that takes place at the site of the space to be a model for work that can happen in an institutional context.

GW: What about your project for the biennial, *The Third Party*? Can you describe the project, its parameters, its genesis, and your hopes for it in the context of the biennial?

DW: *The Third Party* originated exactly through the processes mentioned above. It consists of a mobile interview cart that is on wheels so that it can be pushed around the museum and be placed in front of different works of art. The cart has two chairs facing each other with a small table in between. On the cart I interview people whom I seek out about whatever work of art the cart is parked in front of. I choose the pieces. For the biennial I am going to be interviewing people within walking distance of the museum. My hope for this piece is that it will spark some of the same interesting debates that happen through Agitprop.

GW: In a statement explaining the purpose/function of Agitprop, you write of two competing interpretations of Duchamp's *Fountain*, how it simultaneously opens up art for the "untrained" while also reaffirming the social permission given to the artist to designate something as art. In light of this, you write that Agitprop "invert(s) this positioning by placing the 'gallery' in the position of the work of art." Can you elaborate on the idea of the gallery occupying the place of the artwork? I'm particularly interested in your linking Agitprop to the tradition of the readymade/sculpture.

DW: Obviously, I acknowledge a Beuysian reference first. Galleries, other than being spaces of display and economic exchange, are social spaces, so on one level Agitprop is a social sculpture. On another level the physical space is important to how the social interactions take place. I guess it could be called architecture, but most of the process of shaping the space was reductive. The "readymade" conditions of the space tend to encourage commentary and heated debate from visitors about anything happening in the space or about the space itself.

Also, if it's called a work of art, then the activities that take place inside (and outside) the container can be varied according to need. The space has been transformed into such diverse forms as a garage sale, a performance space, a diner, a studio, an office, a classroom, and an exhibition space. It allows these forms to function as tools of engagement. ∎

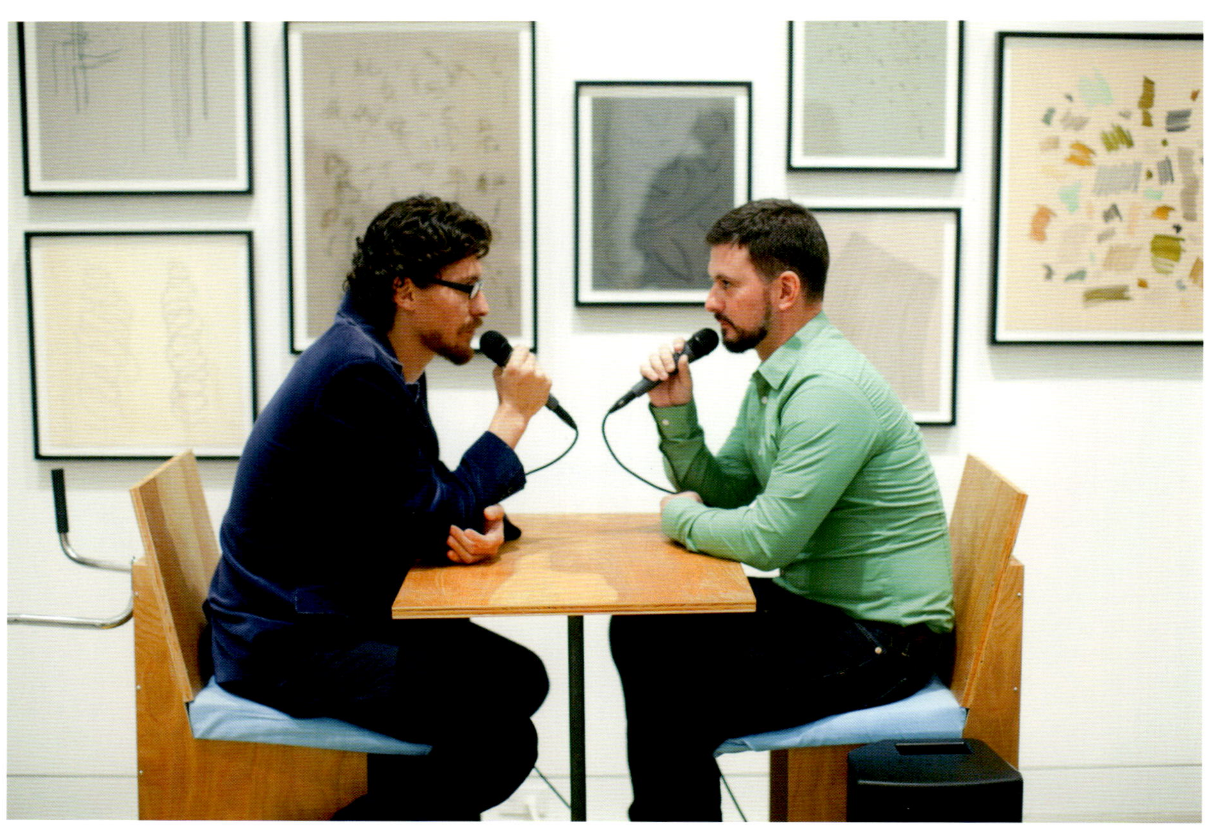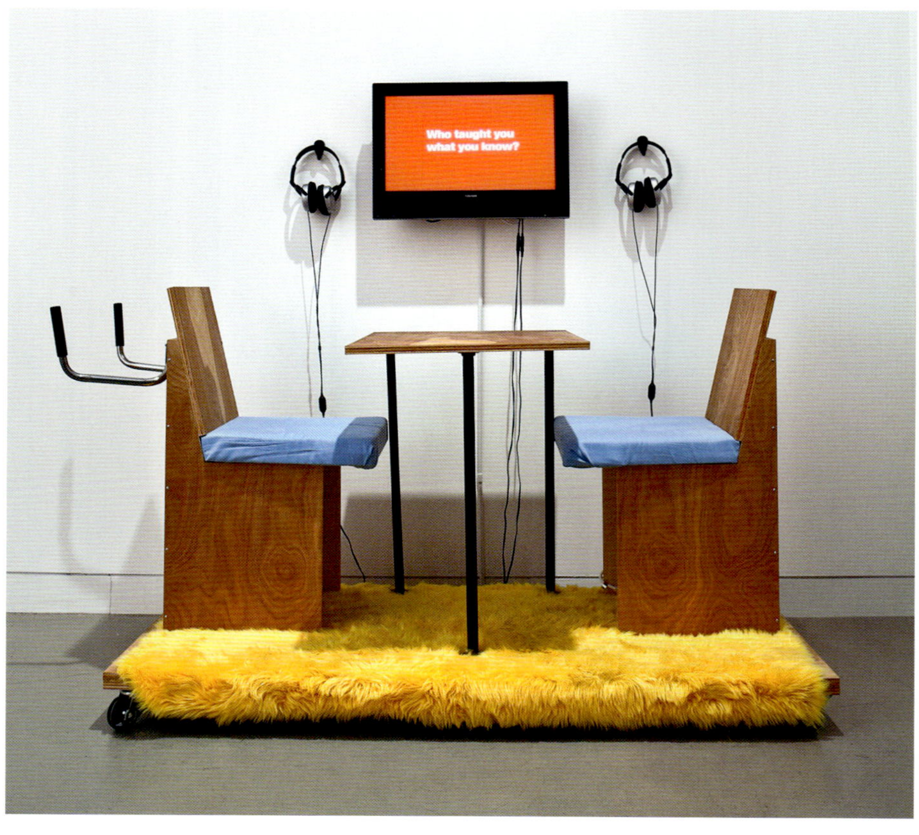

***The Third Party*, 2010** — cat. no. 3
Interview cart in use and on view during 2010 California Biennial

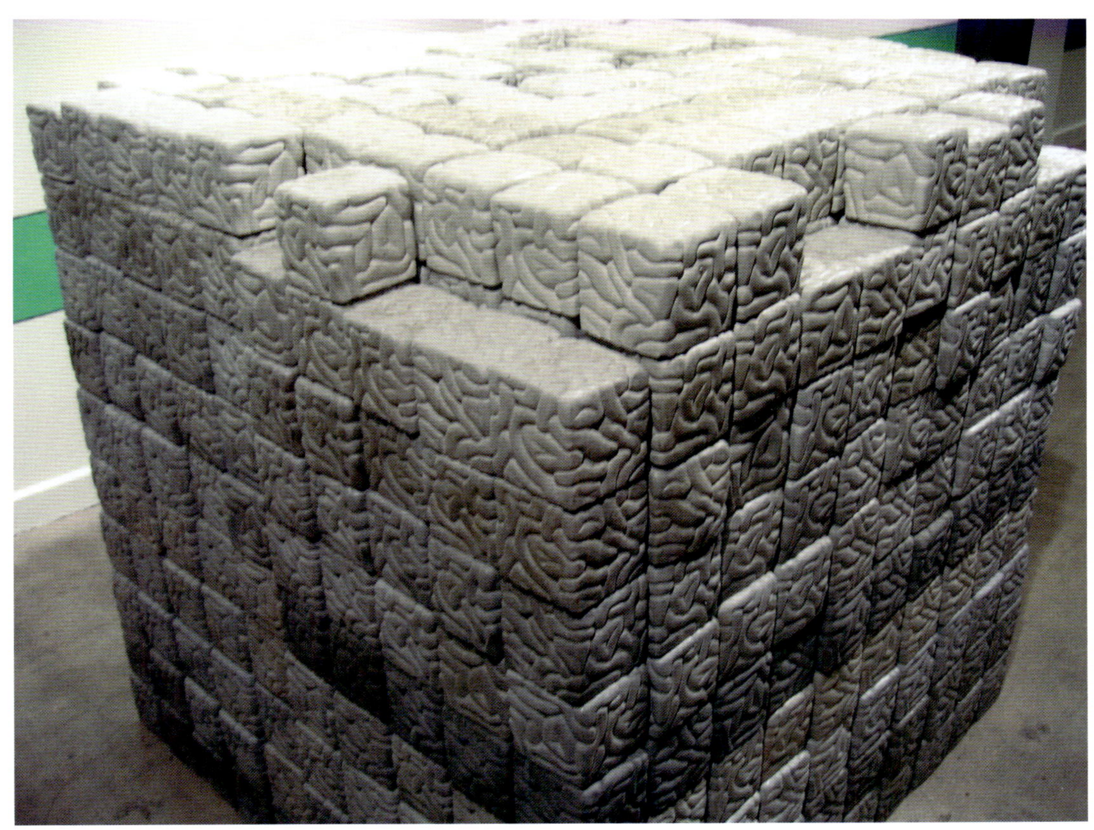

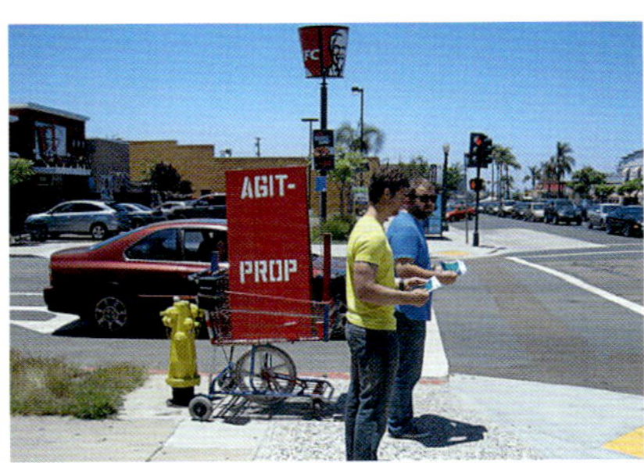

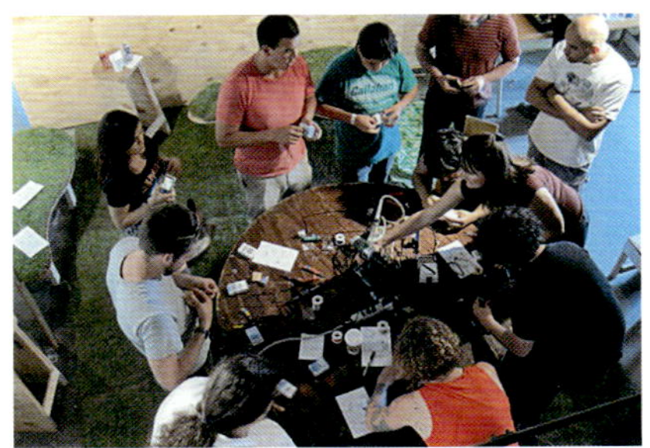

Bottom
There Goes the Neighborhood, 2010
Volunteers distributing maps and information about the four-day event
Courtesy of Agitprop

Top
Brain Trust: Sculptural Stock in Agitprop, 2009
Installation view, ART Produce Gallery, San Diego
Courtesy of Agitprop

Bottom
There Goes the Neighborhood, 2010
Volunteers distributing maps and information about the four-day event
Courtesy of Agitprop

There Goes the Neighborhood, 2010
"Turn Up Everything" workshop by Michael Trigilio
Courtesy of Agitprop

Gil Blank

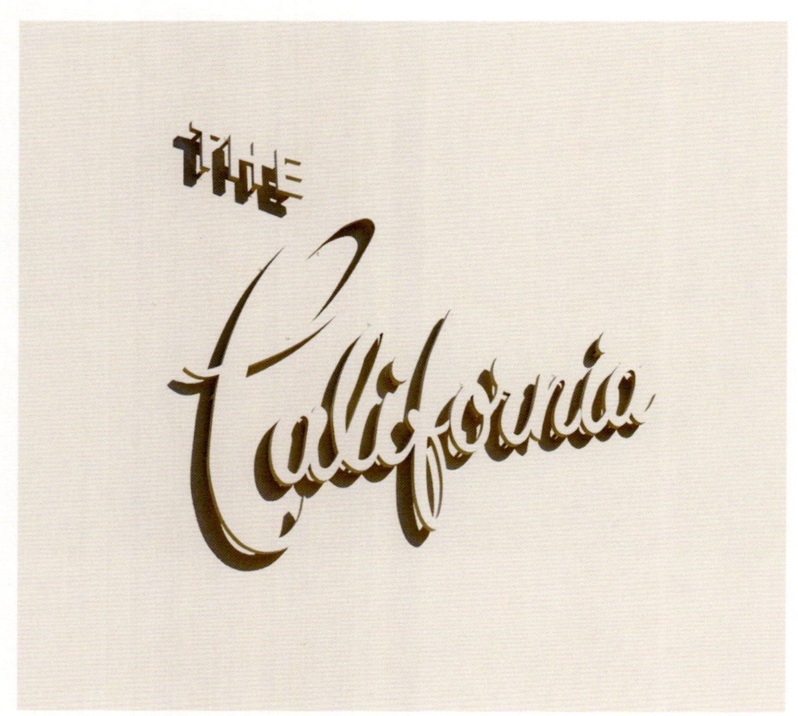

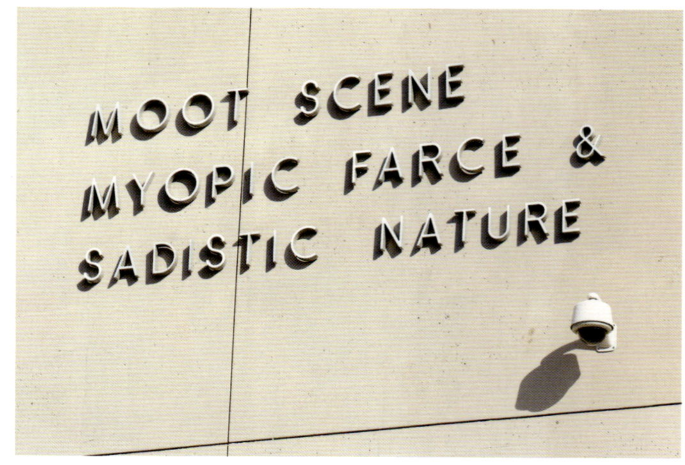

No Title, **No Date** — cat. no. 4
No Title, **No Date** — cat. no. 5

Interview with Sarah Bancroft

SB: **Tell me about your central project for the biennial,
Wiederholungszwang, and how it fits within the larger
structure of your work.**

GB: It's an extended, multiyear and multipart cycle of photographic works that reckons with the passage of time—an
attempt to move backward and forward through it, using
one group of images as a pivot for that action. The thirty-
six dark gray bricks in the installation make up one early
stage of that cycle, and although this is the first time that
they'll be exhibited, it marks a culmination of several years'
work on the project. Also, maybe it's a new beginning.
I think you'll see what I mean by that recursive, cyclical
nature.

I had the bricks made over the summer of 2010 from
industrially processed graphite, and each has an image
laser-engraved onto it of the old waterfront in Portland,
Maine. Those images were first downloaded from a
webcam in 2004. Throughout that year I was continually
looking northward each day, to a sight that I found alternately beautiful and banal. The image depicts what the
early American settlers of the town considered to be the
"best general view," which is to say a grand and clarifying
picture of a great future, boundless as the ocean that it
looked out over.

My original experience of that view, if there can be anything original about either the view or its remote and digi-
tized download, was vicarious: I was far away from Maine
at the time, but the view became my own, even as it was
always clearly of an experience that I could never join.
After spending the subsequent years living with the images—reckoning with the infinite regress that they came
to embody—I had to find a way to materialize that exile,
to crystallize the desire within them, as in all images, that
otherwise is only implicit.

By engraving the ephemeral data onto bricks made of
elemental carbon, I'm harnessing an absurd promise of
technology to make the most permanent form of image
that I could conceive. The bricks are solid and utterly in-
ert, whereas the initial image—itself born of an equally
absurd wish for presence or communion—was always just
a phantom trace. That duplication though was one more
of many false starts. I've since proceeded to reimage the
bricks by electronically scanning them, thus returning
them (again) into traces, which are subsequently printed
out once more, as another generation. I'll then scan those
as well, continually repeating the cycle, as I make my way
back in technological time through various historical im-
aging processes, so that materially each new cycle bears
all the distortions and artifacts of degradation that come
from each of its previous generations. The action becomes
manifold—the making and viewing of the art unfolds for
both you and me as a new event, in real time—even as
the "original" is borne further and further away, most likely
toward a black monochrome.

SB: **That idea of time informs many of your works.**

GB: All of them.

SB: **But you decline to date most or even title them. Why?**

GB: I work with images precisely because I find the ambiguity
inherent to them to be fractious and unknowable, experience's own best model. So the false sense of specificity
that comes with titles can be maddening to me. I just don't
believe that images can ever really typify anything. To pin
them down epigrammatically feels like a lie to me, no matter how plain or vague the title—never mind something as
excessive as *My and My Beloved's Abandoned Sleep*. The
link between photographs and dates is doubly problematic, something I've tried to model in *Wiederholungszwang*,
which simultaneously extends and annuls the photographic
hope of stilled time.

Wiederholungszwang translates from the German as
"the compulsion to repeat": if one workable definition of
trauma is a missed encounter or lost history, it follows that
such an experience can never be adequately recovered or
re-*presented*, only endlessly repeated, even as every such
repetition bears you further away from it. Looking at these
images reproduced again in a different form, or as new
objects, each new viewer experiences for herself another
step in the same course of separation, which is scripted as
a new but diminished event.

SB: **In addition to *Wiederholungszwang*, we're also including two other photographs in the exhibition that have
been digitally altered yet very much speak to place.**

GB: But only indirectly, maybe in the same way that *Wiederholungszwang* speaks to dislocation, if in a different
voice. Each of the two pictures was made in Los Angeles.
They're color, I guess, but drained of most of it, and show
signs but are stripped of their referents. One is an ana-
gram of an icon, and the other is a shadow of itself.

The material thing-ness of the bricks has its counter in
the flat super-images of the color photographs, which are
seamless, bright, and cold to the touch. The data within
them have so much on offer, all of that terrible hope conveyed by an intensely present image, which of course can
never be anything even remotely present. For all their
hyperspecificity—the crisp image, the tightly defined
tonal values and layout, and even the framing—they still
recede into that deep silence, the push-pull tension of
wanting so badly to be there, to be here and now, to know,
and yet to end up with nothing to show for it. ∎

Born 1970 in Morristown, New Jersey;
lives and works in Santa Monica and
New York. A graduate of Stanford
University (BA, 1992), Blank has had
solo exhibitions at Ville D'Images,
Vevey, Switzerland; LaMontagne
Gallery, Boston; Mandrake, Los
Angeles; and Andrew Roth Gallery,
New York. He has participated in
group exhibitions at Blum and Poe,
Los Angeles; Cardwell Jimmerson
Gallery, Los Angeles; Presentation
House Gallery, Vancouver; Lawrimore
Project, Seattle; White Columns, New
York; CB Roppongi, Tokyo; Galerie
Rodolphe Janssen, Brussels; Paula
Cooper Gallery, New York; and MoMA
PS1 Contemporary Art Center, Long
Island City, New York. Blank was a
founding editor of *Influence* and *Issue*,
and his writing regularly appears in
magazines and monographs.

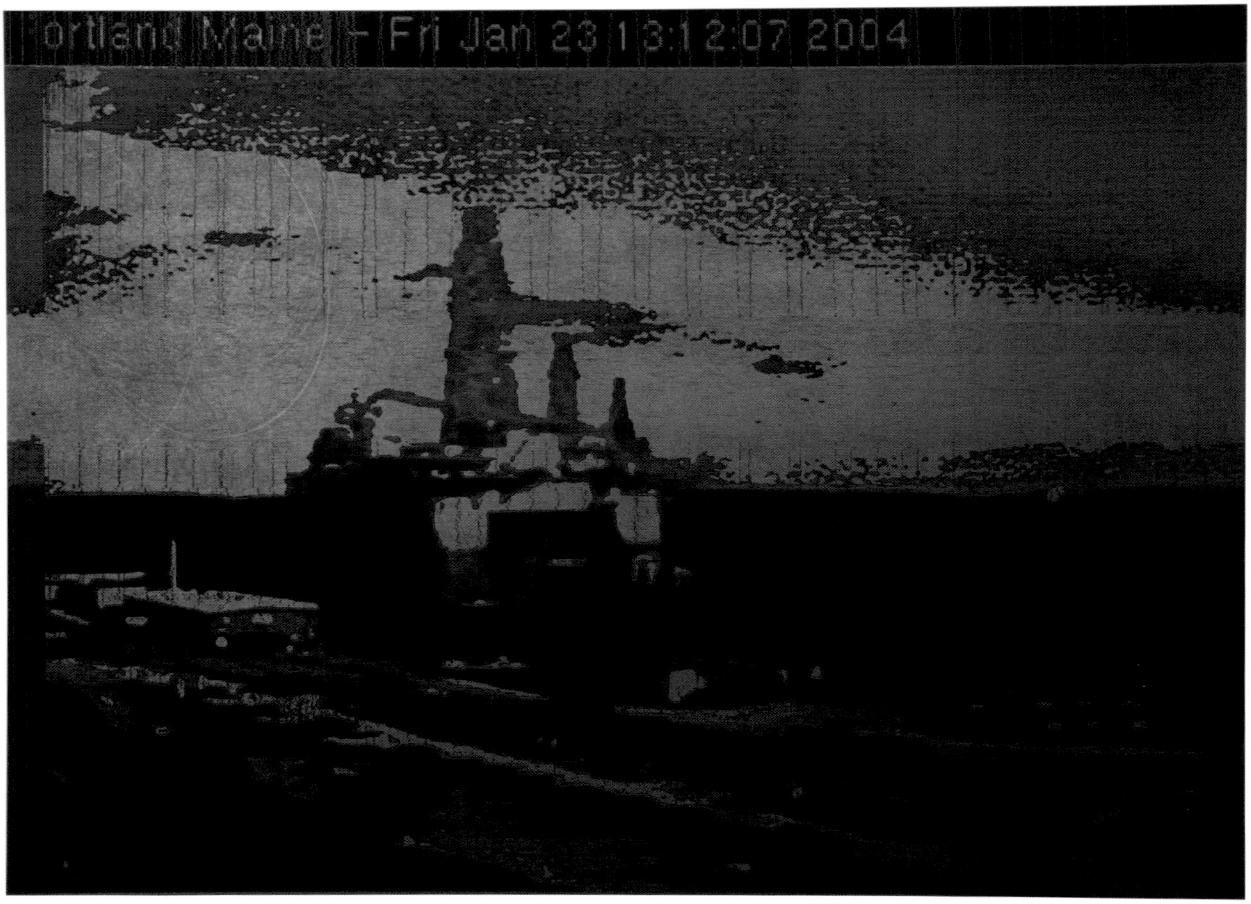

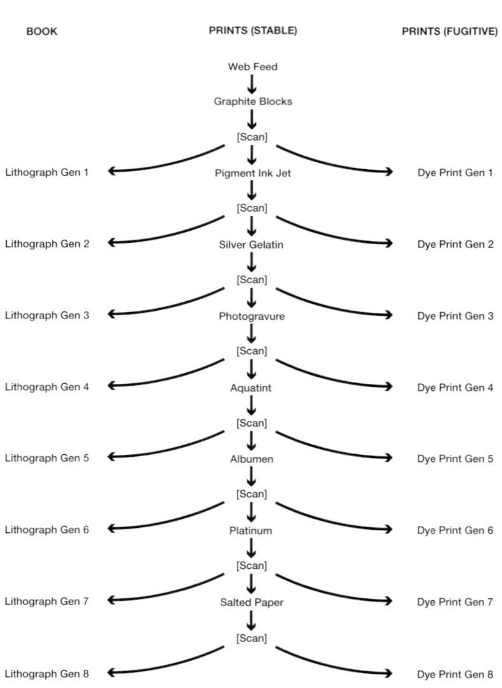

***Wiederholungszwang I.ii.5,* No Date** — under cat. no. 6

Structural diagram of ***Wiederholungszwang***, showing the three main
branches of the cycle
Courtesy of the artist

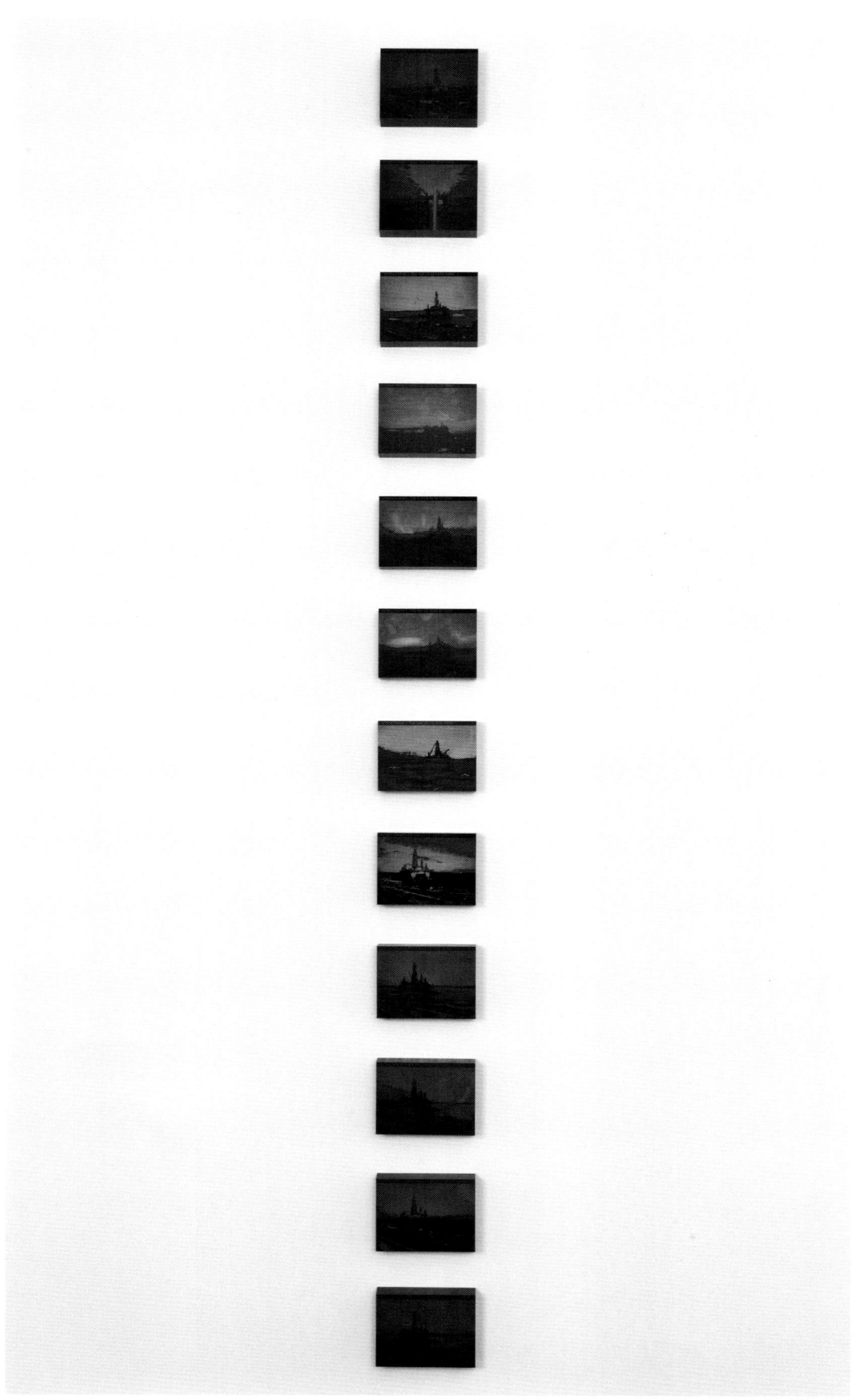

Nate Boyce

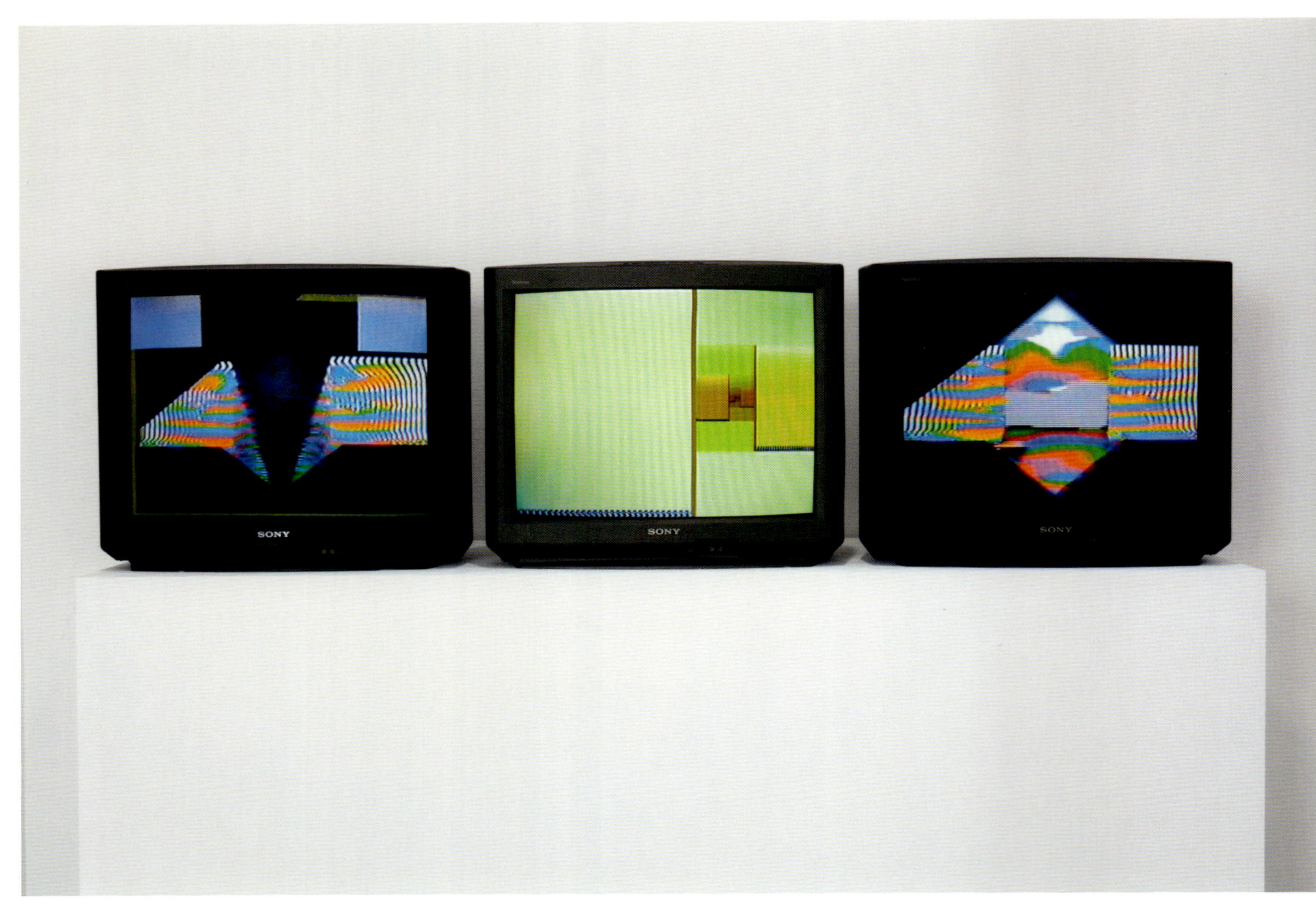

Interlaced Increments, **2010** — cat. no. 9

CF: **Let's start by opening up your work to the larger museum audience. What is the viewer looking at? I ask this thinking that one not versed in the ways of computer-generated graphics and programming may have a difficult time understanding what they're looking at and how something like this is generated, not to mention how it relates to art. Can you explain what the viewer is looking at and what your working methods are for setting up your digital canvas?**

NB: Most of what I do is synthetic—I generally don't use lens-based photographic material or appropriated imagery. In some of the recent pieces, like *Parallel Series I* and *II*, I started by generating basic shapes and colors using consumer-grade video-mixing hardware. These devices have preset patterns for combining and transitioning between images. Instead of using them for their default functions, I feed the signals back into themselves to create a range of different compositions. I'll then take those images and turn them into digitally rendered scenes using 3D animation. I like working within the constraints of these essentially ready-made compositional templates.

I'll often reshoot the image from a monitor numerous times or record it to VHS and then bring it back into the computer and recombine it with the original image. I'm interested in how the fusion of old and new tools gives an ambiguity to the image. It's simultaneously hi-fi and lo-fi, and this complicates the psychological and emotional responses someone might have when they experience the work.

CF: **What kind of genres, movements, concepts, and outside art historical influences have informed your practice?**

NB: I've always been interested in the history of experimental film/animation/video that deals with abstraction and the materiality of the moving image. Structural filmmakers like Paul Sharits and Hollis Frampton have been important for me from the start. Similar to their work, I try to articulate the inherent properties of the medium and foreground the raw materiality of video in an effort to heighten awareness of the act of perception. I'm attempting to create experiences that are viscerally intense but analytical and reflexive at the same time. Before I started working with video, I was making experimental music, synthesizing and processing sounds in a very sculptural way. Serialism in music, and the procedural and systematic approaches to visual art and music in the work of people like Sol LeWitt, Peter Kubelka, and Karlheinz Stockhausen have been influential for me. One of the things about serialism in time-based forms is that it gets at a temporal abstraction, which I think resists the imposition of narrative. I'm attempting to deal with abstraction in a way that doesn't rely on the fact that it's a deconstruction of some representational material. For me, the directionality of extracting representation to arrive at abstraction has been exhausted. I'm trying to reverse that process.

CF: **But even though your practice incorporates manipulated images and technology, the way you speak about your work lends itself to the static arts—say, painting, sculpture, and minimalism. What's the relationship of these disciplines to your work or practice?**

NB: I like to get involved with ideas outside the discourse surrounding new media. I get more inspiration from looking at artists like Sigmar Polke or Lynda Benglis than I do from art dealing with new technology. I like to research art history, and I end up taking these ideas out of context and mapping them to new parameters with new materials. Going back to what I was saying about 3D animation epitomizing the production methods of pop culture, I think it's interesting to use it to reprocess art historical concerns. To some extent, using 3D animation, or any video hardware, feels like a pop cultural reference in itself. For instance, Michael Fried's take on Frank Stella or Robert Smithson's "Entropy and the New Monuments" (1966) are textual points of reference that have interesting implications for what I'm doing with video and animation. In addition to the conceptual concerns that I have, I'm actually interested in thinking formally about pictorial construction. In the 1980s and 1990s abstraction was pretty much a nonissue for new-media art, which seemed to be wrapped up in postmodern issues and identity politics. Part of what I'm doing is seeing what happens when connections are made between abstraction in early video and historically concurrent issues in painting and sculpture. I've always been interested in the early years of video art, when people experimented with abstraction and synthesis, but to me, most of that work really doesn't go beyond technological demonstration.

CF: **What about the theoretical trajectory of art history that examines images in relation to media and culture? Specifically, I'm thinking about Guy Debord's ideas about the spectacle, Marshall McLuhan's media theory that places the focus on the medium rather than content, and more recently, Lev Manovich's theories on "new media" and its cultural implications. How do you see your work in relation to these ideas surrounding the image, media, and technology?**

NB: It's not that I don't think that those conversations are relevant, but I get more from looking into specific art historical or theoretical materials that indirectly relate to those ideas. I'd say that I have a generally anti-illusionistic stance that's informed by aspects of apparatus theory that critique the authoritarian and manipulative properties that are built into the basic mechanisms of cinema as well as theorists of structural/materialist film like Peter Gidal. It's crucial to be thinking about these issues when working with high-end 3D animation and visual effects software, which epitomize the production methods of pop culture. When working with these materials, there's a real danger of unconsciously perpetuating the ideology of consumer culture that uncritically fetishizes technological novelty. For me, these critical discussions are very generative in that they point to ways of working against the normative uses and aesthetic modes built into the tools. ■

Born 1982 in Shawnee, Kansas; lives and works in San Francisco. Boyce graduated from the San Francisco Art Institute (BFA, 2006). His work has been exhibited at the CCA Wattis Institute, San Francisco; Bemis Center for Contemporary Art, Omaha; Deitch Projects, New York; the New York Underground Film Festival; Jack Hanley Gallery, San Francisco; the Exploratorium, San Francisco; Galerie Neue Alte Bruecke, Frankfurt; and the San Jose Institute of Contemporary Art. Boyce was an artist-in-residence at the Headlands Center for the Arts in Sausalito, California, in fall 2010.

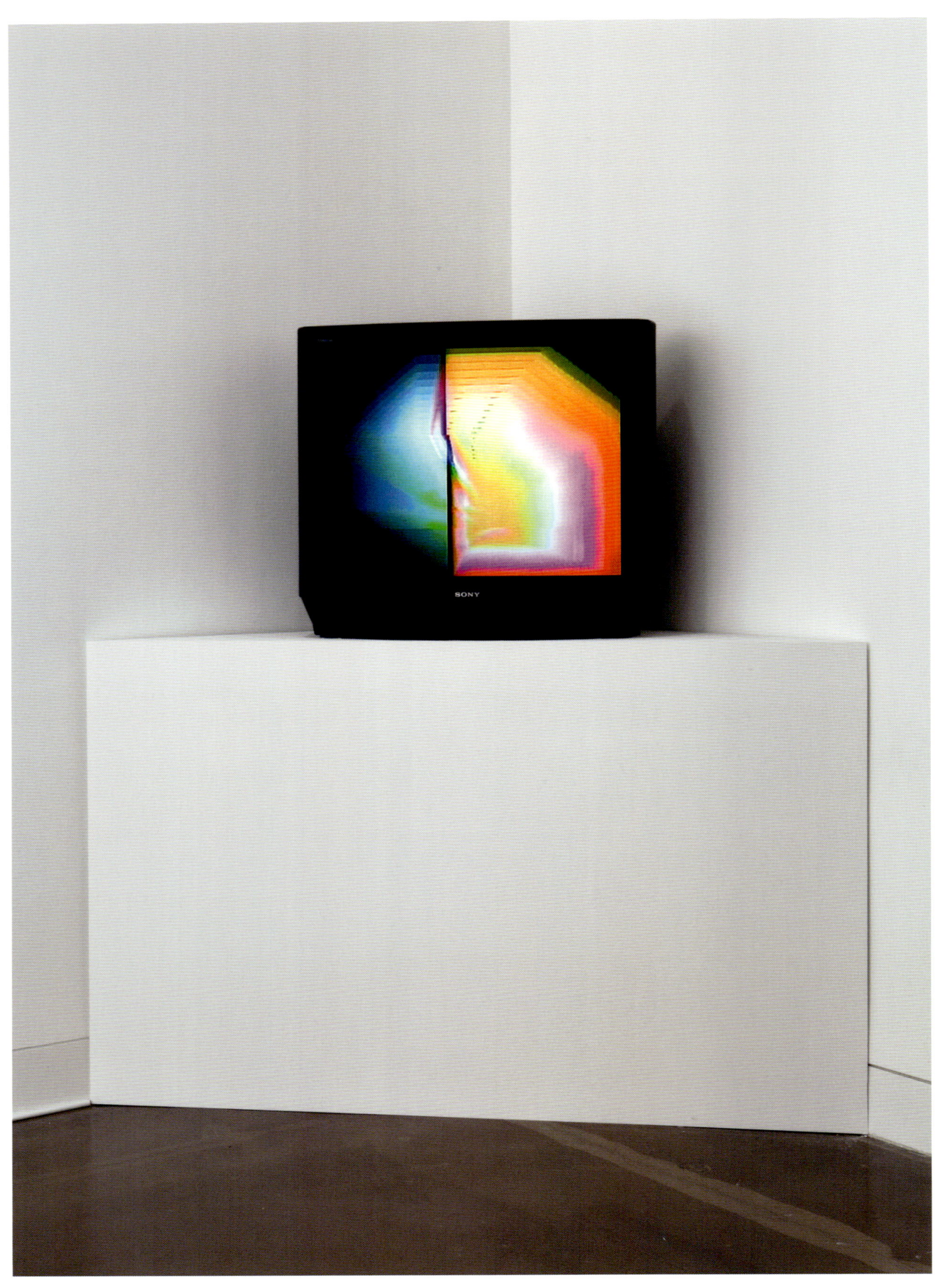

Parallel Series II (Zoom, Rotation, Collision), **2010** — cat. no. 10

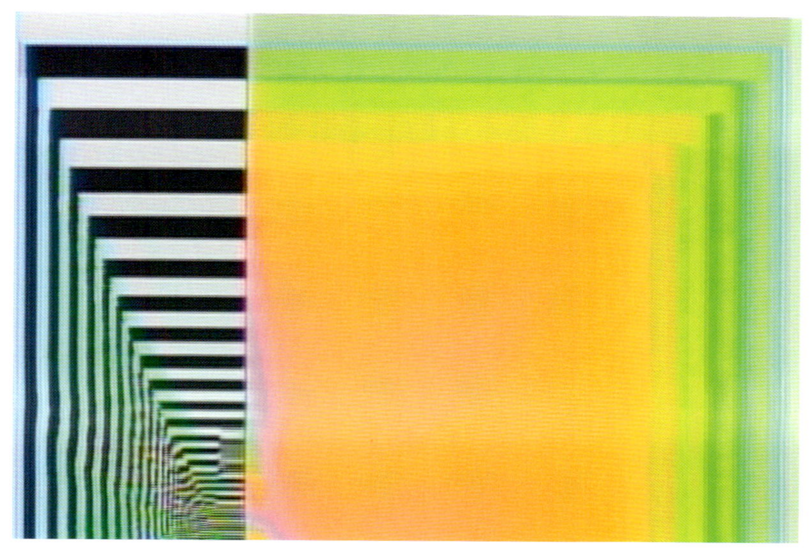

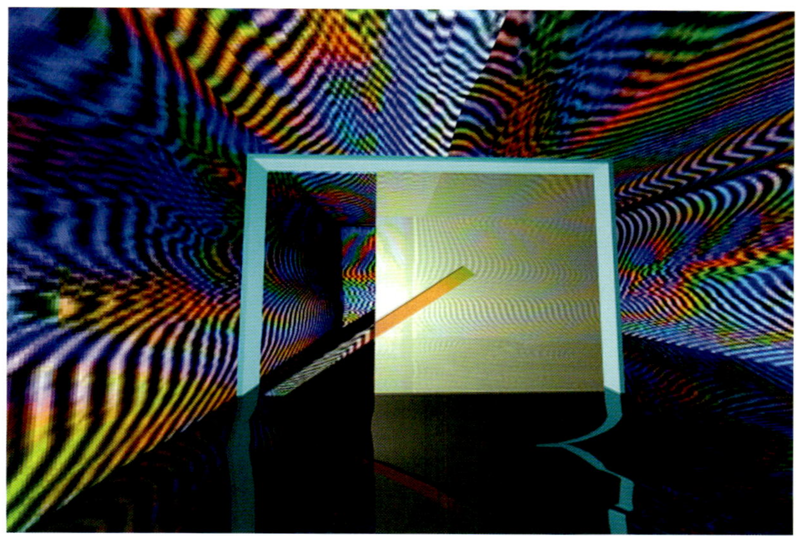

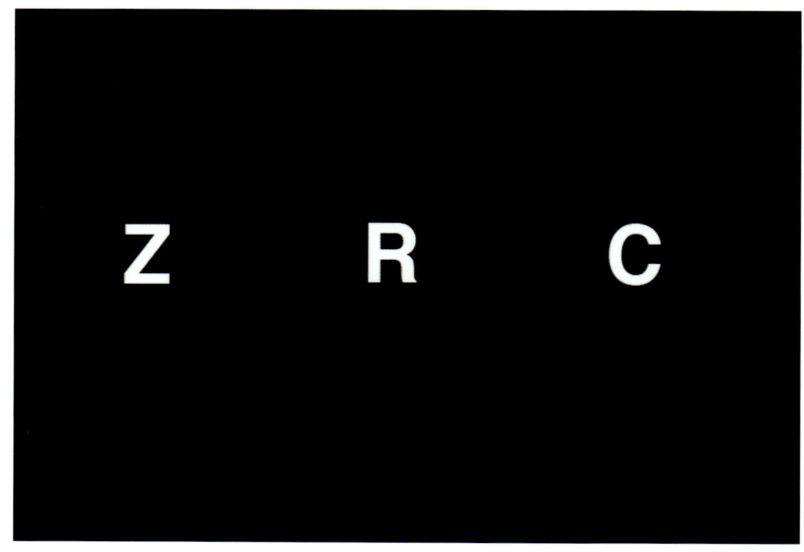

Stills from *Parallel Series II (Zoom, Rotation, Collision)*, 2010 —
cat. no. 10

Luke Butler

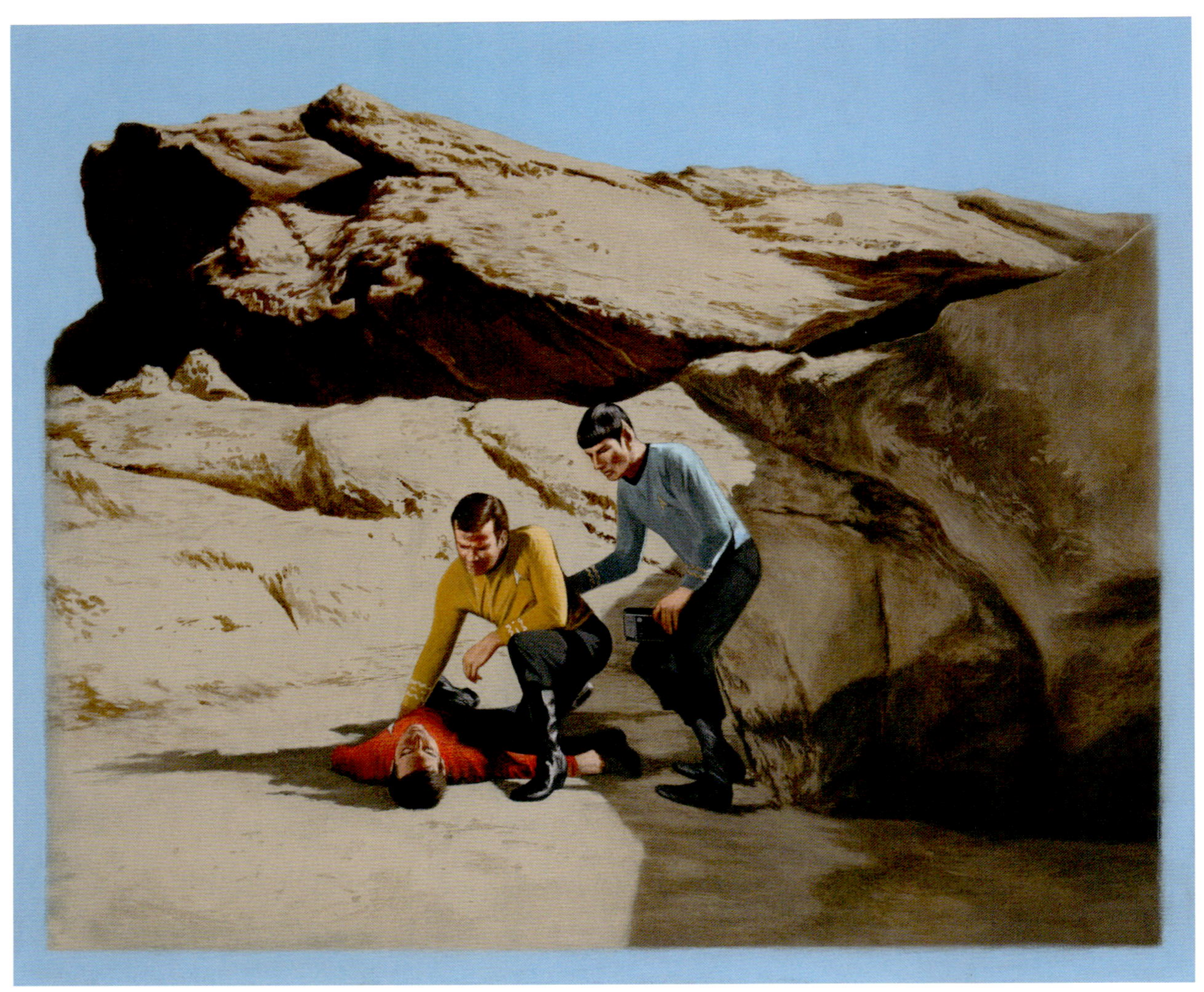

Landing Party II, **2009** — cat. no. 13

Interview with Stacie Martinez

SM: **How would you define your work?**

LB: I make paintings and collages that contemplate masculinity and mortality as seen on TV. In speaking the bright, two-dimensional language of popular culture, my work both celebrates and antagonizes the heroic figures of my youth.

We live in a world seen and shaped through popular culture. It is its own sort of reality, a remarkable and reliable point of connection with other people. I still love my heroes and action figures—even if I can see around them now, I can never quite look away either. My artistic endeavors represent an opportunity for us to work together.

SM: **Tell me a little about how the Enterprise idea first came to you.**

LB: When the original *Star Trek* episodes were released on DVD, I was amazed at the clarity of the imagery—quite a bit more vivid than it had ever been on reruns after school or at 1 a.m. What an amazing privilege to have these great staples in my grasp, whenever I wanted them, like a twenty-four-hour kitchen full of cereal. At any and every instance of Kirk's struggle and pain, I began to spy a great pantheon of pathos, of noble, virtuous, and outrageous suffering—shallow, absurd, and poignant all at once.

I think these images work because they are out of context. As photo- or video-based extractions, they would be too close to their source. But as paintings on canvas, made carefully and faithfully, something else emerges—a meditation on sorrow, loss, anxiety, confusion, and vulnerability. I think these become as much about pathos as about the fantastic, legendary figures in the picture, and certainly they are about the strange yet entirely natural combination of the two.

SM: **You seem to have captured, in essence, Captain Kirk's humanity.**

LB: I am constantly impressed by how culturally unaccustomed men are to introspection and vulnerability. Men aren't asked to look at themselves publicly. So there is something funny and productive to me about forcing it, about using men as a vehicle for openness, anxiety, ambiguity. The hero must always win, but he must fall first. Isolating him there, in his cycle of agony, makes for a story that starts in his world and hopefully illuminates ours. It helps that William Shatner is such an energetic, ardent actor. If someone else had played Kirk, the character could have seemed hollow and generic, and *Star Trek* might not have made it. Shatner fills Kirk to bursting with humanity.

SM: **Why Pietàs, Saint Sebastian, and religious symbolism today? Even if you didn't set out thinking, "I'm going to make work with religious iconography," there's no denying that it's embedded in the subtext.**

LB: I took an AP art history class in high school, with Ms. Betsy Goldberg, who still comes to my shows! This class was my introduction to all sorts of histories, not least that of Catholicism and its arsenal of iconography. It is amaz-

ing to me how much of Western art history absolutely depends on the Catholic Church, and more amazing still how alien that seems in the present. Going into a gallery now, one sees very little of all that precedes us. I find that rupture rather provocative. I am not a traditionalist. I think artists should do only what they are most interested in, whatever that is, however it works. I happen to be drawn to heroic narratives. My skepticism of heroic invulnerability doesn't reduce my fascination. I try to use a visual language that is appropriate to the heroic idiom, and I try to explore all the cracks where reality peeks through.

I have to admit that I backed into painting Pietàs. I made this work because I thought it would be funny and resonant, that it was both an absurd and entirely proper thing for me to do. The iconography of suffering is somewhat built in. It was only well into the work that I identified it in the manner of Saint Sebastian or the Pietà, realizing that in depicting a universal figure of pathos, I had wandered into a most hallowed tradition.

On that note, I think entirely too much can be made of an artist's intentions. Art is a journey, a living thing. One must have intuition, trust in what one wants to do, and not try to nail everything down before setting out. Ideas only generate art; the reality of seeing it through changes it. Some of the most vital aspects of one's work become visible after the fact.

SM: **The work conjures a reaction that is simultaneously nostalgic and humorous, which I think taps back into your comments about universality.**

LB: For all of my life *Star Trek* has been on TV somewhere, and I think people know it whether they were into it or not. It was a staple of afternoon and late-night reruns, in the time before cable and Internet and the fragmentation of culture into subdivisions and preferences of seemingly limitless variety. *Star Trek* is of the same world as Walter Cronkite— a main artery, not a diffuse capillary system. TV of that era may appear cheap and disposable, but what of it lingers does so because it was made well. Papier-mâché rocks are less unconvincing than bad storytelling!

As a teenager growing up in SoHo in the eighties, I yearned for things that connected to reality, even if only the dopey, pedestrian world around me. Mass culture felt distant and oblivious, animated by the spirit of entertainment executives. Gallery art seemed to me like it existed beyond some Olympian barrier of inscrutability; it did not stir my curiosity. I gravitated to things like Robert Crumb, whose drawings were about raging hormones and dirty streets, and to the Ramones, Beastie Boys, and Public Enemy, music that was collaged out of the urban landscape. My dream was to make art about the world I knew, art that a smart, curious person not necessarily steeped in art conventions could appreciate. ∎

Born 1971 in San Francisco; lives and works in San Francisco. Butler attended the Cooper Union School of Art (BFA, 1994) and California College of the Arts (MFA, 2008). He has had solo exhibitions at Kantor Gallery, Los Angeles, and Second Floor Projects and Silverman Gallery, both in San Francisco. He has also participated in numerous group exhibitions, including shows at ABC No Rio, New York; Galerie Georg Kargl, Vienna; the Institute of Contemporary Art, Boston; and the Eagle Tavern, San Francisco.

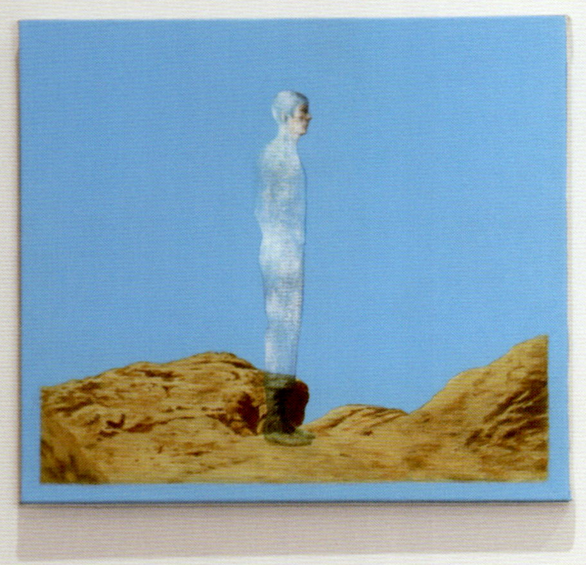
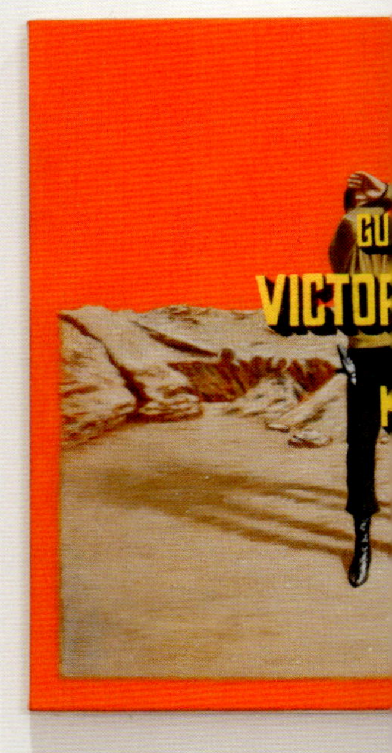

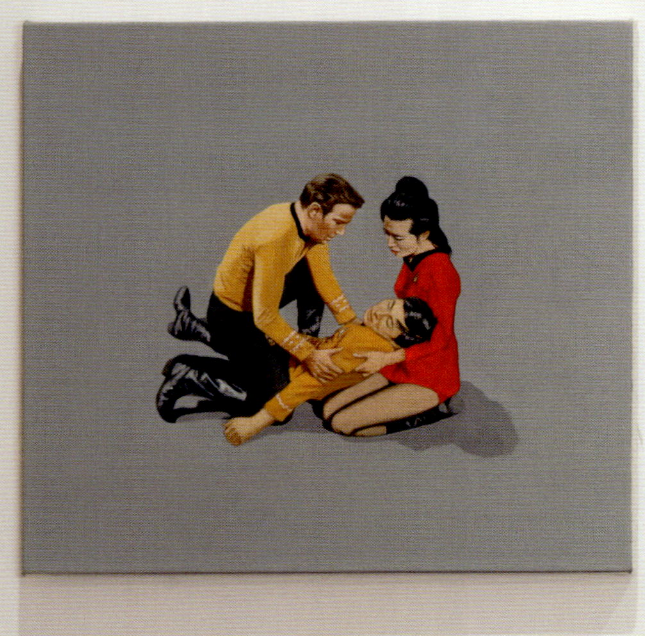
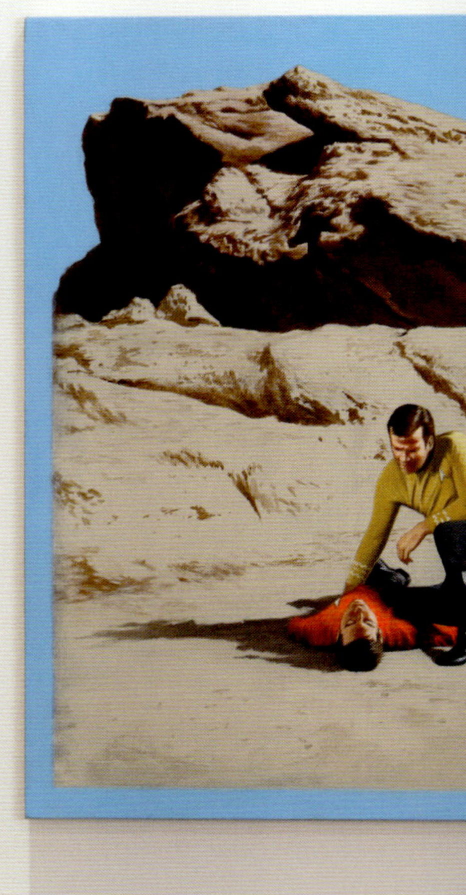

Top left to right
Spock, **2010** — cat. no. 15
Vic Tayback, **2010** — cat. no. 16
Captain XIII, **2009** — cat. no. 12

Bottom left to right
Captain, Crew IV, **2010** — cat. no. 14
Landing Party II, **2009** — cat. no. 13
Captain X, **2008** — cat. no. 11

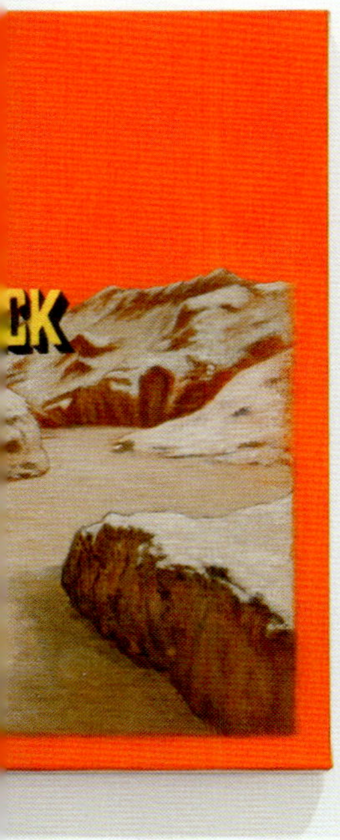
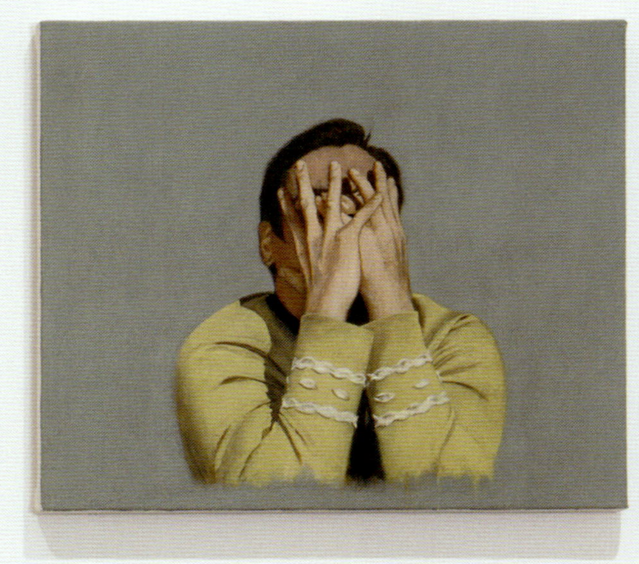
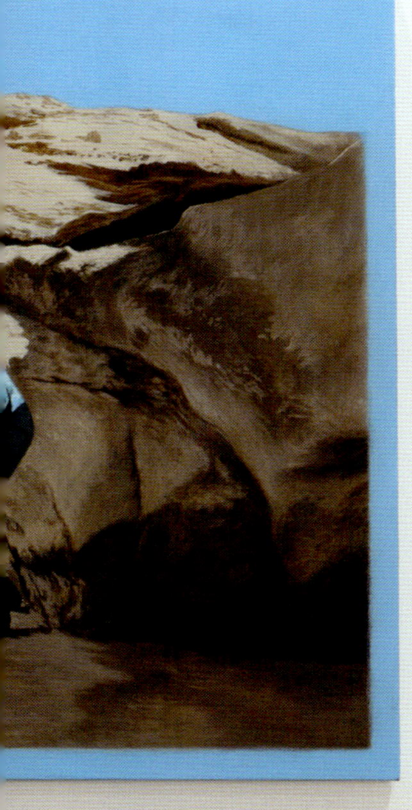
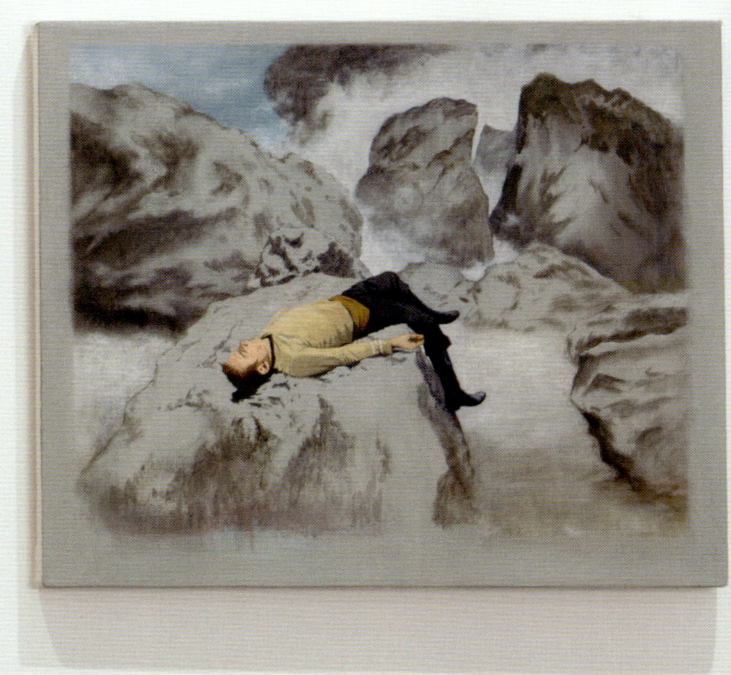

Juan Capistran

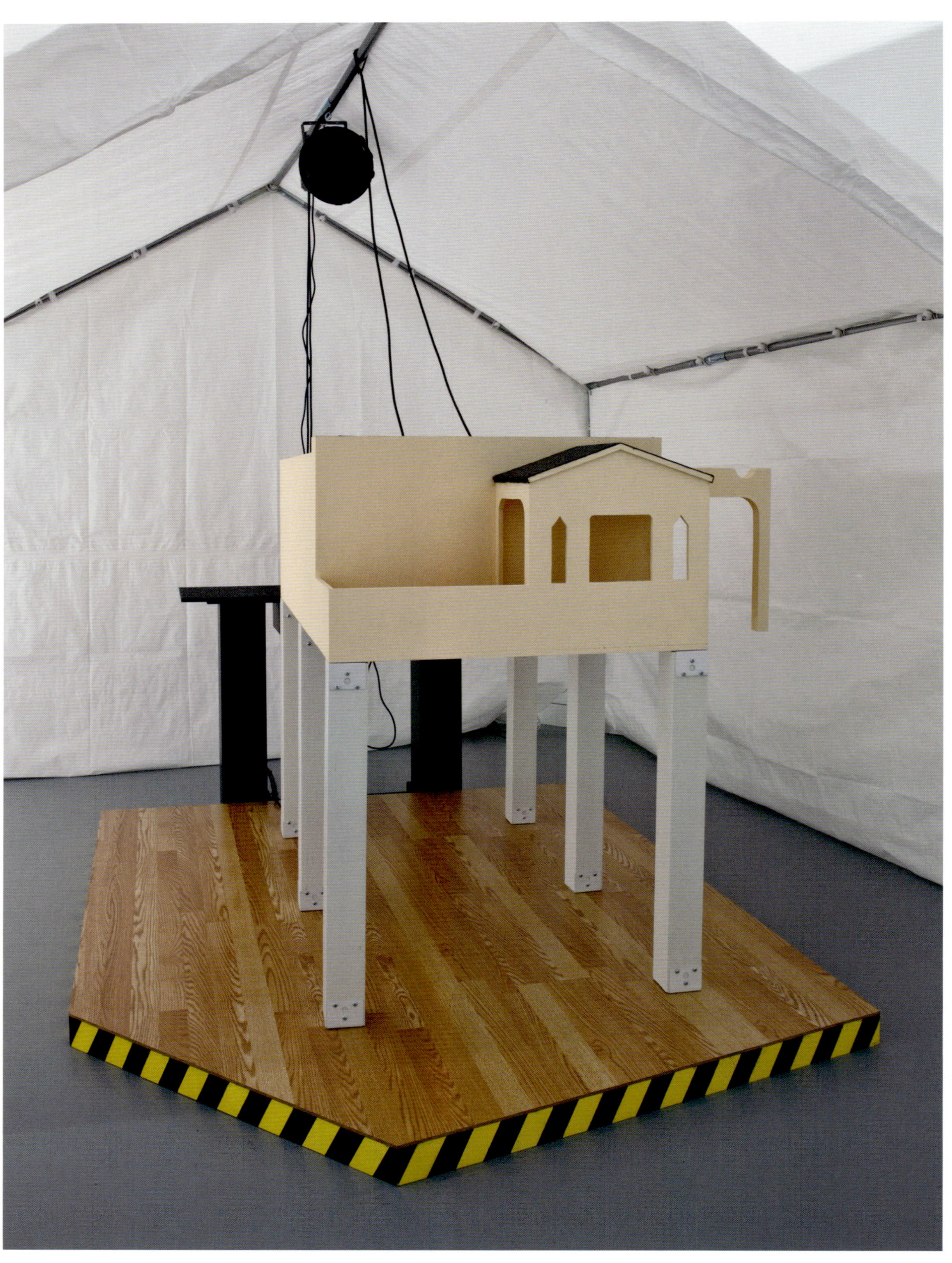

***This Machine Kills Fascists or Labor Sets You Free (Love Is the
Message)*, 2010** — cat. no. 17

Interview with Stacie Martinez

SM: **Let's talk about the work you're making for the biennial. When we spoke, you made reference to a tabernacle. Describe the installation/performance.**

JC: The work is composed of two major parts, a sculpture installation and a sound performance. The installation is located within a large, ten-by-twelve-foot tent structure and consists of a scaled-down re-creation of the dance floor from the Hacienda nightclub, which was located in Manchester, England. On top of the dance floor sits a large reproduction of the home I grew up in, which is located in south Los Angeles. The house is a typical Spanish colonial revival home that has been stuccoed, and it sits atop modernist-style stilts and is fitted with a three-hundred-watt sound system that is connected to a mobile DJ system. The audio that is played through the sculpture varies from manipulated sounds to historically significant songs and music associated with various underground subcultures. With the music playing and the lights flashing, the viewer enters a space that becomes a call to arms. It is a new revolution, and there is plenty of room to dance! Rousseau said something like, without action, all pleasure, all knowledge is nothing but a postponed death; we must not cease from toil until we have created a free space. There is a formal reference to a tabernacle in the installation, but the work is not a religious space. The installation operates as a temporal space, a "house," a "home," a "sanctuary" created by a displaced group, similar to a tabernacle.

SM: **You were born in Guadalajara, Mexico; you came to the United States when you were three; and you now practice in Los Angeles. How is your work tied to your own experience?**

JC: The work comes from a personal narrative. It comes from my experience in a part of Los Angeles that has been in constant flux. It's a narrative that is local and global at the same time. It is about a life that was, is, and could be. I was born in Mexico but really have no connection to it besides my parents. I grew up in South Central Los Angeles when it was still predominantly African American. I experienced the influx of Latin American immigrants and the "black flight" that followed. It has become a place of multiple identities and endless possibilities.

SM: **Home/hacienda. Place/space. These seem to be dominant themes in your work, and this project in particular appears to stem from the idea of creating one's own space. Can you expand on this?**

JC: I am interested in how space is taken over and claimed as one's own—a sidewalk, an empty lot, a house. I'm interested in how groups of people can come together, create alternative spaces and economies and exist autonomously outside of a hegemonic culture. How can we take what we have or don't have and produce a place where one can exist and operate in the in-between space?

SM: **After the performances for the opening events, how will the work change? How do you envision visitors will experience your work, and what would you like them to take away from the installation?**

JC: There are multiple ways to experience the work. With the performance, the viewer has more of a physical experience and connection with the work. For the rest of the time, the work operates in a more subtle way. I want people to think about the space in which one lives: how one navigates through that space and what one does with that space. ∎

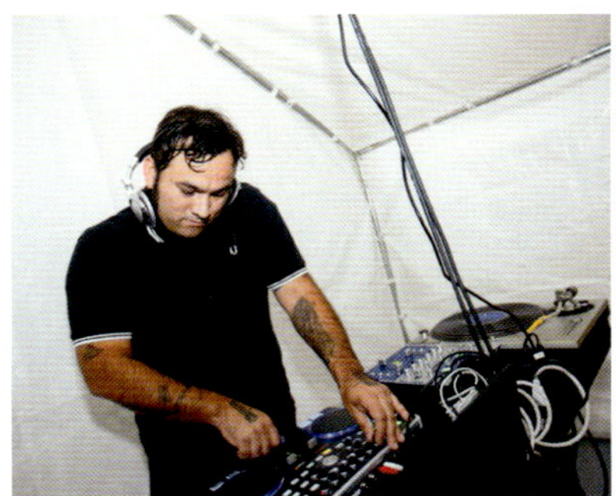

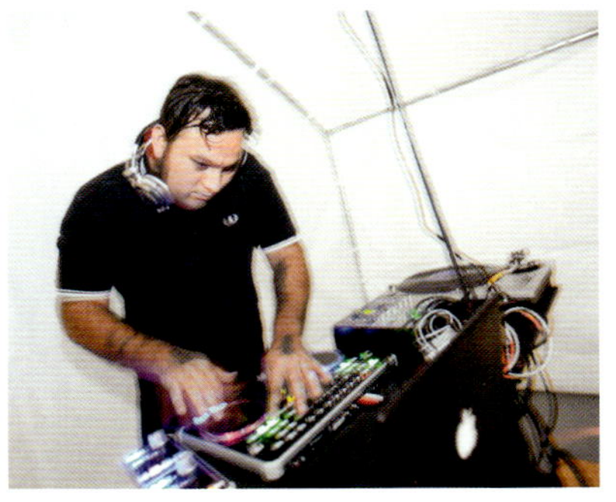

Born 1976 in Guadalajara, Mexico; lives and works in Los Angeles. Capistran attended Otis College of Art and Design (BFA, 1999) and the University of California, Irvine (MFA, 2002). He was awarded a California Community Foundation fellowship for the arts in 2009. His work has been exhibited nationally and internationally, at venues including the Bronx Museum, Bronx, New York; the Los Angeles County Museum of Art; the Museo Tamayo, Mexico City; Chisenhale Gallery, London; CAM Contemporáneo, Guadalajara; and Kurimanzutto, Mexico City.

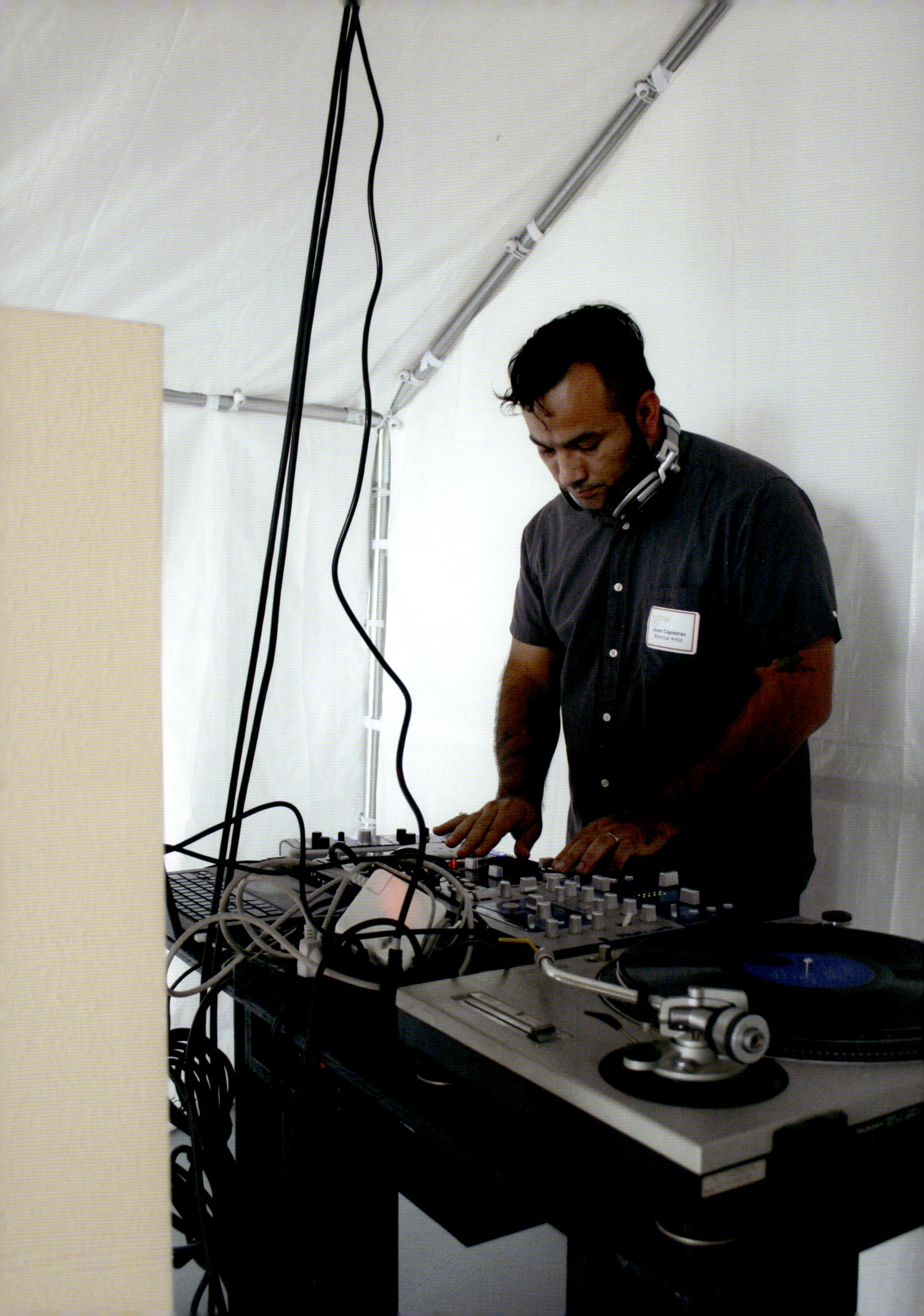

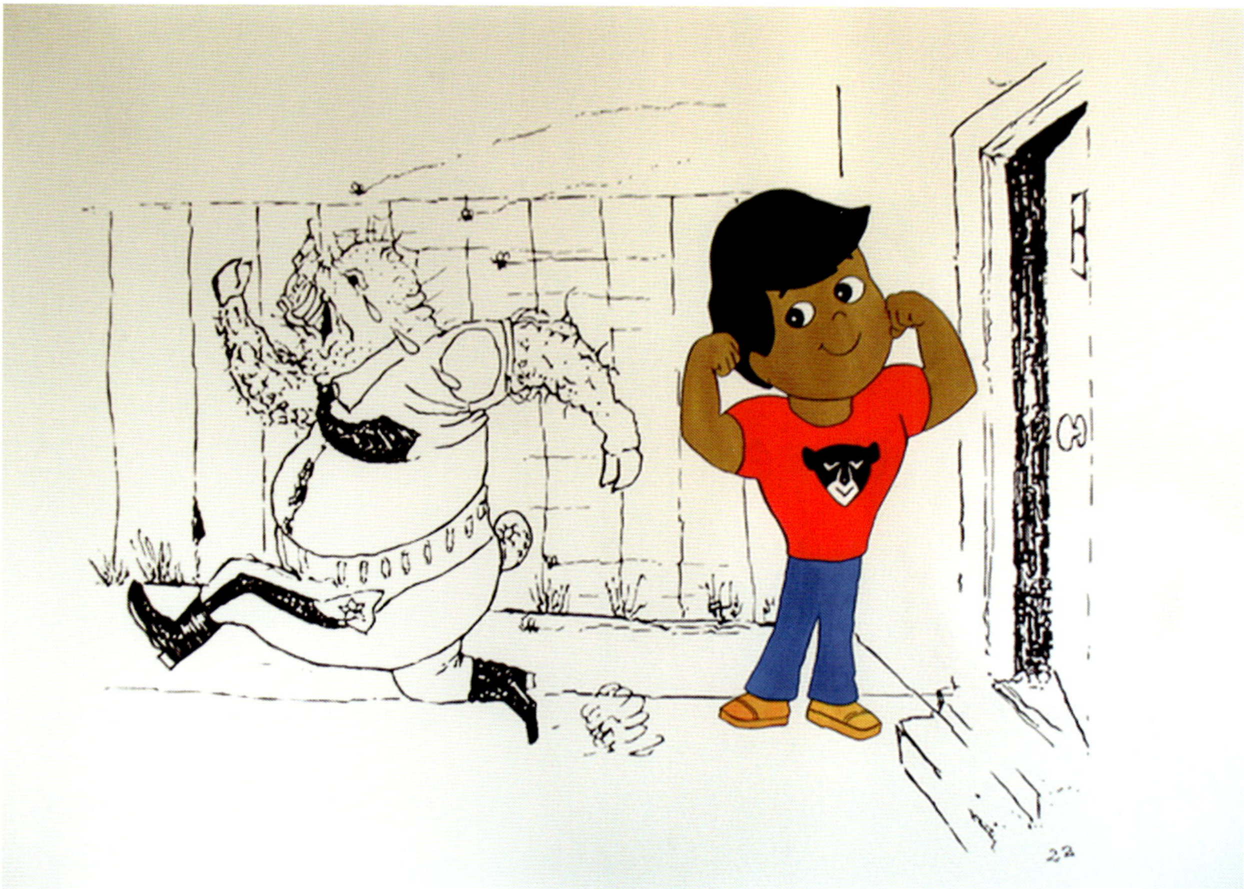

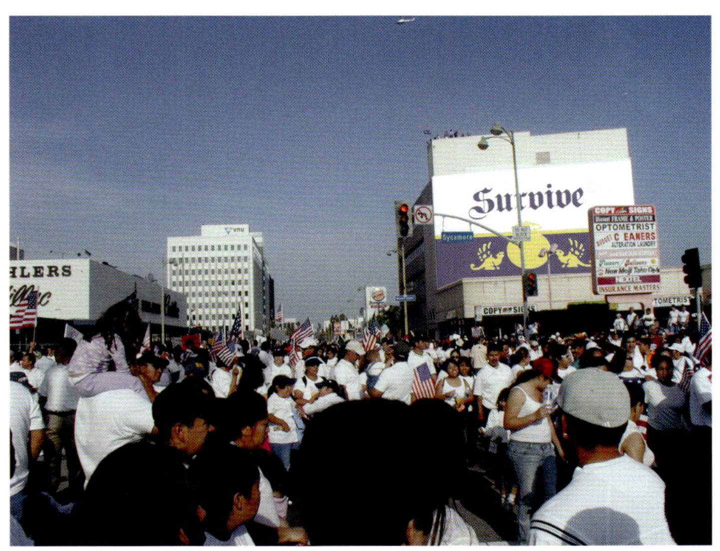

From the series *Sympathy for the Devil/Eat the Rich or 13 Point Program to Destroy America*, 2010
Ink and watercolor on paper
30 × 40 in. (76.2 × 101.6 cm)
Courtesy of the artist

What Makes a Man Start Fires? 2008
Altered photograph
Dimensions variable
Courtesy of the artist

This Machine Kills Fascists or Labor Sets You Free (Love Is the Message), **2010**— cat. no. 17
Installation and performance during the 2010 California Biennial

Zoe Crosher

Practice
Photography, installation, book projects

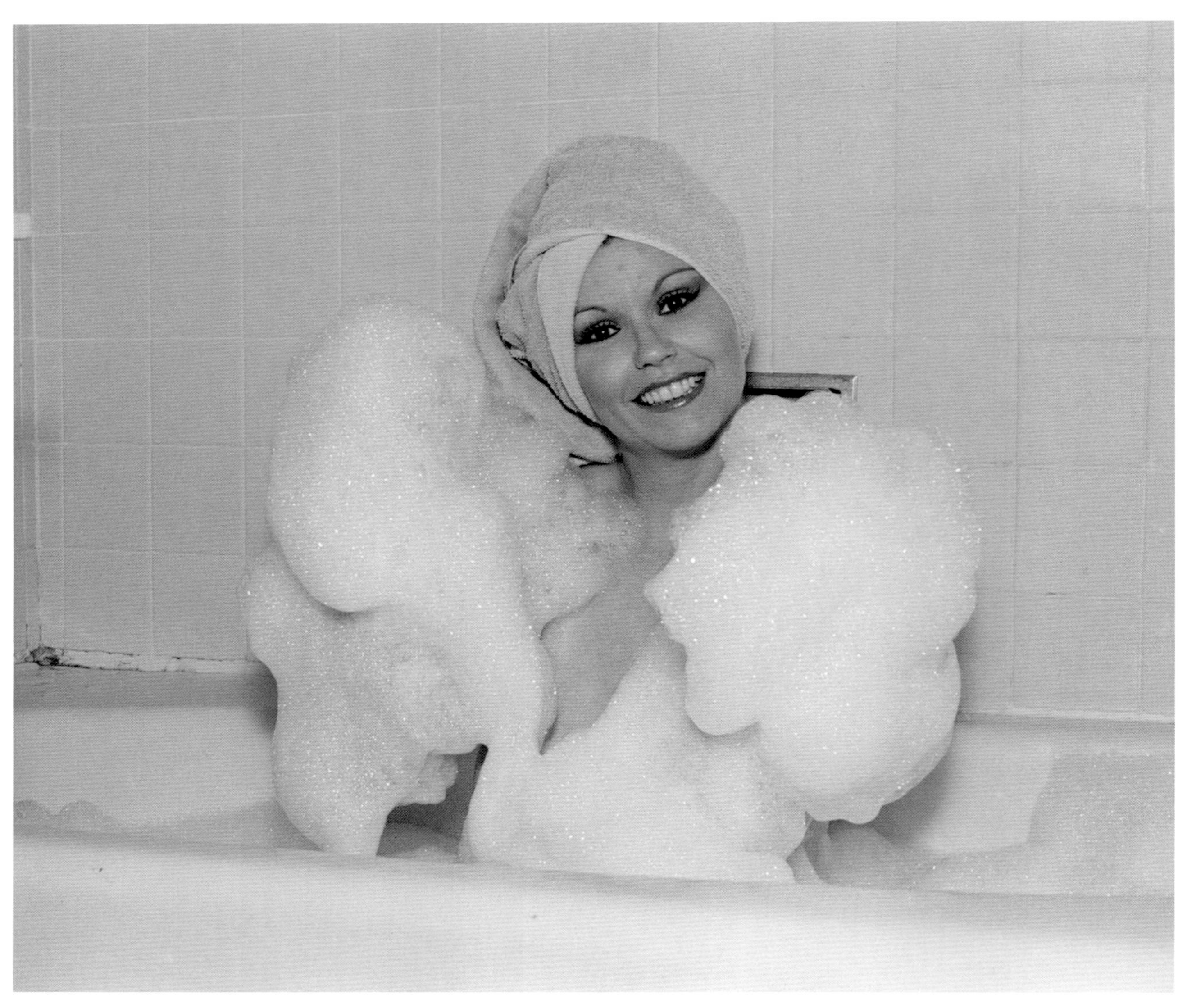

Like Miko Smiling for Christopher Williams, **2008** — cat. no. 18

Born 1975 in Santa Rosa, California; lives and works in Los Angeles. Crosher graduated from the University of California, Santa Cruz (BA, 1997), and California Institute of the Arts (MFA, 2001). Her work has been exhibited internationally in Vancouver, Rotterdam, Los Angeles, and New York. She is the subject of two monographs: *Out the Window (LAX)* (2006) and *The Vanishing of Michelle duBois*, to be published by Aperture in 2011. Crosher has served as a visiting faculty member at the University of California, Los Angeles, and at Art Center College of Design and as an associate editor at the journal *Afterall*.

Interview with Sarah Bancroft

SB: Your work with the photographic archive of Michelle duBois is well known—although little exhibited in California—and has gone through three iterations. The two previous incarnations and exhibitions were the *Reconsidered Archive of Michelle duBois* and the *Unraveling of Michelle duBois*. You are now focusing on the *Unveiling of Michelle duBois*. Can you describe these explorations and presentations of the archive, how they relate to one another or have progressed from one to the other?

ZC: So far, the Michelle duBois project has loosely gone through these three iterations, with each successive installation a site-specific and expanded version of the last. The first round, the *Reconsidered Archive of Michelle duBois*, started off in a much more academic place, inspired by unintentional art historical references (the *CindySherman-esque* and the *Like Christopher Williams* pieces extracting meaning from uncanny parallels given how the images actually *looked* and when they were made, as well as the materiality of the archive itself). This period focused heavily on the physicality of the actual archive, emphasizing the backs of duBois's snapshots and the fronts of her photo albums.

The question became how does one take this mass of photographs, ultimately *things*, and go beyond a simple re-presentation, beyond simply adding more strange images to the preexisting and already fetishized world of the amateur photograph? As I am obsessed with the fiction of a singular image or approach to history, I realized that mining the concept of the archive, and this archive in particular (given its bizarre meanderings and wonderings), had a way of exposing the fissures that I was interested in, from the end of the analog/materiality to questions of what to include/not include in the metanarrative to what Jan Tumlir calls the "Kodak-inspired Kabuki."[1]

A satellite approach to shifting accumulation emphasizes my larger concerns of the impossibility of any singular notion of "truth" to be found in either the photograph or, by extension, the photographic archive. The fiction of a total, singular historical record—not just official and public history, but that most twentieth-century notion of the individual—is exposed by its dynamic nature. They run on parallel tracks, the impossibility of collecting and recording one's entire life (or a nation's entire history) through photographs and obsessive recordkeeping. And this is where the second round, the *Unraveling of Michelle duBois*, has resonance, "by re-photographing, scanning and reorganizing duBois' slippery self-portraits of costumed, performative sexuality into a re-contextualized archive"[2] that almost becomes the same size as, if not larger than, the original archive. Borges's allegory about mapmaking, in which the map of the kingdom when unraveled takes up the space of the entire kingdom, is an important inspiration (originally introduced to me during my time working with *NTNTNT*).[3] As is my obsession with the amateur (with its root word *amor*), manifested in the amateur photographer. Motivated by the very obsolescence it is trying to outrun, the/her/my compulsion to photograph and record, by its nature, is its undoing.

And such a bittersweet compulsion becomes so viscerally apparent when one is faced with some of these duBois images, so beautiful and at the same time so horrendous.

SB: Who is Michelle duBois? How did you come to work with the archive?

ZC: A few facts: Michelle duBois, a name that was just one of her five aliases, turned tricks to sustain her travels throughout the Pacific Rim during the 1970s and 1980s. She worked the noon to 10 p.m. shift. She took on many guises and kept fanatical photographic documentation of her dramatic transformations. Until one day she didn't. I generally try to give out as few facts as possible, and thankfully rumors abound.

SB: Your biennial installation features imagery from the spectrum of the archive—the narratives created around "reconsidering," "unraveling," and "revealing," and/or the impossibility of locating a static subject. The installation also relates to an upcoming artist's book. How does the book further the project?

ZC: The current "unveiling" actually has five elements: the biennial is one component, and the book plays a part in most of these elements. They will all be on view this fall.

1 — At the California Biennial, the unveiling of the process for the forthcoming book will be presented in a mock mock-up of pages from the book layout. These will be shown alongside existing framed and unframed images that reference the photographic, the analog format and its disappearance, both literal and metaphoric. Also included are previous editions done for Invisible-Exports in New York City in February 2009 (Artist-of-the-Month, *Almost Okinawa from "In & Around the Fronds"*), and the current "disappearing" edition (*The Vanishing of Michelle duBois*, 2010), done for Aperture.

2 — At Charlie James Gallery in Chinatown, the *Unveiling of Michelle duBois* installation commences at the end, with *last four days and nights in Tokyo*. Here is where the obfuscation of and total access to the fantasized image of Michelle duBois are given equal weight.

3 — Also in Chinatown, at Dan Graham, there will be an installation that emphasizes the self-reflexive collecting aspects within the archive and within the fantasized context of Chinatown, itself an L.A. fantasy of Asia. Also to be included are a number of images from the archive that are almost the same.

4 — At Emma Gray's new space in Culver City, Emma Gray HQ, there will be an installation with just the backs of photos and the alias images.

5 — Finally, writer Lara Taubman and I are collaborating on a script that unveils the narrative, which will be performed by an ingenue Canadian actress. She'll read from a script in a rented room at the Pagoda Hotel on Broadway in Chinatown. Sitting on the bed, with her back to the audience, the actress will perform, in a dusky darkness, collapsed texts adapted from notes written by duBois, transcripts of video interviews with duBois, along with splices of various collected anecdotes, reviews, responses, and articles about the lives that duBois led. ■

1. Jan Tumlir, "Femme Fatale: Zoe Crosher's Reconsidered Archive of Michelle duBois," *Aperture*, no. 198 (Spring 2010): 37.

2. Press release for *The Unveiling of Michelle duBois*, Charlie James Gallery, Los Angeles, October 2010

3. See Jason Brown and Zoe Crosher, eds., *NTNTNT* (Valencia: California Institute of the Arts, 2003). The Borges story referred to is "On Exactitude in Science."

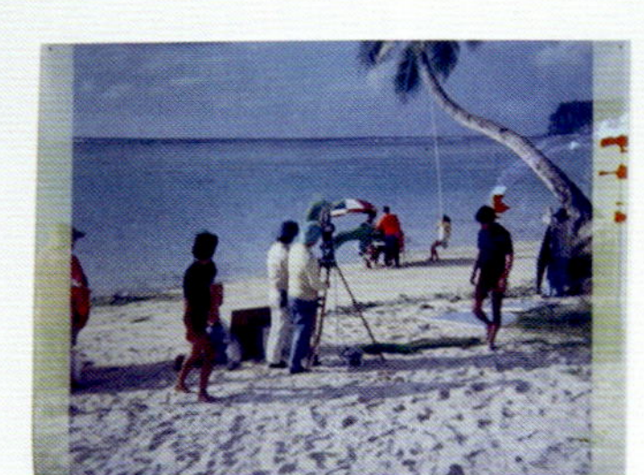
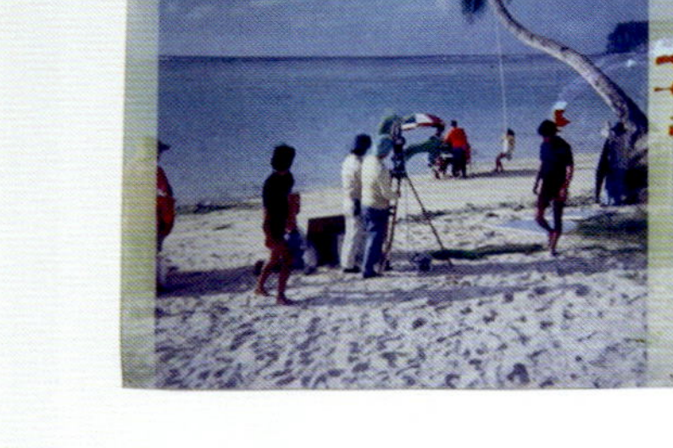
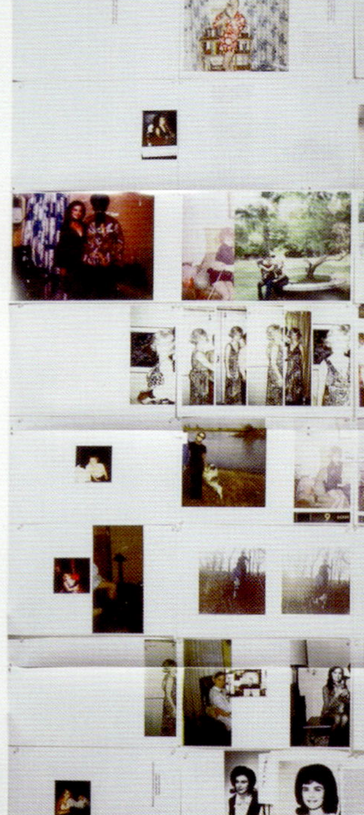
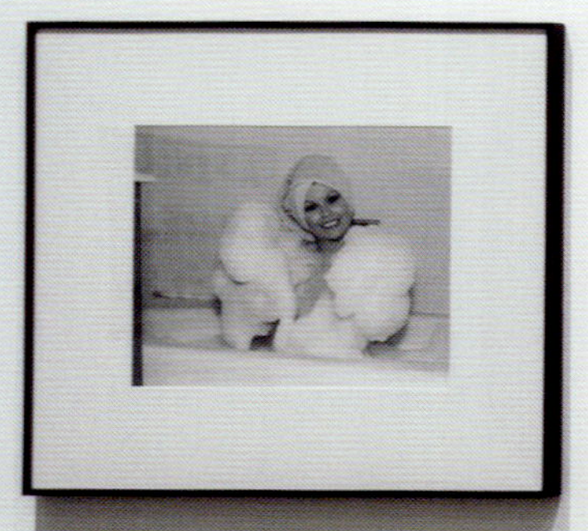
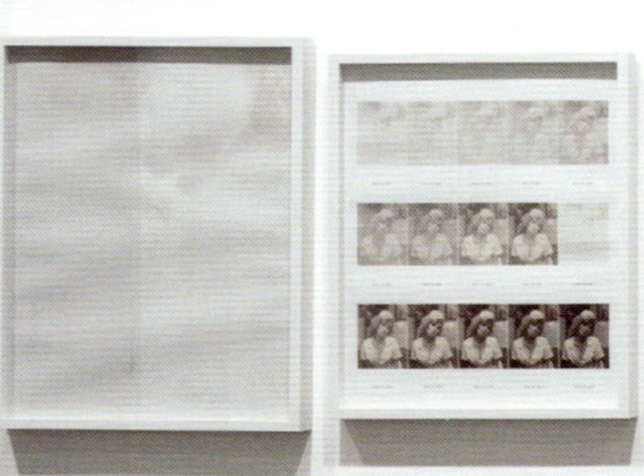
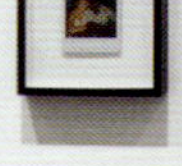

Like Miko Smiling for Christopher Williams, **2008** — cat. no. 18
Final Image from the Disappearing of Michelle duBois, **2010** — cat. no. 21
Her Fantasy Film Shoot on the Beach, **2010** — cat. no. 22
The Vanishing of Michelle duBois, **2010** — cat. no. 25
Looking Another Way, **2008** — cat. no. 19
Mock Mock-up, **2010 (in collaboration with Juliette Bellocq)** — cat. no. 24
Super Foto (Me), **2009** — cat. no. 20
Kodak Color Film, **2010** — cat. no. 23

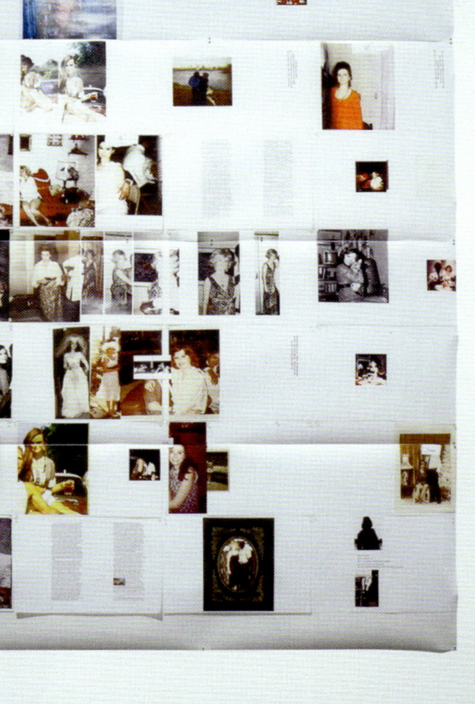

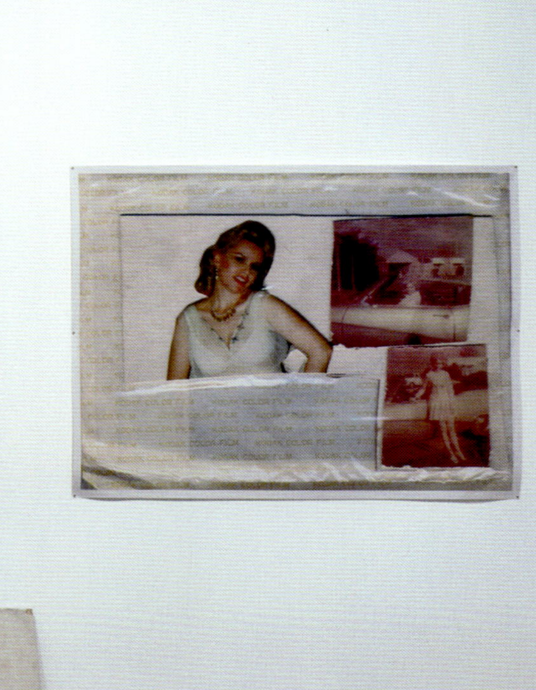

KILAT
cuci cetak
SUPER
FOTO

Brian Dick

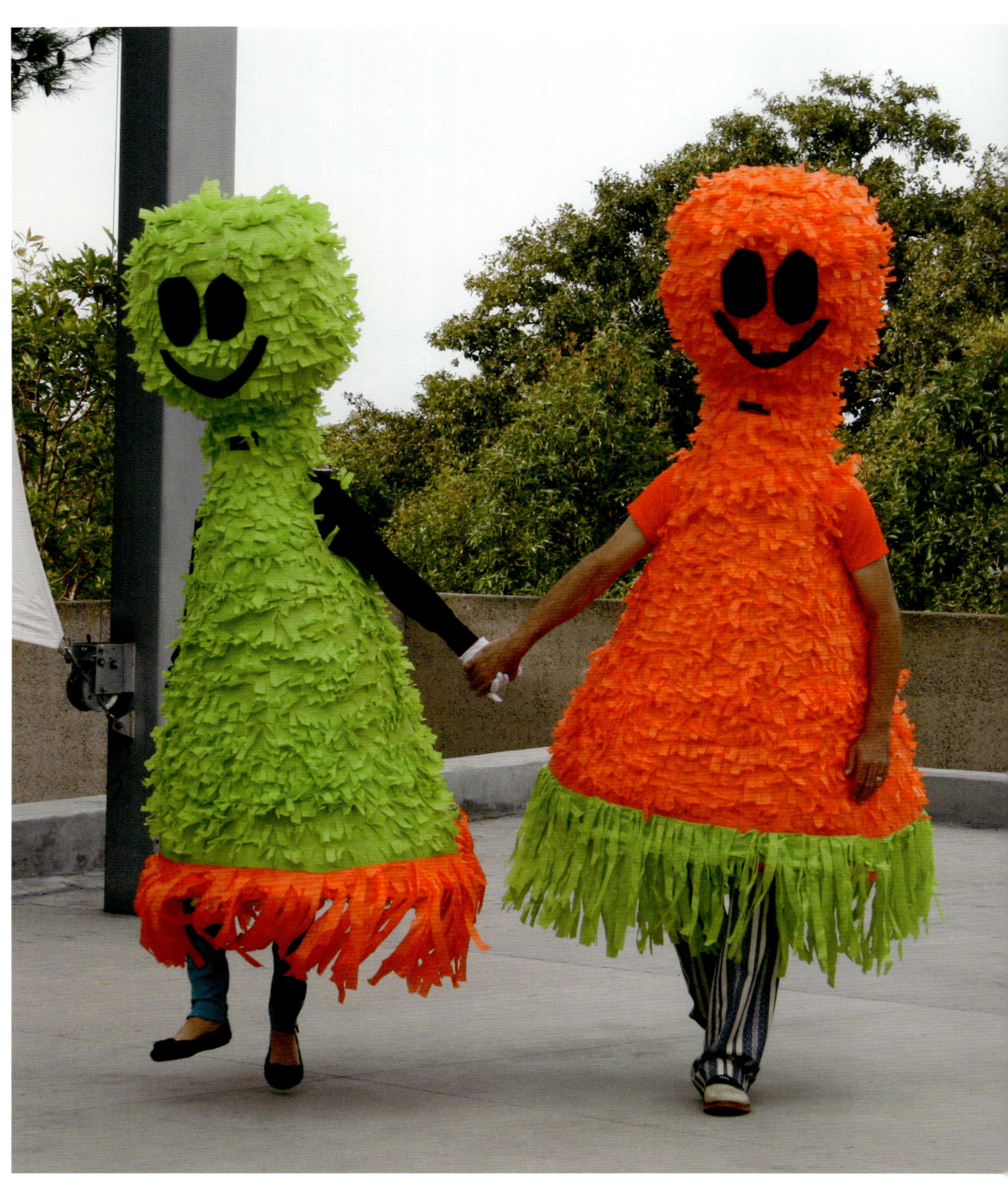

The Nationwide Museum Mascot Project Presents: OCMAscot, **2010 (in collaboration with Christen Sperry-Garcia)** — cat. no. 26

Interview with Katherine Lukacher

KL: When it comes to creating and implementing an artistic concept, you seem fascinated by the idea of building and rebuilding, especially with found or adopted materials. By utilizing these vastly different types of materials, what are you allowing yourself to explore?

BD: I like when things fall apart in a funny or interesting way. I am taking what would normally be considered practice or private space and putting it in a public context, allowing for all the false starts, mistakes, and happy accidents to be out in the open. I suppose it is a process of creating equality between artist and audience if they are interested in playing along.

In relationship to the Mascot Project, that idea gets pushed as far as I have been able to push it. At its best, the Mascot Project functions as a spontaneous public forum for random encounters that involve an exchange of creative ideas that help solve problems, implement policy, and (maybe) offer a critique of an institution that is not at all interested in this kind of undisciplined, noncontextualized discourse.

KL: What types of responses have you received from people while you hunted and gathered for the components of your mascot outfit and then once you activated it? How will **Orange County** differ from your previous venues?

BD: Usually we just disappear into the background. Really, it looks a bit like a scavenger hunt. We've found components for the mascots in thrift stores, dumpsters, and dime stores and gotten them from friends of friends. When we explain what we are doing, people are usually charmed and willing to help. When we are wearing the costume and doing whatever activities go along with that, people react pretty much like they would to any costumed character you'd see at an amusement park or fair and are generally disarmed and charmed by the costume (unless they are freaked out by it, which has also happened). Christen Sperry-Garcia, my collaborator, initially worried about trying to make the mascot relevant to the venue. What we discovered very quickly was that if the mascot was accepted it did not matter what it looked like or if it appeared to be relevant to the particular location or not. The only practical considerations that we have adopted over time are making sure that the mascot costume has good visibility and is relatively comfortable to wear. It's all one big evolving experiment, and neither of us knows what will happen or how this one will be the same or different from our previous experiences.

KL: For the 2010 California Biennial you also plan on doing a "car cozy" or, in this case, a "van cozy." A cozy is typically used to keep a teapot warm, while in your work *Hot Rod Car Cozy* (2000), you seem to be playing with the idea of keeping a hot rod warm. What are you exploring in this "cozying" process?

BD: The cozy idea was always about transformation or disguise. In the same way that "clothes make the man or woman," putting on the cozy, in lieu of a new paint job or souping up the car, transformed a regular car into a hot rod but in such a ridiculous way that everyone could be in on the joke.

Also you could actually drive the original car cozy. So to take a car that was as far from anything like a hot rod that you could imagine made the whole thing ridiculous and funny. With the cozy on, the Festiva ended up looking like a clown car or, as one person observed, a luchador mask—not really a hot rod.

As the van will be static at the museum, I have been thinking about ways to address that fact. Do I disguise the van and treat it as a small, neutral space or push its "vanness"? Anyway it is a cargo van and not a travel van. Those travel vans have a long history that gives context to a cozy that would play with that history and culture, including, for example, a sewn "Honk If You're Horny" bumper sticker or an embroidered desertscape stitched on the side. I'm not sure what to do with this particular van. I do know that since I am combining the car cozy with the mascot and the glow-room (recently renamed the Glowfitti Room), the cozy will be an attempt to create continuity among these different works.

KL: When we first met, you made a statement that was quite captivating: "Sometimes you have to sacrifice aesthetics for ten minutes of pathos and joy." Could you explain further how this statement reflects your larger artistic credo and its translation into practice?

BD: For me it is all about the moment of doing. I am not so interested in the work afterward. So whether I am making my bed differently every day or putting up phosphorous-impregnated glow-in-the-dark walls that will hold a drawn light mark or stencil for only a few minutes, I guess it's pretty clear that I am not that interested in longevity.

KL: You visited the **Orange County Museum of Art** in early **June 2010** to explore the space; you also brought along a tote bag. As an artist what do you carry with you when exploring a new space?

BD: A camera and a sketchbook. I am interested in a space only as a technicality. I'd just as soon do the show in my pocket or sit outside the museum with a couple of sketches and explain what might have been to whomever passes by. Or better yet, have a bag of stuff to play with (or use their bag of stuff to play with) and see what we could come up with together. I always find that kind of thinking much more exciting. The stakes are so small that there is no way to fail, and both of us potentially have a beautiful memory. Not very professional, I'm sure, but a lot closer to "pathos and joy." ∎

Born 1963 in Las Cruces, New Mexico; lives and works in Long Beach and San Diego. Dick graduated from the University of California, Los Angeles (BA, 1991), and the University of California, San Diego (MFA, 1995). He has participated in numerous gallery shows, museum exhibitions, and film festivals throughout the United States, Europe, and Japan. In 2008 he participated in the inaugural exhibition of the New Children's Museum, San Diego, *Childsplay,* with a reinvention of Allan Kaprow's *No Rules Except . . .* and *Yard.* In 2009, together with his partner, Christen Sperry-Garcia, he participated in the Bushwick *SITE Fest* in Brooklyn, and in 2010 he was featured in *Here Not There: San Diego Art Now* at the Museum of Contemporary Art San Diego. Dick received the 2008–9 San Diego Art Prize.

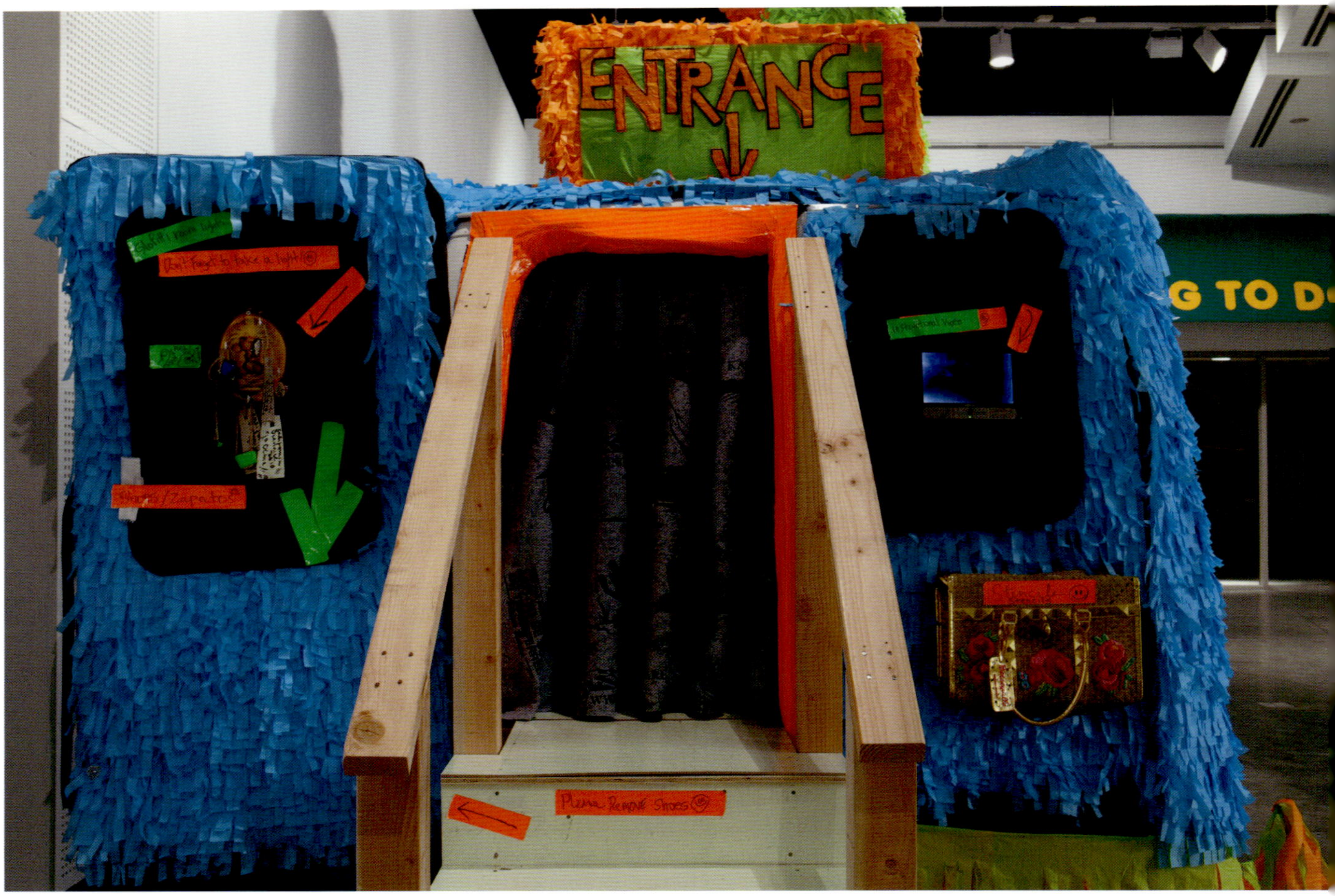

ENTRANCE
Don't Forget to take a light
Please Remove Shoes
TO DO

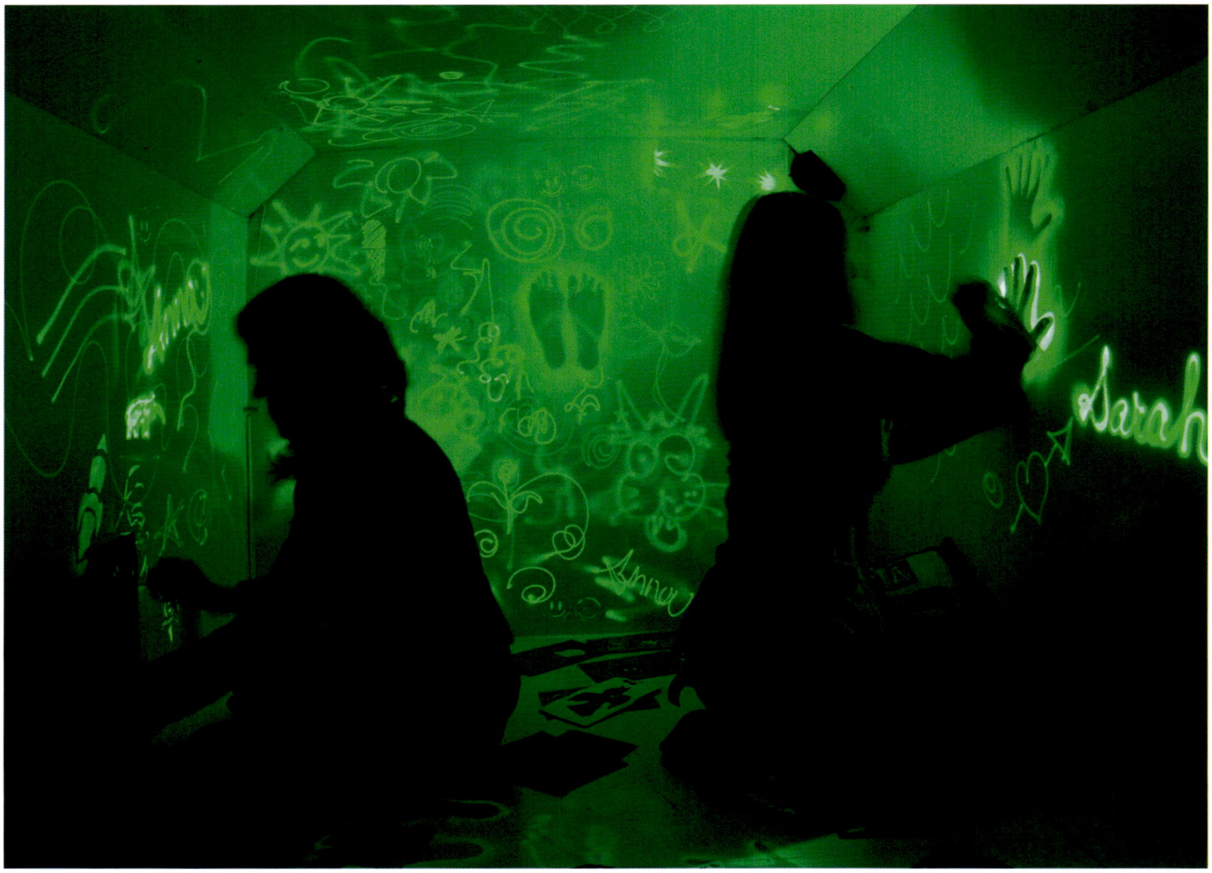

Sarah

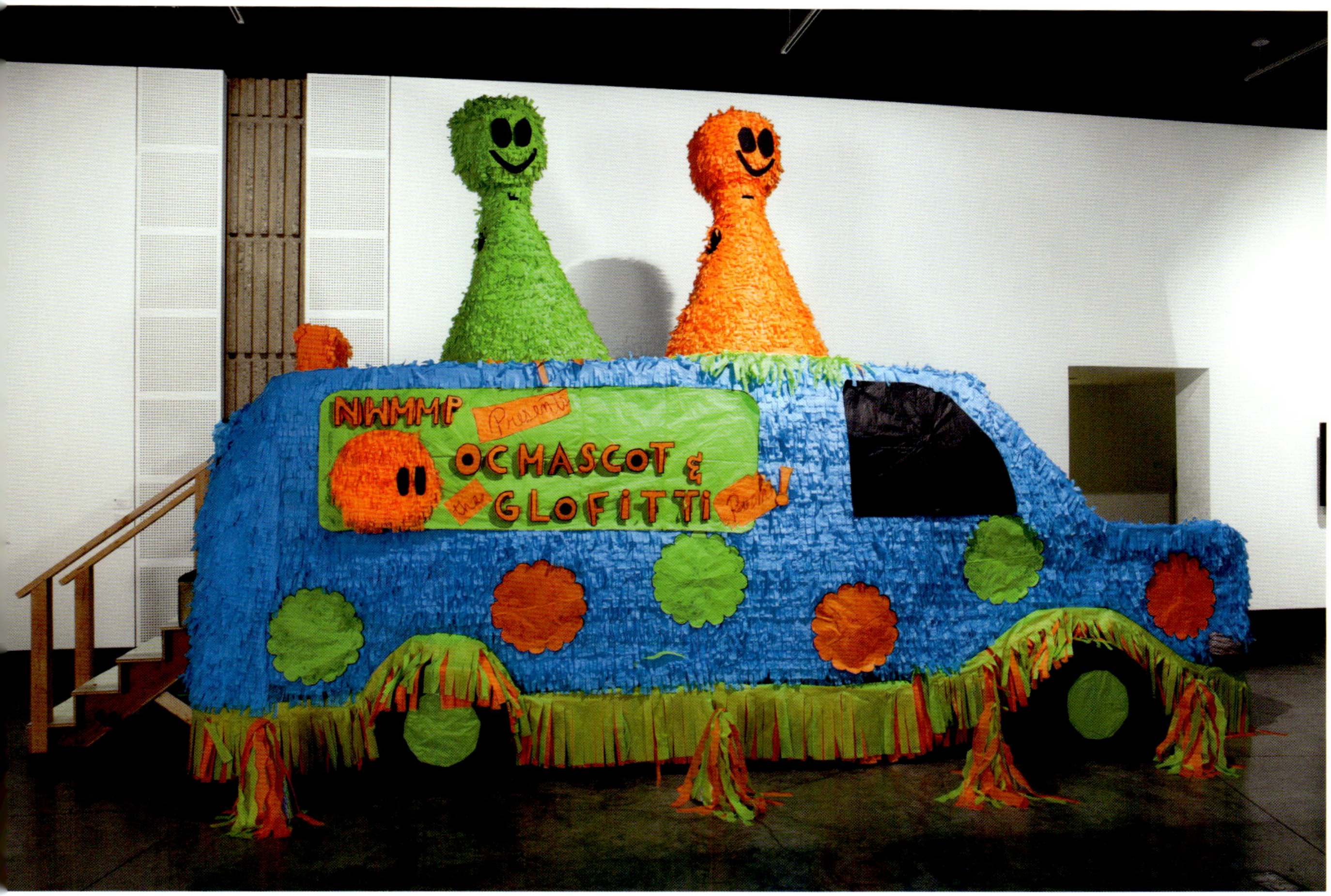

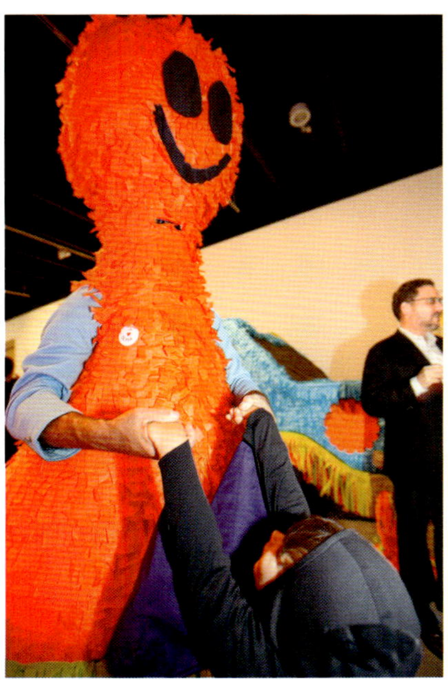

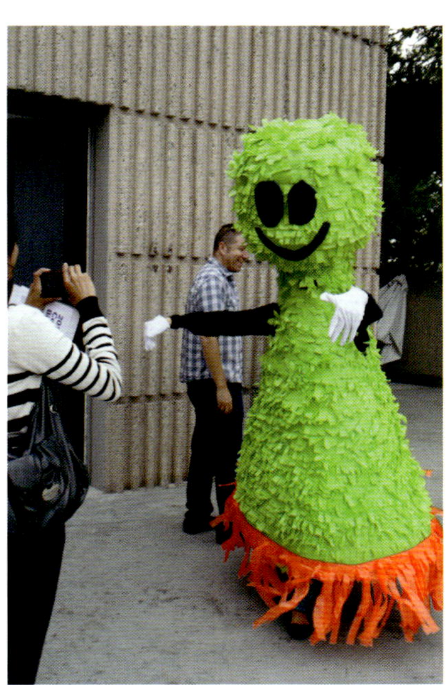

Opposite and top
***The Nationwide Museum Mascot Project's Piñata Cozy with
Glowfitti Room*, 2010 (in collaboration with Christen Sperry-
Garcia)** — cat. no. 27
Piñata Cozy (top) and ***Glowfitti Room*** (opposite bottom)

Bottom
Mascots performing during 2010 California Biennial opening events

Dru Donovan

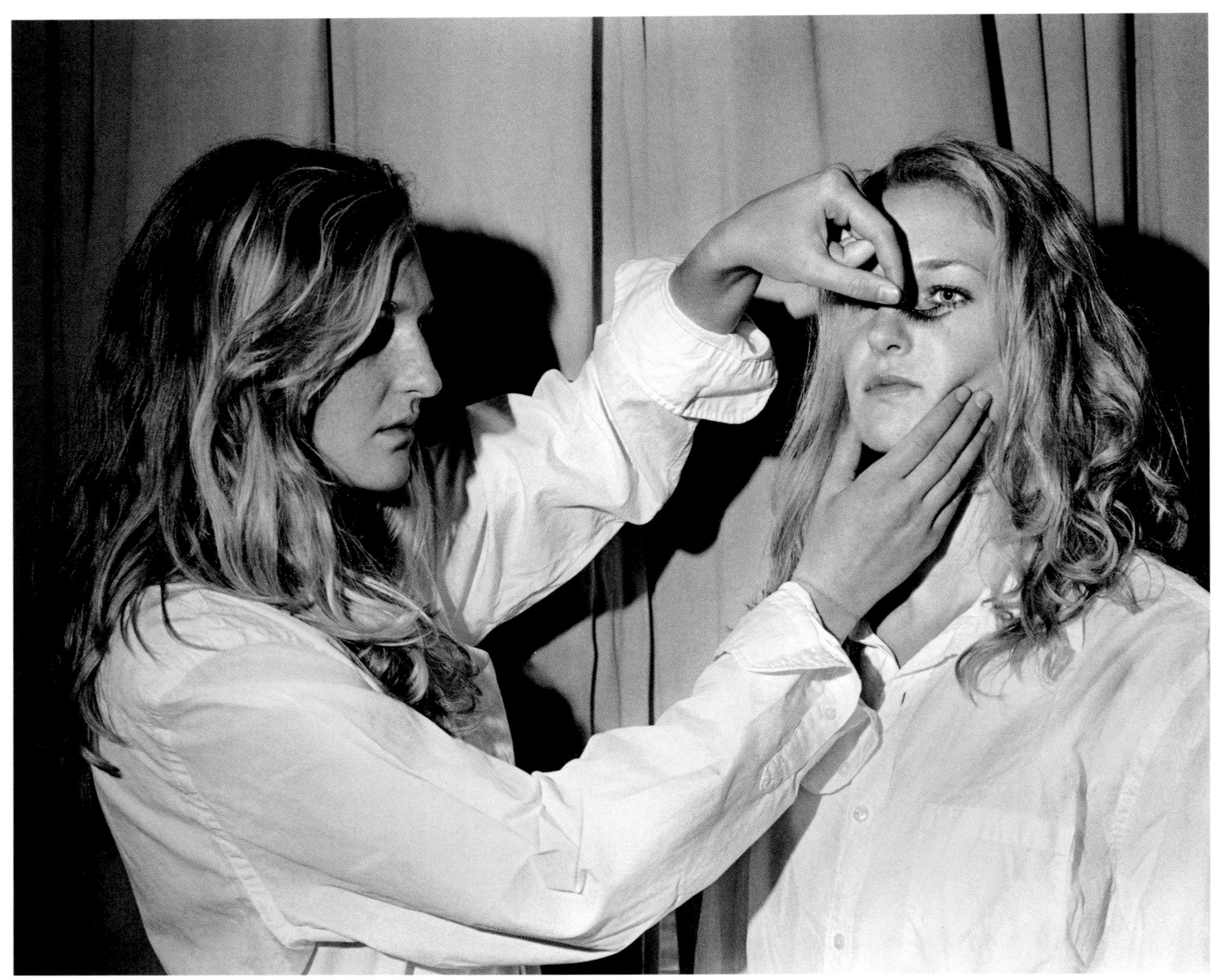

Untitled, 2008 — cat. no. 28

Interview with Grant Wahlquist

GW: **The first body of work in the biennial is a series of untitled photographs. The subjects are diverse, but there seem to be unifying themes and strategies at work. Is there any intentional connection?**

DD: The first body of work aims to explore the way in which we take care of ourselves and of one another, examining our need for physical contact, how we show affection, and ways in which we investigate and present our bodies. I cultivated a way of working in which images supported one another through aesthetics, light, form, and situational ambiguities. I am not relying on a specific place or creating a body of work that falls under one title or photographing a specific group of people.

The image of the young man in the midst of a headstand was one of the first images in which I began to employ this directorial working method. While riding my bicycle, I came across a local teenage dance troupe that practiced at night in a park. After watching them over a period of time, I recognized that I wasn't interested in documenting the group themselves but was interested in the way that their practice informed how they developed or gained control of their bodies and movements. After making this image, I needed to see other ways in which people controlled, or lost control of, their bodies.

Perhaps for obvious reasons, I became intrigued by bodybuilding. The level of discipline a bodybuilder must have in order to sculpt the figure exemplifies an obsession with control in which both the mind and the body must be extremely disciplined and work in conjunction with each other in an attempt to reach a prescribed perfection. While I was photographing the bodybuilder, she revealed details about the portrayal of the feminine image through tanning, costuming, nails, and hair, as well as transformation of muscle and loss of fat. I started to think about what we apply to and remove from our bodies in order to construct or project identity.

GW: **Do you consider them to be portraits? I'm particularly interested in the images of twins. The experience of working with subjects who have such a close tie must have been interesting.**

DD: The images are portraits to a point, in the sense that they are images that portray people but not in the traditional sense of having an image that solely reflects the subject in some context. Rather, the images are completely constructed scenes in which I dictate the situation and portray the subjects in a context that I create. Although the work doesn't strive to articulate a particular individual identity, it's really important to the work that the situations are real. There is a big difference between photographing twin sisters and photographing two women who merely look alike.

Working with the twins was a really interesting experience because of their deep connection. At one point when I was making that photograph, I asked one of the twins to hold the other's face and look directly into her eyes. My flash broke, so I stopped photographing to fix it. After a minute or two I looked up and saw that one of the twins was still holding the other's face. Their eyes were locked as if in a trance. It is this connection, this uncontrollable element, that I can't make up when photographing.

GW: **The images from the second body of work, Lifting Water, are restagings of images that you created while caring for an ailing friend. I'm very interested in the process that resulted in these images. In particular, what purpose did restaging the initial images serve? How did the casting process work?**

DD: After my friend died, I didn't understand what had happened or how to deal with the loss. Although I had been with him and his family throughout the illness, what I experienced didn't seem real. My thought was that if I could see the situation over and over again then maybe I could make sense of this uncontrollable life experience. I decided to reenact that time to see if I could figure out what had actually happened from a different perspective.

I put an ad on Craigslist asking for models—any sex, age, size, or race. It wasn't important that any of the models look like anyone involved during the illness. I knew I couldn't, nor did I want to, replicate it exactly. I hoped I could get at least one model involved who had gone through a similar experience. One of the first people to respond had taken care of his mother and sister when they died. He knew exactly what I was thinking about.

Three Sundays in a row I rented the same motel room and assembled a cast in which the main character stayed the same and the "caretakers" changed. I asked the cast to reenact very small scenes that I remember so clearly: help him out of bed, walk him to the bathroom, give him a glass of water, help him back into bed, change his shirt, wash his back.

I would be conflicted about the outcome of the project. I wanted the reenactment to fail because it would prove that this loss changed every part of my reality and nothing could re-create or replace it. A resolution to this pain couldn't exist. Yet I wanted my intent to totally succeed in order to represent a universal experience. If the work was no longer my experience, then maybe I would feel relief. In the end the experience and the work did both. The work feels real and fake at the same time. By making the photographs, I was able to see what illness and loss looked like. ∎

Born 1981 in Saint Paul, Minnesota; lives and works in San Francisco. Donovan graduated from California College of the Arts (BFA, 2004) and Yale University (MFA, 2009). Her work has been exhibited at Humble Arts Foundation, New York; Transformer Gallery, Washington, D.C.; Gallery 339, Philadelphia; Play Space Gallery, San Francisco; and Blind Spot, New York. Donovan was selected for *reGeneration2: Tomorrow's Photographers Today* at the Musée de l'Elysée and was included in *Wallpaper* magazine's "Graduate Directory: Students to Watch."

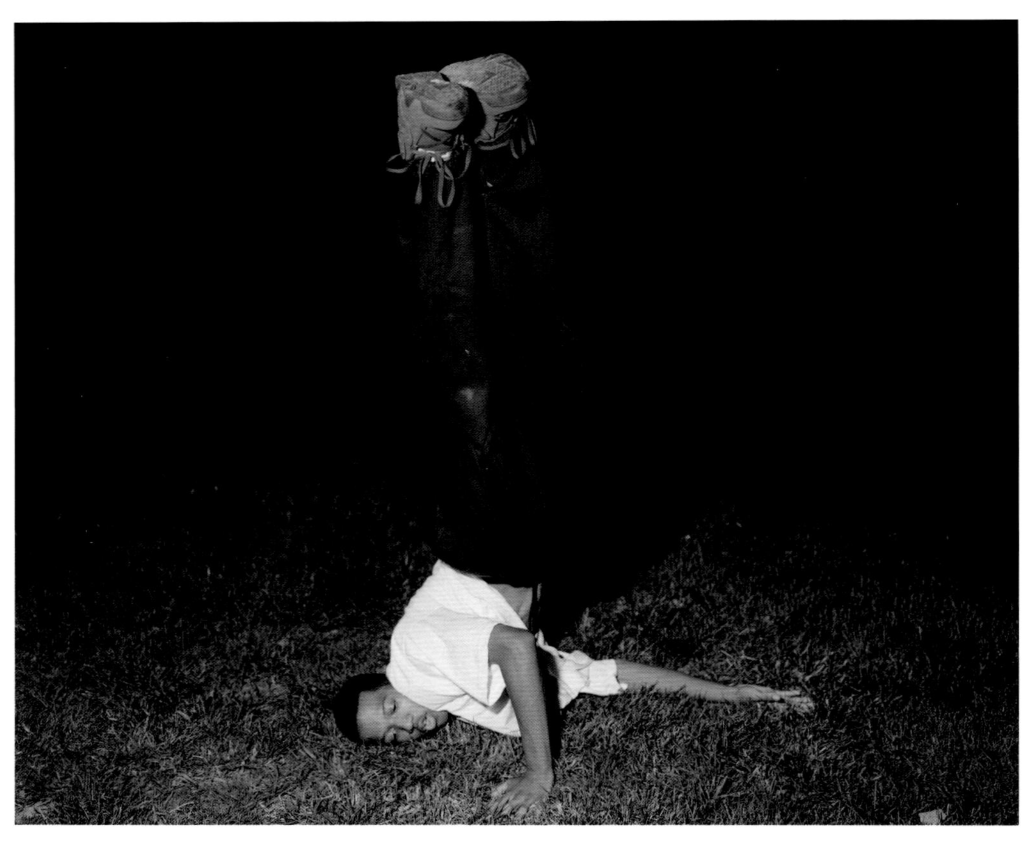

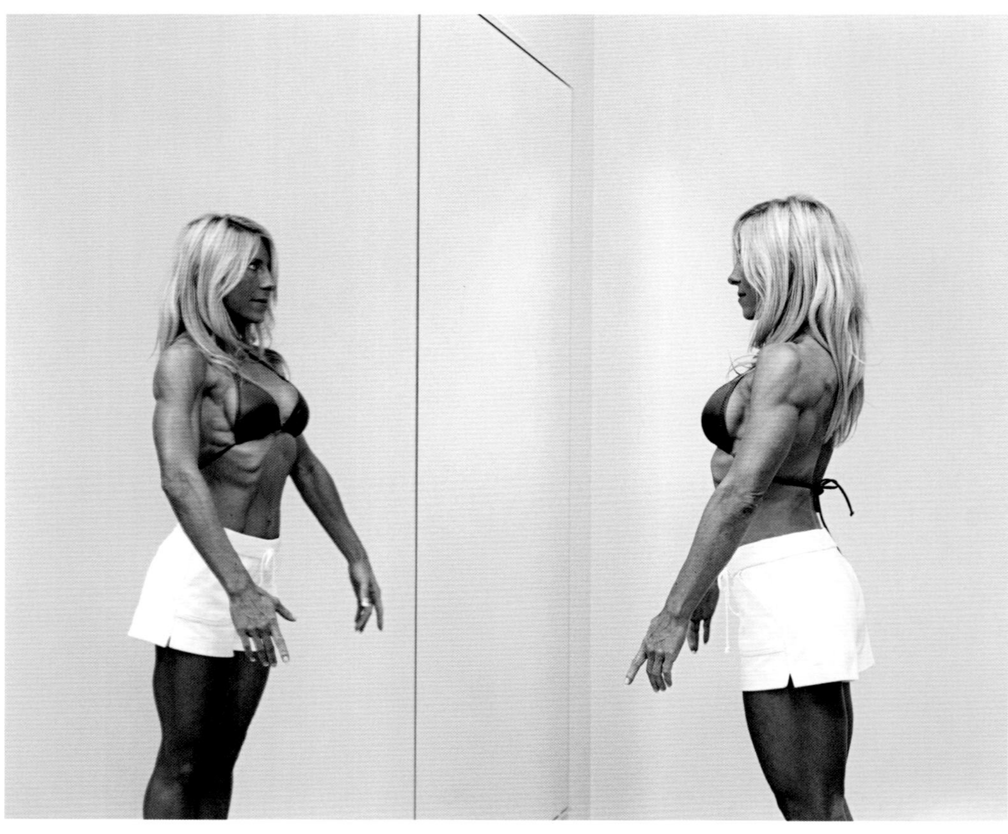

Untitled, 2008 — cat. no. 29
Untitled, 2008 — cat. no. 30

50

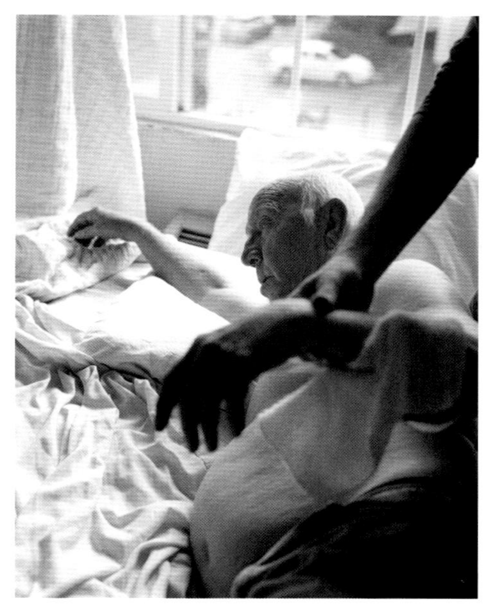

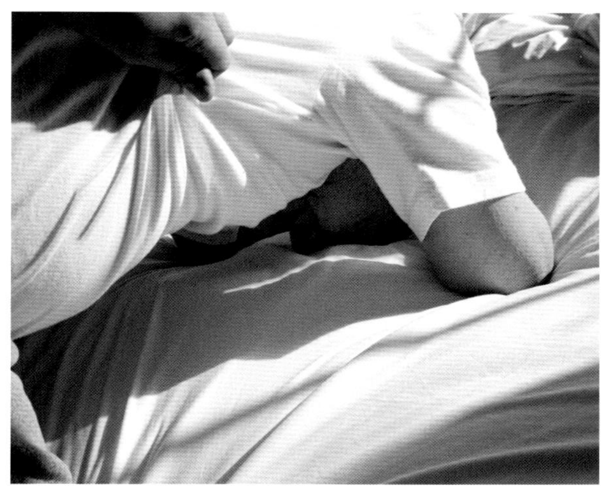

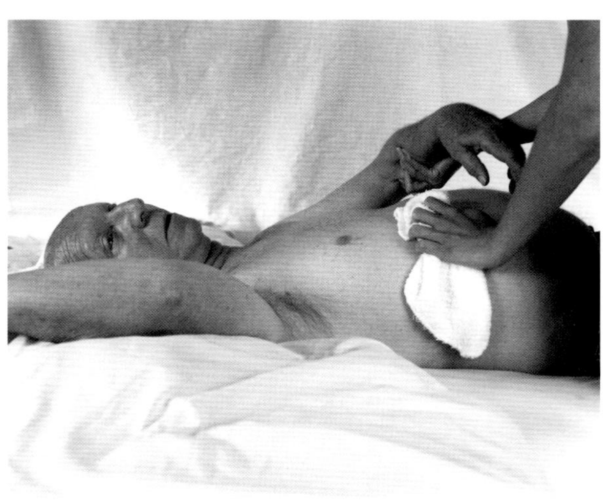

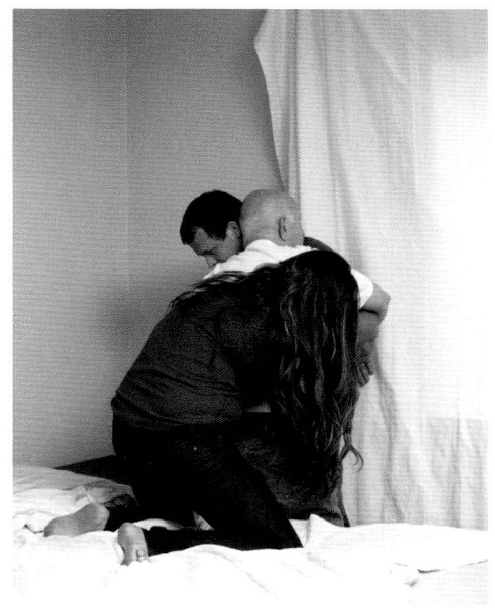

From the series Lifting Water
Untitled 5, **2010** — cat. no. 31
Untitled 6, **2010** — cat. no. 32
Untitled 20, **2010** — cat. no. 34
Untitled 17, **2010** — cat. no. 33

Mari Eastman

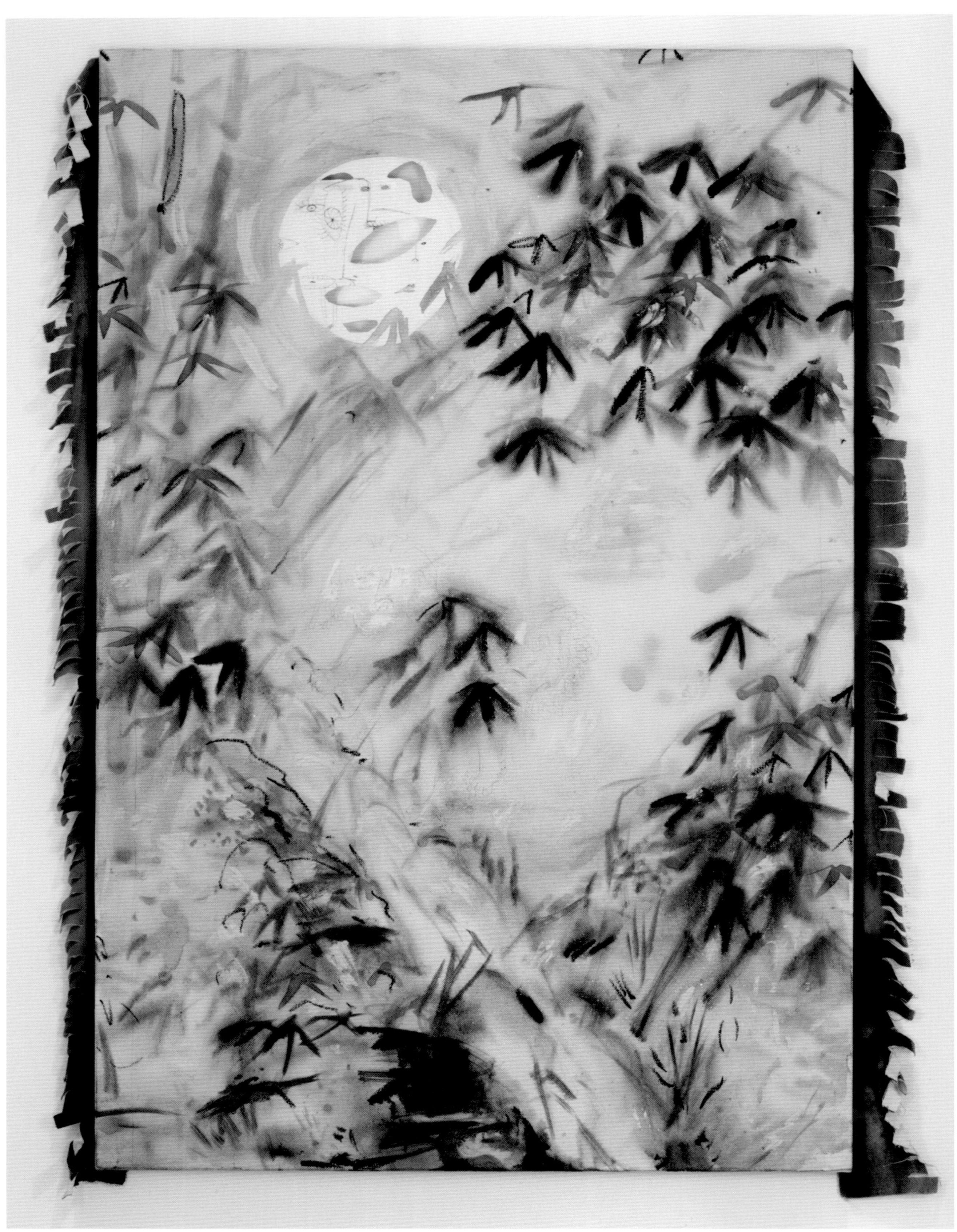

Moonscape with Fo-Dog, **2010** — cat. no. 40

Interview with Chloë Flores

CF: **Your work often contains various cultural and art historical references, ranging from modern art (gestural oil stick marks and cutouts in the canvas), to Asian art (Chinese landscapes and hanging tapestries), to craft (glitter and collage). *Moonscape with Fo-Dog* (2010), one of your paintings in the biennial, is a good example of this. What's the significance of these references, and where does your interest in these various styles stem from?**

ME: Well, I am half Japanese, and I grew up in Asia (Singapore, then Japan) surrounded by ceramics, carpets, carved furniture, and animals from Bali. My mom is a huge enthusiast of decorative arts and would take us to all sorts of places so that she could buy woven textiles and other artifacts. She would also buy back-alley silver in Vietnam, stuff left by the French that was likely stolen or looted. I remember when I was six or seven and sat at the dinner table across from a hanging indigo blue Chinese carpet depicting a deer under a tree with a crane flying above. Actually they still have it. It's amazing. I guess that's where the decorative elements stem from.

CF: **What about the modern elements? We talked earlier about the modernist resurgence in painting that's prevalent right now. What's your relationship to this resurgence?**

ME: I think anyone interested in painting is invested in the ideas surrounding early modernism and ab-ex [abstract expressionism], whether you believe in them or not. Maybe it's like the relationship of current psychotherapy practices to the theories of Freud. Those philosophies basically defined the activity as it exists today, even if we consider some of the ideas behind them naive.

For instance, there's a real nostalgia for utopianism (in painting). Save the world through painting! Create a universal language through painting! Transmit pure emotion through painting! And so on. When I was in graduate school, we would sneer at people who talked about the "journey," and I completely absorbed that postmodern skepticism. In fact, when I teach now, I'm surprised that the ideas are back, with all sincerity, and that my students are skeptical of the skepticism and irony that were the hallmark of much of the work that came to prominence when I was in school.

I do feel envious—I wish I had that charge—the notion that I can make the world a better place through painting. No wonder those Maleviches are so awesome! The reality is that at my core I believe painting is my own selfish activity—that is, completely self-indulgent and pleasurable—and while I hope others like it, I do it for me. I make the painting look good in a way that looks good to me. And the insecure part of me cares what others think and hopes that my abilities are good enough to pass muster.

CF: **It's interesting that you bring up naïveté. Much of what has been written about your work categorizes it as having whimsical, romantic, and girly elements—words that are often associated with adolescence and naïveté. The obvious reason for these characterizations would**

be your use of glitter, images of animals, and references to popular culture. Beyond these conspicuous components, why do you think these qualities are continually attributed to your work?

ME: Hmmm. Well, one of the first pieces I did when I was twenty-six, straight out of grad school, was called *Horse Crazy*. It was an installation in my bedroom with glittery paintings, drawings, and ephemera of horses. That piece set the tone in terms of writing.

But I don't know. Just the other day in my jewelry class I heard an older lady (sixties?) tell another, "But inside I feel I am still fourteen." My mental age is older than fourteen (that was a bad year for me), but I can identify with that statement. And I imagine that others can too. So part of me thinks that there's something to it—the writing about my work being girly. The feminist part of me thinks, "So, because I paint animals, clothing, jewelry, and decorative arts, my work is 'girly'?" What do mature women like? Beige power suits? Nude self-portraits? Girly is a way of dismissing things that are not overtly masculine, aka real serious stuff. Girly is not sexualizing myself in my work. Not overtly sexual must equal presexual. Ironically, sexualized paintings of men, unless they are graphic, are also considered girly/adolescent.

This could also apply to the other paintings that I have in the biennial, the model series. I really love fashion magazines although I know that on some level they are no doubt evil and bad for me. I have a habit of flipping through magazines before I paint. I like the crazy, fast, trashy, inspiring creativity of fashion. Models are the most trivial thing, but I'm really into them. I love hearing model gossip—what they are like in real life, how to pronounce their names, etc. I know it's lowbrow, but I can't help it. Recently, I've been reading about Matisse and his models, who were live models and not photographs like my ghetto version. I'm trying to combine the trivial pop culture with early modernism. It's a pun.

CF: **Do you consider your work this way?**

ME: Whimsical, yes. Romantic, yes. I guess it depends on how you define it. It sounds pejorative to me, but maybe it secretly signifies awesome stuff! Ironically, in my actual girlhood, I was a tomboy who hated dolls and wore only pants.

CF: **What kind of experience do you hope to elicit from your viewer?**

ME: Pleasure. A temporary freedom from oneself. The best of what I experience when I paint. ∎

Born 1970 in Berkeley, California; lives and works in Los Angeles. Eastman studied at Smith College (BA, 1992) and the School of the Art Institute of Chicago (MFA, 1996). Her work has appeared in exhibitions at the Contemporary Arts Forum, Santa Barbara; the Honolulu Academy of Art; the Japanese American National Museum, Los Angeles; the Berkeley Art Museum; Museum Morsbroich, Leverkusen, Germany; and the Hammer Museum, Los Angeles. Eastman has had one-person shows at Emily Tsingou Gallery, London; Sies + Höke, Düsseldorf, Germany; Galleri Nicolai Wallner, Copenhagen; Sprüth Magers Projekte, Munich; and Karyn Lovegrove Gallery, Los Angeles.

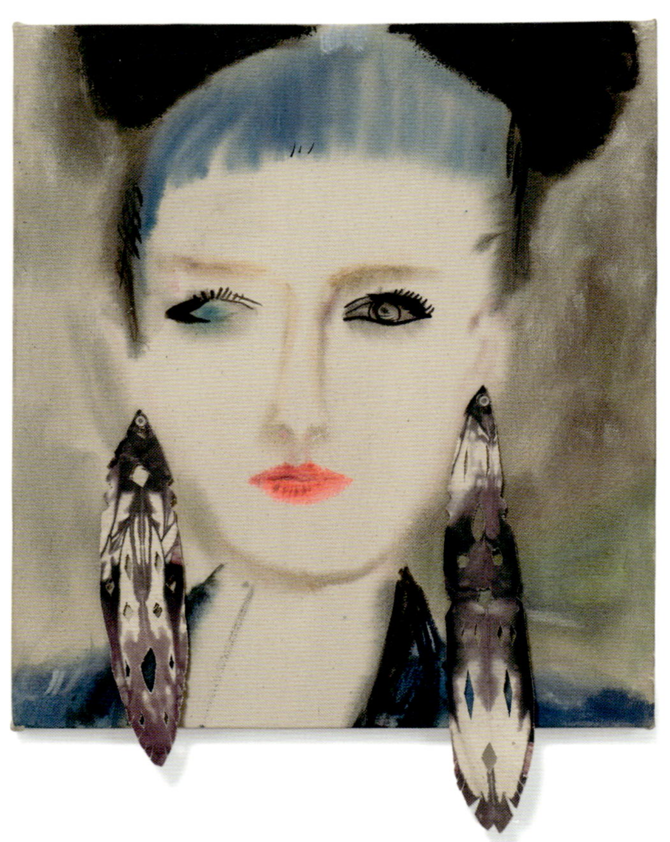
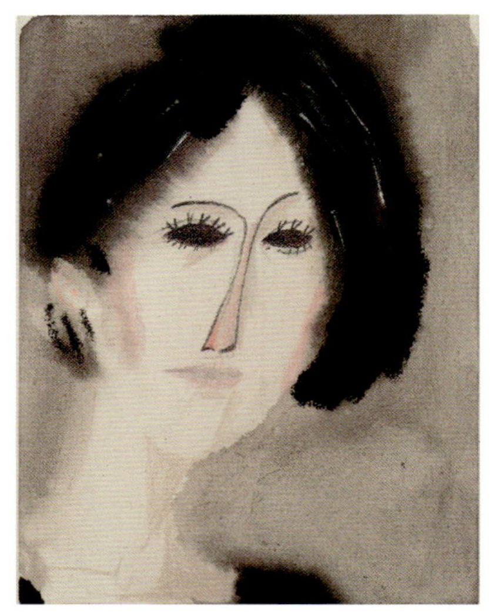
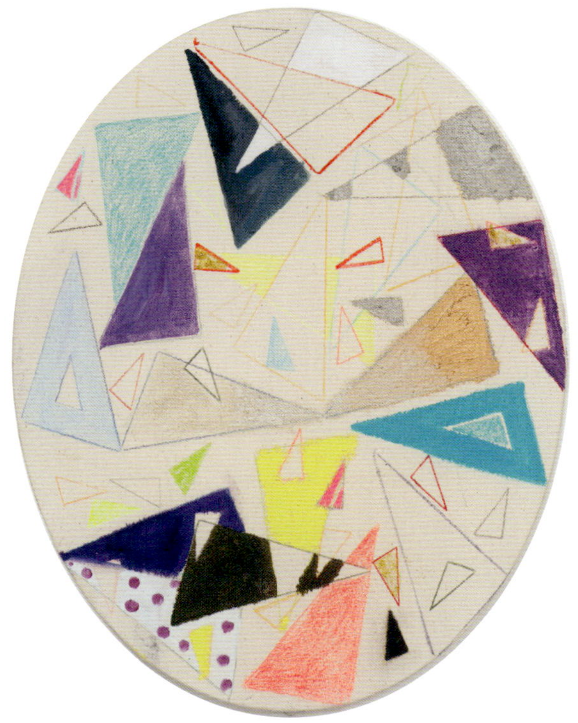
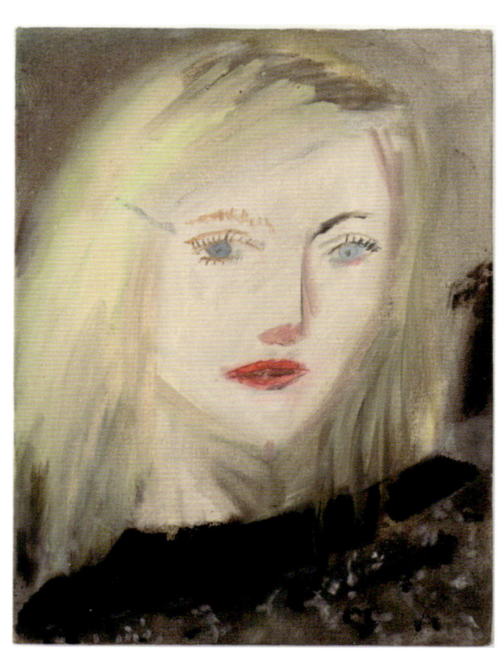

Clockwise from top left
***Model #03, Odile,* 2010** — cat. no. 39
***Model #01, Anne,* 2010** — cat. no. 37
***Model #02, Carolina,* 2010** — cat. no. 38
***Triangles,* 2010** — cat. no. 41

Opposite
Installation view
***Carved portrait of a woman,* 1995–2010** — cat. no. 35
***Standing figure with black hair,* 1995–2010** — cat. no. 36

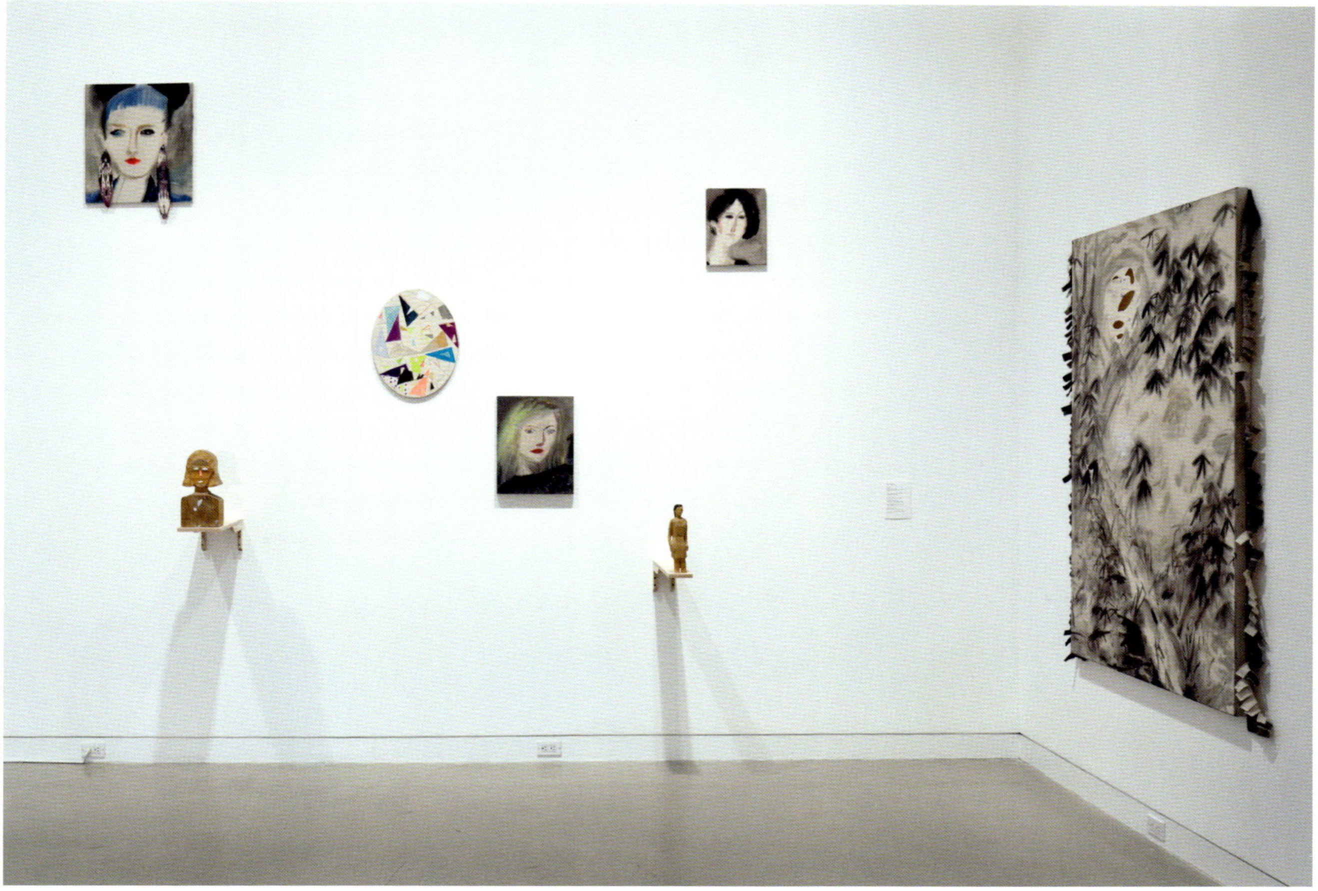

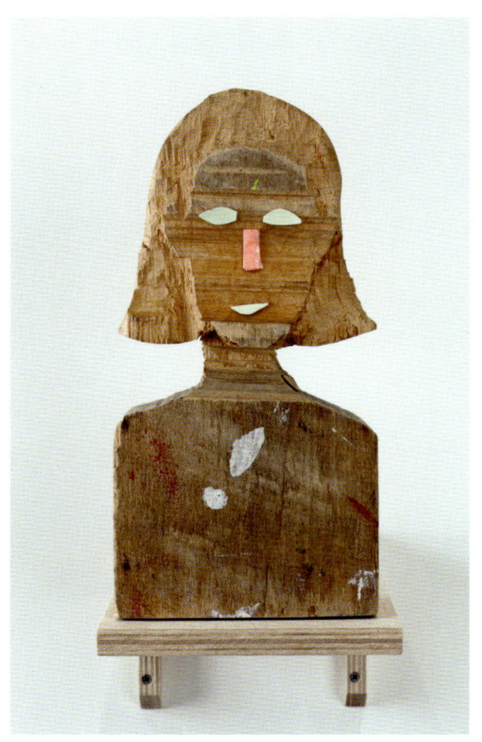

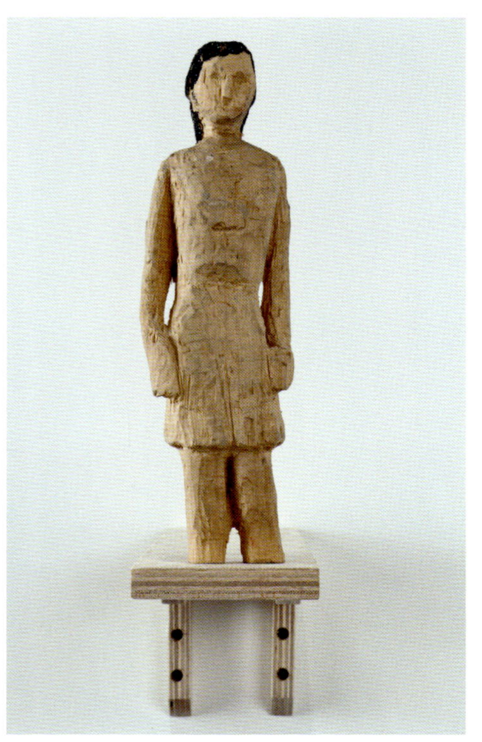

Electronic Disturbance Theater/b.a.n.g. lab

Practice

Artivism, tactical poetries, "continental"—as in inter-American—philosophies and soundings, new-media theater, border disturbance (art), public cultural studies, augmented and speculative cartographies, queer technologies, transnational feminisms, digital zapatistas, codeswitches, dis/locative mediums, intergalactic citizens . . .

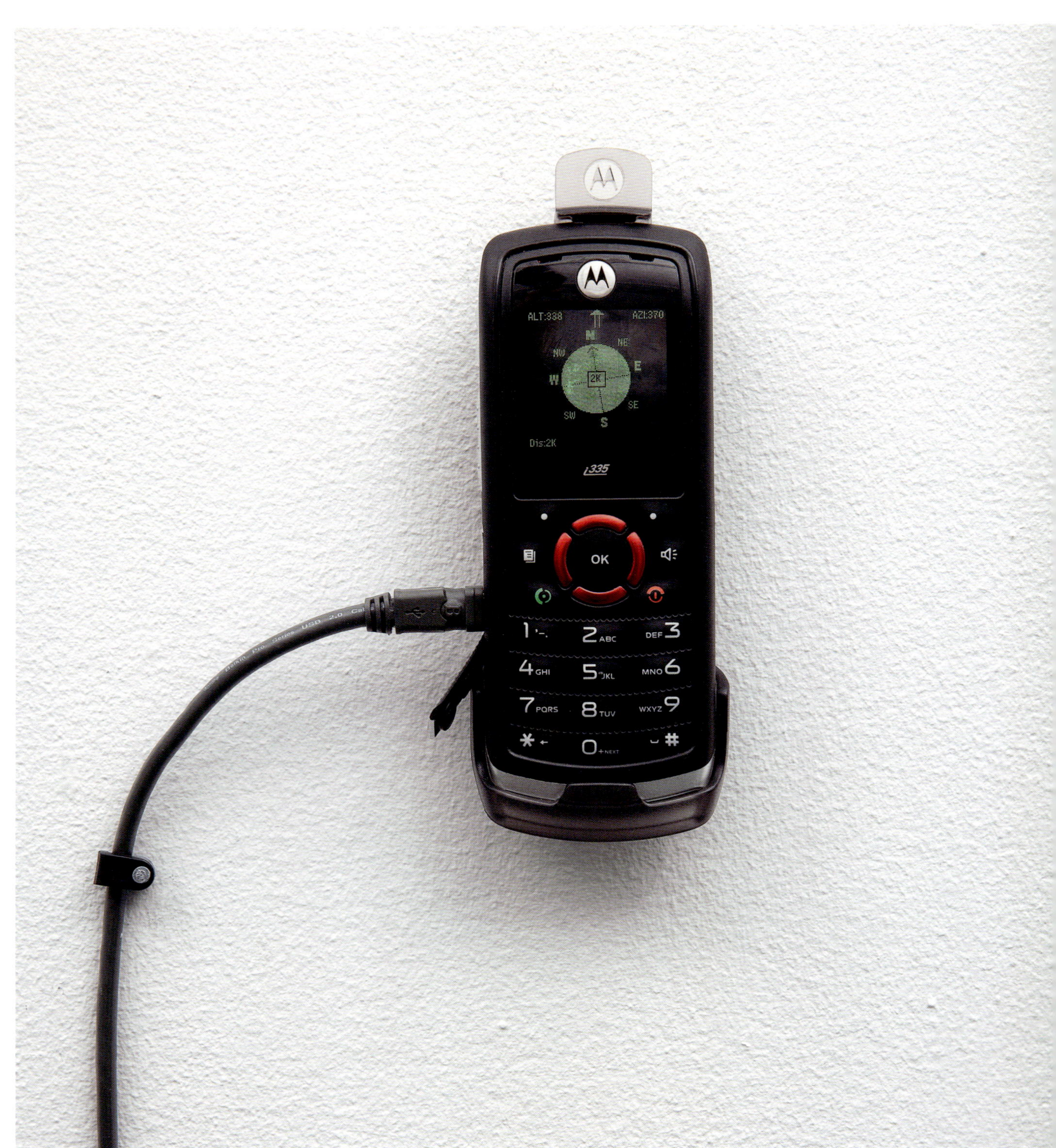

***The Transborder Immigrant Tool (TBT)*, 2007–present**
(detail) — cat. no. 42

Interview with Grant Wahlquist

GW: For the biennial, a version of the Transborder Immigrant Tool (TBT) will be on display. Can you explain a bit how TBT works and the status of its implementation?

`Ping Poems:` TBT is a walking tool, a "global poetic system," *pace* Laura Borràs Castanyer and Juan Gutiérrez. It allows a user to locate the nearest water cache left by human rights groups by way of a simple compass interface that points to the water cache and clocks its distance. It also provides audio poems as sustenance. TBT flows between the reality of a landscape and a virtual locative world based on satellites, software, cell phones, and poetry. There's now a fully functioning version of TBT that's ready to be deployed, and we're going to begin the process through workshops with NGOs and humanitarian organizations.

GW: The sit-in as a strategy of nonviolent civil disobedience usually involves actual bodily activity. What happens when it is transposed to the digital realm? What meaning does "nonviolence" take on in the absence of bodily presence, when the virtual sit-in emphasizes the use of aliases that obscure the activist's identity?

`Reload:` In Electronic Disturbance Theater's practice of "electronic civil disobedience" (ECD), data bodies are linked to real host bodies (we are always transparent about who and where we are). The data bodies that join the performance are not anonymous; every protester's IP address (computer address) is as discernible as the facial features of someone standing on a street corner participating in nonviolent protest. At the same time, EDT has always promoted that ECD should occur in conjunction with traditional CD actions. And now, with robust cell phones, many people doing nonviolent actions on the streets can join the ECD gesture—truly bringing data bodies and real bodies together.

`Data Fluids:` ECD should be understood as occurring not only in the digital realm, because the digital/physical dichotomy is a false one. ECD involves a number of physical components, from the hardware that the web page is displayed on and that the JavaScript runs on to the human body that activates that code. As such, it is important to understand ECD as a new form of civil disobedience that seeks to intervene in the mixed physical/digital worlds that people inhabit.

The ECD practitioner gains a more fluid form of embodiment. Participants in a virtual sit-in are not necessarily restricted to the same rules and protocols of gender, sexuality, race, religion, location, class, ability, and age that they may experience in a physical sit-in, as their physical forms are usually not described in their data bodies or http headers. The use of any communications technology—be it a web page or a GPS-enabled cell phone—opens up one's body to partial organs, prosthetic augmentation, and organs without bodies. Our increasing interdependence with these technologies only underscores the need to engage them as part of our physicality to circumvent the reinscription of quotidian oppressions into the so-called digital realm.

GW: In an op-ed that appeared in the *San Diego Union-Tribune*, you state that TBT is part of an attempt "to create art that sounds beyond museums, chat rooms, lecture halls, and laboratories." TBT obviously exists in the midst of a concrete political situation and as a form of political activity. How do you feel about it being exhibited in the context of the biennial? Are you at all concerned that the context of a biennial will shift or obscure what TBT "means"?

`Ecstacies:` As surely as TBT is bound to a transparency of practice that refuses the false security of anonymity, it is bound to the ethical opacities and vagrancies of an aesthetics-politics of mixed metaphors and blessings. We envisioned this project as having an infinitely translucent capacity to navigate the Sonoran and Chihuahuan deserts, viral media coverage, multinational debates on immigration, gallery, museum, and performance venues. . . . In the historical moment in which we wander, like those that preceded it, "social drama" and its representations remain dynamically intertwined. . . . We revel in "ecstasies of influence"—prior or contemporaneous artistic and activist experimentation that demonstrates the inseparable "emergencies" of aestheticsethicspolitics. Thus, for instance, we'd hazard the claim that TBT resonates with projects by bioartists like Critical Art Ensemble, by performance artists like Orlan and Guillermo Gómez Peña and the BAW/TAF, by new-media artists like the Institute for Applied Autonomy, by Latin American conceptualists like CADA of Chile and Los Grupos of Mexico, by poets ranging from the U.S. transcendentalists to past and immediate undertakings in conceptualisms and documentary poetics, by scholars of global ethnic studies, which created or are creating new assemblages in the world that redraw the boundaries of the real and the imaginary. What TBT "means" is still shapeshifting, but we welcome this biennial's contributions to the project as an Austinian "performative."

GW: A great deal of media attention has been paid to the project. Was this surprising to you, or was it anticipated or desired? How has it informed the evolution of the project?

`Morph US:` The project's viral media coverage was not unanticipated. One of EDT's earlier performances of electronic "civil disobedience"—SWARM at ARS Electronica, which degenerated into a battle with the DOD (Pentagon)—was covered on the front page of the *New York Times* (October 31, 1998). The attention TBT garners brings to mind that incident. We wagered that art could weigh in on—and morph—cultural debates. This said, at certain junctures, we have cringed at the sensationalized commentary on TBT.

The project pings a plethora of discursive registers. At the very least, we envision it as having the potential to raise awareness about a humanitarian crisis at the Mexico-U.S. border (and beyond). We agree that undocumented entrance into the U.S. is a topic of paramount importance but not for the reasons that most contend. We came to this project with shared conviction: Not on our watch. We will NOT inhabit the "privilege of unknowing" that people are dying needless deaths in the U.S.'s southern borderlands for lack of water and direction. Right-wing media has repurposed the project, nestling its critique of it into the larger context of an antieducation, antiresearch, anti-LGBTQ, anti-immigrant, anti-Latin@, anti-Muslim agenda. The outrage generated over alleged taxpayer money used on TBT has been vociferous and manipulative. Publics reading or listening to right-wing news have been given inaccurate synopses of the project. Nevertheless, the hate mail and death threats that we have received are inexcusable—they corroborate our theory that the backlash against TBT is of a piece with yet another toxic wave of U.S. culture wars. The homo- and transphobias, xenophobia, misogyny, and racism directed at us have been so thick that we could cut their lump sum with a knife and butter both sides of our bread for years to come (that is, if that sum were not so rancorously rancid). Still, in the past six months we have begun to view the project's viral coverage as the "first phase" of TBT's deployment; it represents the project's paradoxical success as a "conversation piece." Our hope: that one in one hundred people will move beyond reactionary rhetoric to ponder—for better or for worse—TBT's impetus.

GW: I was struck by two statements you made to the media in the course of the controversy. First, when you declined to be interviewed by Fox News, you stated that your aesthetic diverges so much from the network's that such an interview would not be productive. In a similar vein, in your *Union-Tribune* op-ed, you described TBT as a "poetic gesture," as "poetry in motion." Can you elaborate on your use of the terms *aesthetic* and *poetic* in these contexts? How do you understand the relationship between aesthetics and politics in your activities in general and with this project in particular?

Alter-Poesis: The location of the poetic in TBT exceeds the boundaries of the individual poems uploaded onto the project's phones. Paraliterary, TBT aspires to reread continental lineation. Mary Pat Brady describes the border as a "state-sponsored aesthetic project"; her description returns us to Jacques Rancière's compelling theses on aesthetics, politics, and ethics. To search for the "other history" of the border's performance, we don't have to look far . . . the boundary's shifting "aesthetic" fortunes in the era of the North American Free Trade Agreement and Homeland (In) Security alone are staggering and include obsessive media coverage of the so-called archetypal figure of the "illegal." Media outlets like Fox News deploy a formulaic image loop: recycled landing strips besieged by crossers, the vigilant Border Patrol officer who anxiously scans the daytime horizon with binoculars or stalks nocturnal borderlands with infrared goggles. . . . Our "aesthetic," which diverges sharply from this repetition compulsion, propels us, and by extension TBT, in the direction of alternative ethics and politics. We seek inspiration in the current humanitarian efforts of organizations like Border Angels and Water Station, Inc., but we also strive to channel history (with a modest lowercase *h*), tracking, for instance, the original tenets of Henry David Thoreau's appeals to higher law doctrine via "civil disobedience," the Underground Railroad's North Star flying, disparate civil rights movements' liens on futurity, the Sanctuary Movement's safe-housing, Zapatismo's "world in which many worlds fit" . . .

Simultaneously we call upon poetry's better days as a queer technology, not bound to the mandates of Reason (with a capital *R*), but rather to the always already unfinished business of "circumference" and the "tangential."

The poems that Carroll has written for TBT roughly fall into two sets—the first interested in linguistic experimentation, in conceptual isms and base material isms, and the second, a conceptual exercise in toto bound to the cipher of "desert survival." You will hear selections from each of these sets and their translations (into Spanish, Taiwanese-inflected Mandarin, Greek, German, Russian . . .) on the cell phones installed at OCMA.

Codeswitch: All of the project's poems move within the orbit of earlier beta actions of electronic civil disobedience (ECD) by Electronic Disturbance Theater (EDT). For instance, in 1998 Carmin Karasic (one of the cofounders of EDT) and Stalbaum developed FloodNet in response to the December 22, 1997, Acteal Massacre in Chiapas, Mexico. This new mode of online communication tuned into the "lower frequencies," amplifying gaps in data, making visible the invisible by disturbing government and corporate servers with intentional requests for nonexistent information. Highlighting the dadaist-meets-Kafkaesque force of power's response, Stalbaum frames the "404_file not found" gesture within the arc of conceptual network-art (net art) history: "FloodNet is an example of conceptual net.art that empowers people through activist/artistic expression. By the selection of phrases for use in building the 'bad' URLs, for example using 'human_ rights' to form the URL 'http://www.gb.mx/human_rights.' The gesture prompts the server to return messages like 'human_ rights not found on this server.'" With twenty-twenty hindsight, we could read these "error logs" as EDT's outing of the military-industrial complex's "explicit poetry."

You Q-T!: We see the intersection of our aesthetic and our politic in the speculative gesture. Many of our conversations about TBT present it as an ethical act of staging possible futures of transnational communities and augmented border crossings. It can be seen as "Science of the Oppressed." We often speak of TBT as a "Queer Technology," after the project by artist/theorist Zach Blas that seeks to create speculative alternative technologies based on queer knowledge and desire. There is no reason to assume that everyone crossing international borders in a few years will not have a GPS with which to queer their passage. ∎

Many thanks to the following friends and comrades who lent TBT their voices and trans[ ]lational hearts and minds: Yanoula Athanassakis, Zé Carroll-Domínguez, Jordan Crandall, Jenny Donovan, Lili Hsieh, Petra Kuppers, Zac Monday, Patricia Montoya, Chloe Sanossian, Tatiana Sizonenko, Oliver Ting, Gabriela Torres, Steve Willard, Zona Yi-Ping Tsou, and Felipe Zúñiga.

Electronic Disturbance Theater (EDT) was founded on December 22, 1997. b.a.n.g. lab was founded on October 4, 2005.

EDT/b.a.n.g. lab's Transborder Immigrant Tool (TBT) represents a collaborative project by artists Micha Cárdenas, Amy Sara Carroll, Ricardo Dominguez, Elle Mehrmand, and Brett Stalbaum. TBT, a GPS cell phone last-mile safety tool and poetry device for finding water caches left near the United States–Mexico border by human right groups, was the winner of the Transnational Communities Award, funded by Cultural Contact (Endowment for Culture, Mexico–United States). TBT also has received funding from CALIT2 and the UCSD Center for the Humanities. TBT was included in the exhibition *Here Not There* at the Museum of Contemporary Art San Diego and in City Centered, a Festival of Locative Media, in San Francisco. In June 2010 Printed Matter Inc. released a pamphlet of the group's writings titled *SUSTENANCE: A Play for ALL Trans [ ] Borders*.

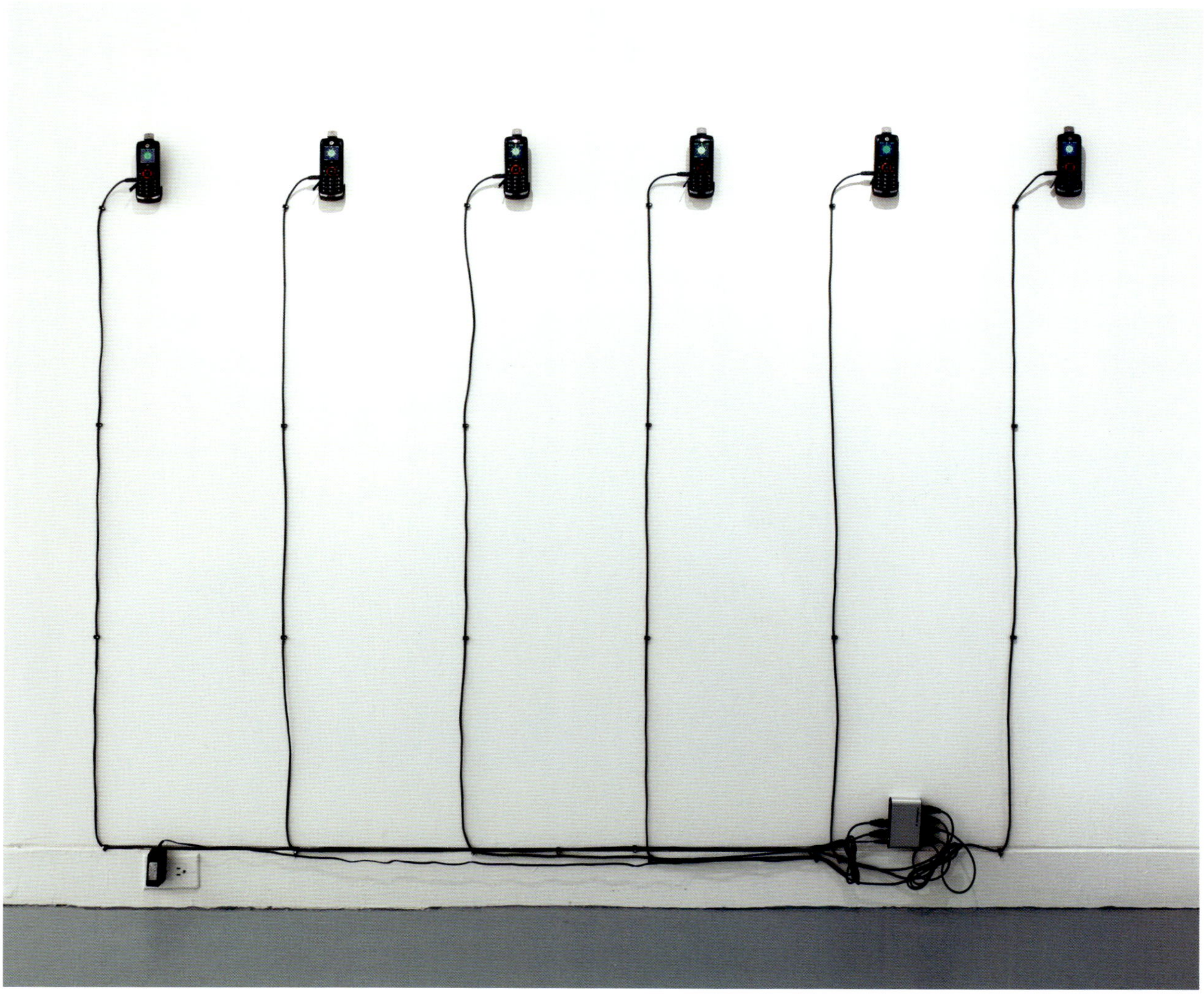

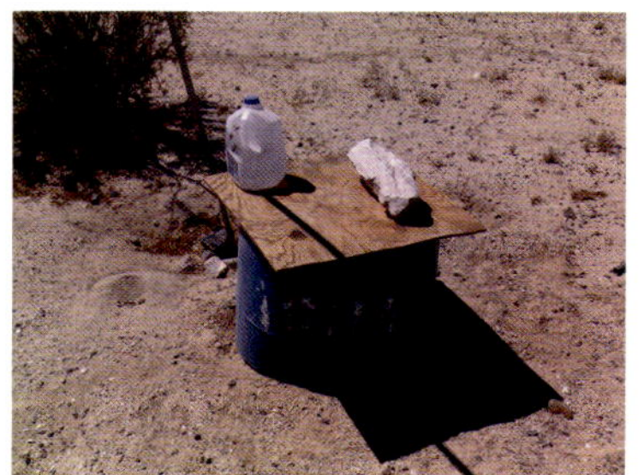
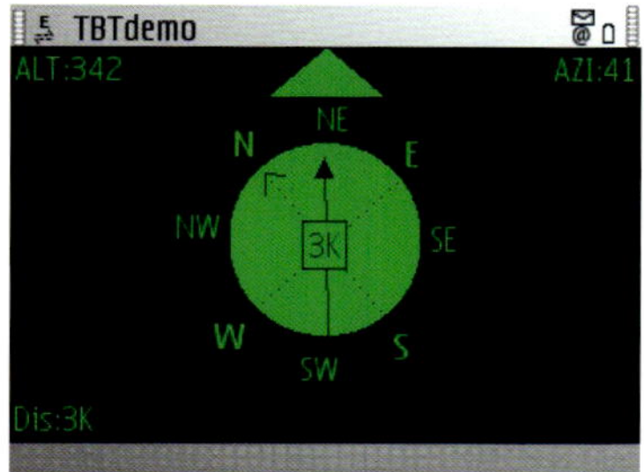

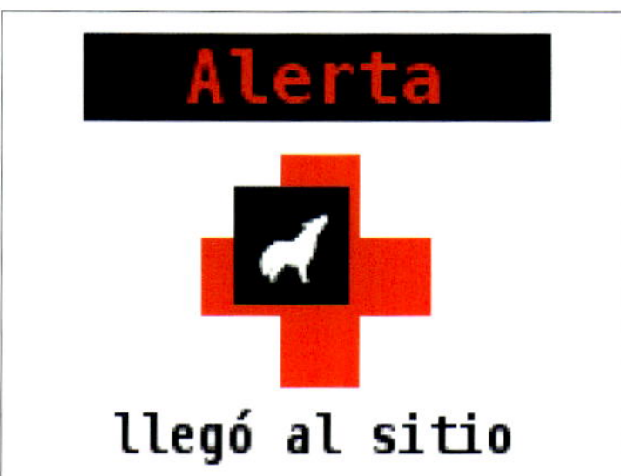

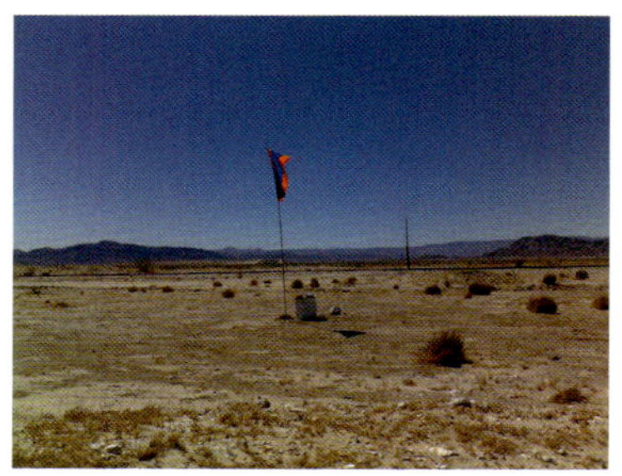
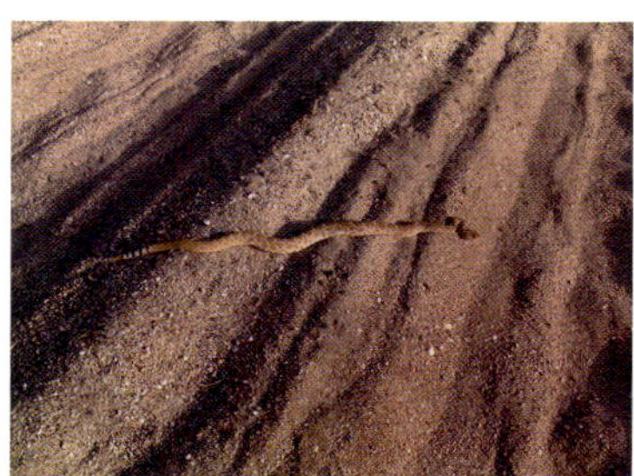
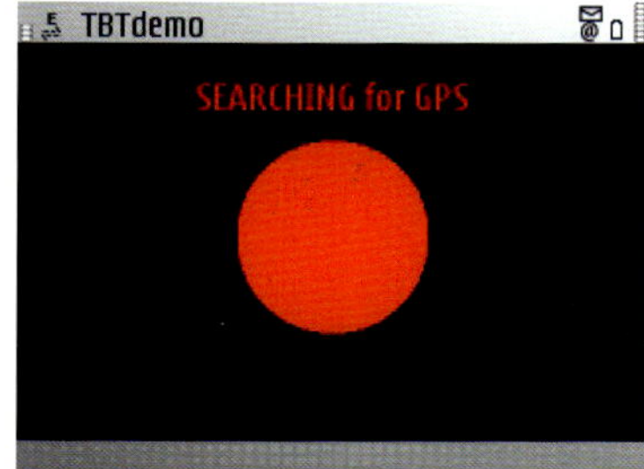

***The Transborder Immigrant Tool (TBT)*, 2007–present** — cat. no. 42
Installation view and screen grabs

Carlee Fernandez

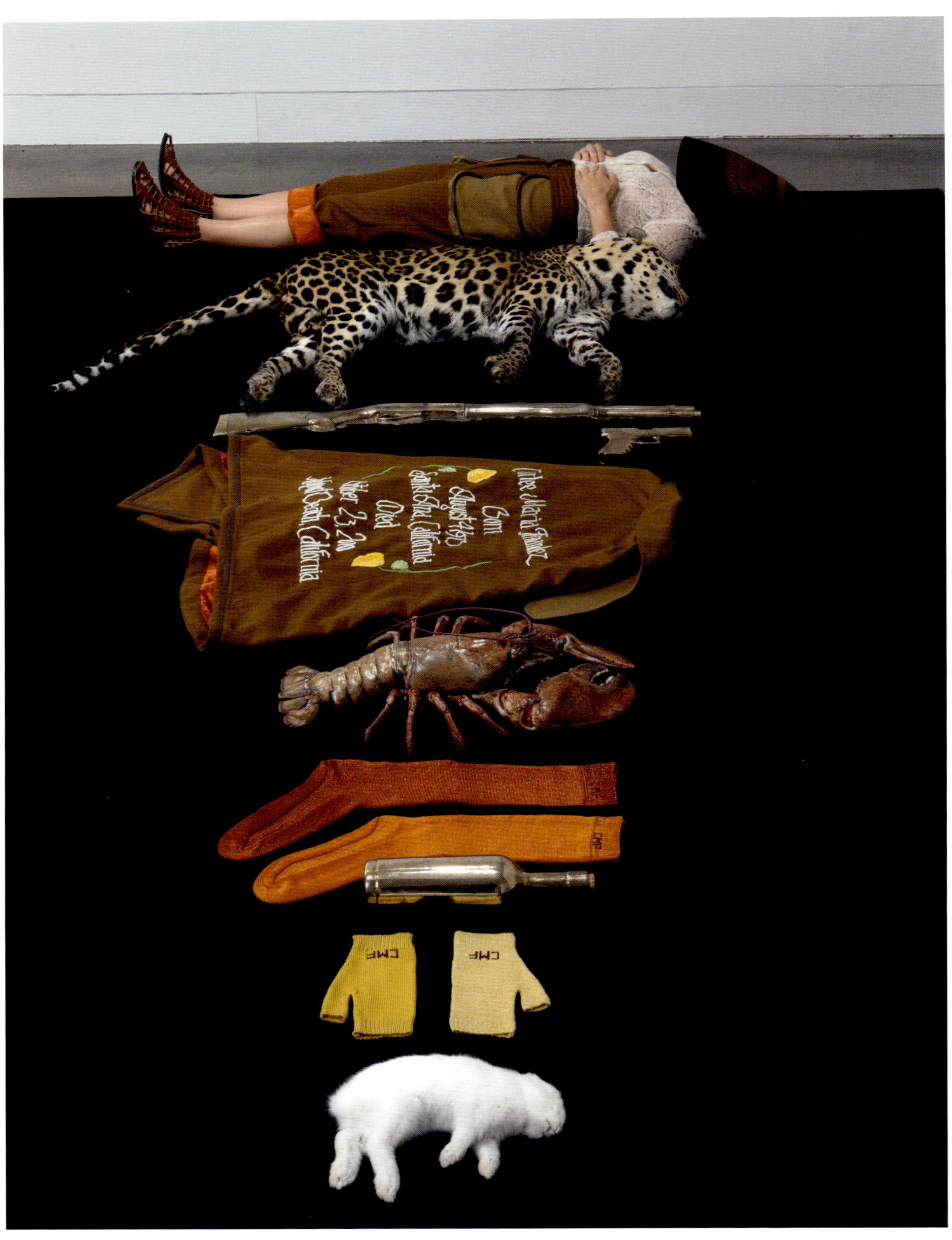

Above and opposite
Life after Death, 2010 — cat. no. 43

Interview with Stacie Martinez

SM: Let's talk first about the taxidermy—it's not every day that you see a leopard in an art museum. Your work explores the theme of nature and has recently involved a taxidermic element, as exemplified by your project for the biennial. How does this become crucial to the work itself?

CF: I have a huge affinity for animals. At an early age my mother taught us to find beauty in both the living and the dead through our numerous pets and plenty of taxidermy hanging on the walls of our home. So I've always felt very comfortable with taxidermy and relished using it in my work.

The human and animal figure is very important to my art making. I tend to refer to the figure as an organic form that in itself is very sculptural and lends a great deal to my work. In this piece it's a taxidermic leopard, among other taxidermy, as well as my own human body.

Taxidermy allows my work to involve a natural element and formally deal with the positive and negative space that the piece has to offer—spaces that are inherent to any body, really. In my past work I have fit taxidermic forms into one another or cut open the form to expose the hollow interior cavity. Taxidermy is simply a skin over a hidden fiberglass form. Part of my work in these pieces had to do with redefining the interior space of taxidermy: an implosion experience, in some sense. Now the work is on a grander scale, and it's more of an explosion experience.

In *Life after Death* (2010), the taxidermic forms simply interact with one another, lying side by side in the context of the grander space. Taxidermy troubles viewers' perceptions: what was dead now appears to be living. My work feeds into that, plays with it. By choosing to use untraditional taxidermy poses—freshly dead poses—I hope to create a trompe l'oeil effect in the interplay of life and death.

SM: Your biennial installation appears to be part mystical burial, part archaeological excavation. Can you talk a little about your intent?

CF: Visually, I want this piece to appear as if a burial had just been unearthed and categorized for viewing. Or as if a historical painting had been broken up and separated into its constituent parts for display. Conceptually, I want the piece to be items for my next life. If I could have authority over it, what would I wear? What would I bring? Which items would represent me? Which items would I want to live with? What would I eat? I looked at ancient burials and came up with my idea of what was needed and desired. I created my ultimate burial, with beauty, fantasy, and utilitarianism.

The interplay between death and life—you might even call it "rebirth," in some sense—has always been a part of my work. The cycle of life: from death comes life, and vice versa. My last body of work, World according to Xavier, was definitely a reference to that idea: the birth of my son, the death of me. *Life after Death* presents the same thoughts but this time more in a dreamscape manner, a dream landscape of a rebirthed me, with all the items I need to survive in a new world.

SM: In past works your body has been an element in the photographic process—performative, yes, but ultimately photographic. This is the first time you will perform live. Why the shift?

CF: To me there isn't much of a shift. I always approach my art in the same manner: attention to space, the form, and the visual. If I really think about it, "performance" in this piece is a step short of photography in the scheme of my work. The performative aspect falls under the same constants as my photographic work. I'm holding a pose within a sculptural context. This time instead of five minutes holding a pose, I'm holding the pose for six hours.

As a sculpture, the piece will be mainly viewed without my body. My body is an added element that appears occasionally during the run of the exhibition. An extra added element to further the trompe l'oeil effect, and also to further the idea of connections between life and death, between taxidermic forms and living forms. The pants, blouse, hat, and sandals will be laid out in position for me to fill with a human body form. But in a sense I feel like the whole piece is my attire. My body fits the clothes, but it's the whole piece that I wear. ∎

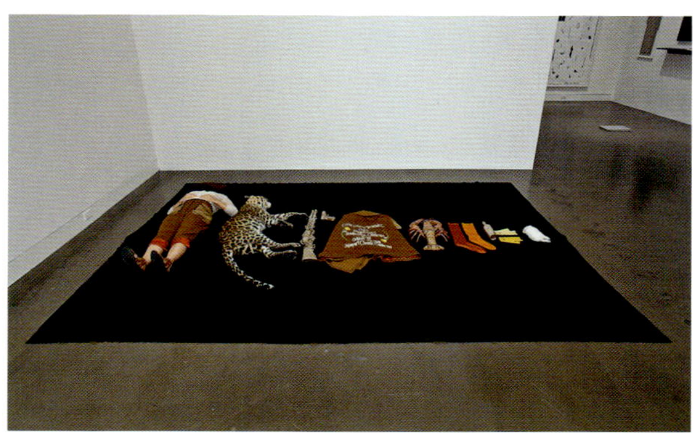

Born 1973 in Santa Ana, California; lives and works in Los Angeles. Fernandez is a graduate of California State University, Fullerton (BFA, 1997), and Claremont Graduate University (MFA, 1999). She had a solo exhibition at ACME., Los Angeles, in 2010, and her work was featured in the Los Angeles County Museum of Art's exhibition *Phantom Sightings: Art after the Chicano Movement* in 2008. Her work has been exhibited at UCR Sweeney Art Gallery in Riverside, California, and at Villa Arson in Nice, France, and is in the permanent collections of the Los Angeles County Museum of Art; Nerman Museum of Contemporary Art, Overland Park, Kansas; and the San Jose Museum of Art. Fernandez received the 2008 California Community Foundation Fellowship.

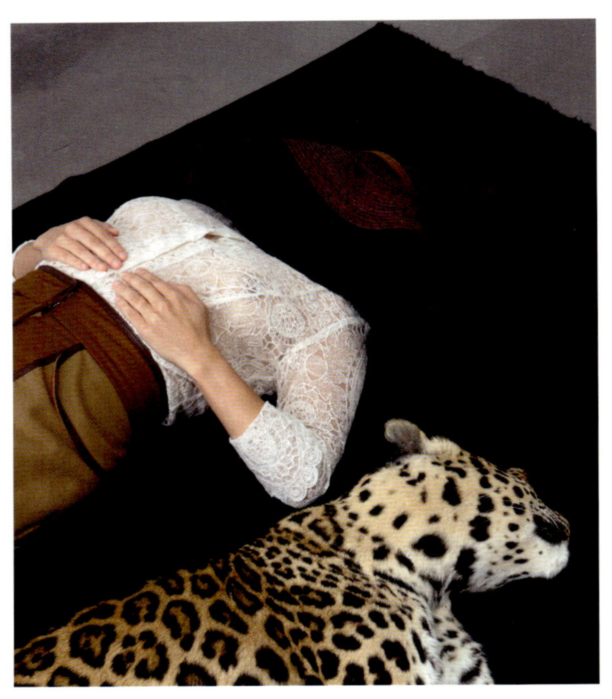

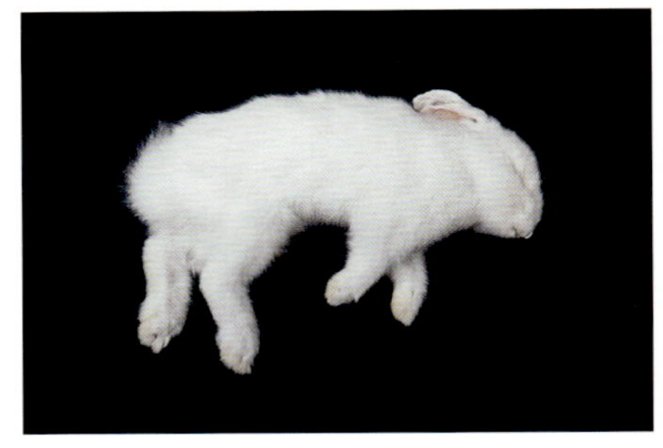

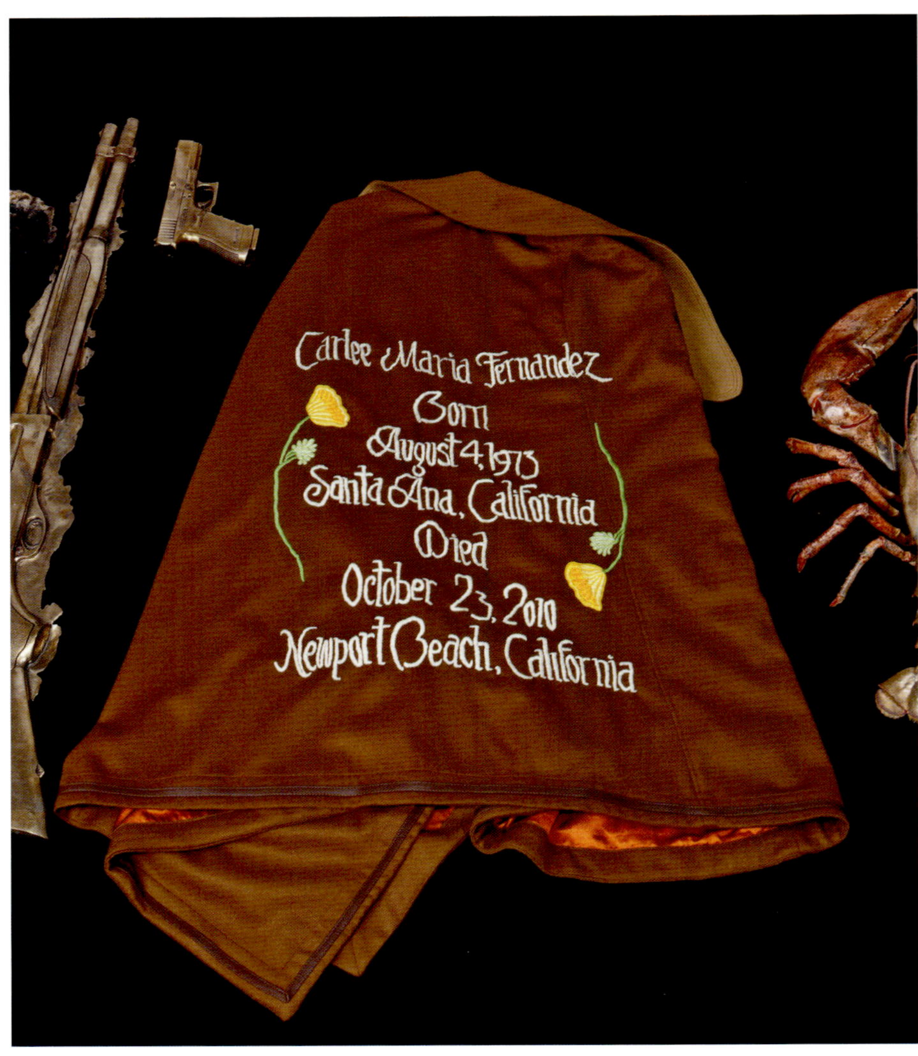

Carlee Maria Fernandez
Born
August 4, 1973
Santa Ana, California
Died
October 23, 2010
Newport Beach, California

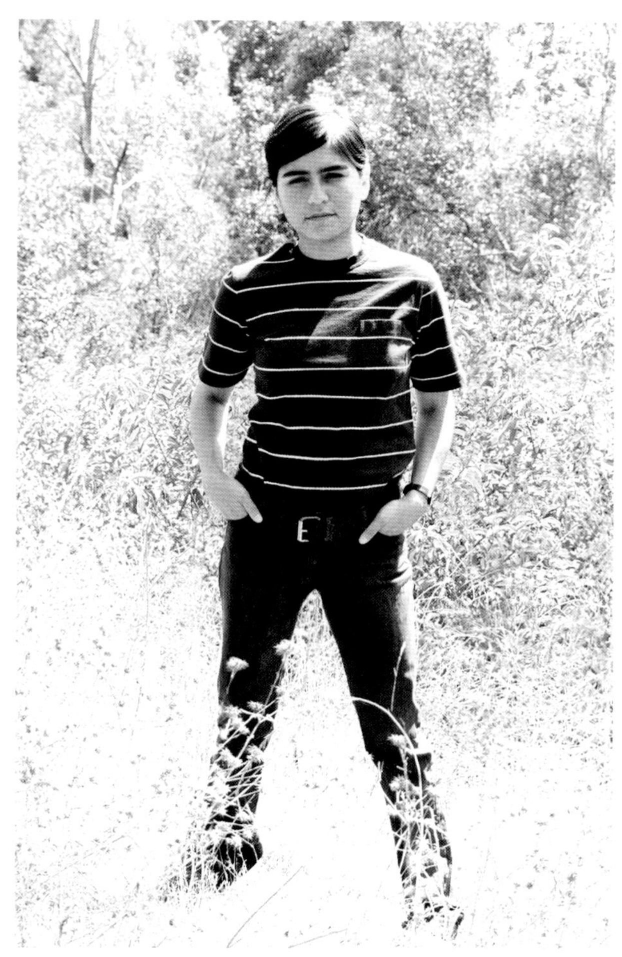

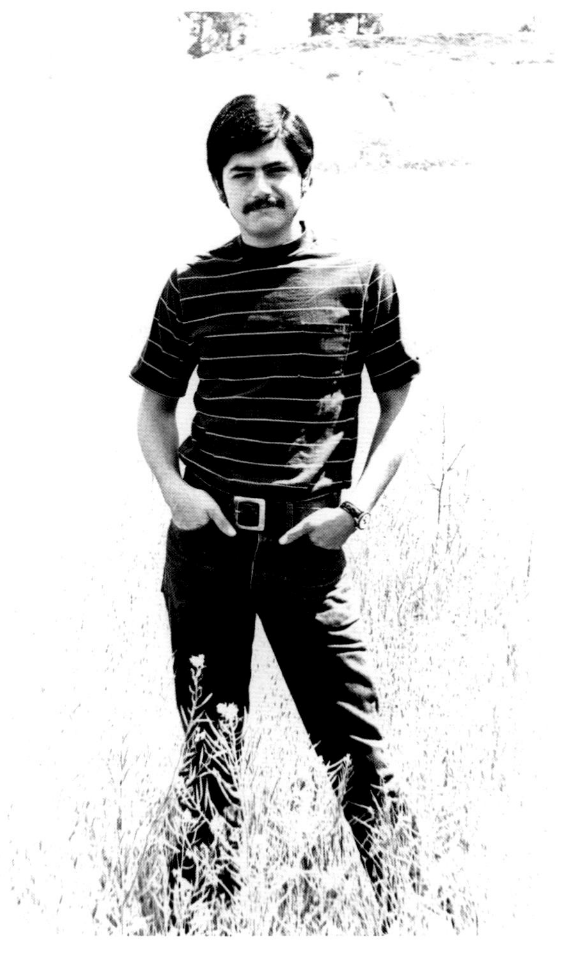

Opposite
Life after Death, **2010** (details) — cat. no. 43

Above
Self-Portrait: Portrait of My Father, Manuel Fernandez, **2006**
C-prints
18 × 12 in. (45.7 × 30.5 cm) each
Courtesy of the artist and ACME., Los Angeles

Finishing School

Practice
Finishing School's interdisciplinary approach addresses contemporary sociopolitical and environmental issues through playful models of participation that often test the boundaries of artistic practice

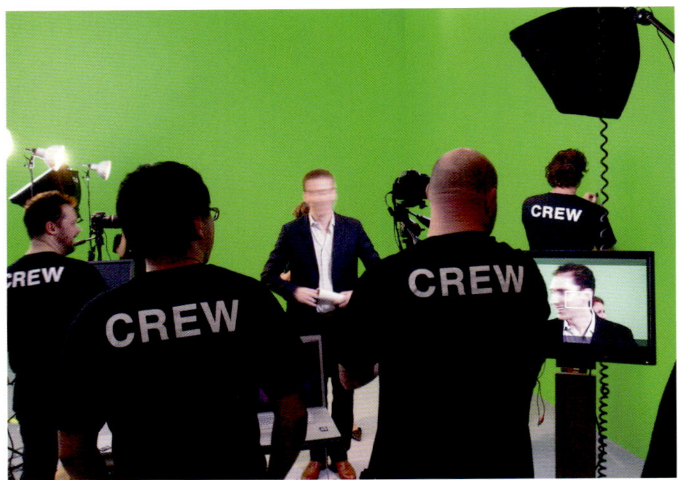

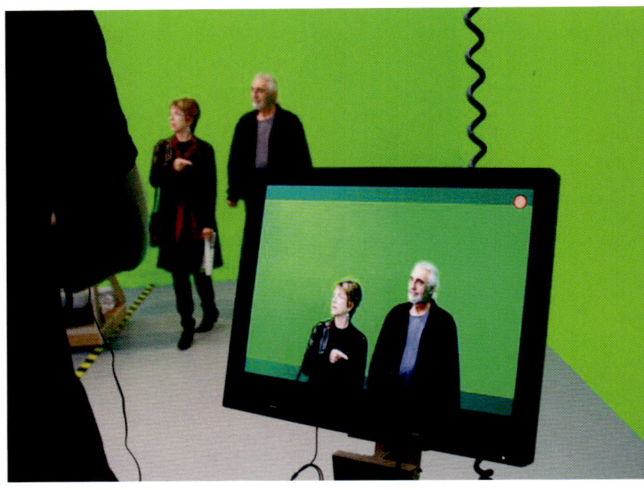

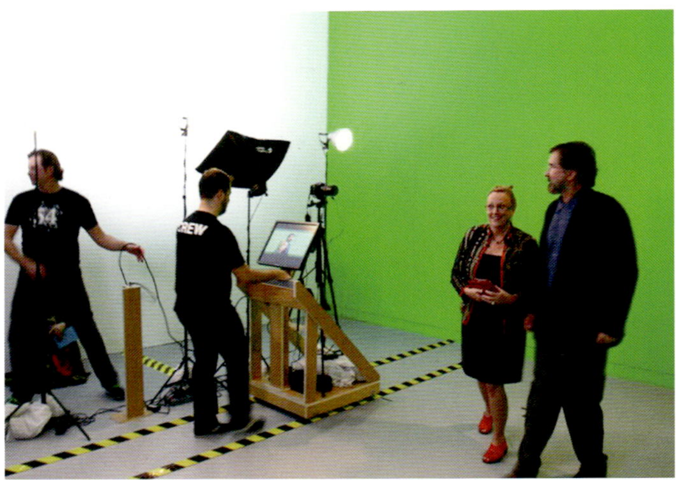

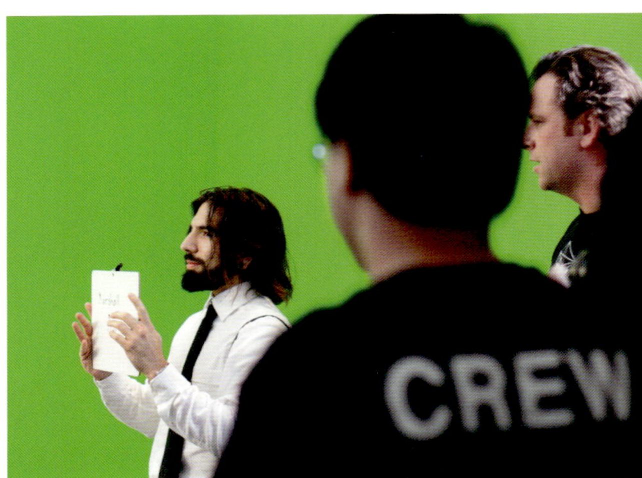

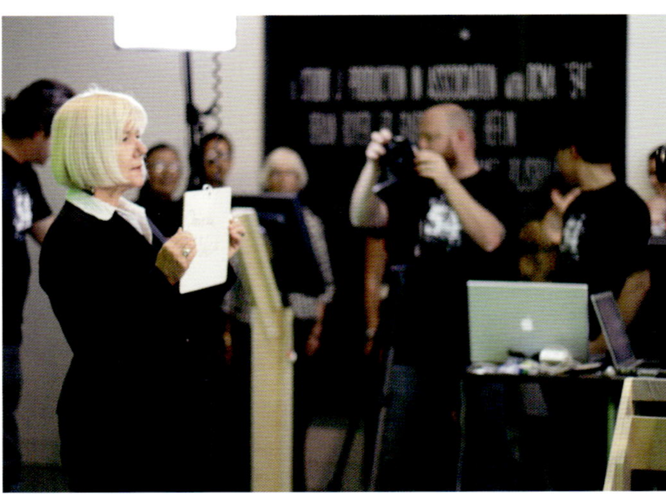

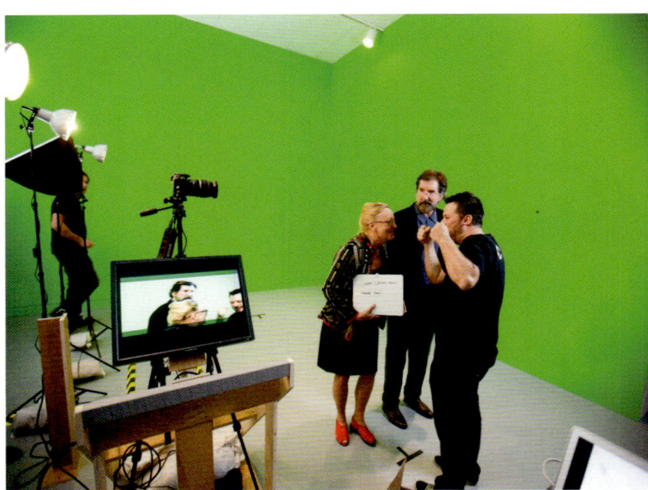

54, 2010–11 — cat. no. 44
Filming during 2010 California Biennial opening events

CF: Can you give us a short introduction to your project *54*?

FS: For the 2010 California Biennial, we will begin production of *54*, our new participatory film project. The project explores the complex socioeconomic and political landscape of biennials, using the invitation to participate in one biennial (the 2010 California Biennial) as an opportunity to critique the very model through the critical cinematic dramatizing of another biennial (the 2011 Venice Biennale). *54* employs relevant biennial histories and narratives, investigates the role of biennial audiences as participants, and speculates about the impact biennials have on culture. *54* is about the biennial experience as much as it is about the two specific biennials addressed in the project.

The film portion of the project blends narrative, cinema verité, and improvised experimental cinematic styles. Intervention, homage, appropriation, and collaboration are important tactics in the making of the film. This project is becoming too absurdly complex. Which is perfect. *54* is a multifaceted project without traditional boundaries between the process of making the film, the film itself and related ephemera, and the interactive installation in which it will be presented as a completed project. *54* is our most far-reaching project to date, both conceptually and geographically.

Visitors to the California Biennial are encouraged to participate as actors in scenes filmed at the museum and surrounding locations scheduled during the course of the exhibition. Additionally, participants are invited to meet us in Italy, where we will also be filming in and around the Venice Biennale in June 2011. You should come with us. Seriously.

CF: Let's talk about the residency format as a model for your practice. How does it compare to, say, being invited to participate in a thematic exhibition that already places your work within a broader contemporary art historical context.

FS: The residency format is a preferred structure for our practice. There are many differences. For example, exhibitions are typically highly controlled and static structures that serve to support a curatorial thesis, whereas a residency can be open and responsive to audience and institution and, most importantly, is measured over time and experience. "Smooth vs. striated" to quote Deleuze and Guattari. Time, fluidity, experimentation, and direct engagement are common luxuries in residencies that we relish.

CF: There's a strong performative aspect in practices such as yours, in which the focus is on participation, collaboration, and active audiences. There's a theatricality to it. You're performing, the participants are performing.

FS: Yes, performance, participation, collaboration, and audience activation are important to social practice, which provides personal, open-ended contact; accountability; and intimacy with the artists and their ideas: dialogue that is human, interpersonal, as opposed to dialogue that is solely mediated in the form of a work of art. Also, people love to role-play. We try to capitalize on that. Children naturally do

this. We try to bring that to our work as well. The audience can help us figure things out. That isn't always the case, but we try . . .

CF: So it's a true collaborative interaction. Or collaborative performance. In which the audience also performs. Who informs your practice in this regard?

FS: Yes, placing the audience in the playful line of fire fosters accountability and reflection of ideas. As a practice, collaborative interaction has a rich history and many blueprints for social and political interactivity and shared authorship. We are indebted to so many: Bertolt Brecht, Allan Kaprow, Andrea Fraser, Group Material, and Critical Art Ensemble to name a few artists and collectives. We are also informed by the writings of Paulo Freire and bell hooks, educators and theorists who promote parallel strategies regarding praxis, agency, and power.

CF: What about the role the film plays in your project?

FS: The film provides a lens to address biennial issues. We're trying to make it interactive. We want to share the filmmaking/viewing experience. We want the audience to be in the film with us; we want the audience to travel with us to make the film; we want the audience to play a role in editing the film.

CF: What is the film about? Can you also discuss the hypercube symbol found in some of the project images?

FS: *54* is sci-fi drama [laughter]. Psychological sci-fi drama [more laughter]. We would like to partially think of this as the film being made in Federico Fellini's *8 1/2*. We have been drawn over the years to *8 1/2*, a film about filmmaking and a film about Fellini making that specific film. We also enjoy how Fellini inserted autobiographical layers into the film and his display of process and critique of the very system that supported his film. Some of these elements will be present in our film.

Seriously, *54* will be a nonlinear film presented ultimately in an installation context, masked as a sci-fi narrative. Critically speaking, *54* is a film about biennials and a film about these specific biennials (California and Venice).

The hypercube symbol is important to us. We created a 54-path hypercube as a sacred/political mark for the film's internal mythology. It also represents the number of paths (scenes) presented in the film, the relationship between various time and space dimensions presented in the narrative, and the various tiers to the project as a whole.

CF: What about affect? On the very basic level, why include participants? Why interact? Why engage? What is the desired effect?

FS: The answer is simple. Selfishly, it makes the ideas, inquiry, and experience more meaningful for us as a practice and hopefully for the audience as well. There is a dialogue happening in real time, in the trenches. We are always surprised by the results of a project. The audience always adds to the dimension of an idea in ways that we never anticipate. We love that!

CF: It feels good.

FS: It does feel good. Conversely, artists and institutions traditionally wrestle with the effectiveness of didactics as a strategy to educate and elaborate on a work of art in lieu of the artist's own physical presence in the display space and willingness to engage in dialogue with the public at large. There can be a vast disconnect between an artist's work and the general public, a frustration that we have all experienced. Enter Finishing School: this is the territory that we like to inhabit.

CF: **You're dealing with the problematics of accessibility of conceptual art . . .**

FS: From the beginning, we have struggled with the internal politics of delivery and the internal politics of dialogue between audience and artist. We really try to break down the barriers between us and them. For example, the quotation in the beginning of our catalog for *Saturday School,* our first project, quoted Charlie Brown's teacher: "wah wah wah wah." That's how the art world is perceived: "wah wah wah wah." They put this stuff up on the wall, and you look at them and it's like, "what does this stuff mean?" What does that do for somebody who isn't trained? Addressing the relationship between each project and its audience is important to our practice. Because our interests are broad, we are constantly wrestling with the idea of effective accessibility of concepts with consideration of the context of each of our projects.

CF: **Let's talk about critical reflection being made on the biennials in this project.**

FS: We are interested in the aspirations and discontents of aesthetic judgments, boundaries as artists, institution, audience, nation-states, and the public regarding biennials. Also, the economic, historical, social, and political relevance of biennials as an insulated system and to society as a whole. Our lofty goals are to create lasting critical reflections for us, the multiple exhibition audiences, participants, and bystanders concerning the role of biennials in contemporary culture. We also want to temporarily redirect some of the flow of creative communication and power of the biennial experience into the hands of the project participants, the public at large, and the film/installation audience as the vehicle for critical reflection. This project spans multiple exhibitions: the one we have been invited to, the one we are intervening in, and the one in which we hope to present the completed iteration. The critical reflection will be distributed among multiple audiences and the three exhibitions, linked by the film.

CF: **So you're redirecting the power of critical reflection into the hands of the audience?**

FS: Sure. Because this is an open-ended project, we are equally interested in how it will end.

CF: **Why choose the biennial format to create this type of critique?**

FS: Because it's the biggest stage and there's the greatest amount of risk, on everybody's part: our part, OCMA's part, the multiple audiences' part. Can we use one biennial to criticize another and, in the end, evaluate the entire system? We want to challenge the institution and compel it to be self-reflective and consider a new paradigm.

Ultimately we felt that the best way to make this criticism was to do it from within. An often-stated criticism of institutional critique is that it is supported and presented in museums and galleries, even with its critical stance toward them. Additionally, it's said to be a complex game in which only select artists, theorists, historians, and critics can play, leaving the general public alienated and watching from the sidelines. In this project we are keenly aware of our position and have willingly placed ourselves as the target of our own criticism. ■

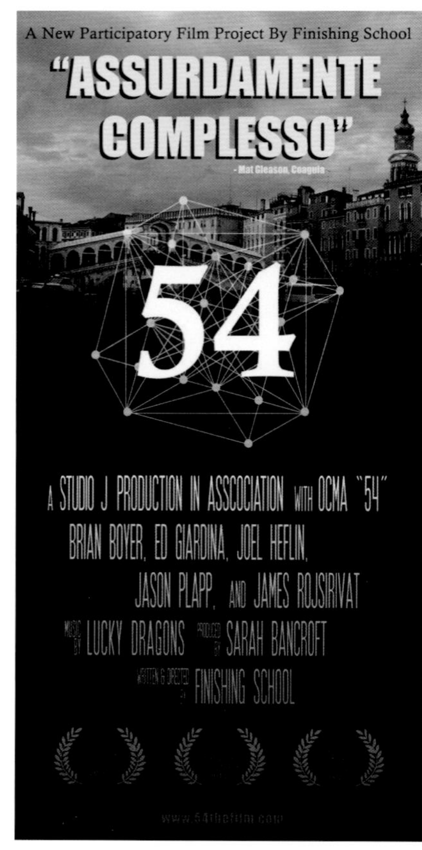

Movie banner for *54*

Established in 2001, Finishing School is a Los Angeles–based interdisciplinary artist collective composed of Brian Boyer (b. 1975, Downey, California); Ed Giardina (b. 1972, Torrance, California); Joel Heflin (b. 1974, Portland, Oregon); Jason Plapp (b. 1976, Knoxville, Tennessee); and James Rojsirivat (b. 1974, Bangkok, Thailand). Finishing School has presented projects at the Museum of Contemporary Art, Los Angeles; Los Angeles County Museum of Art; LACE, Los Angeles; Walter and McBean Galleries, San Francisco Art Institute; Polvo, Chicago; Contemporary Museum, Baltimore; Center for Architecture, New York; and Art Interactive, Cambridge, Massachusetts, as well as internationally.

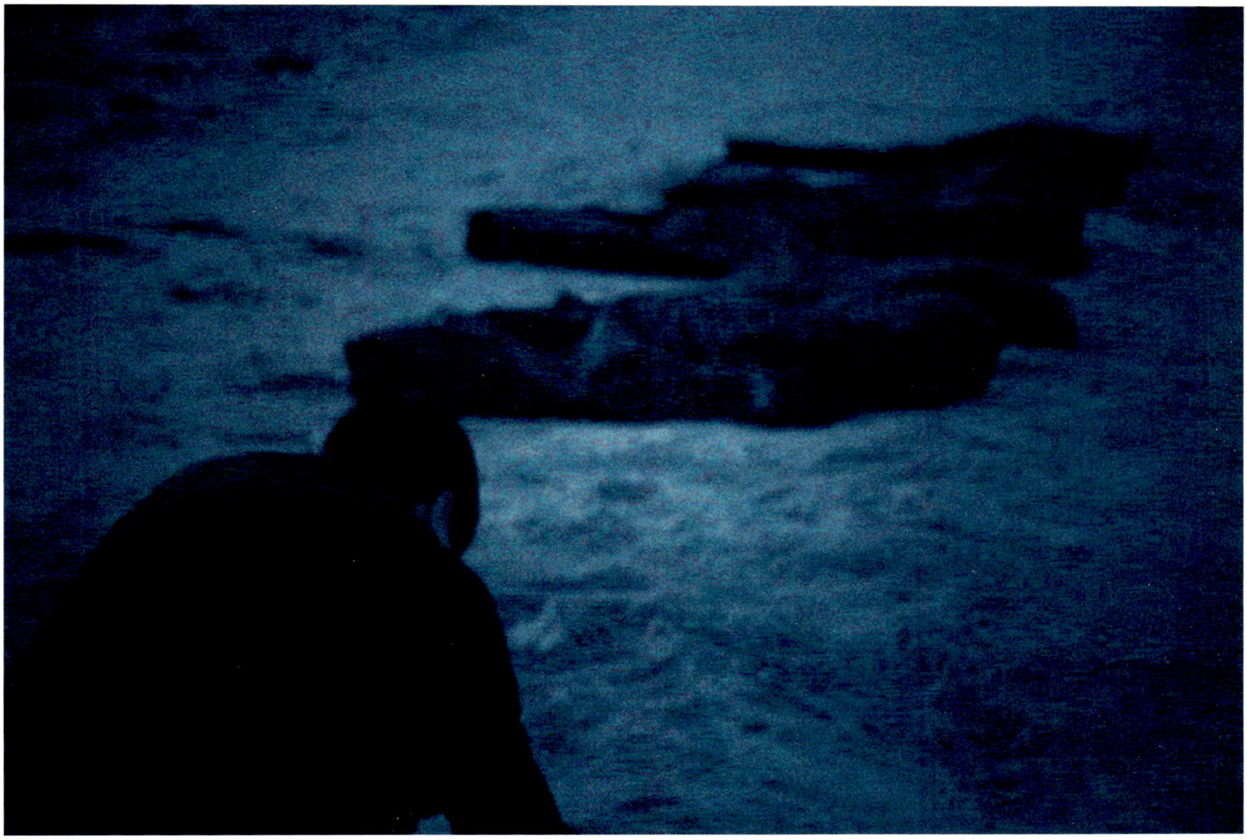

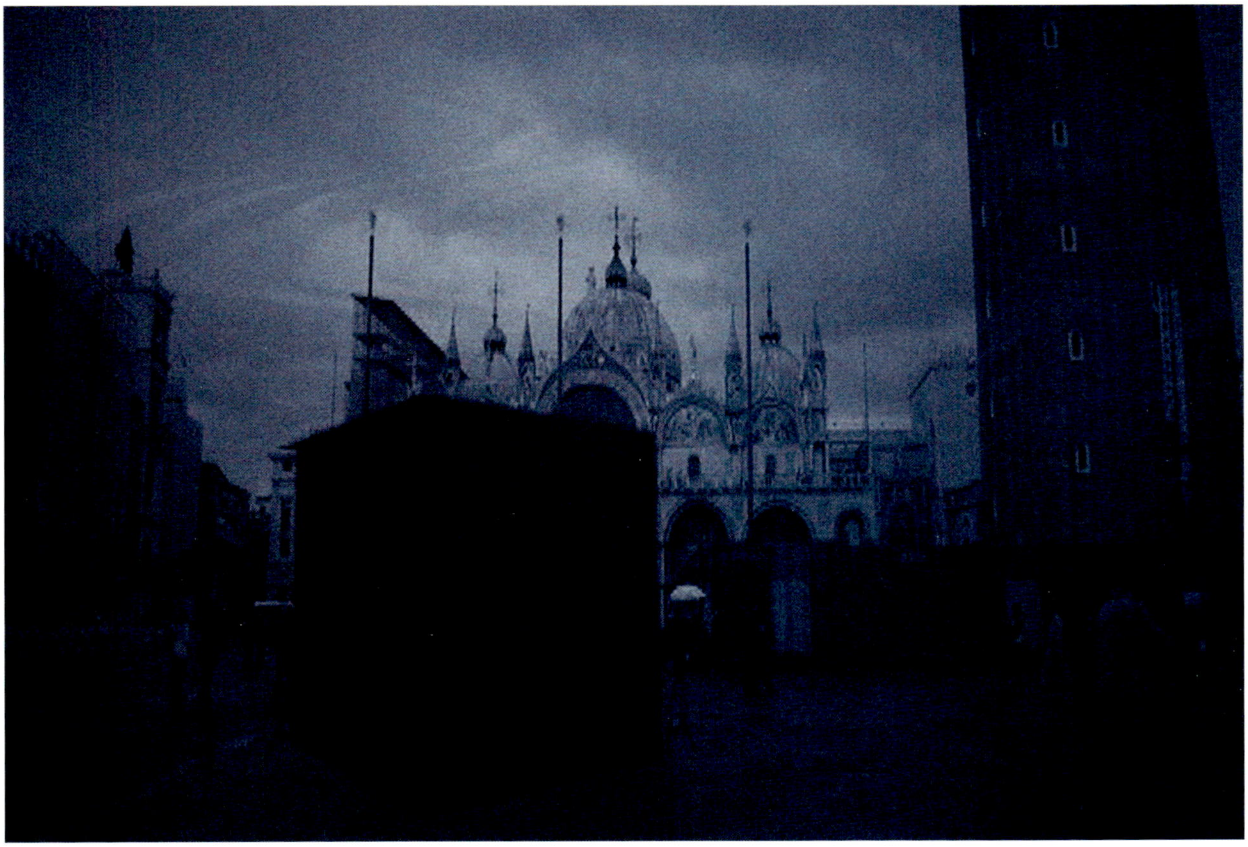

Stills from *54*, **2010–11** — cat. no. 44

Eve Fowler

Practice
Photography, artist's books, collage

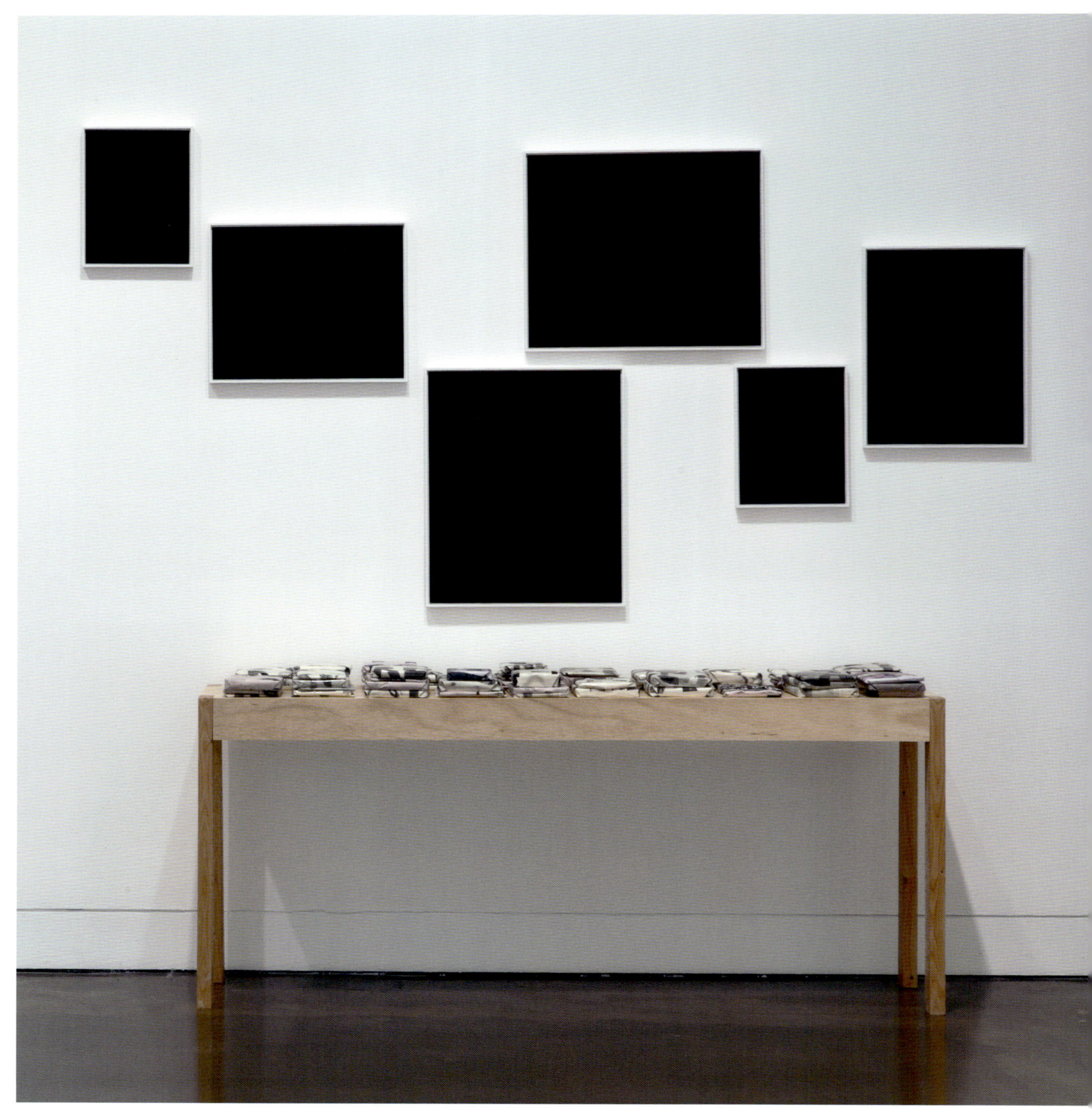

Above, on wall
***Woman from Behind in Hotel Room Naked*, 2009** — cat. no. 46
***Woman Seated Naked*, 2009** — cat. no. 47
***Woman Waiting*, 2009** — cat. no. 50
***Two Friends at Home*, 2009** — cat. no. 45
***Woman Standing Shirtless in a Doorway*, 2009** — cat. no. 49
***Woman Sleeping*, 2009** — cat. no. 48

Above, on table
See pages 70–72 for title, 2010 — cat. no. 52

Opposite
***A Sign of More*, 2010**
C-print
30 × 40 in. (76.2 × 101.6 cm)
Courtesy of the artist and Horton Gallery, New York

Interview with Stacie Martinez

SM: **How did the idea for the black photographs first come to you?**

EF: The idea for the black photographs came to me for several reasons. Making figurative work representing a subject can be difficult. I tried to be as responsible about representing the people I chose to photograph as I could. I chose to photograph people in my community, the queer community, who are self-possessed and powerful. I think most of the photographs that I made function in the way that I want them to in terms of how the subjects are represented. About two years ago a collaborative piece I made with Math Bass called *Gloria Hole* (2008) turned up on a porn site in Japan. Around that time I was looking at the photographs of Sigmar Polke. Although I am also interested in references to black paintings and traditions of radical nonrepresentation, I was more influenced by a series of photographs Polke made in 1975 called the São Paulo series. The photographs, almost completely black, were taken when Polke ducked into a bar while trying to escape a sudden downpour. He unknowingly ended up in a gay bar.

The images and what was written about them in the exhibition catalog MOCA published in 1995 were also interesting. In the images gay men embrace but are almost completely obscured in blackness by Polke's darkroom processes. I thought it was interesting that an underrepresented group was even further obscured/erased. When a figure does appear in Polke's photographs, it is often obscured, but what I found really telling were the essays by Paul Schimmel (only referring to the photographs as abject and never even mentioning that they were of people or that the bar was a gay bar) and by Maria Morris Hambourg (who beautifully describes the photographs, the men embracing, and the darkroom process but never questions why these subjects in particular are obscured more than any others in Polke's work). Neither essay questioned the erasing of the subject.

So I thought about that erasing in terms of what I have tried to do with my work and thought about ways to turn deleting into another kind of visibility. It seems counterintuitive to say that black photographs are about visibility, but I think drawing attention to the difficulty of representation works in this case—it starts a conversation. The process of taking the photograph remains the same. The subject is still the queer community, but the image is printed until it is black, obscuring the subject. The titles describe the content, leaving the viewer to imagine what is there.

SM: **One could argue there is a sense of loss, of poignancy, in your work—this blocking/obscuring of the subject— both in the black photographs and the book project. You indicated, however, that you see it more as an act of memorialization and protection.**

EF: There is obscured information in both projects and in other works of mine. This works to include people who have a certain amount of information and exclude those who do not. With the book project the obscuring or wrapping of the books occurred organically. I wrapped

twenty or so books from the One Institute to give as a gift. I wrapped them in Xeroxes of collages that were in my studio. A friend who is an artist and curator (A.L. Steiner) asked to include them in a show in New York.

After that I decided to wrap all the books in my library that were purchased from the One Institute and catalog the information in a way that would recognize these mostly forgotten writers. I recently heard an interview in which someone said that the movie *Sunset Boulevard* was the perfect combination of satire and respect for/of Hollywood. This project works for me in a similar way—if you look at the books on my blog or read the title of the piece, you can see both respect and not necessarily satire, but irony. I think that's important to point out because, although I deeply respect the authors of these books, sometimes I am looking at the books with a sense of humor. Some of the ideas in these books have become outdated, but the evolution of ideas that came from these books is important.

Not all but many of the authors are underrecognized. I'm interested in these feminist and lesbian writers either because the writing is good or because they were so out of the closet publicly when it was still very risky and difficult to be out. I think it is important to recognize these writers. The title of the piece includes the name of the author, publisher, year of publication, and information about the text or the writer. When the work is shown, the information about the books is available, as it is in this catalog, and accessible to whomever might want to investigate these books. ∎

Born 1964 in Philadelphia; lives and works in Los Angeles. A graduate of Temple University (BA, 1986) and Yale University (MFA, 1992), Fowler is cofounder of Artist Curated Projects in Los Angeles. She has had solo shows at Horton Gallery, New York; Thomas Solomon Gallery, Los Angeles; and Julie Saul Gallery, New York. She has participated in group exhibitions at Tulane University Art Gallery, New Orleans; Leo Koenig Inc. Projekte, New York; the Hammer Museum, Los Angeles; New Langton Arts, San Francisco; and Yerba Buena Center for the Arts, San Francisco. Her work is in the collections of the San Francisco Museum of Modern Art; the New Museum, New York; and the Smithsonian Institution, Washington, D.C.

The Sophie Horowitz Story, Sarah Schulman, 1984, the Naiad Press Inc. "We all knew Laura Wolfe. She was part of a group known as Women Against Bad Things. The New York Post headline read **ANTI-AMERICAN, COMMIE, LEZZIE BLOOD-THIRSTY PIG** over a copy of Laura's high school graduation picture. I cleared a place on my desk and tacked her photo to the wall." **We'll Do it Ourselves: Combating Sexism in Education**, Barbara Yates, Steve Werner, David Rosen, 1974 University of Nebraska Press, Lincoln, Nebraska. Contents include: The Portrayal of Women In Children's Books on Puerto Rican Themes, The Oppression of Gay People, Literature and our Gay Minority, Organizing Women's Studies, A Question of Survival: The Predicament of Black Women, The Gay Student Group, Afterthought: Lesbians As Gays and As Women. Also fantastic front and back cover. **Wives Who Love Women**, Jane Scott, 1978, Walker and Co. New York. In this book a fifty-year-old woman comes out as a lesbian with the help of her husband. Takes place in L.A. **So Long As There Are Women, Nine Lives of Women Who Prefer Women,** Elula Perrin, William Morrow and Company, Inc., New York, 1980. The first chapter is titled You dirty dyke. Elula Perrin owned the nightclub Katmandou in Paris. **Gullibles Travels**, writings by Jill Johnston. 1974, Links Books New York, NY. CONTENTS; The Red Baroness in America, The Rightful Air to the Thrown, The Genius I've Squandered in Bed, Marykissmas & A Hippy Nude Year, Great Expectorations, There'll Awe Ways Be an England, Oh Vade & Moder Goddelijk, In Excessive Deo, Gullibles Travels, Strange Degli Innocenti, Busted: Illegal Attire in the First Degree, Could I Have a Light, Elektra, Reconsidered, The Yearly Mellowdrama, More Orphan Than Not, Call It a Day & a Day It Was, Holier Than Me, Hic Et Ubique, A Fair to Meddling Story, Tender Gluttons, As Anybody Lay Dying, Kraut Fishing in Amerika, Resurrection for 40 Cents, Springjoyce, Atroxatrashajokajaxatrocious, Obsoletely Unadulterous, Writing into the Sunset, Delitism, Stardumb, & Leadershit, Women & Film, Hurricane Bella Sweeps the Country, The Holy Spirit Lucid in New York, R.D. Laing: The Misteek of Sighcosis, Time Wounds All Heals, Agnes Martin: Surrender & Solitude. **Sunday's Women: Lesbian Life Today** by Sasha G. Lewis. Here are the real-life joys and problems of growing up gay, coming out, coping with friends and family, living with a lover's children and creating a supportive lesbian family. This book presents a comprehensive portrait of 70's lesbian womanhood. Beacon Press, Boston. **Riverfinger Woman** Elana Nachman recounts what it was like to be a young gay woman in the 60's. It deals with what is real and what is imaginary. daughters, inc., Plainfield, Vermont. **They Will Know Me By My Teeth**, Elana Dykewoman, With the publication of They Will Know Me By My Teeth (1976), Elana changed her surname to "Dykewoman," at once an expression of her strong commitment to the lesbian community and a way to keep herself "honest," since anyone reading the book would know the author was a lesbian. The stories and poems in the collection are written from within the lesbian community, addressing such issues as surgical breast reduction, masturbation, class, inventing creation myths, and mythic lesbian communities. **A Woman Appeared to Me**, Renee Vivien. An autobiographical account of her love affair with Natalie Clifford Barney. Published in Paris in 1904. Jeannette H. Foster translated it into English. Cover and title page are by Tee A. Corinne. Naiad Press, Inc., Tallahassee, Florida. **Lesbian Lives, Biographies of Women from The Ladder**. Edited by Barbara Grier and Coletta Ried. In 1955, in San Francisco, eight women met and formed the daughters of Bilitis. In 1956 that group began publishing The Ladder. This book includes the biographies of over 75 lesbians such as Sappho, Edna St. Vincent Millay, H. D., Collette, Queen Christina of Sweden and Amelia Earhart. **Sapphic Songs Seventeen to Seventy**, Elsa Gidlow. A collection of poems and amazing photographs of Elsa Gidlow throughout her life. Looking boyish, with cats, naked–from 17 to 70 like the book says. She wrote lesbian poems in 1919. She really put herself out there. **Elsa Gidlow** (1898–1986) was a poet, who in 1923 published the first volume of openly lesbian love poetry in the United States: On A Grey Thread. She promoted alternative spiritualities including Buddhism and Goddess Worship. In the 1940s she founded a rural retreat center, The Druid Heights Artists Retreat, in Marin County, California. She lived there until her death in 1986. Wikipedia lists Neil Young, Alan Watts, Ansel Adams and feminist theorist Catharine MacKinnon as friends of Elsa Gidlow. **The coming out stories**, foreword Adrienne Rich, Editors Julia Penelope Stanley and Susan J. Wolfe. Coming out stories published in 1980-Things were really different 30 years ago. Brave people who seem tormented tell their stories here. Not a lot of joy here but interesting info. Persephone Press, Watertown, Mass. **Lesbian Images**, Jane Rule. This is a study of the work and lives of 12 well-known women writers (Radclyffe Hall, Gertrude Stein, Willa Cather, Vita Sackville-West, Ivy Compton-Burnett, Elizabeth Bowen, Colette, Violette Leduc, Margaret Anderson, Dorothy Baker, May Sarton and Maureen Duffy. 1975, Doubleday & Company, Inc. Garden City, NY. **Retreat: As it was! A Fantasy** by Donna J. Young, Naiad Press inc., 1979. Cover by Tee A. Corinne. Retreat-A world of women beyond your imagination? What it was like before the men came. The cover is the best part of this curious gay sci fi work of fiction. **Nighthawk**, Artemis OakGrove. Lace Publications, Denver, Colorado. 1987 described on its back cover as a "sexy novel about dangerous, inner city women…who play for keeps." The cover illustration, by Vickie, is amazing and looks like a G.B. Jones drawing. You can see the cover at lesbiantreasures.blogspot.com. **sexism-it's a nasty affair**, jeanne cordova. New way books Hollywood, 1974. This book is in lower case from front to back, as are many feminist books written around this time. Everything about this book is great, the art, the cover, the writing & the font. Jeanne Cordova was the president of the L.A. daughters of Bilitis and founded Lesbian Tide. **The Lesbian Body**, Monique Wittig. Beacon Press Boston. 1973. Author's Note: Le Corps Lesbian has lesbianism as its theme. A theme, which cannot even be described as taboo, for it has no real existence in the history of literature. Male homosexual literature has a past, it has a present. The lesbians, for their part, are silent-just as all women are as women at all levels. When one has read the poems of Sappho, Radclyffe Hall's Well of Loneliness, the poems of Sylvia Plath and Anais Nin, La Batarde by Violette Leduc, one has read everything. Only the women's movement has proved capable of producing lesbian texts in a context of total rupture with masculine culture, text written by women exclusively for women, careless of male approval. Le Corps Lesbien falls into this category. **Goddess of Lesbian dreams**, poems and songs of fran winant, 1980, Violet Press, New York, NY. Arlene Raven wrote the following on the back cover; "Read this book awake at night. Imagine that the moon has replaced the sun with her light. Walk outside to your own "Sacred Grove" your own place of waking dreams. And on your way, move through your own form, Becoming Womanbeast, bird-fly-or take a taxi driven by a "Goddess of Lesbian dreams." Recognize her (give her a tip). There are drawings with photographs of women taking pictures in trees, a song about winning the lottery and poems with titles like "Lesbian Nights". This is book is a lesbian treasure and was the inspiration for the title of my blog lesbiantreasures.blogspot.com. **Our Right To Love, A Lesbian Resource Book**, produced in cooperation with women of the National Gay Task Force. An illustrated comprehensive guide for lesbians, students, teachers, parents, feminists, legislators, counselors, and movement organizers. Editor: Ginny Vida, Media director, National Gay Task Force. 1978, Prentice-Hall, Inc., Englewood Cliffs, New Jersey. Andrea Dworkin, **The New Woman's Broken Heart**, 1975, Fog In The Well, East Palo Alto, California. A collection of short stories. Here's the title story: morning broke. I mean, fell right on its goddam ass and broke. no walking barefoot if you care about yr feet, kid. I waited and waited. no call came. I cant say, the call didnt come because it wasnt a question one really. it was a question of any one. it was a question of one goddam person calling to say I like this or that or I want to buy this or that or you moved my heart, my spirit, or I li yr ass. to clarify, not a man calling to say I li yr ass but one of those shining new women, luminous, tough, lighting right up from insi one of them. or some of the wrecked old women I know, too late not to be wrecked, t many children torn right out of them, but st I like the wrinkles, I like the toughness of th heart. one of them. not one of those new ne new girl children playing soccer on the boys team for the first time. young is dumb. at lea it was when I was young. I have no patience with the untorn, anyone who hasnt weather rough weather. fallen apart, been ripped to pieces, put herself back together, big stitche jagged cuts, nothing nice. then something shines out. but these ones all shined up on outside, the ass wigglers. I'll be honest, I do like them. not at all. the smilers. the soft voices, eyes on the ground or scanning oute space. its not that I wouldnt give my life for them, I just dont want them to call me on th telephone. still, business is business. I need one of them, the ass wigglers, to call me on the phone. editors. shits. smiling, cleaned u shits. plasticized turds. everything is too lor or too short or too angry or too rude. one eve said too urban. Im living on goddam east 5 street, dog shit, I mean, buried in dog shit, police precinct across the street sirens blaze day and night, hells angels 2 streets down, toilet in the hall and of course I have colitis constant diarrhea, and some asshole smiler says too urban. Id like to be gods editor. I ha a few revisions Id like to make. so I wait. not quietly, I might add. I sigh and grunt and groan. I make noise, what can I say. my cat runs to answer and then demands attention absolutely demands. not a side glance eithe but total rapt absolute attention, my whole body in fact, not a hand, or a touch, or a little condescending pat on the head. I hiss. why not, I mean I speak the language so to speak which brings me to the heart of the matter. ladies. for instance, a lady would pretend sh did not know exactly what to say to a cat tha demanded her whole life on the spot. she would not hiss. she would make polite mute gestures. even if she were alone, she would as if someone was watching her. or try to. sh would push the cat aside with one hand, pretending gentle, but it would be a goddam rude push you had better believe it, and she would smile. at the window. at the wall. at th goddam cat if you can imagine that. me, I his thus, all my problems in life. the ladies dare not respect hissers. they wiggle their goddam asses but hissers are pariahs. female hissers male hissers are another story altogether. fo example, one morning I go to cover a story. I go 1500 miles to cover this particular story. now, I need the money. people are very coy out money, and the ladies arent just coy, they are sci fi about money. me, Im a hisser. I le it but I need it. only I dont want to find it der the pillow the next morning if you know at I mean. I dont wear stockings and I want buy my own hershey bars. or steal them self at least. Id really like to give them up ogether. but I wouldnt really and its the only cial lie I tell. anyway I pick my own health zards and on my list sperm in situ comes mewhere below being eaten slowly by a urmet shark and being spit out half way ough because you dont quite measure up. an attitude, what can I say. except to mind the public at large that the nstitution is supposed to protect it. so I go cover the story and the ass wigglers are out large numbers. I mean they are fucking nging from the chandeliers, and there are andeliers. ritzy hotel. lots of male rnalists. whither they goest go the ass gglers. so its a conference of women. and point is that this particular event occurred cause a lot of tough shining new women ve demanded this and that, like men not ng inside them at will, either naked or with truments, to tear them up, knock them up, at them up, fuck them up, etc. and suddenly, ladies have crawled out of the woodwork. I go to pee in the classy lounge where the lets are, and one of the ass wigglers doesnt k to me. I mean, Im peeing, shes peeing, so o the fuck does she think she is. so the line drawn. but its been drawn before. in fact its en drawn right across my own goddam sh, its been drawn in high heeled ladies ots trampling over me to get into print. I an, I cant make a living. the boys like the s wigglers. so I work you know. I mean, I king work. but theres work I wont take on, e certain kinds of ass wiggling at certain ecific moments. the crucial moments. like en the male editor wants that ass to move ck and forth this way and that. as a result, I what is euphemistically referred to as a or person. I am ass breaking poor and no rson either. a woman is what I am, a hisser, oddam fucking poor woman who stays ddam fucking poor because she doesnt fuck rious jerks around town. its the white glove ndrome. the queen must be naked except for e white gloves. while hes fucking her raw e has to pretend shes sitting with her legs sed proper and upright and while hes ting with his legs closed handing out work signments she has to pretend shes fucking n until she drops dead from it. yeah its ugh on her. its tougher on me. I dont mean this to be bitter. I dont know from bitter. its e that morning fell flat on its ass and when rning breaks its shit to clean it up. and I nt much like sleeping either because I have hnicolor dreams in which strangers try to me in very resourceful ways. and its true at since the ass wiggler snubbed me in the let of the ritzy hotel I get especially upset

when I go to pee in my own house (house here being a euphemism for apartment, room, or hovel--as in her own shithole which she does not in any sense own, in other words, where she hangs her nonexistent hat) and remember that the food stamps ran out and I have $11.14 in the bank. bleak, Arctic in fact, but not bitter. because I do still notice some things I particularly like. the sun, for instance, or the sky even when the sun isnt in it. I mean, I like it. I like trees. I like them all year long, no matter what. I like cold air. Im not one of those complainers about winter which should be noted since so many people who pretend to love life hate winter. I like the color red a lot and purple drives me crazy with pleasure. I churn inside with excitement and delight every time a dog or cat smiles at me. when I see a graveyard and the moon is full and everything is covered with snow I wonder about vampires. you cant say I dont like life. people ask, well, dont sweet things happen? yes, indeed. many sweet things. but sweet doesnt keep you from dying. making love doesnt keep you from dying unless you get paid. writing doesnt keep you from dying unless you get paid. being wise doesnt keep you from dying unless you get paid. facts are facts. being poor makes you face facts which also does not keep you from dying. people ask, well, why dont you tell a story the right way, you woke up then what happened and who said what to whom. I say thats shit because when you are ass fucking poor every day is the same. you worry. ok. she had brown hair and brown eyes and she worried. theres a story for you. she worried when she peed and she worried when she sat down to figure out how far the $11.14 would go and what would happen when it was gone and she worried when she took her walk and saw the pretty tree. she worried day and night. she choked on worry. she ate worry and she vomited worry and no matter how much she shitted and vomited the worry didnt come out, it just stayed inside and festered and grew. she was pregnant with worry, hows that? so how come the bitch doesnt just sell that ass if shes in this goddam situation and its as bad as she says. well, the bitch did, not just once but over and over, long ago, but not so long ago that she doesnt remember it. she sold it for a corned beef sandwich and for steak when she could get it. she sold it for a bed to sleep in and it didnt have to be her own either. she ate speed because it was cheaper than food and she got fucked raw in exchange for small change day after day and night after night. she did it in ones twos threes and fours with onlookers and without. so she figures shes wiggled her ass enough for one lifetime and the truth is she would rather be dead if only the dying wasnt so fucking slow and awful and she didnt love life goddam it so much. the truth is once you stop you stop. its not something you can go back to once its broken you in half and you know what it means. I

mean, as long as youre alive and you know what trading in ass means and you stop, thats it. its not negotiable. and the woman for whom it is not negotiable is anathema.for example, heres a typical vignette. not overdrawn, underdrawn. youre done yr days work, fucking. youre home. so some asshole man thinks thats his time. so he comes with a knife and since hes neighborhood trade you try to calm him down. most whores are pacifists of the first order. so he takes over yr room, takes off his shirt, lays down his knife. thats yr triumph. the fuck isnt anything once the knife is laid down. only the fuck is always something. you have to pretend that you won. then you got to get him to go but hes all comfy isnt he. so another man comes to the door and you say in an undertone, this fuckers taken over my house. so it turns out man 2 is a hero, he comes in and says what you doing with my woman. and it turns out man 2 is a big drug dealer and man 1 is a fucking junkie. so you listen to man 1 apologize to man 2 for fucking his woman. so man 1 leaves. guess who doesnt leave? right. man 2 is there to stay. so he figures hes got you and he does. and he fucking tries to bite you to death and you lie still and groan because you owe him and he fucking bites you near to death. between yr legs, yr clitoris, he fucking bites and bites. then he wants breakfast. so once you been through it enough, enough is enough. ah, you say, so this explains it, whores hate men because whores see the worst, what would a whore be doing with the best. but the truth is that a whore does the worst with the best. the best undress and reduce to worse than the rest. besides, all women are whores and thats a fact. at least all women with more than $11.14 in the bank. me too. shit, I should tell you what I did to get the $11.14. nothing wrong with being a whore. nothing wrong with working in a sweatshop. nothing wrong with picking cotton. nothing wrong with nothing.I like the books these jerko boys write. I mean, and get paid for. its interesting. capital, labor, exploitation, tomes, volumes, journals, essays, analyses. all they fucking have to do is stop trading in female ass. apparently its easier to write books. it gives someone like me a choice. laugh to death or starve to death. Ive always been pro choice. the ladies are very impressed with those books. its a question of physical coordination. some people can read and wiggle ass simultaneously. ambidextrous.so now I'm waiting and thinking. Anne Frank and Sylvia Plath leap to mind. they both knew Nazis when they saw them, at some point. there were a lot of ass wigglers in the general population around them wiggling ass while ovens filled and emptied. wiggling ass while heroes goosestepped or wrote poetry. wiggling ass while women, those old fashioned women who did nothing but hope or despair, died. this new woman is dying too, of poverty and a broken heart. the heart broken like fine china

in an earthquake, the earth rocking and shaking under the impact of all that goddam ass wiggling going off like a million time bombs. an army of whores cannot fail-to die one by one so that no one has to notice. meanwhile one sad old whore who stopped liking it has a heart first cracked then broken by the **** ladies who wiggle while they work."the new womans broken heart" copyright © 1978, 1979, 1980 by Andrea Dworkin. All rights reserved. First published in Heresies, Vol. 2, No. 3, spring 1979. *A lesbian feminist anthology, AMAZON EXPEDITION,* edited by Phyllis Birkby, Bertha Harris, Jill Johnston, Esther Newton and Jane O'Wyatt. 1973, Times Change Press, Washington NJ. Includes The Comingest Womanifesto by Jill Johnston, The New Misandry by Joanna Russ and The Parable of Mothers and Daughters by Florence Rush. *The Fur Person*, May Sarton, 1957, Holt, Rinehart & Winston. The back cover reads "This charming story is drawn from the true adventures of May Sarton's own cat and recounts his evolution from a Cat-About-Town to a Gentleman Cat and finally his emergence as a genuine Fur Person." Illustrated by David Cartright. *The Lesbian Reader*, 1975, Amazon Press. Edited by Gina Covina and Laurel Galana. This book includes How to Make a Magazine, Toward a Womanvision and Radical Reproduction: X Without Y by Laurel Galana as well as Hands by Maud Haimson, I dream in Female: The Metaphors of Evolution by Barbara Starrett and Waiting for Something to Happen by Jennie Orvino. I may have ripped The Lesbian Love Ethic out of this book to use in a photogram—collaboration with Anna. I did. I found bookmark in this book from the sisterhood bookstore in Los Angeles. *The immaculate conception of the blessed virgin dyke*, Ellen Marie Bissert, 1972, 13th Moon, Inc. Poems by Ellen Marie Bissert. Nice photograph on the back cover. *Class & Feminism, A Collection of Essays from THE FURIES*, Diana Press, 1974, Edited by Charlotte Bunch and Nancy Myron. Essays include: The Last Straw by Rita Mae Brown, Gimme Shelter by Tasha Peterson, Class Beginnings by Nancy Myron, Slumming it in the Middle Class by Giny Berson, Recycled Trash by Coletta Reid, Revolution Begins at Home by Coletta Reid and Charlotte Bunch and Garbage Among the Trash by Delores Bargowski and Coletta Reid. *Lesbian Feminism in Turn-of-the-century Germany* edited by Lillian Feverman and Brigitte Eriksson. 1980 The Naiad Press. This book includes portions of: The New Eve: Modern Education and Old Morality by Maria Janitschek(1906), Of The New Woman and Her Love: A Book for Mature Minds, Elisabeth Dauthendey(1900), The Truth About Me, E. Krause from Yearbook of Intermediate Sexual Types(Leipzig, 1901), Are These Women?, Aimee Duc (Berlin,1903), What Interest does the Women's Movement Have in the

Homosexual Question? By Anna Rueling (Berlin, 1904). **Lesbian Nuns Breaking Silence** edited by Roesmary Curb & Nancy Manahan, Naiad Press, 1985. "Lesbian nuns I know are going to dance! In convents this book will go around like hotcakes, just the way THE HITE REPORT did. Everybody read it. Lesbian nuns will be more self-conscious about this book. They're also going to be listening for the response from other members of the community and praying to God it's okay." **To the man reporter from the Denver Post**, Poems by Chocolate Waters, Eggplant Press, 1975. Some of the poems in this book appeared in Lavender Woman, off our backs, Desperate Living, Women's Press, So's Your Old Lady and Big Mama Rag. There's a nice pencil drawing of vagina in a landscape. **Mother, Sister, Daughter, Lover** Stories by Jan Clausen, 1975, The Crossing Press, Trumansburg, New York. "Jan Clausen is a lesbian lover editor clerical worker non-biological parent political activist runner writer." **Loving Women, The Nomadic Sisters**, Illustrated by Ann Miya, 1976. An illustrated sex manual for lesbians. Great drawings. **Old Dyke Tales**, Lee Lynch, The Naiad Press, Inc., 1984. **Fernhurst, Q.E.D, and Other Early Writings**, Gertrude Stein, 1950, The Banyan Press. Stein is the author of one of the earliest coming out stories, Q.E.D. (published in 1950 as Things as They Are), written in 1903 and suppressed by the author. The story, written during travels after dropping out, is based on a love triangle she joined while studying at Johns Hopkins in Baltimore. The triangle was complicated in that Stein was less experienced with the closeted social dynamics of romantic friendship as well as her own sexuality and any moral dilemmas regarding it. Stein maintained at the time that she detested "passion in its many disguised forms". The relationships of Stein's acquaintances Mabel Haynes and Grace Lounsbury ended as Haynes started one with Mary Bookstaver (also known as May Bookstaver). Stein fell in love with Bookstaver but was unsuccessful in advancing their relationship. Bookstaver, Haynes, and Lounsbury all later married men. (Blackmer 1995, p. 681-686)Her growing awareness of her sexuality began to interfere with the bourgeois values implicit in her medical studies[citation needed] and would have put her at odds with contemporary feminist theory and opinion[citation needed], and Q.E.D. may have assisted her with understanding her scholarly and romantic failure. However, Stein began to accept and define her masculinity through the ideas of Otto Weininger's Sex and Character (1906). Weininger, though Jewish by birth, considered Jewish men effeminate and women as incapable of selfhood and genius, except for female homosexuals who may approximate masculinity. –from wikipedia-nuts. **Common Lives, Lesbian Lives, A Lesbian Quarterly,** number twenty-one. 1986a. Includes photographs of "desert dykes and dogs" by zana, Lesbian Ritual Art by Ramona Star Scarpace, Tarot Card by Ruth Mountaingrove. Poems titled "Love Me Like You Mean It" and "After a Year of Celibacy" **Tracking Our Way Through Time: A Lesbian Herstory Calendar Journal**, Janet S. Soule, 1984, Sandpiper Books, Chicago, IL. A calendar & journal that catalogs facts, photos, quotes and graphics drawn from lesbians. **True to Life Adventure Stories**, Volume two, Judy Grahn, Editor, The Crossing Press, 1978. "As soon as I received True to Life Adventure Stories, Vol.2, I sat down and read Linda Maries' 'Straight Woman.' When I had finished laughing, I moved on to the wonderful 'Tehuantepec,' and so on through the book. These are stories so real, so vibrant, so outrageous that, yes indeed, they are true to life. An adventure not to be missed."-Alice Walker **sinister wisdom 33**, Fall 1987, editor and publisher Elana Dykewomon, A Journal for the Lesbian Imagination in the Arts and Politics. Contents include A Dyke Geography by Elana Dykewomon, photographs, poems, drawings and stories. **Six of One**, Rita Mae Brown **A Lesbian Estate by Lynn Lonidier**, 1977, Manroot, South San Francisco. Poems by Lynn Lonidier: I Hear You Guarded Two-Sex, Say My Name, A Mother Is A Broken Mustard Jar, Falconess and Lightfoot of Fairies. **the lesbian primer**. liz diamond Illustrations by carol arber. Salem, MA: Women's Educational Media, 1979 **Madame Aurora**, Sarah Aldridge, 1983, the Naiad Press Inc "Elizabeth Beaufort: beautiful, impoverished scholar who has eked out a living as a teacher until deafness and a scandal over a book about love intervene." Early American lesbian scandals. **The Amazon of Letters, The Life and Loves of Natalie Barney**, George Wickes, Popular Library, New York, 1976. Great photographs of Renee Vivien dressed in one of many outfits that helped inspire "Orlando" by Virginia Woolf. **Lesbian Love in Literature** edited by Stella Fox, 1962, Avon Book division, New York. Includes stories by Sappho, Guy de Maupassant, Kay Boyle and Fyodor Dostoevsky. The varieties of Lesbian experience . . . A young boy discovers his dead father has been replaced by a woman, a dissatisfied wife learns that she and her husband love the same woman, a young girl falls in love with father's mistress, a college girl initiates her roommate, a French woman dressed in man's clothes looks for her lovers and a student learns about love from her teacher. Violette Leduc, **Mad in Pursuit**, 1972, Panther Books, London. In the second remarkable volume of her life story, Mad In Pursuit, the war is finally over. A new generation of writers has appeared in Paris, among them Camus, Genet, Sartre, and Cocteau, and every day, they can be seen writing at the marble-topped tables of the Cafe de Flore. Already in her thirties Leduc burns with hero-worship and an obsession to become a celebrated writer herself. When she finds a mentor in none other than Simone de Beauvoir, she is pulled into the center of Parisian literary life -"a beehive gone mad. "In the no-holds-barred style that made her a legend, Leduc paints a vibrant picture of the brilliant minds around her-and the dark passions and insecurities that drove her to write. **young, gay & proud**, 1980, Alyson Publications, Inc., Boston, Massachusetts. Originally published in Australia, under the same title, by the Gay Teachers and Student Group of Melbourne. U.S. edition prepared by Sasha Alyson, Enid Braun and Beth Ireland. A resource for gay youth, teachers, librarians and youth workers. Suggested reading includes, The Pillar and the City by Gore Vidal, **The Young in One Another's Arms** by Jane Rule, The Chairoteer and The Persian Boy by Mary Renault and Maurice by E.M. Forster. **Eating Artichokes**, Willyce Kim, 1972, Printed by the Women's Press Collective. Poems and photographs. Ripening, **An Almanac of Lesbian Lore and Vision** by Lee Lanning and Vernette Hart. Printed in 1981 by Iowa City Women's Press, includes drawings, poems and information about lesbian lore, for example: Lesbian Lore Oestre, the goddess of fertility, is the source of our word "oestrus" for animal sexual heat and the festival Easter which celebrates this generating power". **Love Politics and "Rescue" In Lesbian Relationships**, an essay by Diana Rabenold, 1987, HerBooks, Santa Cruz. "The way to stop the Rescues and begin to equalize power in a relationship is to ask for 100% of what we want 100% of the time **Gay Oppression and Liberation or: Homophobia: Its Causes & Cure**, by the Gay Theory Work Group of the Movement for a New Society, June 1977. Contents include: Caught in the Web: How This Society Oppresses Gay People, Keeping Wimmin's Energy from Wimmin, Separatism for Wimmin and lesbian mothers with male children. **The Sound of One Fork**, Minnie Bruce Pratt, night heron press, 1981. Poems – look up MBP **This Woman**, Poetry of Love and Change by Barbara O'Mary, Times Change Press, 1973. Includes: "Why I am Getting Fired," "How You Oppress Me," "Listening To Women" and "Letter To My Husband." Also includes black and white photographs of Barbara O'Mary, her children and her lovers. **This Woman in America**, by Doraine Poretz, 1978, Bombshelter Press, Hermosa Beach, CA. Poems include: for Barbara, for Edith, for Lyla, for Kate, for Sana, for Mary Ellen, for Susan, for Lily, for Rita, for Sylvia. **Lesbianism and Women's Movement**, Nancy Myron & Charlotte Bunch, Diana Press, Baltimore, Md., 1975. Contents include: Lesbians in Revolt, Charlotte Bunch, Taking the Bullshit by the Horns, Barbara Solomon, The Shape of Things to Come, Rita Mae Brown and Coming Out in the Women's Movement, Coletta Reid. Also includes black and white photographs. **Lesbians Words a Santa Cruz Anthology**, edited by Irene Reti & Sue McCabe. This is a small, self-published collection, edited and produced by local women. "It gives us some sense of historical justice to be able to parti-fund Lesbian Words with reparations money paid to Irene's family by the German government in compensation for the confiscation of their property by the Nazi regime. **Sister Outsider, Essays & Speech** by Audre Lorde, 1984 The Crossing Press Feminist Series. Includes essays The Transformation of Silence into Language an-Action, Learning from the 60's, An Interview Audre Lorde and Adrienne Rich and Sexism: American Disease in Blackface. **Time's Power**, Poems 1985-1988 by Adrienne Rich, W.W. Norton and Company, New York & London, 1989. **Lesbian Teachers an Invisi-Presence** by Madiha Didi Khayatt, State University of New York Press, 1992. **Contrac-with the World**, Jane Rule, the Naiad Press Inc., 1982 **We're Here: Conversations with Lesbian Women** by Angelea Stewart-Park a Jules Cassidy, Quartet Books, 1977. Include-black and white photographs and interviews with women in London and New York. **Pit Stop** by pat parker, the women's press collective, oakland ca, 1973. Photographs by jackie howell, ardena sharks, paula wallace, robin wadsworth. Drawings by wendy cadde-jules and cottie. **Visions Incognito** by Nan-Stern, self published, 1978. Braille on the cover–poems by a blind woman. **Amazon Mothers** by Miriam Saphira, Papers Inc., 19-A book for and about lesbian mothers with really nice illustrations. **Desert of the Hear-** by Jane Rule, 1964, Naiad Press. Desert of th-Heart is a 1964 lesbian-themed novel written-Jane Rule. The story was adapted loosely int-the 1985 film Desert Hearts, directed by Don Deitch. The book was originally published in hardback by Macmillan Canada. It was one o-the very few novels that addressed lesbianis-that was published in hardback form; most books during this period with female homosexuality as a topic were considered lesbian pulp fiction until 1969. At the time th-novel was published, Rule was a lecturer at t-University of British Columbia in Vancouver, and because the novel dealt with lesbianism, her job was threatened.[1]Desert of the Hear-was first republished in paperback form by Talonbooks in 1977., 2010 — cat. no. 52

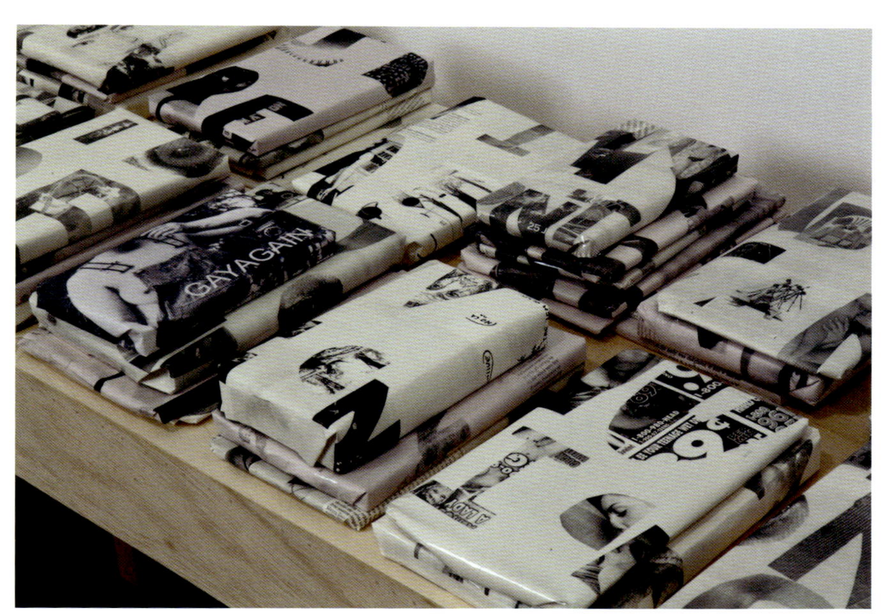

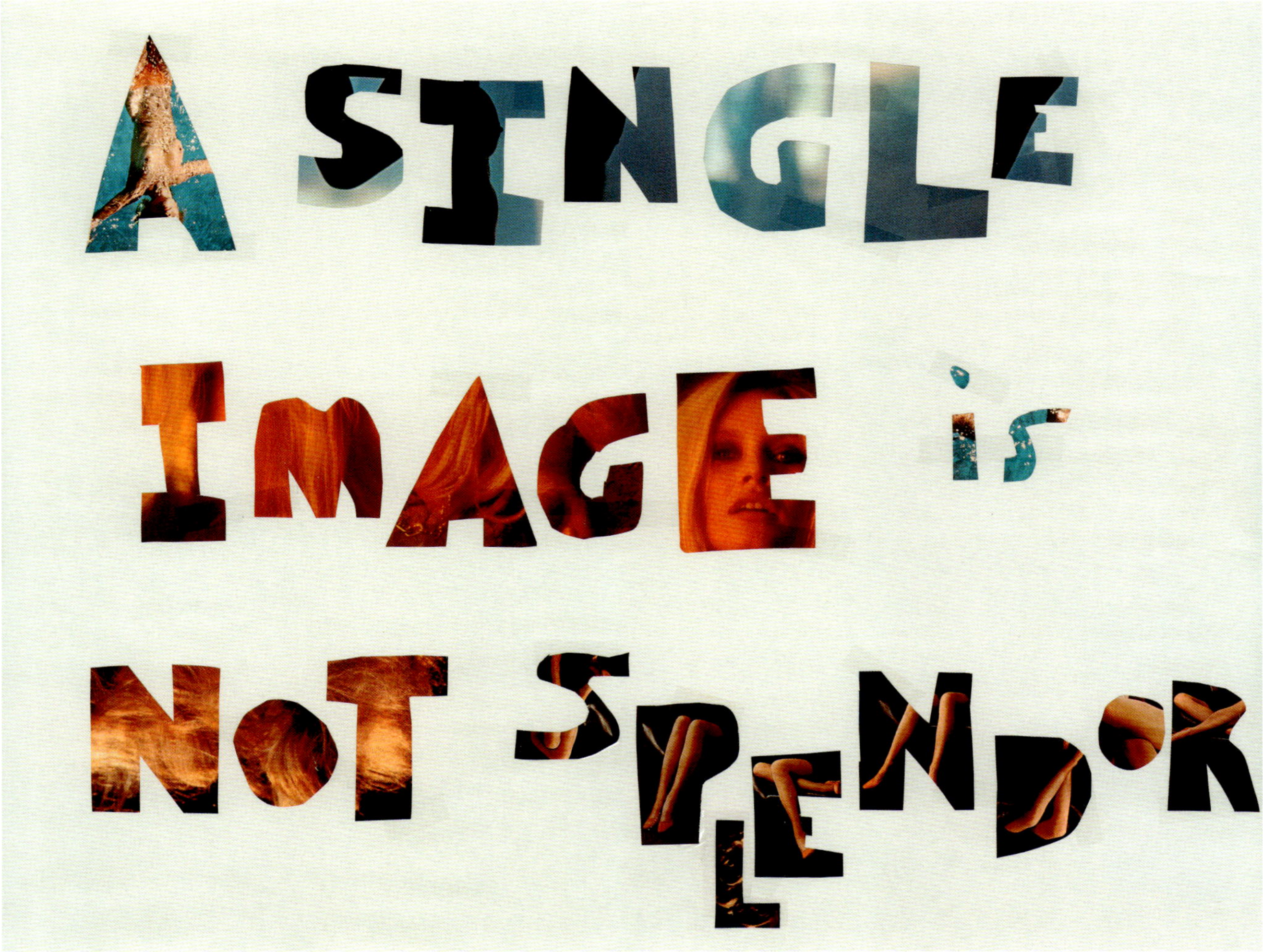

<u>Above</u>
See pages 70–72 for title, 2010 (detail) — cat. no. 52
A Single Image Is Not Splendor, **2010** — cat. no. 51

Rebecca Goldfarb

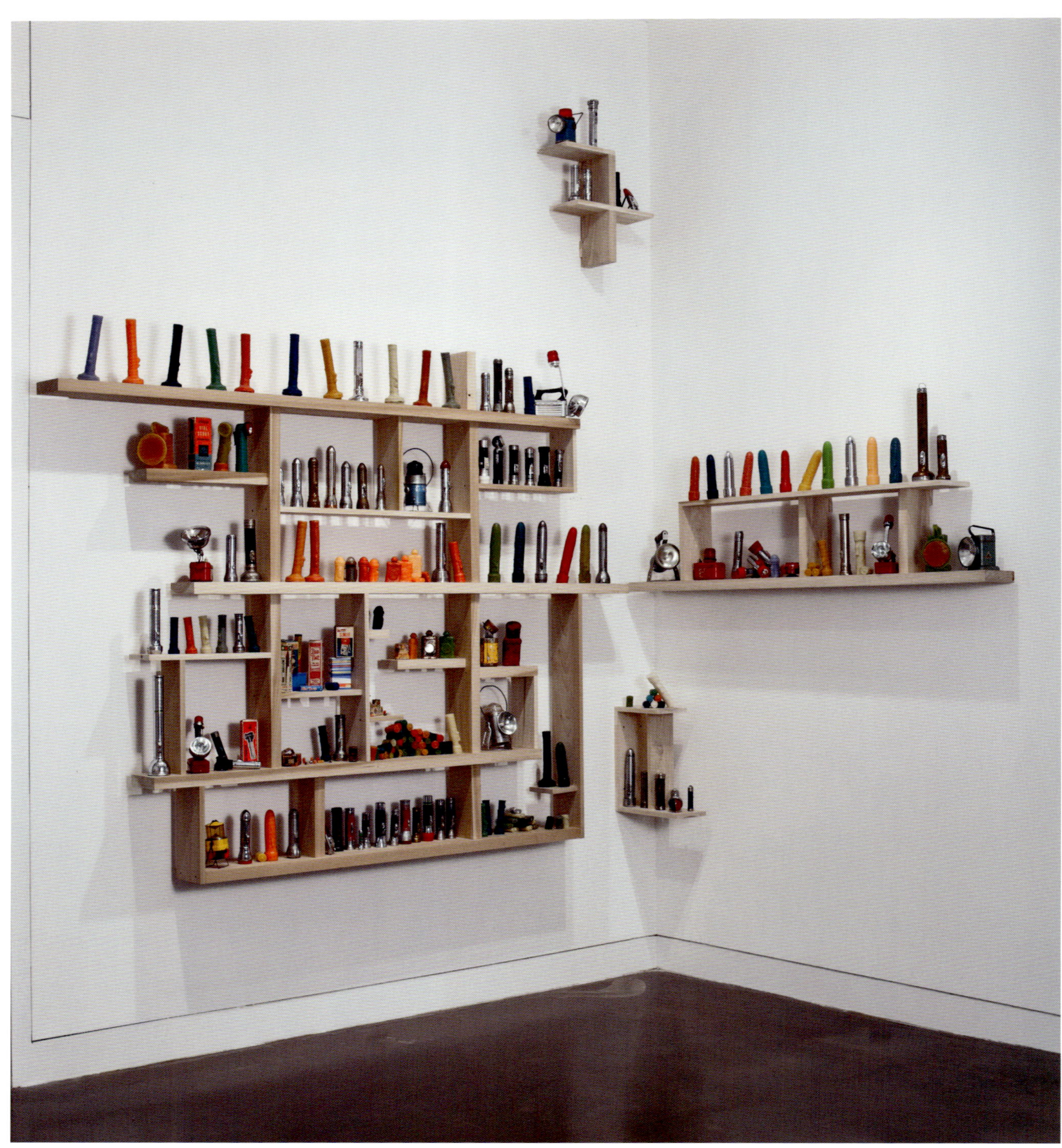

*Traveling through Darkness: Some Sense of the World Turned on When
Flaneur and Collector Meet for the Second Time*, **2010** — cat. no. 53

Interview with Karen Moss

KM: You've worked in photography, installation, and sculpture, but it seems that text (either in the work or in the titles) and subtly constructed narratives are at the core of your artistic practice. Could you please expand upon this?

RG: There's a kind of a master narrative—or monster narrative—at the core. An amorphous or polymorphous creature looking for ways to make itself manifest in the world of things. Language, strings of thought, notions, questions, all these abstractions living within this creature who is continuously searching for a concrete existence. Maybe it's Wallace Stevens's poem "Thirteen Ways of Looking at a Blackbird"—one blackbird and yet so many different ones. Or like Borges's encyclopedic classification of animals. Say I have an umbrella, and it's hovering over my practice. It just doesn't show up in the same way.

KM: *Traveling through Darkness: Some Sense of the World Turned on When Flaneur and Collector Meet for the Second Time* (2010)—your installation of new and vintage flashlights along with their wax casts—comments on authorship and originality, function and dysfunction, the obsession of collecting and, of course, the double entendre of the phallic, uncanny objects. Tell me about this work, how it developed, your intentions, etc.

RG: Was it the *Flaneuse* with her wandering, watchful eye? Or the Collector with her desire to bring the world closer in? Maybe the flashlight itself leads the way—the tool for going into the unknown. The vintage flashlights are buzzing: there's an anthology in every one of those sticks. Backwoods with wolves, the power outage kiss, backpack bottoms and accidents, the ones memorialized in wax, failed ones, phallic ones, the Chevy hoods they've been under. My collection practice creates a context to consider the life of an object, our experience of it, our relationship to it. They're extant, emergent structures that grow as a way to explore the meaning of things.

KM: *Who's Afraid of Fuel, Food and Water* clearly references Barnett Newman's painting *Who's Afraid of Red, Yellow and Blue*; however, your work transcends formalism/minimalism with, once again, your specific choice of objects embedded into the monochromes in a stealthy manner.

RG: Formalism, minimalism, and a nod to pop too? Yes, the work isn't entirely any one of these. The pieces are more than themselves. Representational but hardly. I think it's slippery work, photographs that are more like objects of objects, austere color fields with ubiquitous objects minimally visible to the verge of invisibility. The objects take on a kind of heroic ambivalence, like icons in a dust storm. You could say that they don't advertise well. In choosing the specific object, it's important that it can be easily named. (Like "water bottle," as opposed to "chicken leg and human lung tied together with a shoelace.")

I'm interested in how the object reveals itself slowly over time and how it beckons our attention, or doesn't. This part of my practice is about the act of seeing and thinking. It has an intention of evoking two kinds of experience or spaces for consciousness, one that's envelopment in color and light and another that investigates how the viewer apprehends objects through language.

KM: Your work uses visually engaging materials to construct very specific meanings: it is both aesthetically compelling and conceptually rigorous. How do you balance this in your practice? Do you formulate your ideas first and then choose your materials, or are you initially drawn to particular objects that speak to you, elicit ideas, or imply narratives?

RG: I think that's the resolution: a balanced work. The work may be more balanced than the practice is. At this point in my practice the thought monster that we spoke about is always driving the process, and she's become so well assimilated that her influence is harder for me to see (she's just like much of my work) and she's under my skin as I'm going along now. So the flashlight was an assistant going into the unknown. The object itself didn't entirely lead the way; it rather happily found its niche. And my practice still swings on a pendulum of perceptions—there's always a lot of collaboration that happens between form and concept along the way. Stuff can produce unexpected meaning—evolve beyond intentions I held at inception. ∎

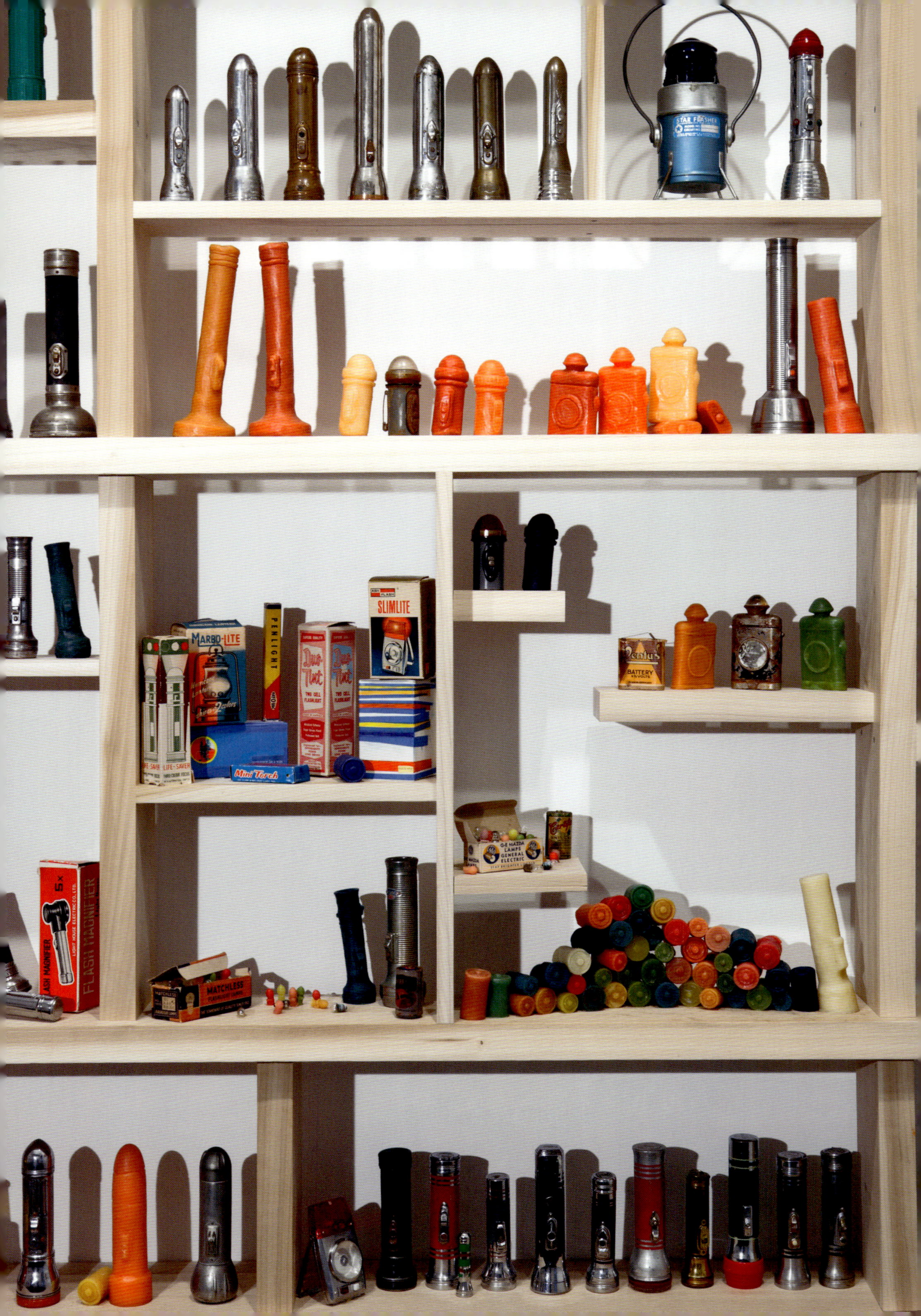

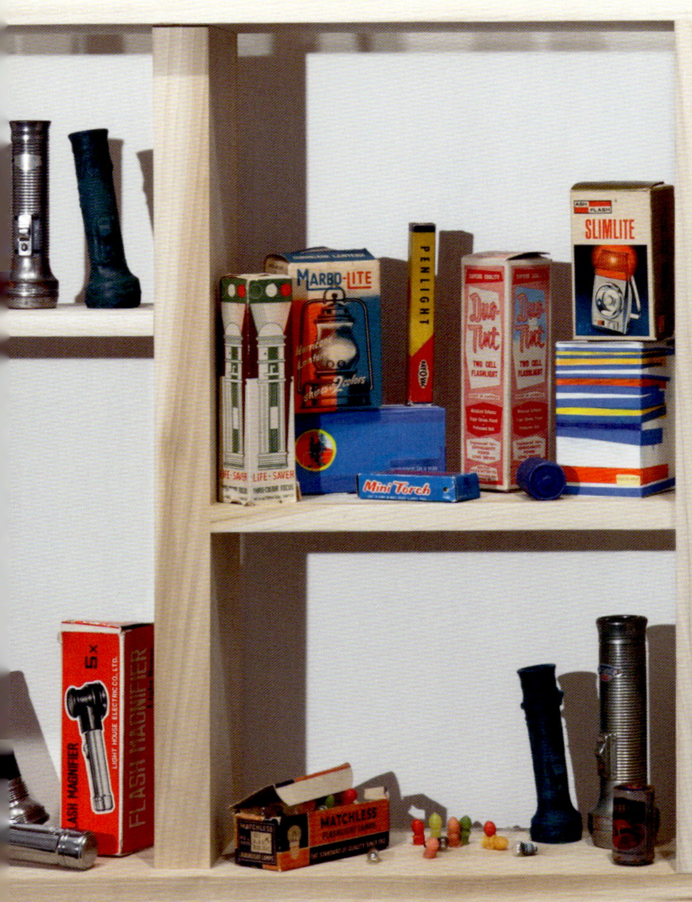
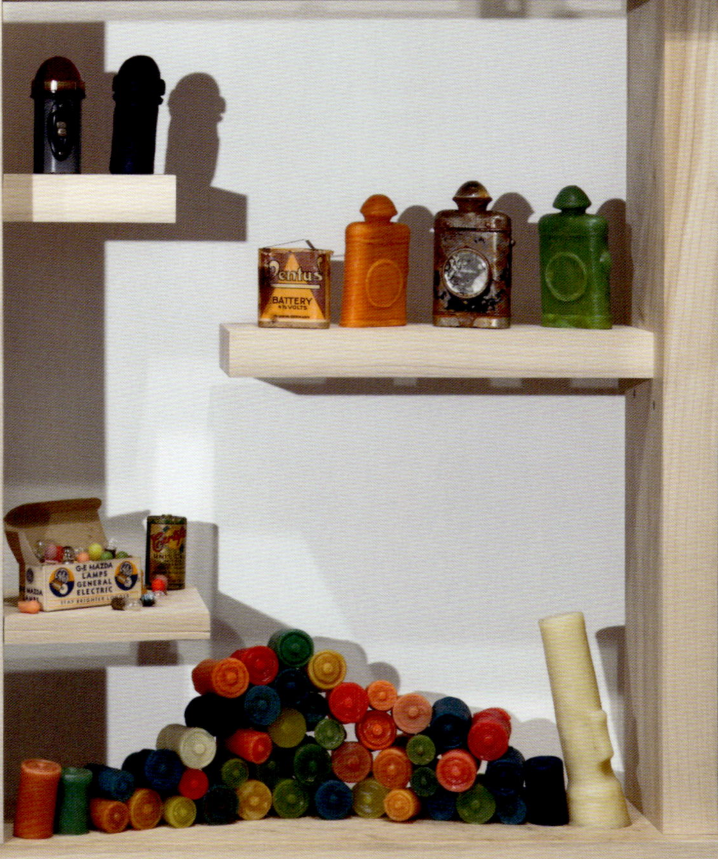
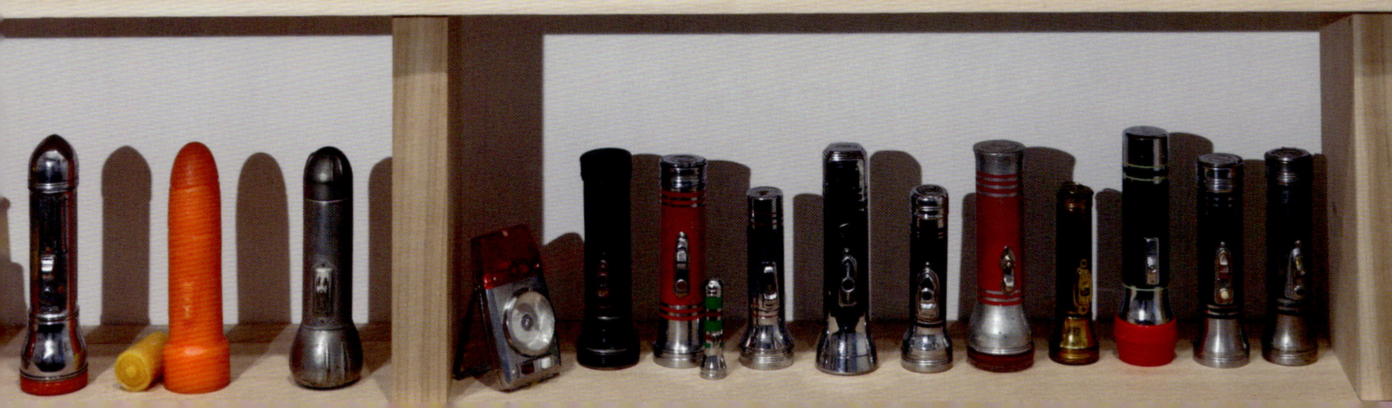

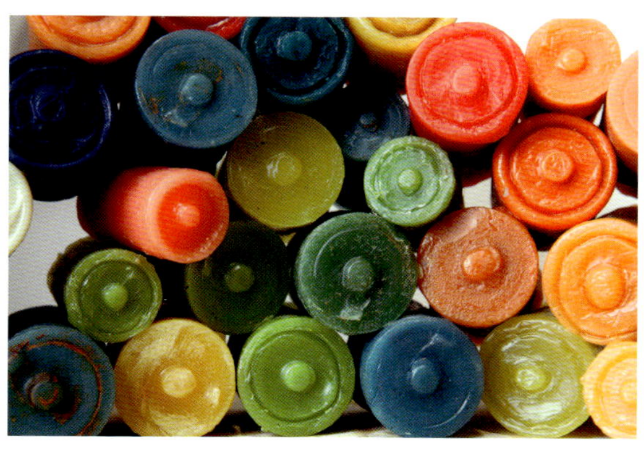

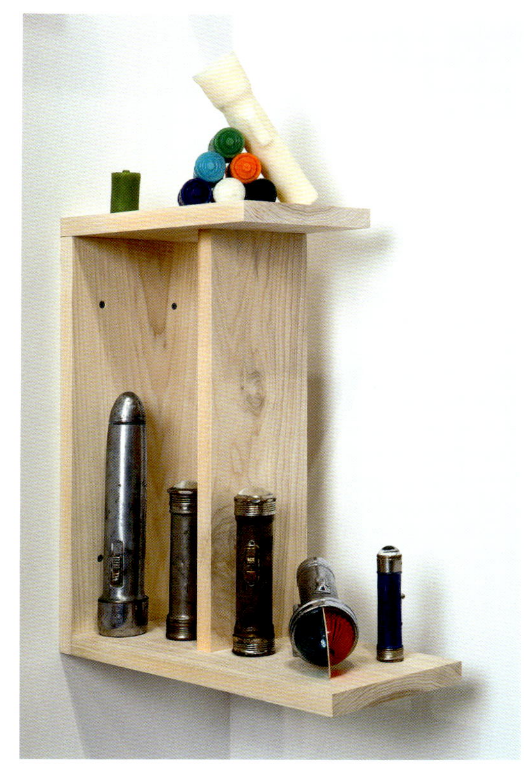

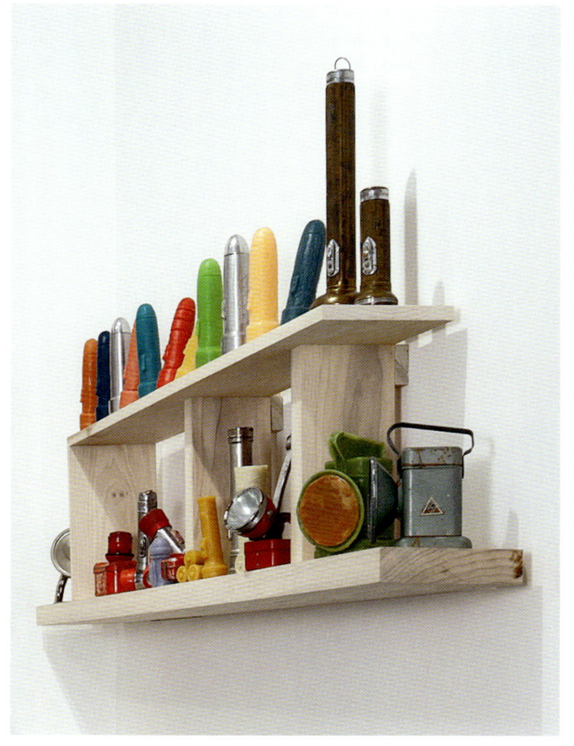

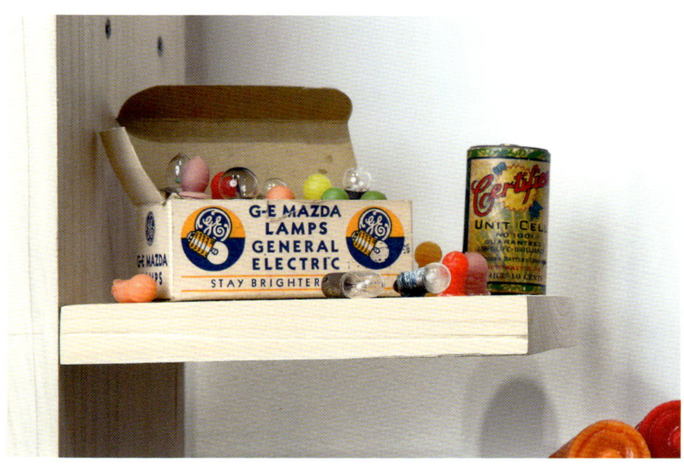

Traveling through Darkness: Some Sense of the World Turned on When Flaneur and Collector Meet for the Second Time, **2010** (details) — cat. no. 53

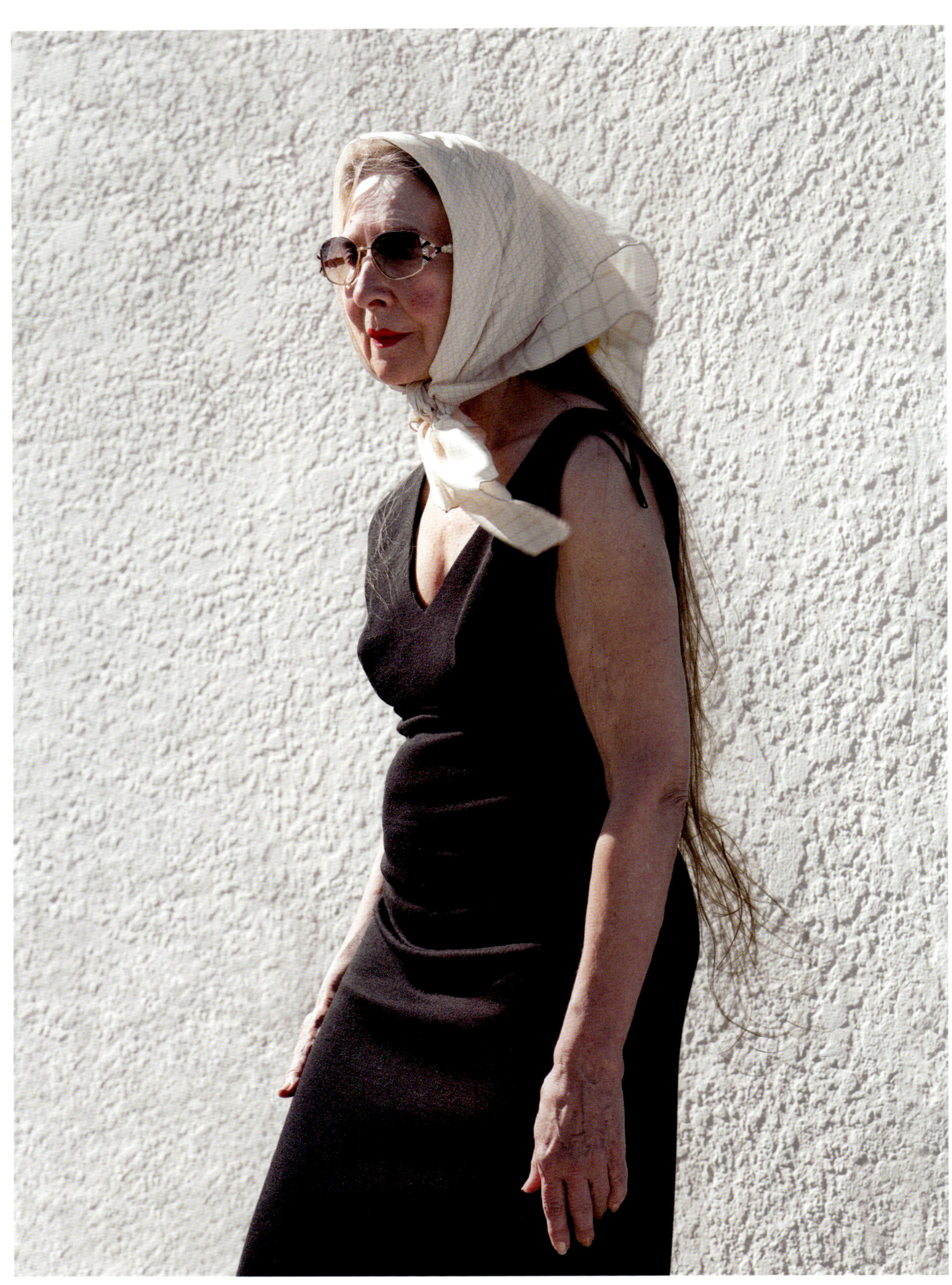

Anonymous, Los Angeles, **2008/printed 2008** — cat. no. 54

GW: **Can you tell me a bit about the suite of photographs that will be shown in the biennial? In particular, I'm interested in the use of the title *Anonymous* in the context of these portraits.**

KG: I'm showing photographs that I've made recently in California; they're part of a series that I call Boulevard. About five years ago I moved from the Northeast to the West Coast, and I was immediately struck by the quality of the light—it's often unforgiving, relentless, and cruel. California sunlight doesn't discriminate between aspiration and failure. It illuminates both equally.

Photography is also kind of cruel. In pictures we unintentionally reveal things that become immovable and fixed in the resulting image. But I find these revelations comforting, as evidence of how we really are. (Thomas Mann once spoke of something he called "erotic irony," which means loving the thing or person you are hurting with harsh analysis.)

These are my street pictures, photographs of people who've been rendered invisible. They might be Hollywood casualties, anonymous Tenderloin drifters, but no matter what their circumstance, they're still subjected to that relentless light. (In Los Angeles they're usually walking while most everyone else drives past, maybe catching a curious glimpse of them for a second or two.)

GW: **Do you think of yourself as a portrait photographer? The tradition of portraiture obviously comes with a host of theoretical and critical associations. To what extent do you purposefully engage with them? Or attempt to evade or avoid them? In particular, I'm interested in the power dynamic operating between the artist, camera, subject, and viewer.**

KG: No, I just think of myself as an artist. Everything artists make has a precedent—we're not creating work in a vacuum, without a historical context. The word *tradition* seems to have negative associations, as if the value of an artwork is directly related to its novelty. I'm not interested in novelty, in cleverness or gimmicks. That kind of work always strikes me as either immature or academic. I'm well versed in theoretical and critical text, but I think those conversations are more interesting to academics. They bore me pretty quickly. Those issues, like the question of the power dynamic between artist and subject, are ones I face every day. It's inherent to the work I'm making. (I once heard a very well known critic speak about figurative art as being too difficult. This very issue of power dynamics makes the work murky territory.) But I'm okay with questions that remain unanswered; I'm comfortable in that murky territory.

GW: **Much has been written about the method by which you executed previous projects such as Poughkeepsie Journal, in which you recruited subjects by placing personal ads in newspapers and collaboratively produced the images. I understand that your working method has changed recently. Can you describe how? What brought about the change, and how do you feel that it has altered the resulting images?**

KG: I walk around, approach people, and if they agree, we make a photograph together on the spot. They appear exactly as I've met them, and it never takes long for us to find that ubiquitous white stucco wall and hard sunlight (my mobile studio). Then we re-create a scene—the act of walking by, waving, hustling for a date, whatever. They often perform enthusiastically, with an enormous, generous spirit. One stranger to another. We improvise and collaborate in a loose, unscripted way so that theater and authenticity are constantly overlapping and indiscernible.

Similarly, with my earlier work, the act of making a photograph itself was a kind of theater. Circumstances were artificial and improvised (subjects responded to newspaper ads), and what emerged was a hybrid between something real and something imagined. Now the idea of theater and transformation includes the way my subjects construct identities and recast themselves within the context of a mythical West. The photographs describe the collision between fantasy and reality—the moment when the myth unravels a little bit. ∎

Born 1969 in Arlington, Massachusetts; lives and works in Berkeley, California. Grannan is a graduate of the University of Pennsylvania (BA, 1991) and Yale University (MFA, 1999). She has exhibited at the Guggenheim Museum, Bilbao; the Palm Beach Institute of Contemporary Art, Palm Beach, Florida; and the Los Angeles County Museum of Art, and she participated in the 2004 Whitney Biennial. Her work has also been featured in numerous publications and is in the collections of the Museum of Modern Art, New York; the Solomon R. Guggenheim Museum, New York; the Whitney Museum of American Art, New York; the Orange County Museum of Art; the International Center for Photography, New York; and the Bard College Center for Curatorial Studies, Annandale-on-Hudson, New York.

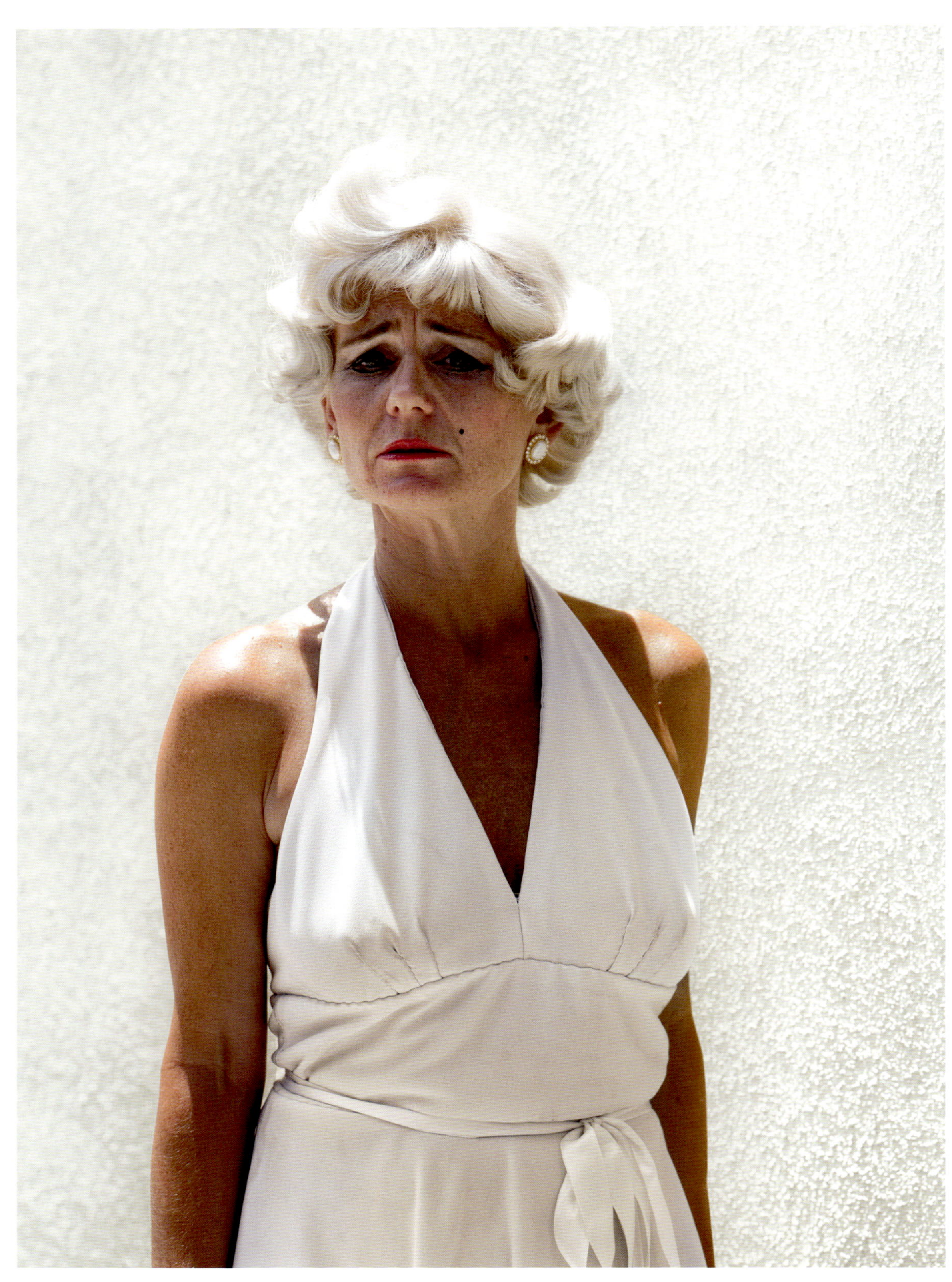

Anonymous, Los Angeles, **2008/printed 2009** — cat. no. 55

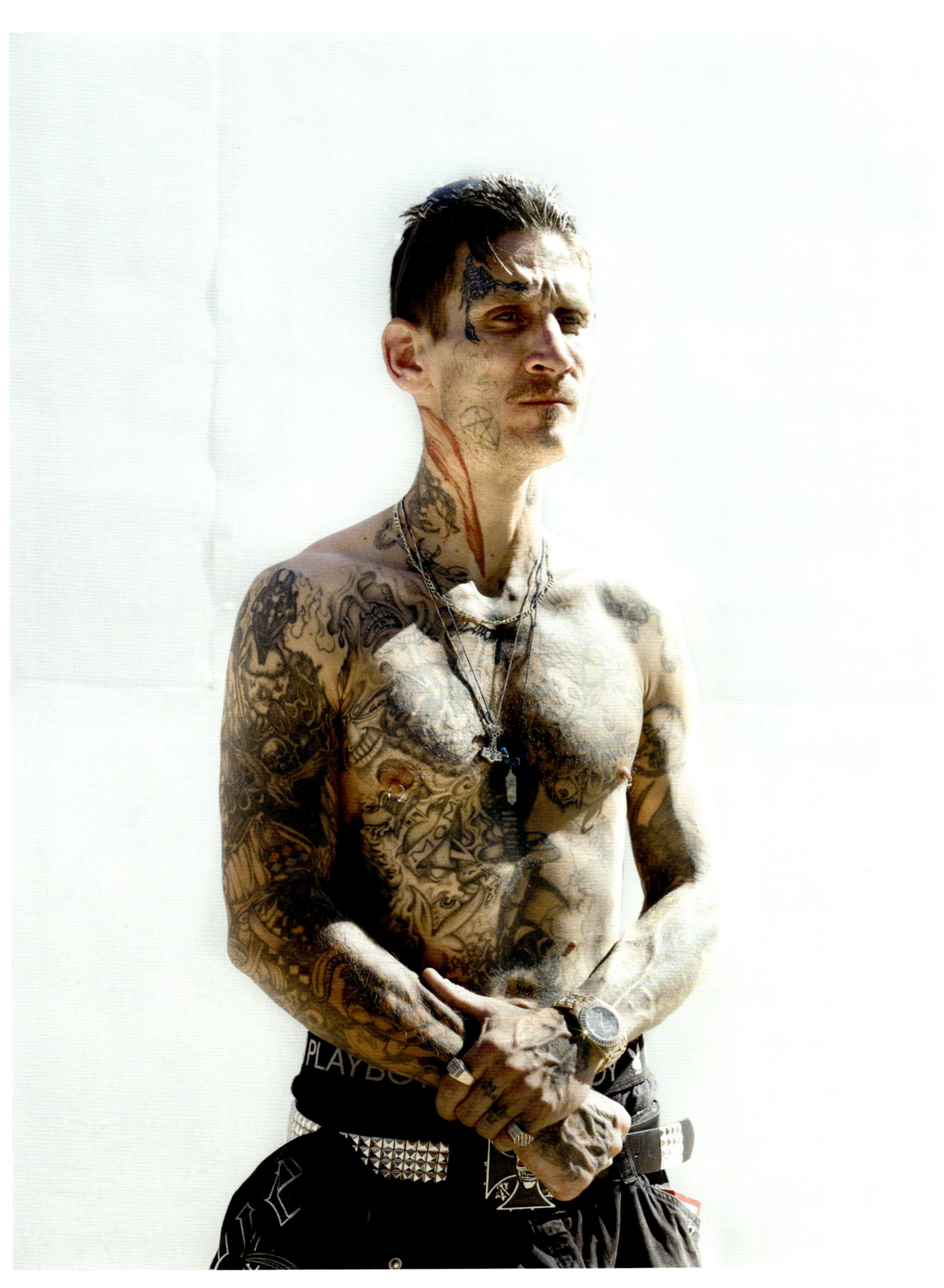

Anonymous, Los Angeles, **2008/printed 2009** — cat. no. 56

Alexandra Grant

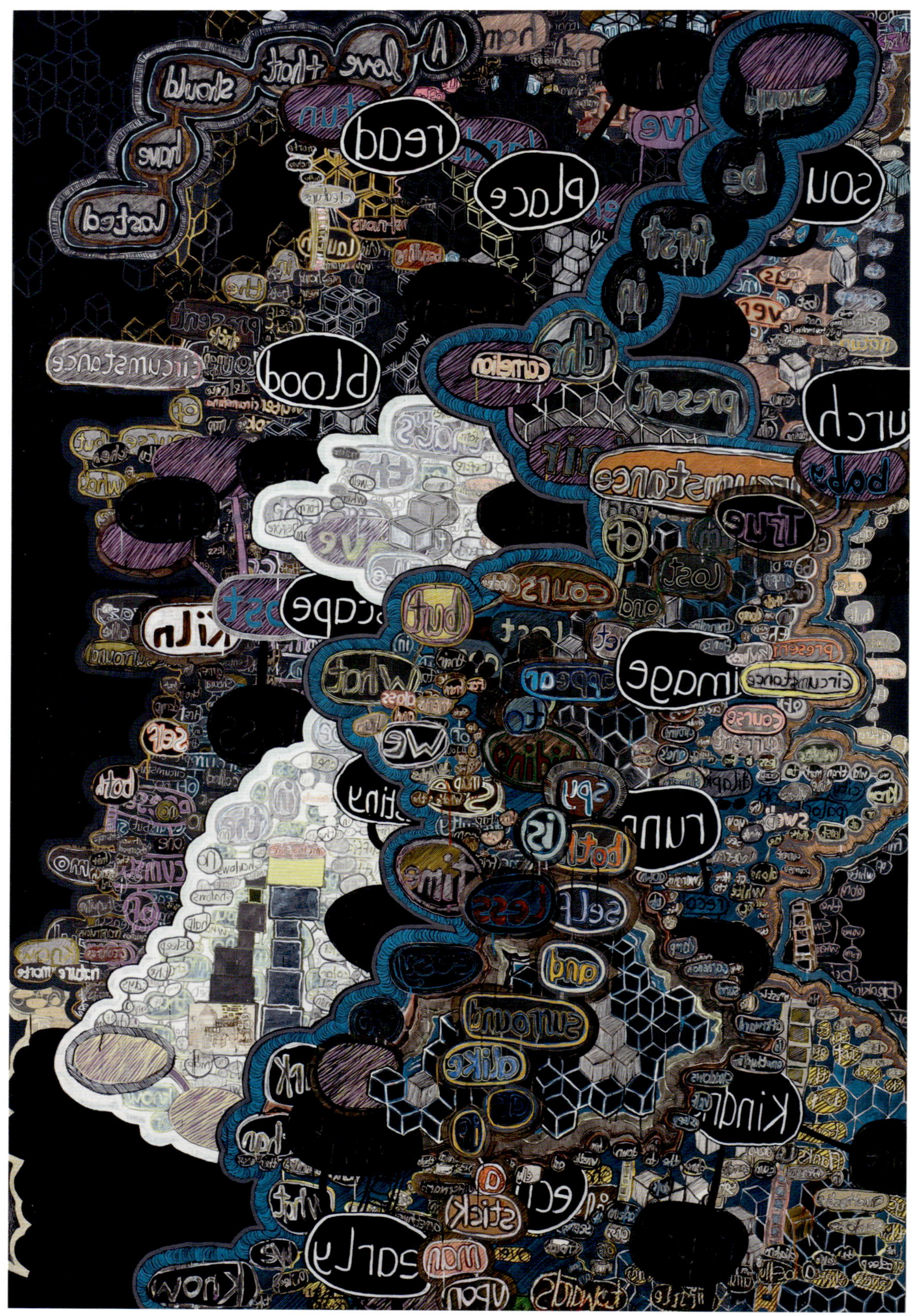

Second Portal (eye) (after Michael Joyce's "Six Portals," 2007),
2008 — cat. no. 58

Interview with Grant Wahlquist

GW: Three works from your Portal series will be on view in the biennial. Can you tell me about the development of the texts that were incorporated into the work?

AG: I imagined the Six Portals as openings into six distinct language spaces. When I described the thematic to my collaborator, the writer Michael Joyce, he suggested that the Portals were doors not only "outward" but also "inward": that each Portal could represent one of the five senses or the mind. Michael wrote a series of sutras, which I used as the scores or scripts for each piece. The formal qualities—color, composition, and architectonic features—were all chosen as visual allegories of the sense. The Portal for "mind," for example, uses spectrums of color to represent a thought bursting through a gray mass of tangled words.

GW: There's a rich tradition of artists combining image and text, particularly in conceptual and postconceptual art. Can you describe your approach to and your interest in using text in the context of what would otherwise be abstract work? I know that you're multilingual and have worked as a translator; do you consider your practice to involve translation in some sense?

AG: The problem of text as image has interested me since I was a child, perhaps because of the cognitive dissonance of moving from country to country and having the experience of trying to decode new languages based on their form and context. I'm intrigued by how artists have related to words (and sometimes *the* word, if you think about religious works) throughout the history of art. Contemporary Los Angeles artists like John Baldessari, Mary Kelly, Ed Ruscha, and Barbara Kruger were as influenced by 1950s advertising (think the VW bug ads in *Life* magazine) as they were by conceptualists like Hans Haacke. My practice began with asking what comes after an advertisement or aphoristic logic-based working methodology, what other visual and linguistic strategies there are. I've been as intrigued by the surrealists and their commitment to breaking narrative as I am by R. B. Kitaj's commitment to both a Jewish literary tradition and color. In my work I see myself as a researcher, interested in writers who I believe "keep the word alive" (to paraphrase Michael Joyce), like Joyce (Michael and James too), Hélène Cixous, and poets like Wislawa Szymborska.

GW: The works in the Portal series have their own brand of balance, whereas the works in your most recent series, Bodies, are structured symmetrically. Was symmetry something that you wanted to explore in general, or does it have a particular relation to the texts that informed that series?

AG: The idea for the Bodies series stemmed from the Portal for the sense of touch, in which I first used symmetry to represent the body, as well as a palette that reflected bodily colors (blood, pus, bile, and so on). For the current Bodies series the translation was from working on paper with acrylic paint to oil on linen and canvas. The material transition completely changed the way I work—from being drawing-driven, the new paintings became about the materiality of the paint, the accretion of gesture. Oil painting, in its physicality and the strength of the color of pigment,

better shows the tension of the subject matter: of bodies as sites of spiritual and intellectual lives, on the one hand (note the symmetry of the cliché), and physical interface with the world (with concerns about beauty, composition, and form), on the other.

GW: You also work in sculpture and video. What makes a particular text seem ripe to be translated into one medium rather than another? How do you negotiate working across different media?

AG: Every piece of mine begins with a text and in response becomes a drawing (two-dimensional) or a painting (often three-dimensional). Often a phrase or form begs further investigation as sculpture—the nimbo series became a spinning cloud of wire words, their shadow projected onto the floor. The introduction of the camera and the dimension of time allows for the documentation of the work as object and its movement (a neon sculpture, for example, oscillates in the lens of the camera because of the behavior of the gas). Video also allows me to introduce recordings of the original texts and play with how the viewer perceives language differently when heard from when it is seen and read.

GW: You've also been involved in the Watts House Project, a "collaborative artwork in the shape of a neighborhood redevelopment" based in the Watts area of Los Angeles. Can you tell me about your experiences with that project? How does it reflect preexisting concerns for you as a person and as an artist?

AG: There is a real focus in the art world today on "public practice." As a studio artist whose focus is on intimate texts, my practice is therefore more private. I use language as image to be open and egalitarian to viewers—anyone can recognize a word even if they can't read it. In working with Watts House Project, my aim was to be an artist-philanthropist and to create another model of what "public practice" could look like, how it could function. Not to work with the community as a material, but to work with a specific group of people (a specific family and other residents and stakeholders on 107th Street in Watts) as a collaborator, offering certain creative gifts (literally the "Love" symbol). As an artist I believe in donating my time and creativity to participate in civic society, to create a space of exchange with a group that wouldn't normally work with artists and architects to realize some of their visions. ∎

Born 1973 in Fairview Park, Ohio; lives and works in Los Angeles. Grant is a graduate of Swarthmore College (BA, 1995) and California College of the Arts (MFA, 2000). She has had solo exhibitions at the Museum of Contemporary Art, Los Angeles, and Honor Fraser Gallery, Los Angeles, and her work has been featured in group exhibitions at the Contemporary Museum, Baltimore; the Center for Contemporary Art, Tel Aviv; and other galleries and museums in the United States and abroad. Grant is a founding board chair and artist with the Watts House Project, an artist-driven initiative to redevelop the homes across the street from the historic Watts Towers in Los Angeles.

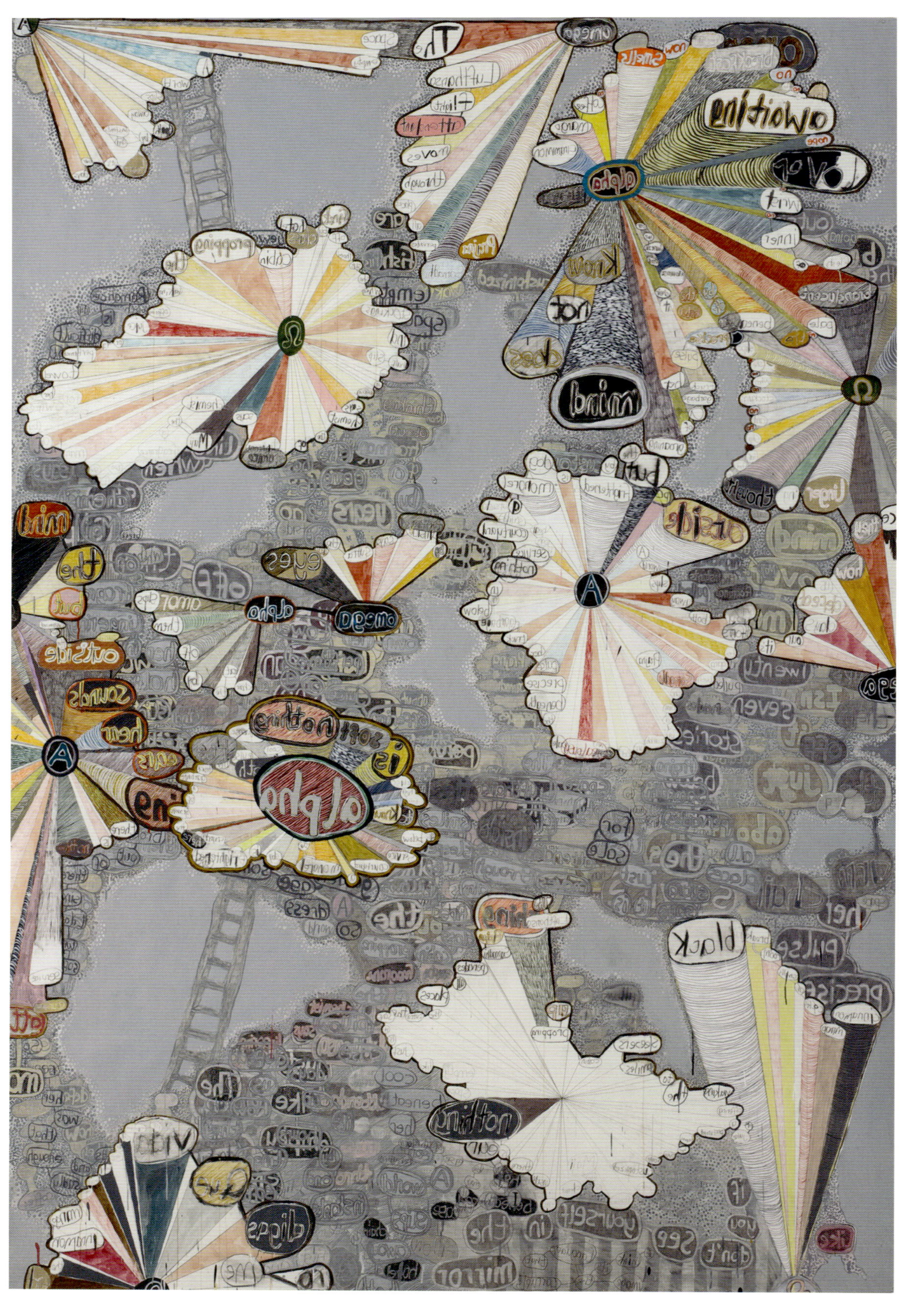

First Portal (mind) (after Michael Joyce's "Six Portals," 2007),
2008 — cat. no. 57

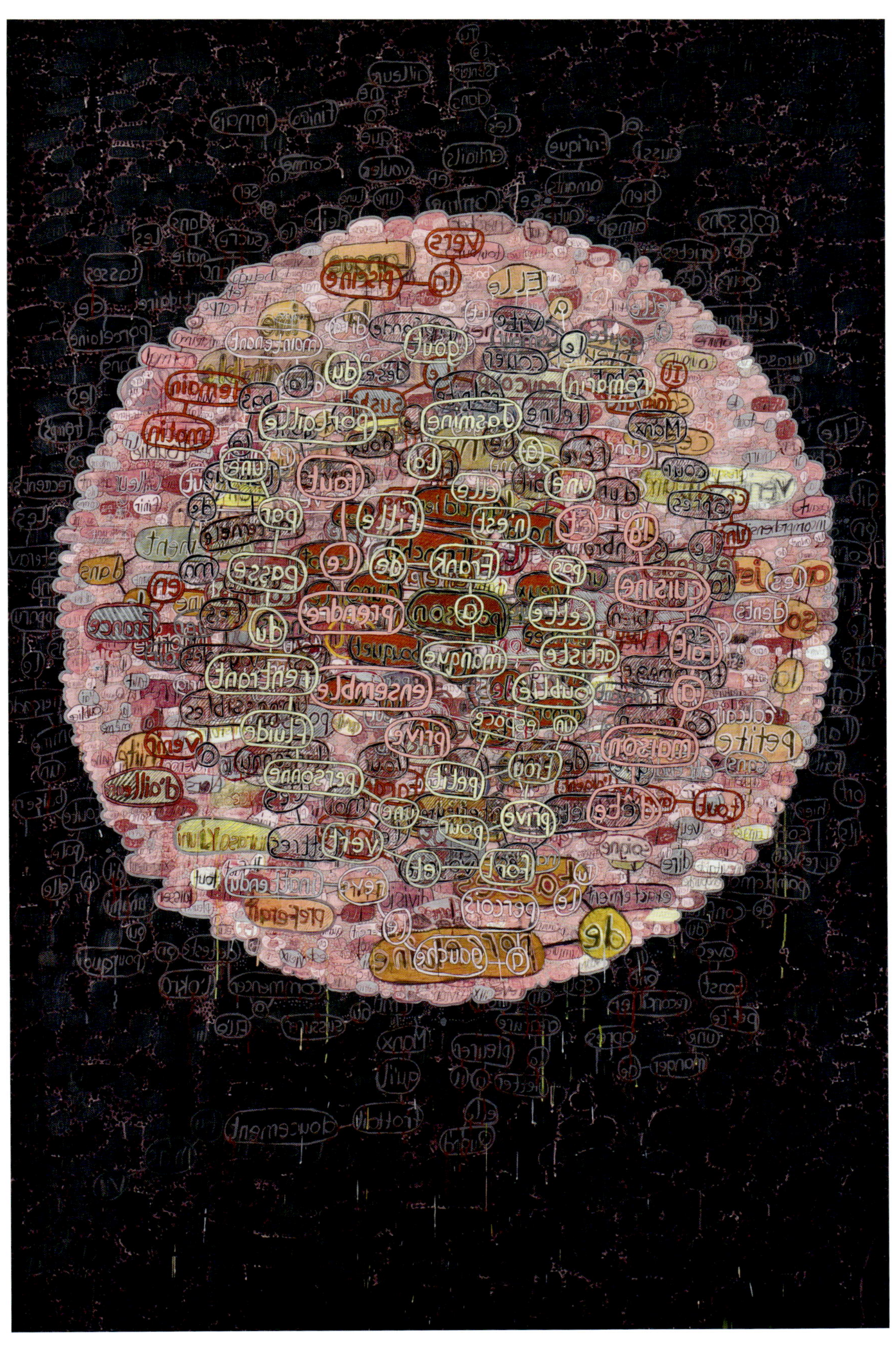

Fourth Portal (tongue) (after Michael Joyce's "Six Portals," 2007), **2008** — cat. no. 59

Sherin Guirguis

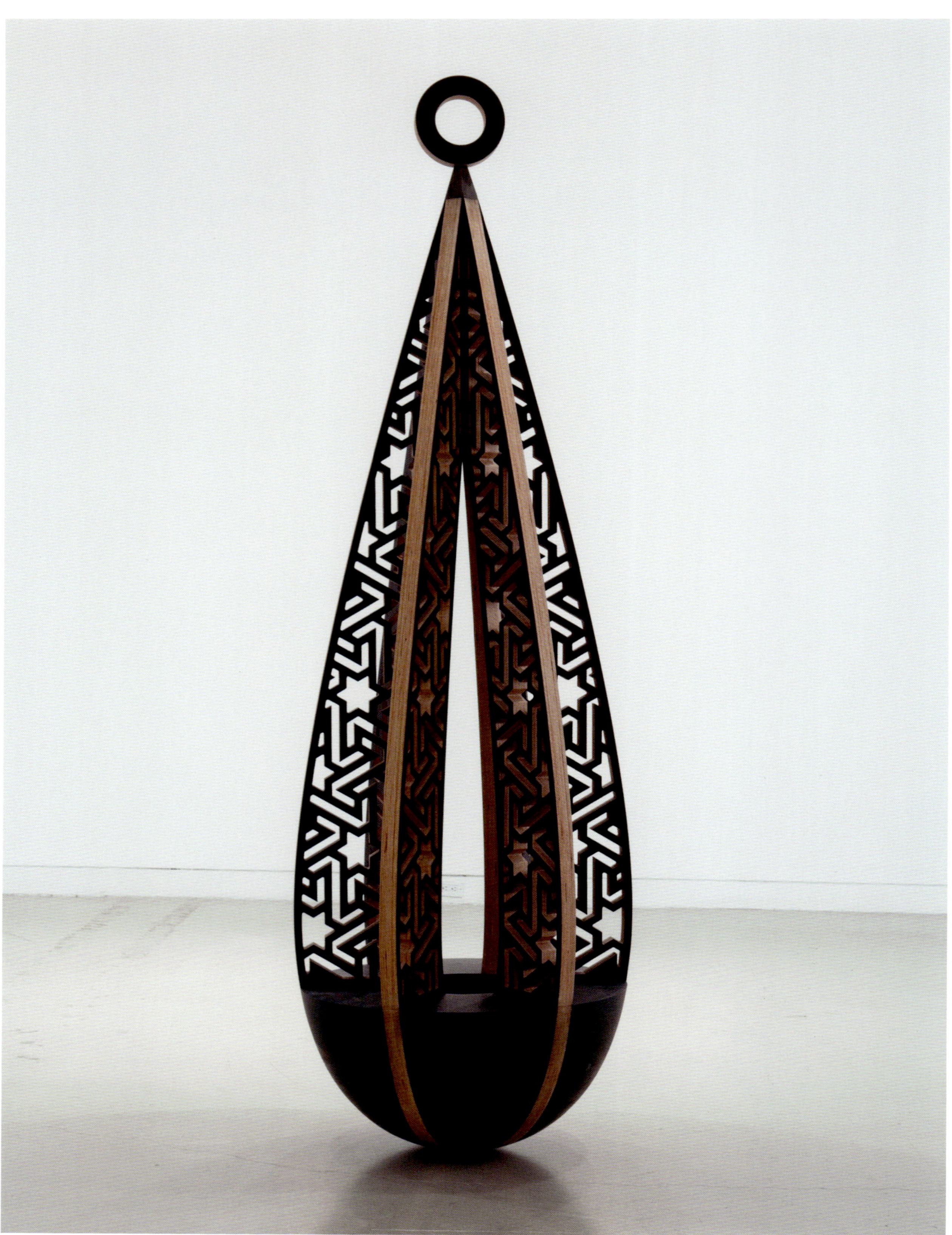

Bein El-Qasrein, **2010** — cat. no. 60

Interview with Sarah Bancroft

SB: I thought it was important to include examples of both your painting on paper and your sculpture in the biennial. Tell me about the new work that will be on view.

SG: My work is a hybrid of various contradictory elements, both formal and social. I was raised in Cairo and have lived for over twenty years in Los Angeles. My work engages both formal and social concerns by juxtaposing the reductive Western language of minimalist aesthetics with that of Eastern ornamentation. It investigates the frictions between the contemporary and the traditional, the reductive and the ornamental, and the public and the private. For the biennial I'll be including a large-scale triptych painting on paper and a kinetic sculpture.

The painting, *Untitled (Dome)* (2010), is a blue-green dome-like shape created by moving ink and watercolor rapidly across the surface of the paper. The form is then superimposed with explosive cloud silhouettes that have been hand-cut into ornamental Arabic designs. The edges of the cloud are then gold-leafed.

Originally modeled on a pair of Bedouin earrings, the sculpture, *Bein El-Qasrein* (2010), is fabricated out of walnut and plywood that has been carved with Arabic *mashrabeya* patterns. The piece reenvisions the ornamental and decorative origins of the earring through the formal lens of minimalism. The earring's kinetic, swaying movement works on several different levels. It can reference the physical narrative of a woman's body as she walks down the public street, asking the question "What does it mean for a woman to occupy this space art historically and socially?" In this sense, the swing of the earring repositions the display of the feminine only so far as it relates to the social ordering of desire. At the same time, the instability and unpredictable nature of the movement can be seen as a reflection of the sociopolitical relationship between East and West. Based on how the viewers interact with the piece, it could rock gently and rhythmically or violently and erratically. *Bein El-Qasrein* is the second in a series of three sculptures, the first of which was exhibited at LA><ART earlier this year. The third has not yet been fabricated. They are each titled after a book from Egyptian writer and Nobel laureate in literature Naguib Mafouz's Cairo Trilogy.

SB: English-speaking audiences will recognize the titles of the novels in this well-known trilogy as *Palace Walk*, *Palace of Desire*, and *Sugar Street*, all streets in Cairo where the author grew up. Your work, too, formally and conceptually relates to Egypt, your birthplace, even as you've mentioned that Egyptian identity is difficult or impossible to define or is defined by "diaspora."

SG: It does so through the hybridization of East and West. My work has always been grounded in Western minimalism. However, I returned to Egypt after a ten-year absence and realized that my relationship to the place and the culture had shifted dramatically. All of a sudden I felt like a stranger in my own country. I found myself in the position of the "other" both as an Arab in America and now as an American in the Arab world. This led to me thinking about the notion of tracing one's identity within a diaspora.

SB: You've often indicated that the paintings operate on three levels: through the painting component, the architectural screen motifs, and the foil or bomb imagery. Can you comment on this? (I'm thinking about your comments that within the works on paper, the painting is the public component, the screen is the private sphere, and the bomb is the third [catastrophic?] element.)

SG: Yes, the paintings are composed of three main elements, a *mashrabeya* pattern (wood screens that were originally used in harems as a type of window and then eventually made their way into homes all over Egypt and the Middle East), the explosive clouds, and paint. I find the *mashrabeya* screens to be inherently contradictory objects as they represent both fear and desire. They are built to hide and protect the private lives and property that exist behind them, yet they are formally seductive, and architecturally they draw the eye. They exist in the space between the private and the public. The cloud forms, which exist in the pubic realm, are based on images of explosive and catastrophic forces (bombs, storm clouds, fire, smoke, etc.). They elicit fear of the catastrophic and a desire to control one's environment through coercion. Finally, the paint articulates the intermediary moment when all these elements collide. It also references the private, solitary practices often associated with women's work.

SB: The works themselves espouse or encapsulate this idea of fear and desire at once. The work is formally arresting, yet it is not abstract; it is very grounded in current events, in place, in personal and global concerns of history and politics.

SG: Yes, all of those things factor into the work; they are the issues I'm interested in. My choice of materials, scale, imagery, and symbols is made to reinforce the conceptual ideas and literary interests that underlie the work. ■

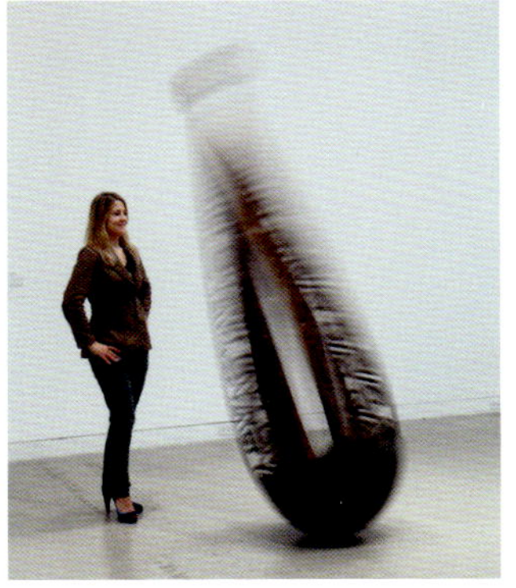

Born 1974 in Luxor, Egypt; lives and works in Los Angeles. Guirguis is a graduate of the University of California, Santa Barbara (BA, 1997), and the University of Nevada, Las Vegas (MFA, 2001). She has had solo projects at LA><ART, Los Angeles, and Patricia Faure Gallery, Santa Monica. Selected group shows include *Quadruple Consciousness*, Vox Populi, Philadelphia; *Under the Knife*, Armory Center for the Arts, Pasadena; *Quickening*, the Museum of Contemporary Art, Tucson; *The Dreams Stuff Is Made Of*, Art Frankfurt, Germany; and *Las Vegas Diaspora: The Emergence of Contemporary Art from the Neon Homeland*, Las Vegas Art Museum and Laguna Beach Art Museum. Guirguis has also participated in a series of public programs in conjunction with the 11th Cairo Biennale.

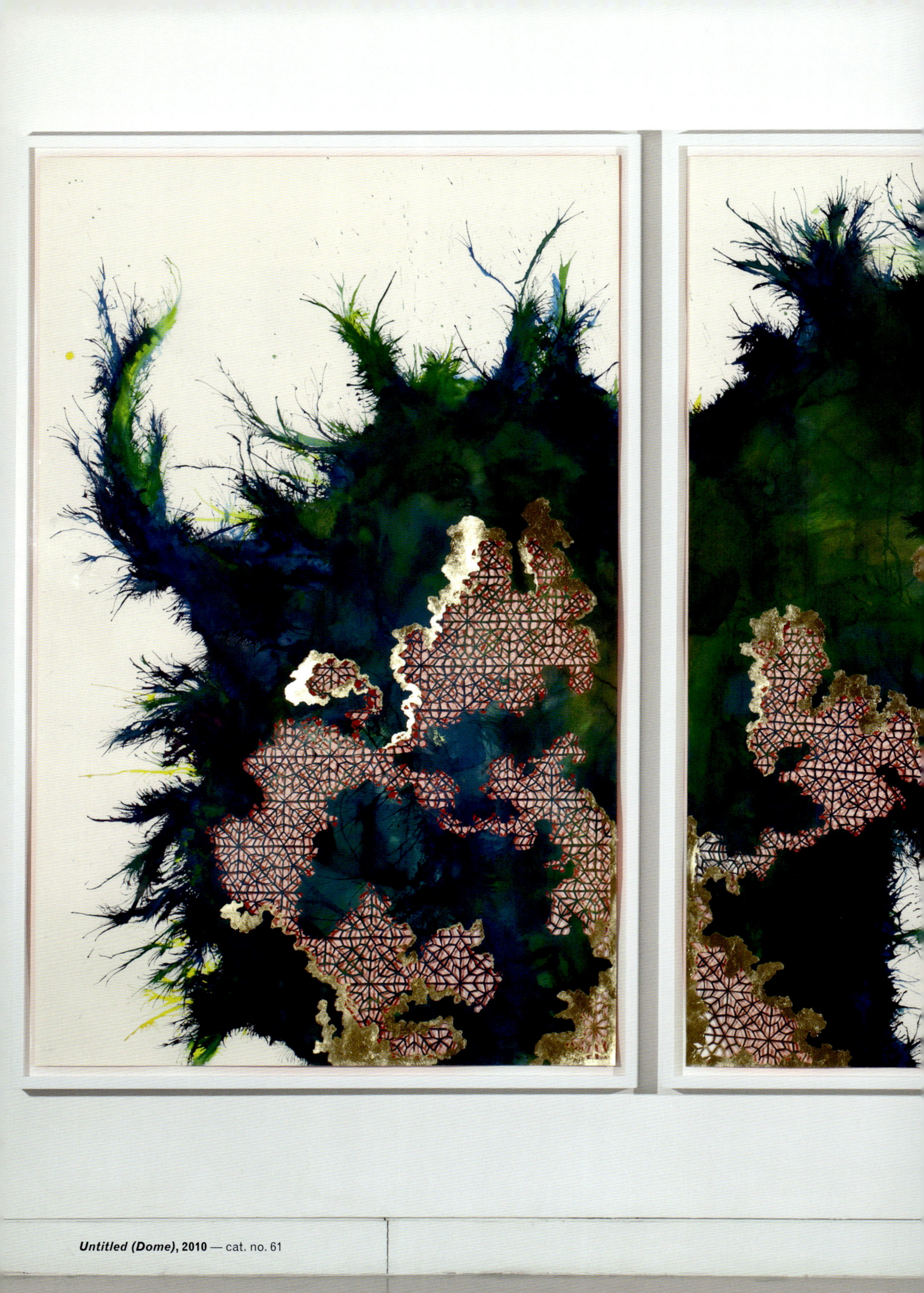

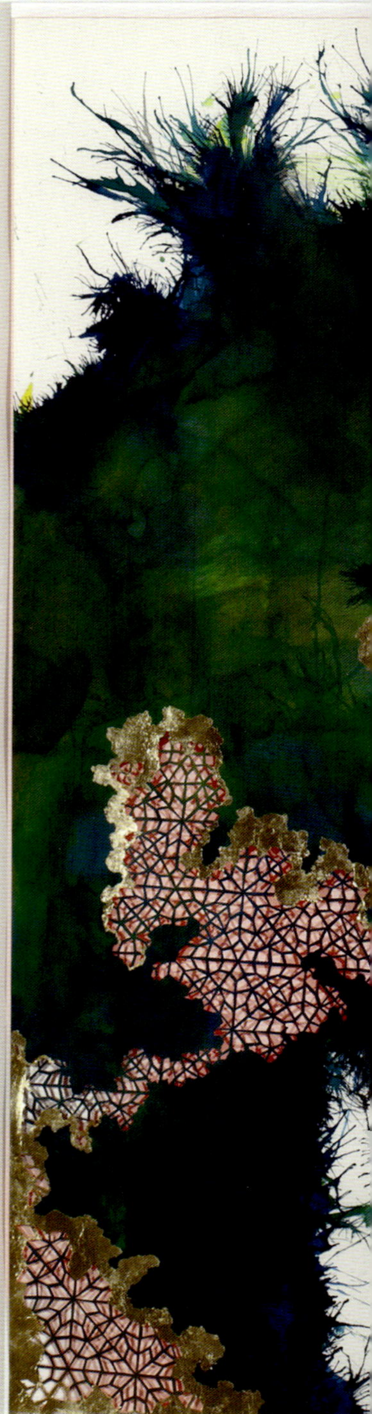

Untitled (Dome), **2010** — cat. no. 61

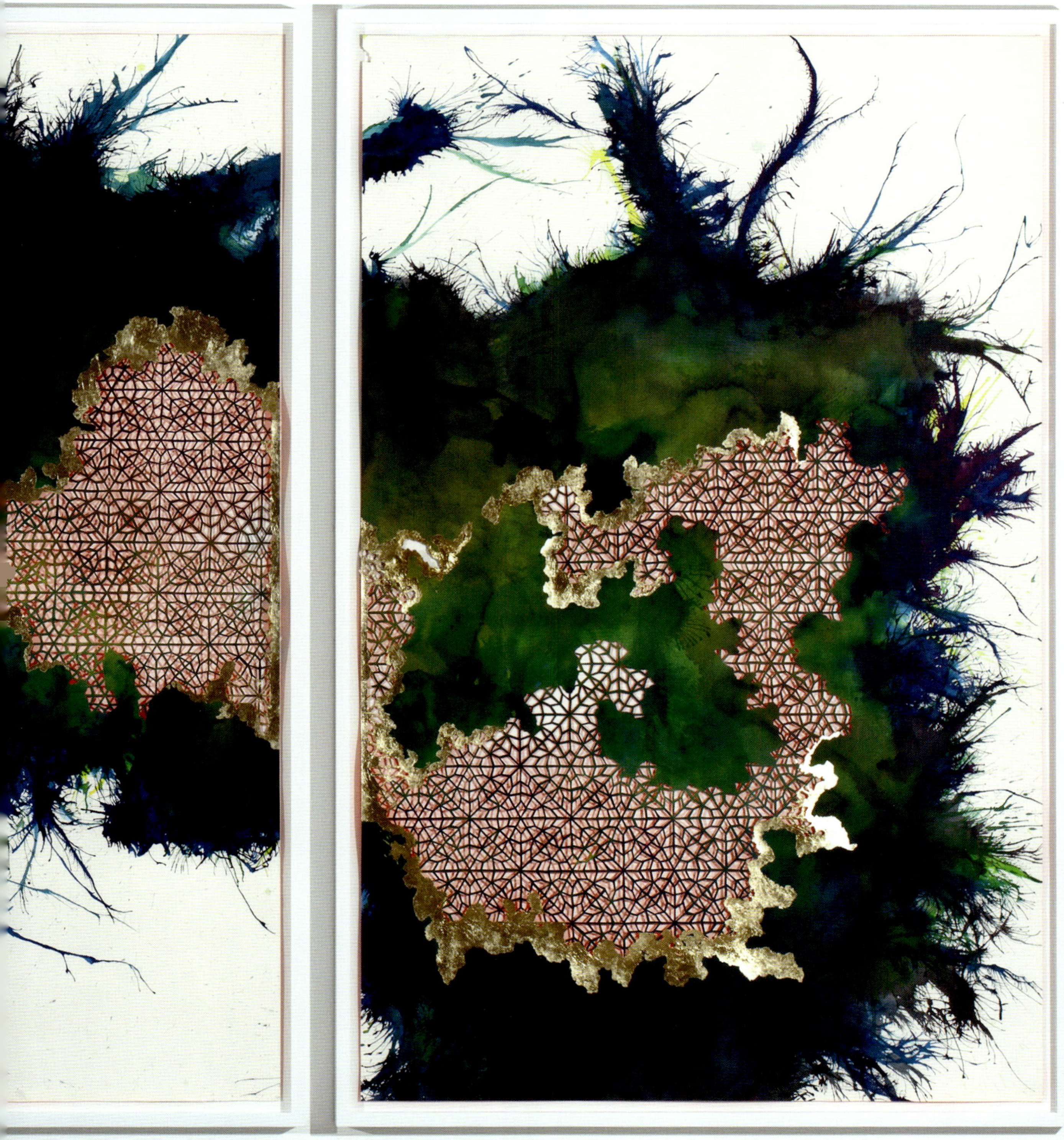

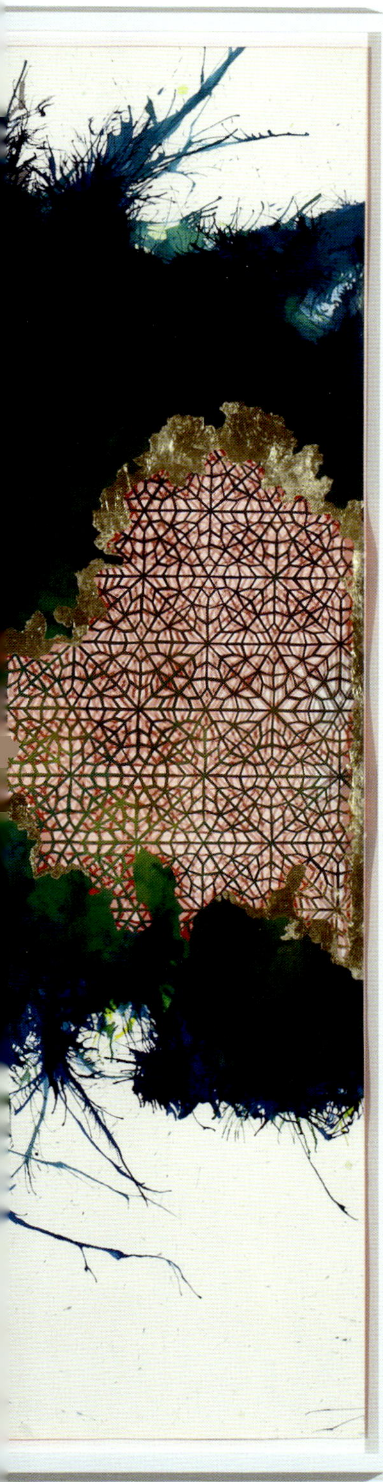

Drew Heitzler

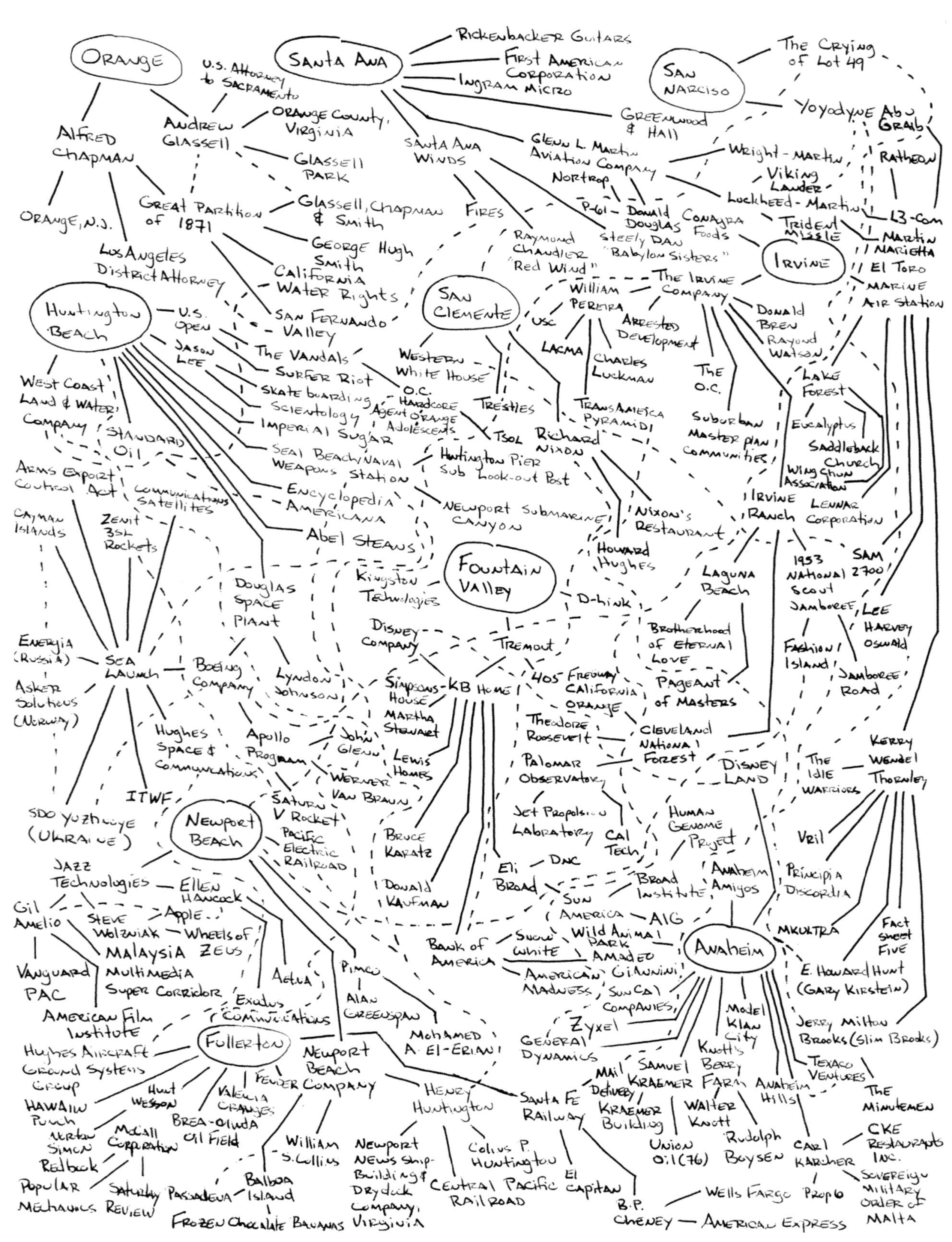

OCMA Stack, 2010 (detail) — cat. no. 62

CF: Much of your recent work presents alternative histories of Los Angeles or, one can say, the city's mythic tropes. What is it about creating alternative histories for or of Los Angeles that interests you?

DH: The narrative of history is essential to the development of ideas like truth or morality. More accurately, it is from history that we as a society develop a common sense. And yet that narrative of history is a narrative. It's written by the victors and so forth. Furthermore, projection into the past (history) dissolves as quickly as projection into the future. Both are stories. Both are guided by the teller. So in both cases validity becomes an issue of power, of who is doing the telling. I don't present my version of the story as anything but my version, and a close viewing of the images presented will reveal gaps in my narrative, even absurd ideas, that sit next to more grounded assertions. There is no truth here, or even much common sense. But it looks good, and that is usually enough.

CF: For your piece for the biennial, *There Is Always Money in the Banana Stand*, you line the walls of the gallery space with framed images that relate to Orange County. Would you say that this work presents an alternative history, and if so, what alternative history is it presenting?

DH: Again, it isn't really about creating an alternative history, but about presenting a group of images that become intertwined through their relationships, legitimate and otherwise, to one another and to the history of Orange County. Subdivision of land and housing development are central motifs, as they are central to the history of this place. With that in mind, KB Homes, the nation's leading home builder, is used as a starting point from which things quickly spin out to include the television show *Arrested Development*, Disney's three little pigs, Martha Stewart, Countrywide Home Loans, Mischa Barton, Sambo's restaurant, the California Wing Chun Association, Fashion Island, John Glenn, Nixon, the Wild Animal Park, the Huntington Beach surfer riot, and the Norton P-61 aircraft, to name just a few.

CF: You mentioned that the images in this series, like most images you use, are appropriated from the Internet. You then frame them, giving the images an art value, when in fact one can understand the value of your work as being rooted in the concept of the work, not in the object itself. Similarly, Kaufman and Broad (KB) manufactured and sold affordable housing in suburban America, but its bigger contribution was selling a concept, one that perpetuated the ideas of the "American dream": anyone can afford to own a home. I'm wondering if you can talk about perceived value of objects in relation to this body of work?

DH: All value is perceived. No one has cornered the perception market yet, but plenty have tried and continue to try. In regard to perceived value, as with most everything else, history is one of our most powerful framing devices, and as I stated above, history is malleable. It's flimsy stuff. If we can't even rely on history to give us an idea of truth, then what good are dreams, American or otherwise? All the ideas out there that people rely upon to make decisions, real decisions about food and shelter, are based on trust in invisible forces. The hand of god. The market. Metaphysics. Magic. Why not trust art? It's just as reliable as anything else.

CF: Right! And the art market is just as reliable as the housing market . . . which brings me to my next question. There's a thread running though this body of work that seemingly connects the current economic crisis with the real estate and art markets, especially in light of the unanimous approval by the Community Redevelopment Agency for the Broad Art Collection, slated for downtown Los Angeles. What are your thoughts on this interconnection, and how do you see it being played out in *There's Always Money in the Banana Stand*?

DH: Well, everything is connected. And while failing markets and downtown development are on everyone's minds, this work has more to do with a place, and how that place is being defined, as opposed to a specific economic moment. I took the title *There's Always Money in the Banana Stand* from a particularly funny episode of *Arrested Development*. This show, the story of a dysfunctional family and their equally dysfunctional home-building company, is a perfect example of how, in the popular imagination, Orange County is synonymous with the housing bubble and all the fraud that those two words imply. So the subdivision of land and the development of housing are the place to start when presenting a historical narrative of this place through images, or a narrative image of the place through history, or an imaginary history of the place through narrative, or all three.

CF: Art is often taken so seriously that humor is lost on the viewer. Can you talk about the humor in your work?

DH: Woody Allen once said that he made funny movies because he was scared of death. Humor is how we talk about the uncomfortable stuff, and it offers unique opportunities when done correctly. The jester calls the king a tyrant and keeps his head. Jack pisses in Peggy's fireplace, and everyone laughs. ■

Born 1972 in Charleston, South Carolina; lives and works in Los Angeles. Heitzler is a graduate of Fordham University (BA, 1993) and Hunter College (MFA, 2000). His films and projects have been screened and exhibited internationally at the Swiss Institute, the Sculpture Center, Anthology Film Archives, and P.S.1 Contemporary Art Center in New York; Blum and Poe, Redling Fine Art, China Art Objects, TRUDI, and LA><ART in Los Angeles; Zacheta National Gallery of Art, Warsaw; Kunstmuseum St. Gallen, Saint Gall, Switzerland; and Magasin Centre National d'Art Contemporain, Grenoble, France. Heitzler's collaborative film with Amy Granat, *T.S.O.Y.W.*, was included in the 2008 Whitney Biennial.

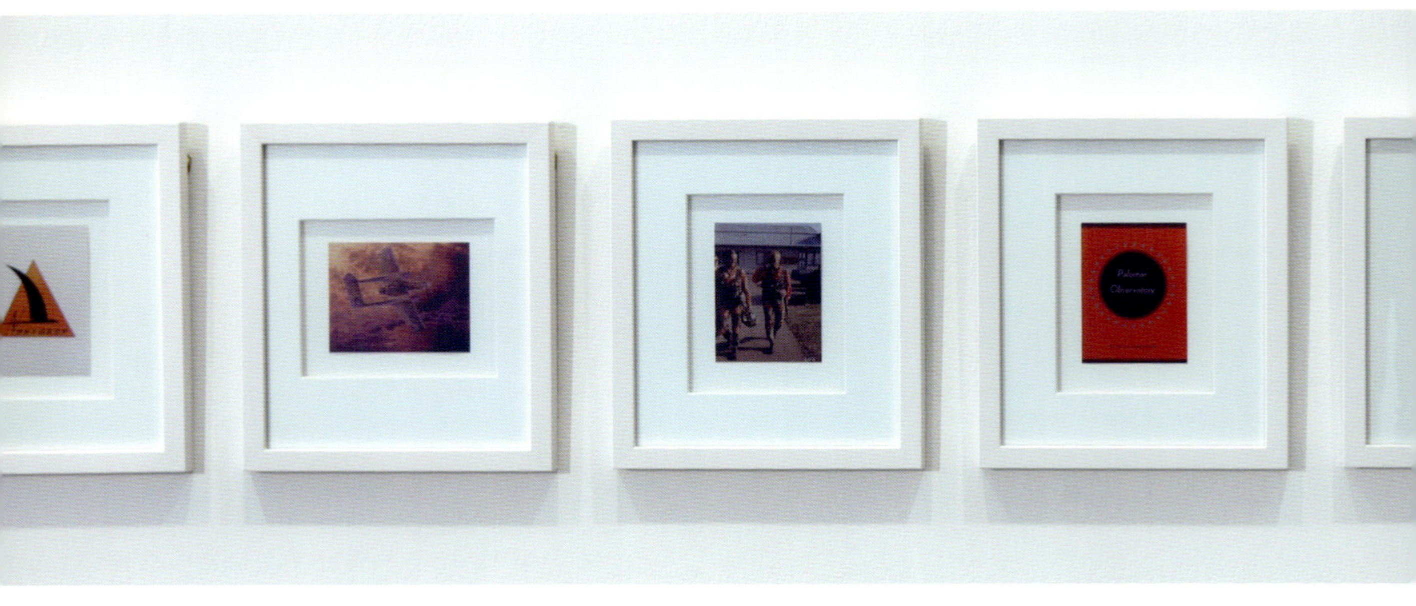

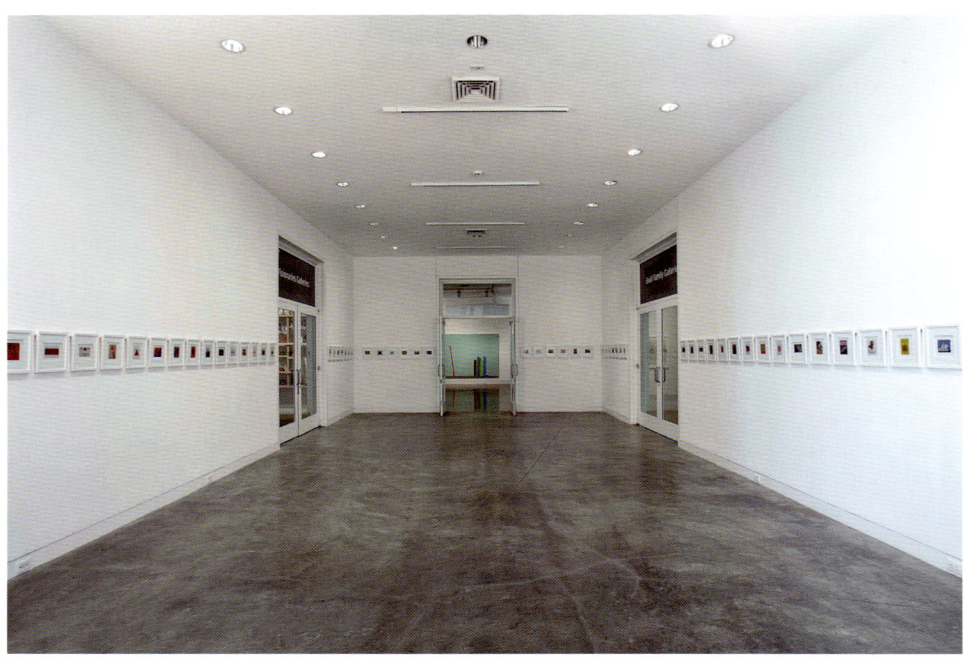

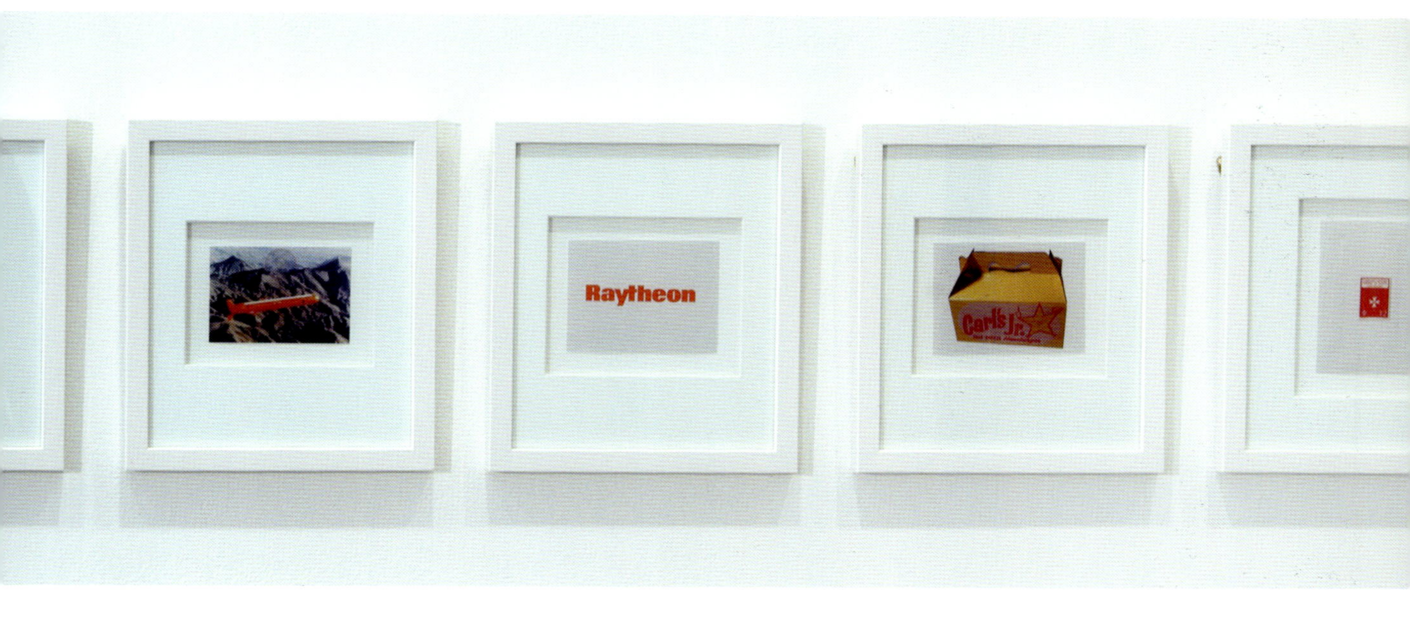

Above and left
***There's Always Money in the Banana Stand**, 2010* — cat. no. 63
Detail and installation view

Violet Hopkins

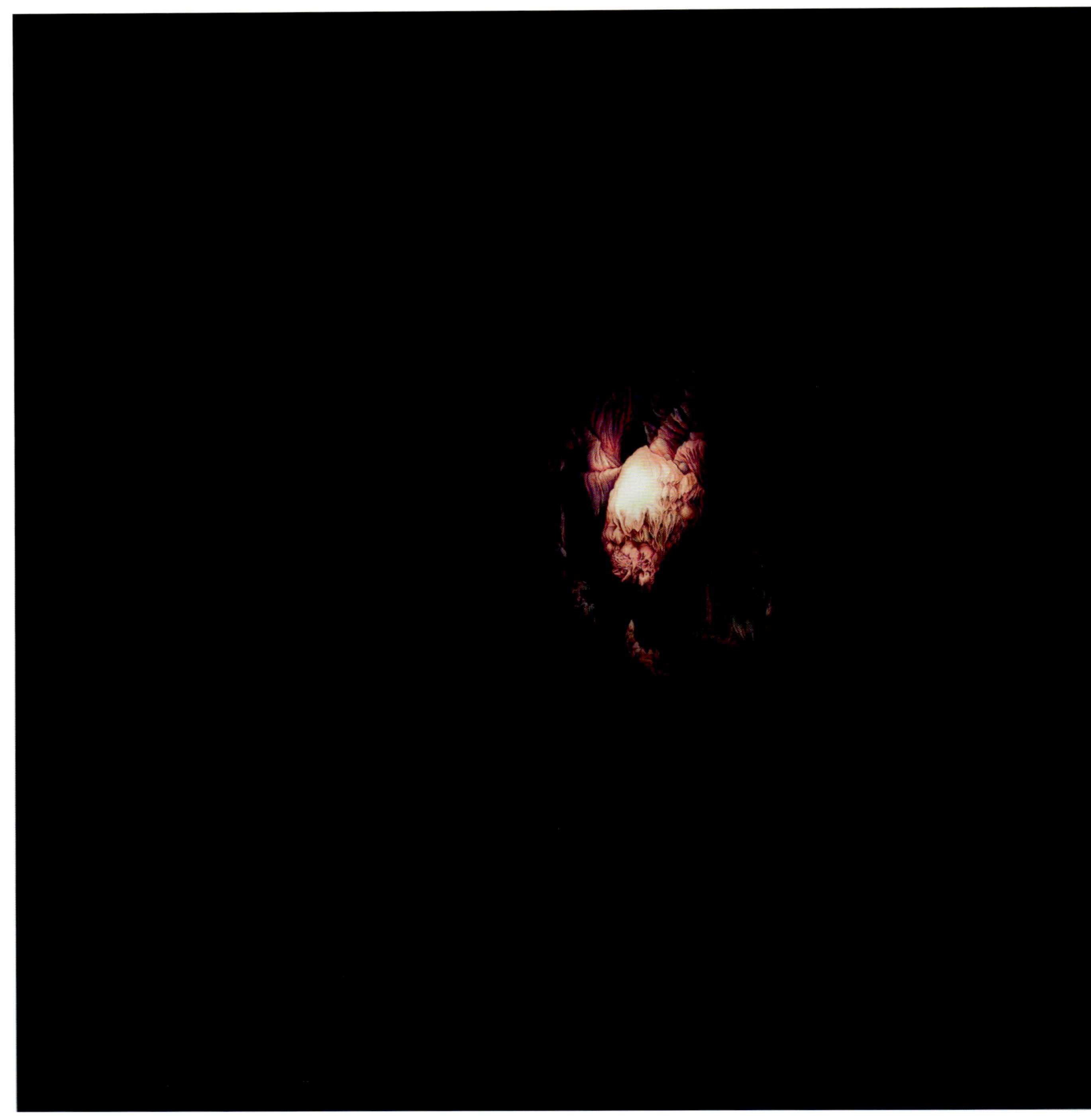

Black Narcissus, **2010** — cat. no. 65

Interview with Anna Brouwer

AB: Your works often appear to reference scientific studies of the natural world, and at the same time they have elements of fantasy that seemingly contradict your methodical approach. How have these two threads developed in your practice?

VH: I grew up watching David Attenborough. Sparse deserts, jungle undergrowth, deep-sea dwellers: I love all that wonder of the natural world stuff. Nature—its complexity, exquisite design, strangeness—is a constant inspiration to me, but so is the photographic representation of the world. My pieces start with photographic references—some my own photos but also vintage postcards, science textbooks, old *National Geographic* magazines, for example. I am loyal to most information in the photographs, such as details, angles, cropping, etc. The color, however, is where I take liberties and where the images depart from the naturalistic. I am fascinated by the variation in the color printing techniques found in these references. The images read very differently from what we see directly with our own eyes. Each era, and its printing method, has its unique tone— sweaty seventies saturation reads so completely differently from the velvety cabro method of the thirties and forties, for example. I like to play with the cultural and emotional triggers set off by these color shifts. In the caves and volcano drawings, I use supersaturated and netherworldly hues that remove them from their original locations. In other work I use more muted tones; in the Golden Record images I mimicked the magenta cast of the faded Kodachrome slides that I used as the source for the project.

AB: You often mix your pigments directly on the paper, which makes your process apparent. How is this important to your work?

VH: When I mix directly on the paper, I make the color its own entity in the composition. The abstract ink marks are like a chromatic key, a direct index of the representational components. They are building blocks of the representational area of the paintings, but I think of them as equally important.

AB: You've mentioned that you look for ways to draw the viewer in to the image. Can you elaborate on your interest in affecting viewer experience?

VH: I approach my work as an invitation to the viewer. I'd like viewers to be able to relate to the work, even mentally enter it, make it their own. I like thinking of the volcanoes and caves as screens for projection. I play with scale too, thinking about how the body relates to the work. With the volcanoes, they are never more than a few inches big. I think of them as a beckoning finger that asks for a kind of intimacy. The caves, in constrast, are large enough to envelop the body. In those drawings, although the entire paper is filled with strokes of pigment, I render only a pocket of light that reveals a small area of the cave.

AB: Interesting, since I think many artists who make two-dimensional work are interested in eliciting responses to their imagery but don't necessarily think about how viewers can claim an image as their own.

In your series of drawings related to the Golden Record time capsules placed on the *Voyager* spacecraft launched in 1977, and in the inkblot drawings in the exhibition, in which you play with the tradition of the Rorschach test, you investigate cultural assumptions about the interpretation of imagery.

VH: Both the photographs selected to be on the Golden Record and the original set of Rorschach cards were used to define us as humans. With the Golden Record, scientists chose 116 images specifically to explain the planet, its civilizations, and its environment to aliens who might come across it. It's an impossible task, especially with so few images. There is a bizarre and faulty logic behind the selections and the scientists' anticipation of how aliens might see us. The images reveal much more about the scientists and the era in which they were chosen. For example, there is a baffling image—an aerial shot of a man measuring an upturned crocodile. What could aliens possibly conclude from that?!?

The original ten Rorschach images were developed as a psychiatric tool to evaluate patients. Again, this set of images has failed in its mission, and now the test is largely discredited. But we are all familiar with the idea of what a Rorschach is. I love it that common responses to the test varied depending on the nationality or culture of the person. The variations in reactions to color and visual imagery, shaded by cultural experiences, are an ongoing interest of mine.

AB: Your work has been described as a balance between precision and abstraction. What inspired your recent shift in the much more free-form and open-ended inkblot drawings?

VH: In much of my work, areas are realistically rendered, but within them organic shapes break down into abstraction—like the smoke within the volcanic eruptions. With the inkblots I wanted to approach image making from the other end of the spectrum. The inkblots are by their very nature not of anything but pigment. They are a product of both chance and manipulation. While I do control the opacity and layering, they are a blind dispersal of colored fluid. They are a solicitation to the human impulse to convert pattern into recognizable images—fossils, vertebrae, genitalia, faces, animals, X-rays, flowers—whatever they might be. Unlike the official test, there are no wrong answers. ∎

Born 1973 in El Paso, Texas; lives and works in Los Angeles. Hopkins is a graduate of the University of Texas at Austin (BFA, 1996) and California Institute of the Arts (2002). She has had solo exhibitions at Foxy Production, New York; David Kordansky Gallery, Los Angeles; and Balice Hertling, Paris. She has participated in group exhibitions at the Galerie Uschi Kolb, Karlsruhe, Germany; the Aspen Art Museum, Aspen, Colorado; Galería Moriarty, Madrid; the Weatherspoon Art Museum, Greensboro, North Carolina; Peres Projects, Berlin; Deitch Projects, New York; David Zwirner Gallery, New York; and Taka Ishii Gallery, Tokyo. Her work is in the collections of the Rubell Family Collection, Miami; the New Museum of Contemporary Art, New York; and the Museum of Modern Art, New York.

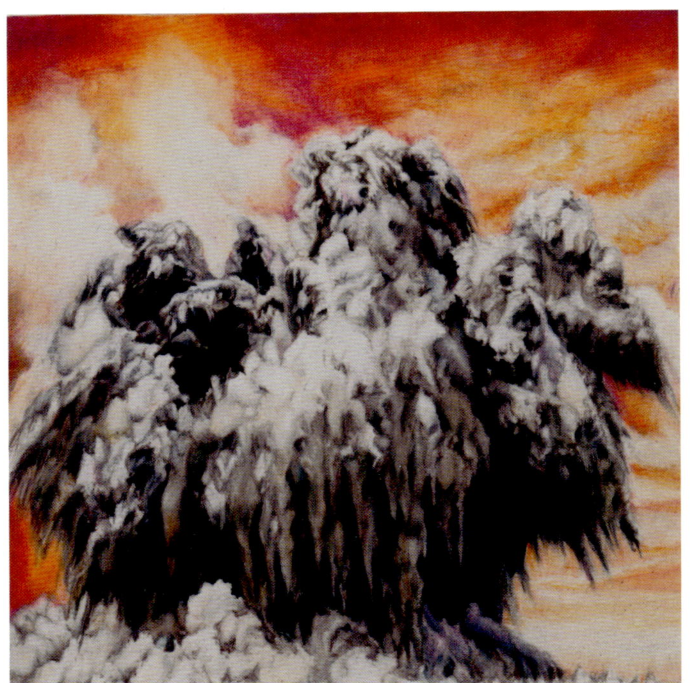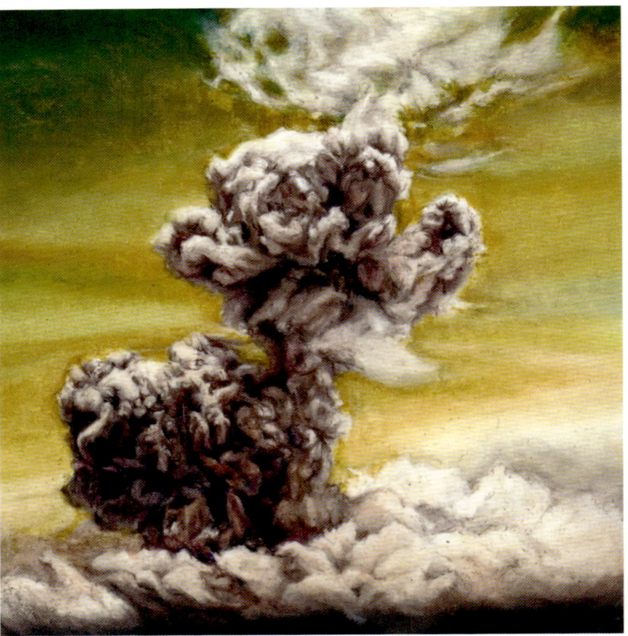

Opposite clockwise from top left
Inkblot 44, **2010** — cat. no. 66
Inkblot 93, **2010** — cat. no. 69

Inkblot 213, **2010**
Ink on paper
19 × 25 in. (48.3 × 63.5 cm)
Courtesy of the artist and Foxy Production, New York

Inkblot 52, **2010** — cat. no. 67
Inkblot 81, **2010** — cat. no. 68
Inkblot 107, **2010** — cat. no. 70

Above
Sing Swan Song, **2010** — cat. no. 72
Crown Gold, **2008** — cat. no. 64

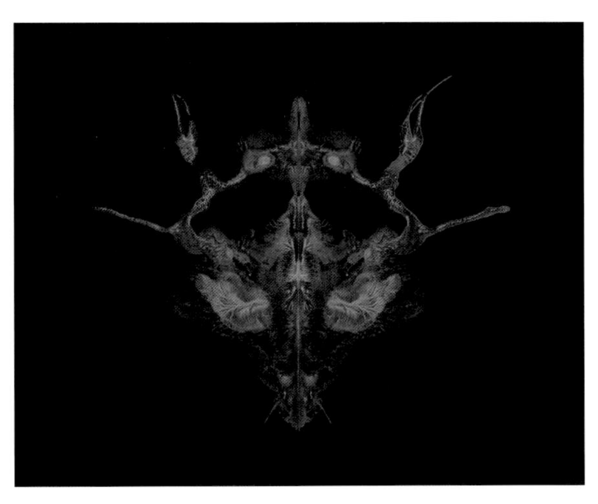
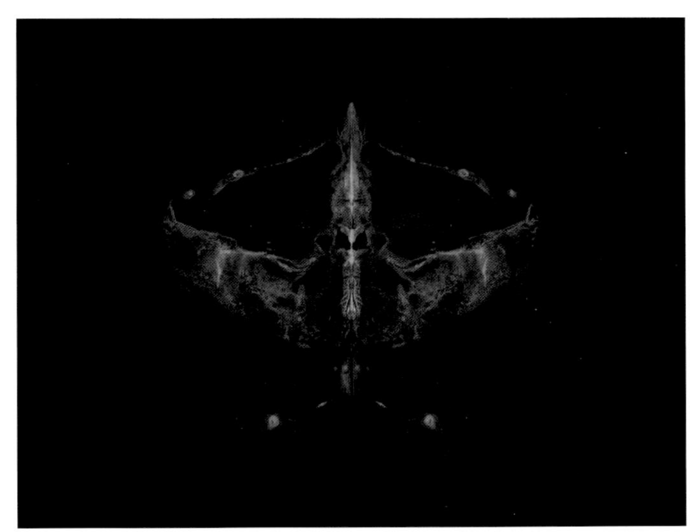
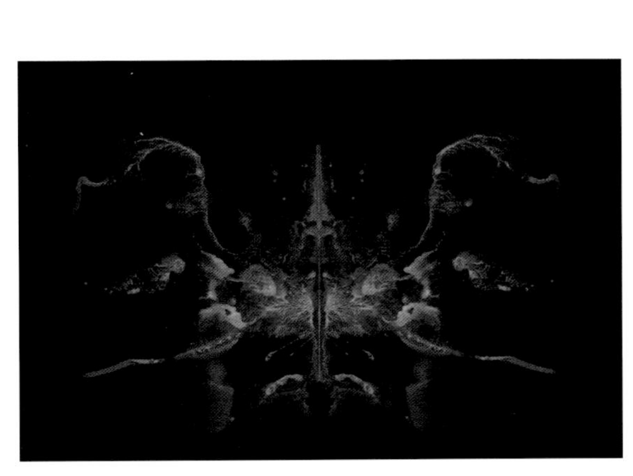
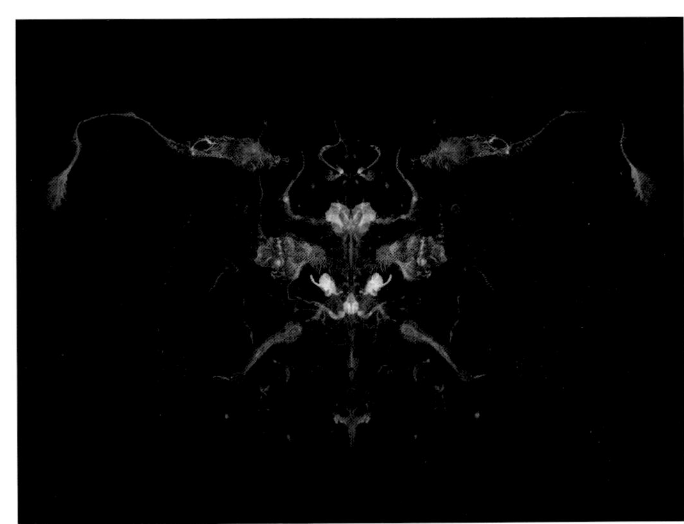
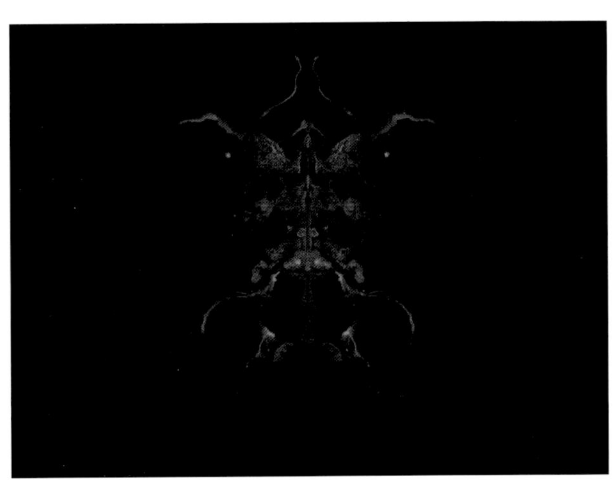
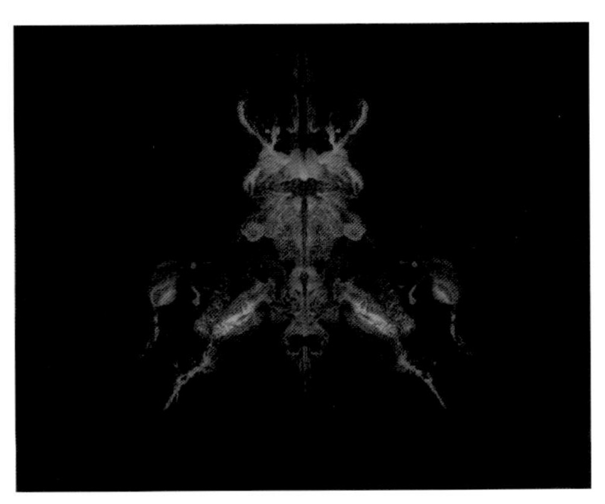

Alex Israel

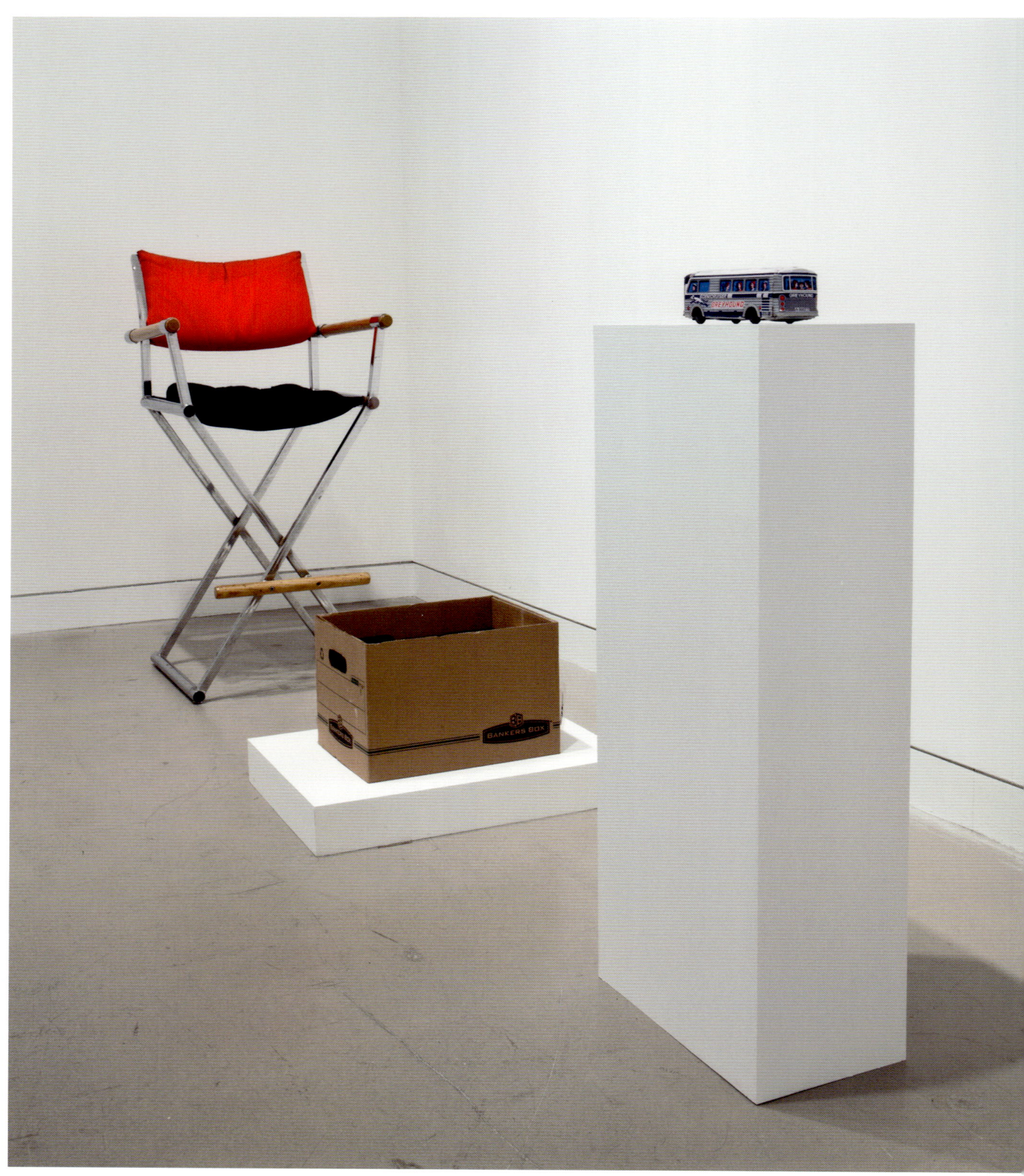

<u>Above</u>
***Property,* 2010** — cat. no. 73, installation view with
(left to right) ***Storyteller*** (cat. no. 73B), ***Sex*** (cat. no. 73C),
and ***Dreams*** (cat. no. 73D)

<u>Opposite</u>
***Property,* 2010** — cat. no. 73, installation view with
(left to right) ***Desire*** (cat. no. 73F) and ***Desire*** (cat. no. 73G)

CF: **I'd like to start by asking you to talk about the city of Los Angeles as a source for the thematic framing of your work. What aspects of L.A.'s cultural landscape influence your work?**

AI: I tend to think that L.A. is only part of the story when I think about sources for the thematic structure of my work. L.A. works for me because I'm from here and because I love living here—I love the city's unique regional culture—but also because it happens to be the place from which entertainment emanates outward on a global scale. My other preoccupation, the other main source for the thematic framing of my work, is art—and there's also a lot of art (a lot that influences on a global scale) that has been made or is being made in L.A. I think the word *framing* is key—and I'm glad you used it. I make frames, sunglass frames in fact. I have a line of sunglasses called Freeway Eyewear. Within the line there are five frame styles that are named after L.A. freeways. The brand itself is a representation of L.A.'s geography—a landscape, so to speak—and the brand's image is meant to reflect the city's history, aesthetic, and moods, which I love. The glasses themselves—and I'm wearing them all the time now—are very helpful when it comes to framing all of this.

CF: **They're iconic . . . which, in some ways, speaks to the cultural iconography and myths of Los Angeles that your work engages to such a degree that one could call it boosterism. Is this what you're trying to achieve?**

AI: Of course.

CF: **Why is it boosterism and not critique?**

AI: Well, that's easy: I'm selling sunglasses and a corresponding lifestyle.

CF: **Let's talk about your project for the biennial. Your installation incorporates objects from Hollywood prop houses, raising the question of what makes art art. Most of the objects easily take the guise of a ready-made, in a recontextualized Duchampian theater installation of sorts. This prop performance includes, interestingly, a few "artworks" that call attention to what one could refer to as their "propness," conveying the gesture of the artist's hand. What is it about the prop that makes it an ideal object of art?**

AI: A prop carton of soy milk, for example, looks banal and everyday enough. Sometimes, however, a prop can be understood only as a prop. For example, at Warner Bros. there is a Maltese Falcon that I've rented a couple of times. It's an amazing thing because it never loses its connection to the film, no matter where it ends up. This is an object that can't escape its "propness." So in an exhibition it stands out as being particularly self-conscious, whereas a carton of soy milk doesn't. The Maltese Falcon in my work may be akin to a kind of gesture or stroke of my hand, sure.

Hollywood props make ideal sculptures because they have to go back. I mean back to the places that I rent them from: Omega Cinema Props, Modern Props, Warner Bros., or Sony, etc. This is incredibly freeing. I get to take ownership of them: I title them and place them in juxtaposition with one another. I even get to take full advantage of their objectness: their volumes and surfaces, the meanings that they carry, and the magical Hollywood histories that have aged them so beautifully in some cases. When the performance ends, I don't have to store or worry about or price or conserve or deal with them.

CF: **As much as your work conflates the roles and functions of objects, it seems that you also blur the lines of what conventionally has been constituted as an artist's practice by obscuring not only roles but systems and markets as well. As an artist your work is situated in installation, video, public art, and sculpture, but you are also the CEO of Freeway Eyewear, the creator and director of the web series RoughWinds, a curator, a blogger, and an art, fashion, and cultural magazine writer-contributor. For you, what makes an artist an artist?**

AI: A beret. ∎

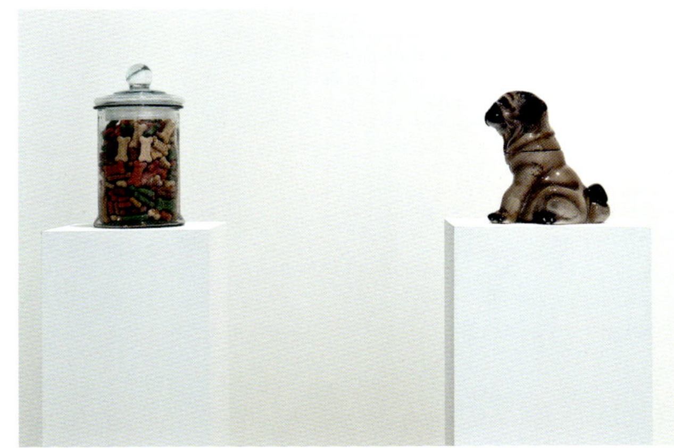

Born 1982 in Los Angeles; lives and works in Los Angeles. Israel attended Yale University (BA, 2003) and the University of Southern California (MFA, 2010). His work has been included in group exhibitions at Kunstverein Braunschweig, Brunswick, Germany, and at Participant Inc., New York. Israel has completed public artworks throughout Los Angeles, and in 2011 he will have a solo exhibition at LA><ART, Los Angeles. He has contributed to *Artforum*, *Purple Fashion Magazine*, and *ForYourArt*, and he edited *Jason Rhoades: Black Pussy Cocktail Coffee Table Book*. He is the founder and president of Freeway Eyewear, Inc. and creator of the web series RoughWinds.

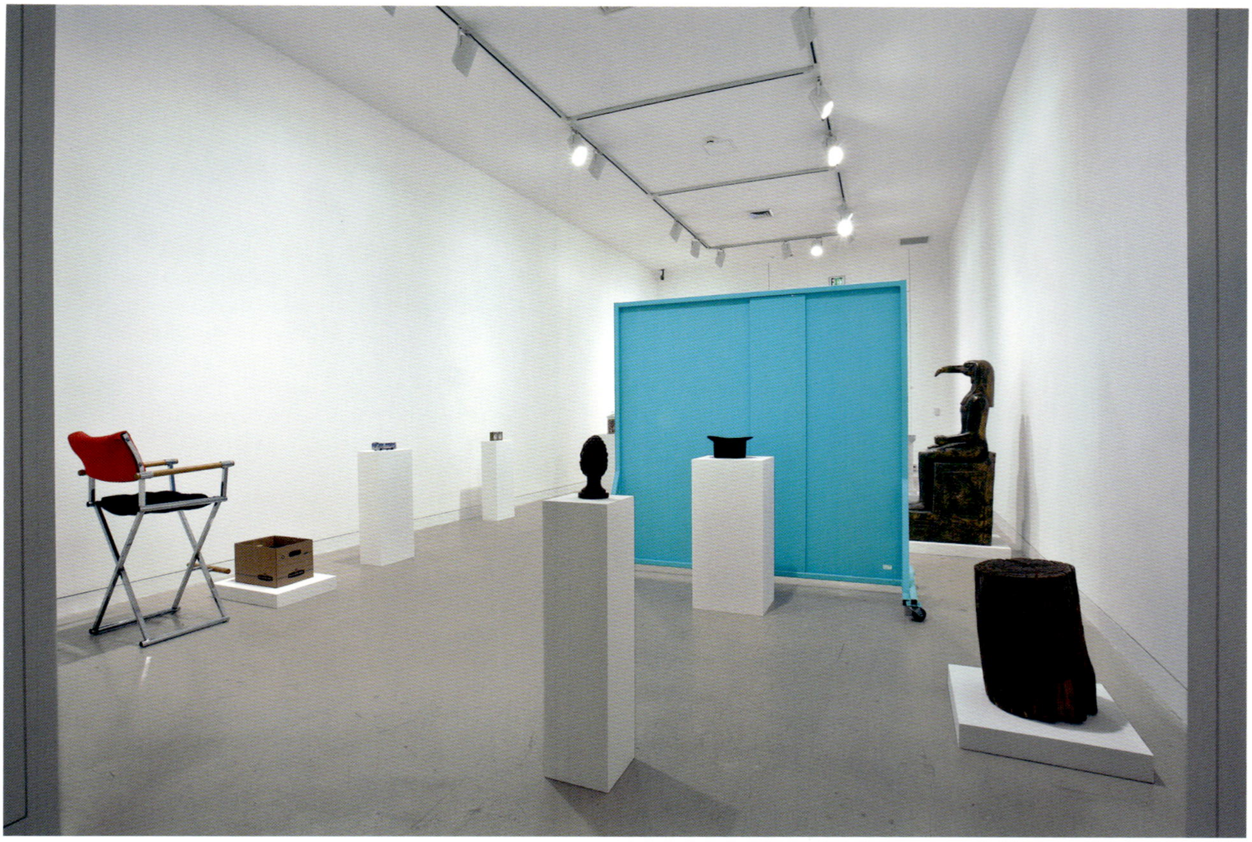

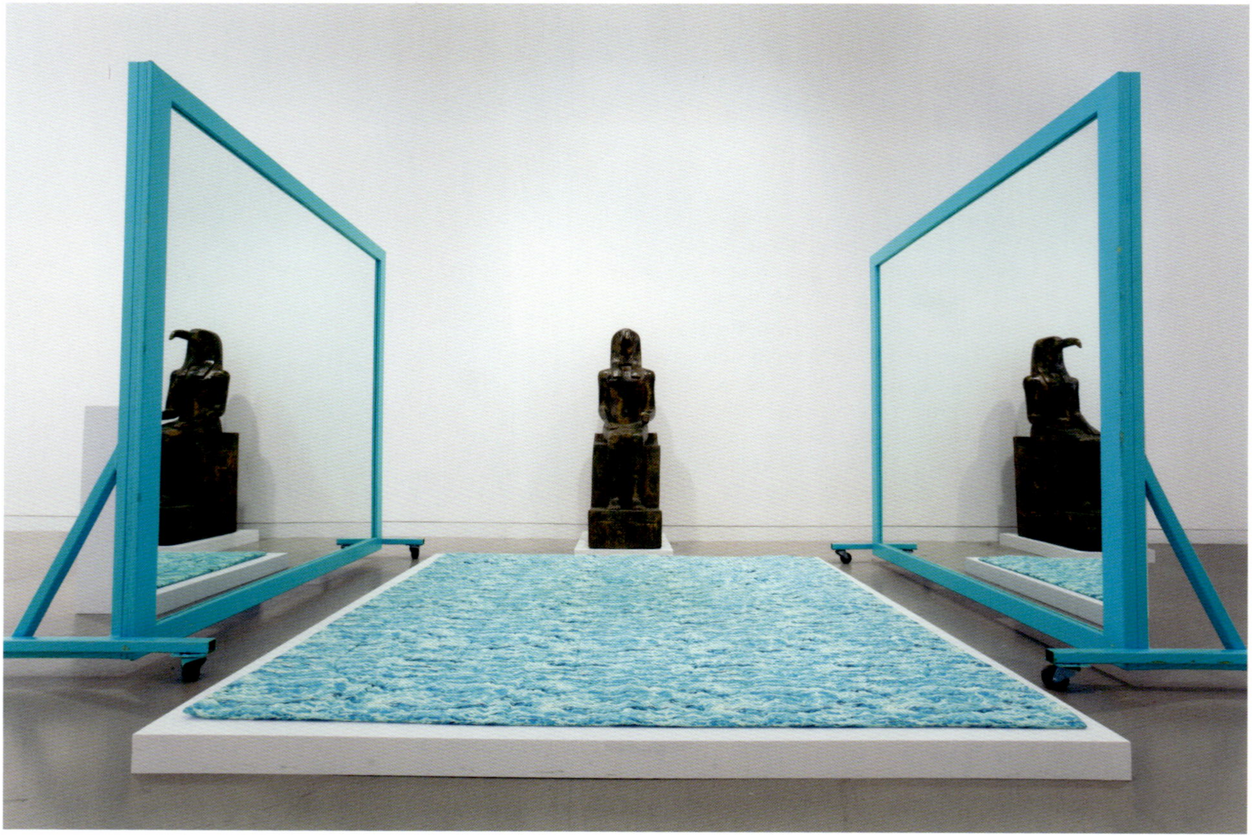

Top
Property, **2010** — cat. no. 73

Bottom
Property, **2010** — cat. no. 73, installation view with (left to right)
Infinity (cat. no. 73O), **Osiris** (cat. no. 73Q), **Pacific** (cat. no. 73P),
and **Infinity** (cat. no. 73R)

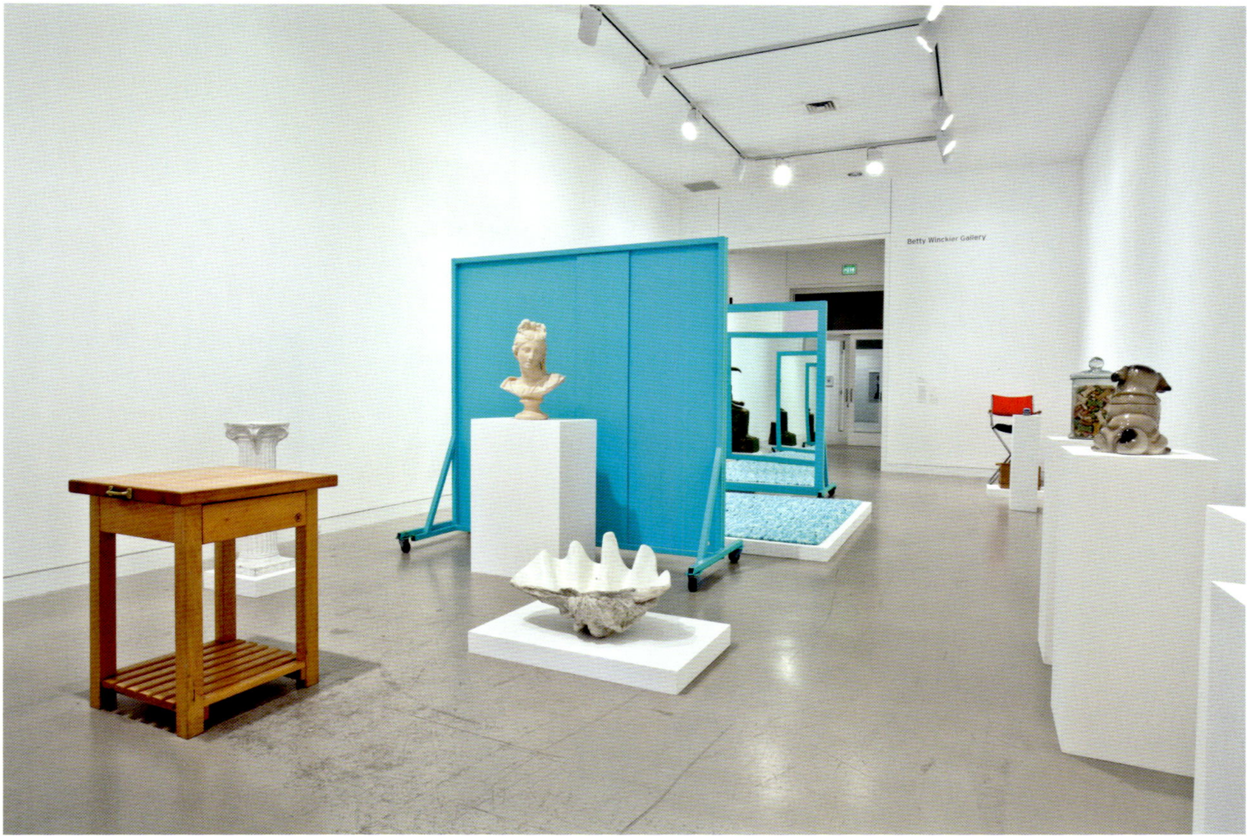

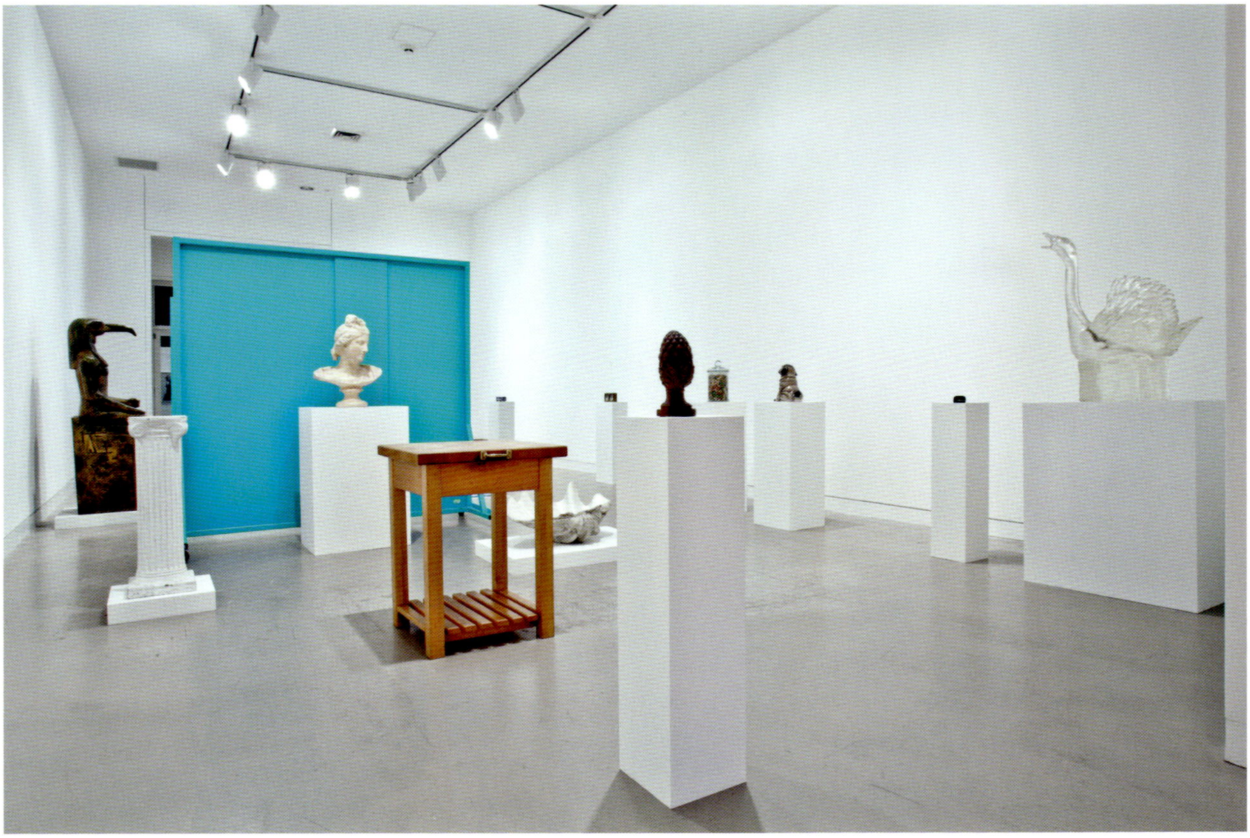

Property, **2010** — cat. no. 73

Glenna Jennings

Practice
Photography, writing, video, curating

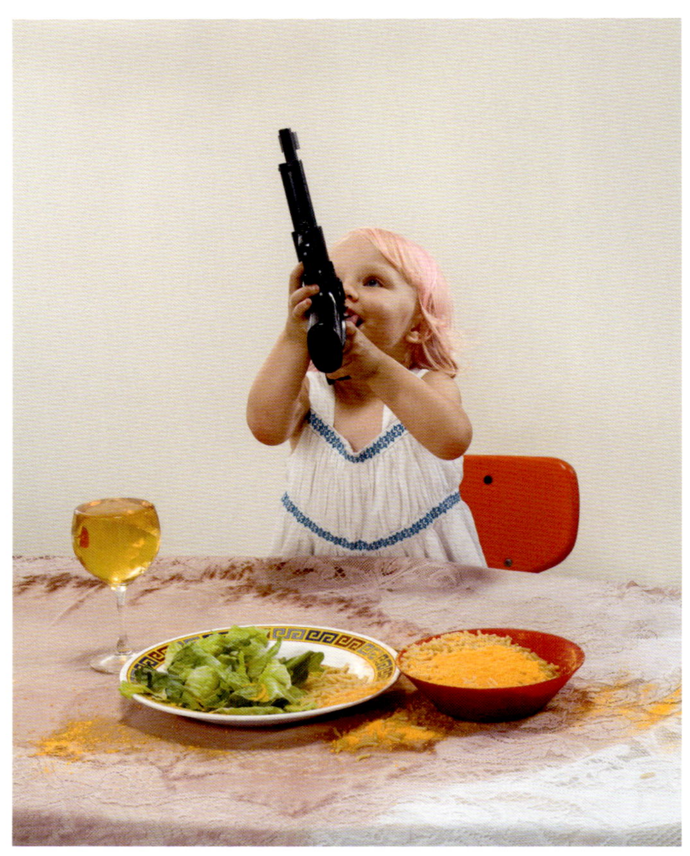

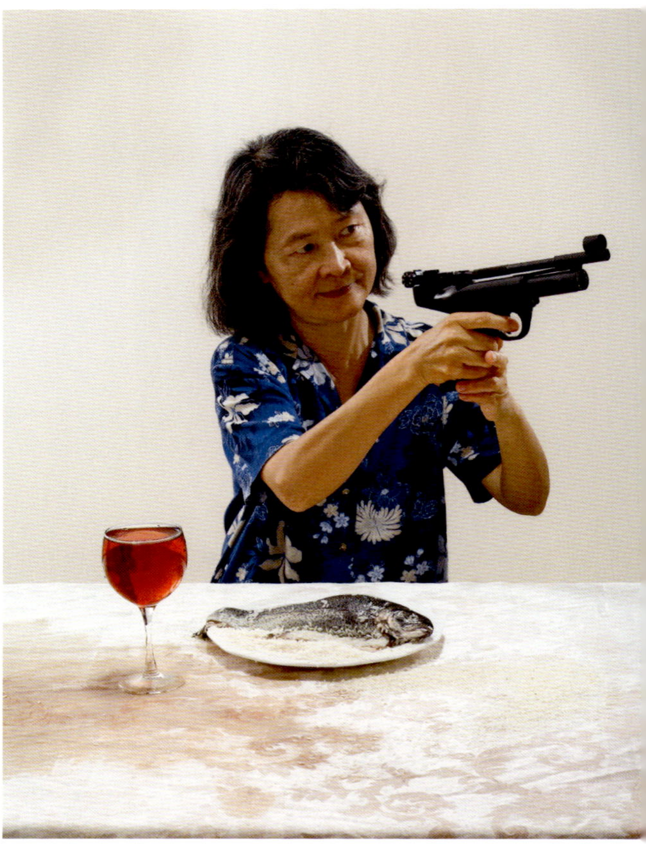

From the series Inheritance
Ellie, **2007** — cat. no. 74
Fang, **2007** — cat. no. 75

Born 1974 in Alpine, California, where she navigated a landscape of monster trucks, chaparral, and soccer moms that still informs much of her practice. She lives and works in San Diego and Los Angeles. A graduate of Pepperdine University (BA, 1995), Art Center College of Design (BFA, 2004), and the University of California, San Diego (MFA, 2010), Jennings has exhibited her work throughout the United States, Mexico, and Europe. She has served as director and head curator of the Geneva-based art collective compactspace since 2004 and is currently the curatorial adviser for San Diego's Periscope Project, a space contemporary art and architecture.

Interview with Stacie Martinez

SM: **If we look at your recent bodies of work Inheritance and Raskolnikov, there are two things that stand out: the fact that they are rooted in your personal life and your interest in global universalities. While these objectives may seem to compete, they actually work together beautifully.**

GJ: I both fear and rely on the "personal" and the "universal" for artistic inspiration and production. Inheritance came about after my father passed away and left me seventeen guns. I had no idea how to deal with these "loaded" objects either physically or ideologically. The resulting portrait work is very personal, not because I consider myself an incredibly interesting subject but because I trust direct sources. The death of a loved one is a common catalyst for artists and writers to consider the expendability of our time in this temporary space.

Raskolnikov—which takes Dostoevsky's text, drops it on its head, and infects it with cheerleading and high school lore—could be viewed as equally personal and self-indulgent. However, my main interest was playing with deconstruction in and around the territory of cultural studies and identity work. These images of thirteen different bodies wearing my high school cheerleading uniform in an array of semi-dystopic suburban spaces could be interpreted in any number of ways, and that interpretation is the task of the translator, who is myself, the subject, and the audience.

SM: **What's the tale behind Likely Stories and other sides, and how does this fit in with the rest of your practice?**

GJ: I found myself in Jacumba Hotel and Spa's Jacuzzi room in 2008, gazing at dewy paintings of kitschy waterfalls and inhaling the ubiquitous rotten-egg scent of sulfur while the Eagles played on a distant jukebox. I had forgotten my camera, so every object took on a greater life as I tried to pack it all into my memory. I come from another backcountry town about twenty miles west of Jacumba and felt it was time for an origins-based project that dealt with the multiple meanings of space and place. Humanistic geographer Yi-Fun Tuan has said, "space made thoroughly familiar becomes place." So I set about becoming as familiar as possible with Jacumba, realizing that I would be up against the whole outsider-insider binary, which I took on by eventually moving into the hotel and spa for a month in 2009.

Likely Stories and other sides takes place within the hotel and surrounding unincorporated community of Jacumba, which is at once any small American border town and an anomaly. After the native Kumeyaay first "discovered" Jacumba's mineral waters, a long series of myths and histories followed, involving cowboys versus Indians, drug dealers versus border patrol agents, illegal immigrants versus various fences—a litany of power struggle metanarratives within a very small mass of earth. The town's heyday occurred in the 1920s, when the new hotel managed to attract celebrities like Clark Gable and Louise Brooks to San Diego's backcountry. That hotel burned down in the 1980s. By that time, the construction of Interstate 8 in the 1960s had basically cut Jacumba off

from heavy commerce and tourism. Since then, it has maintained a population of about five hundred people, who either commute hundreds of miles for work, live off retirement funds, or collect welfare. The "Spa" is basically a social nexus—all gossip and myth pass through its walls and waters.

SM: **The constructed light boxes are a new element in your work. Where does the impulse to make them come from?**

GJ: These thirteen kinetic light-box sculptures are reconstituted from moving waterfall images originally manufactured in China—the kind you find plugged into the wall in Chinese restaurants or perhaps college dorms. The waterfalls were replaced with images shot in and around Jacumba, but the light effects remain. I have long been interested in how kitsch functions in contemporary culture—not as low art, but as a receptacle for each era's collective memory and escapist tendencies. Each of these sculptures started out continents away from Jacumba as one of thousands of identical mass-produced commodities destined for small markets throughout the globe. Their analog technology seemed a perfect fit for dealing with the representation of a small town whose own ego has been damaged by seeming irrelevance.

Likely Stories is a progression from inside to outside, from the body in particular to space in general. Again, I rely on universalities or, better said, larger dichotomies (public versus private, rural versus urban, absence versus presence) in order to make meaning, but in the end each project and each text relies on itself to create these systems of meaning. I start with a point of origin and end up someplace else, which is ultimately all you can ask from photography and writing. Though the myth of global universalities has often been dispensed with, the "personal" image or the idiosyncratic document still aims at the universe, serving as mirror and window.

SM: **You include text from *Likely Stories* beneath the light boxes. Can you discuss the relationship between language and photography in your work?**

GJ: Before I became an artist, I earned degrees in Spanish and English, so language and its translation have always been a part of my practice. I have also been an ESL instructor for over fifteen years, and when dealing with language in the classroom, you see the guts of a communication system and generally seek the simplest route from signifier to signified. But as an artist I am allowed to complicate and obfuscate this route for the purpose of analyzing culture (or simply playing with signs). Yet making images and writing texts are still very different spaces. When you're doing one, you're not doing the other, so there is always a tension (or an all-out battle) between the two acts. In a sense, I picked up the camera as a way to escape words, thinking that images could speak for themselves.

In the end, I see writing and photography as two approaches to dealing with information, as separate but related materials with which to make "stuff." In spite of the physical end product, they are both somewhat "immaterial" practices that involve a lot of staring into space(s) while looking or waiting for meaning to emerge. ■

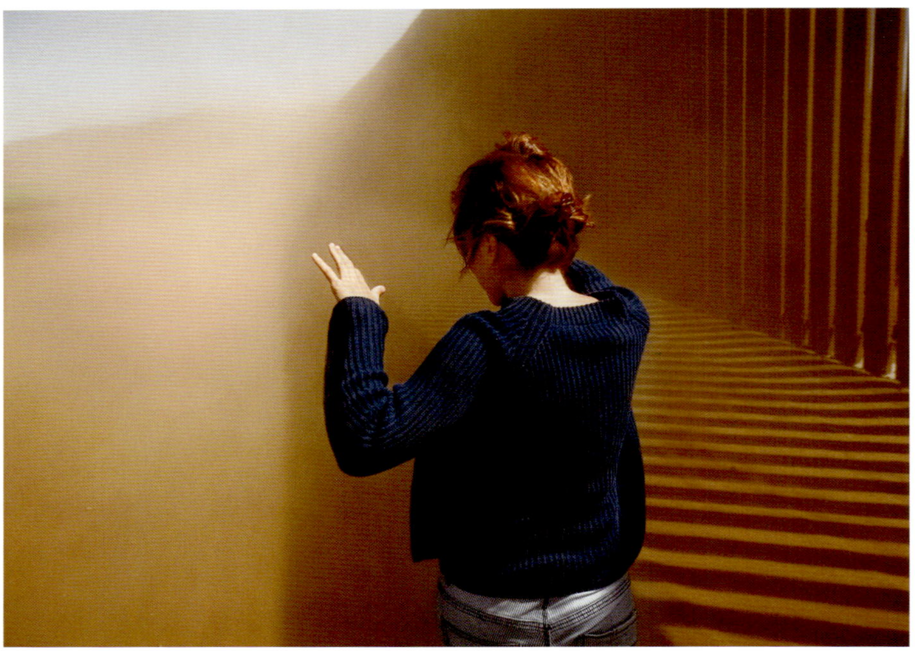

Merve told me to shut the doors. I didn't. I hurried to catch a storm coming in from the other side of the big fence. Now the rough dust lives on my dashboard, a glittering field of plastic and earth that I smuggle across the San Ysidro border two months later. So thick granules of Jacumba end up on Manuel's wet rag. He's the guy that always clears up my view at the petrol station north of Ensenada.

"Aye mujer! De donde viene todo esto?" he wonders.

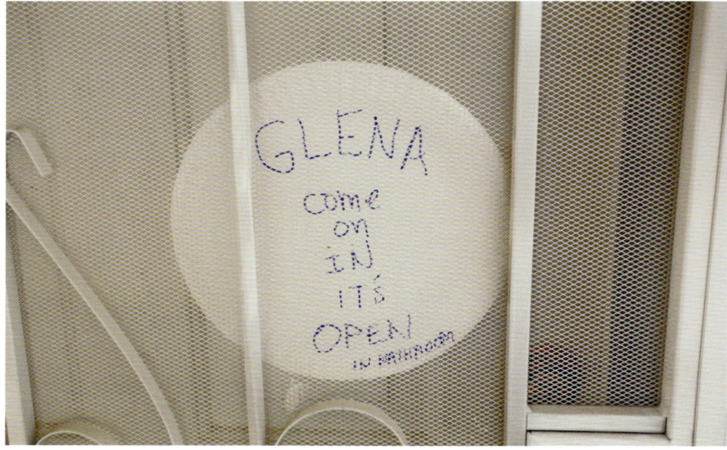

Tim has given me: a Penzoil box filled with over 300 photos from the Pacific Theater of WWII, a broken tripod, beer, a custom 4 x 5 field camera, gun cleaner, William Mortenson's "How to Photograph Women," steak, an Igloo cooler filled with film holders, time, a dead falcon brought down by a bullet the morning I left Jacumba, this paper plate.

Above
From the series Likely Stories and other sides
crossing sides, **2010** — cat. no. 79
in bathroom, **2010** — cat. no. 80

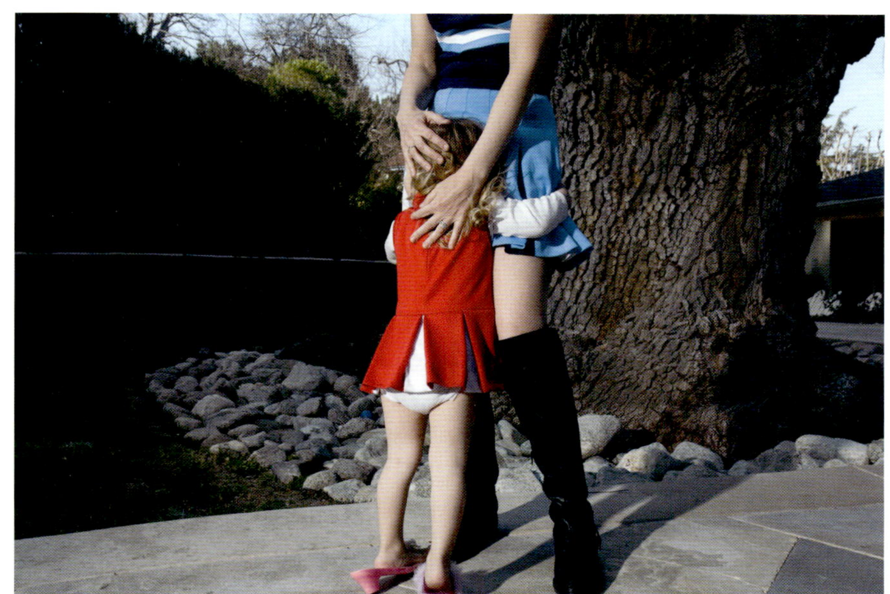

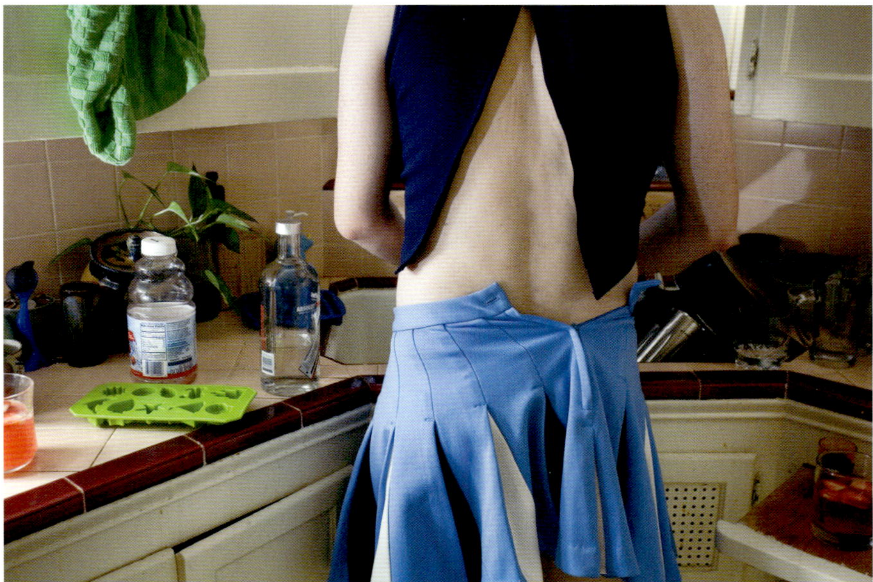

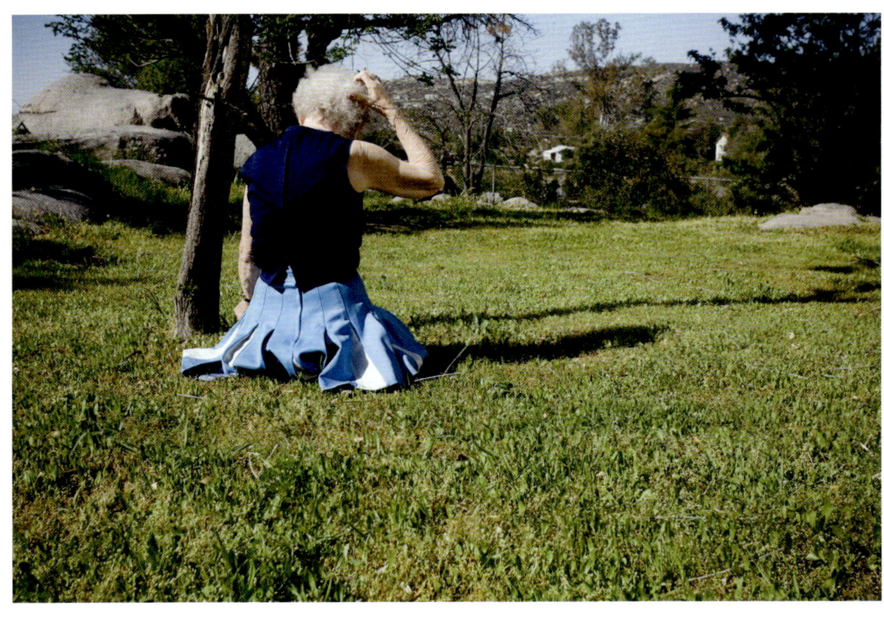

Barry Macgregor Johnston

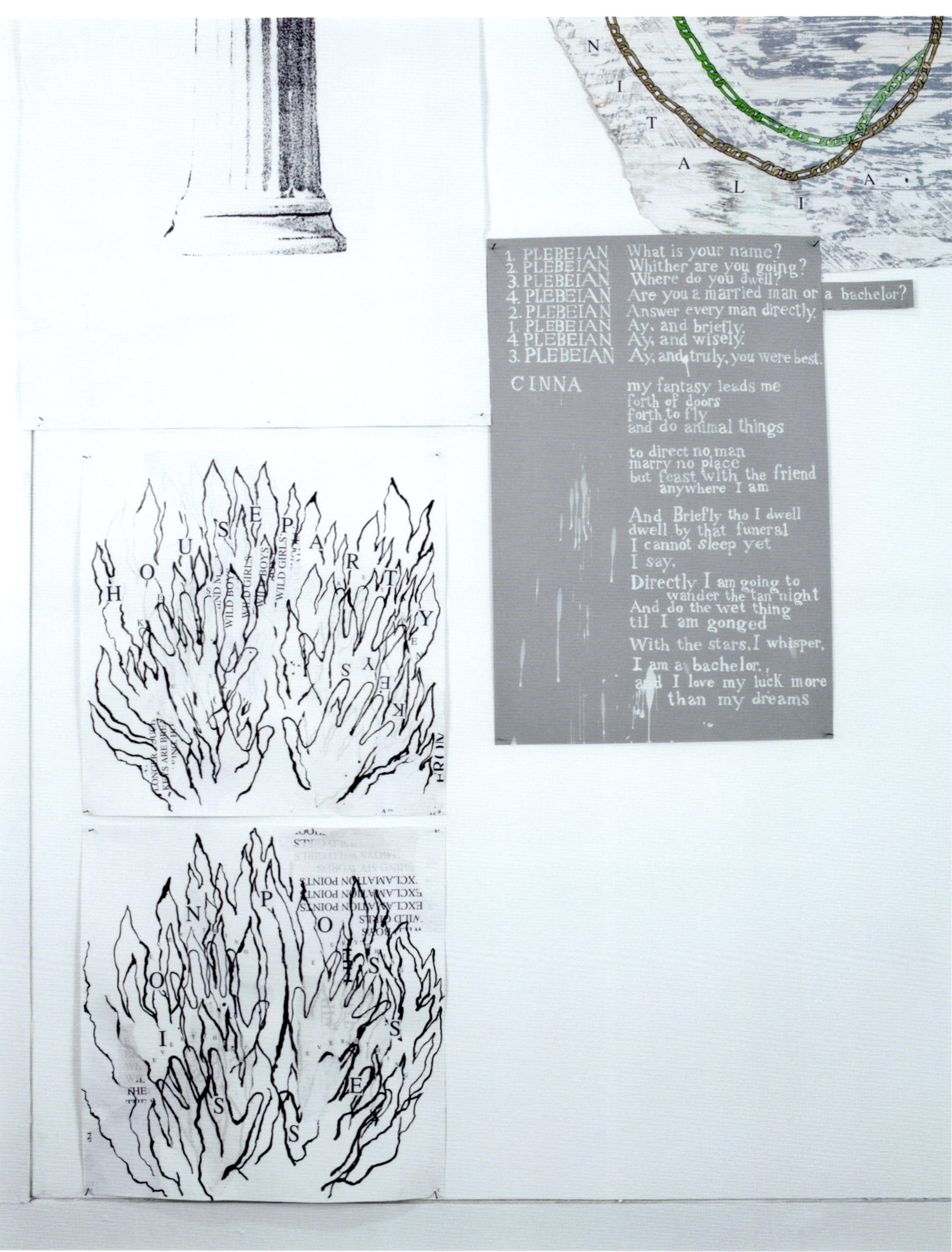

Psychic Curfew, **2010** (detail) — cat. no. 81

Interview with Chloë Flores

CF : **A large part of your practice is situated in performance, which the biennial will highlight. What kind of spaces do you find the most conducive to your practice, and why?**

BMJ : Any place can be conducive to live entertainment, because my goal is complete and violent ignorance of the place and its wishes. Too much of life is dictated by the place it possesses. The question of place is: can we exploit our present condition more than it can exploit us? Actually, the real question is: can live entertainment stop time and therefore destroy space? Or can live entertainment stop time so that we can find, in the intensity of our togetherness, an instant of love that banishes the very possibility that any other place in the world can even exist? . . . And then we must go further and banish the space that we are supposedly inhabiting right now, banish the "here." We are not even here. Live entertainment is all about bodybuilding, building a body for everyone, out of everyone, a body of pure presence. Bodies that are present are nowhere. Pure presence is disappearance. That said, places with less light seem to be better than really bright places.

CF : **An aspect of your practice deals with the ways in which we interpret language. Poetry, for example, is deciphered based on the meaning of words in relation to one another but also the way in which they appear on the page. When poetry is performed or spoken, meaning can be further articulated through inflection, tone, and gesture. How do you see language and poetry functioning in your work?**

BMJ : It goes back to the image of the burning book. The power of language, or one of its powers, is that we can carry it with us at all times, and so a poem does not require any material support—any paper, ink, or voice—to fuel us and constantly inspire us. The fact that we carry language inside us also means that language can be silent, can go undetected, and therefore cannot be confiscated or burned. At the same time it is also the job of poetry to cause books to start on fire, so that they must fall out of people's hands.

CF : **How does that relate to your performances?**

BMJ : I just try to make chorus after chorus of propagandistic slogans.

CF : **Your installation for the biennial evokes a recurring image in your work: the passageway or threshold. A passageway or threshold indicates a point at which we enter or exit a space, whether physical or nontangible. Why is it that the image of the passageway or threshold continually makes its way into your work?**

BMJ: Though the image of the door or the gate or the beaded curtain appears fairly often in my work, I tend to think of everything I do as a door. Poems, entertainment, sculpture—the most important thing is that they should act like exits, arches, out of this world, this world of stuff (this art world), this world of things as they are, and into the realm of how things can be—not how they will be but how they can always be. It definitely has nothing to do with the future.

I want them to be exits from one present time into a different present time, doors through which an alternate possibility can make an appearance. In some way, the material that my work is built from is not even the work. It is for the most part a bunch of junk that remains trapped in the "real world." Yes, most of my work is about assembling material and information from the real world into arrangements, into frames that attempt to invite, to coax some fleeting, unexpected, inhuman, otherworldly possibility to pass through them. So in a certain way, my work is its own context, is in some sense exterior to itself, is barely even art . . . because what I am really concerned with is the possibility of an event, the possibility that material and linguistic arrangements can make an atmosphere where everyone is flooded with a realization of their own power. I guess I am trying to make people and myself feel in some small way the same way that I feel when experiencing the work of some of my favorite artists . . . people like Henry Miller, Bruce Springsteen, Heraclitus, Gabriele D'Annunzio. I can only withstand the work of these bosses for moments at a time, I can read only a few pages—while traveling, for instance, in the car or on the bus on the way to a party—because their effect is to fill me with so much courage and whet my appetite for living to such a degree that I have no choice but to put them down, to shut them off, to run away from them, out, into large groups of people, into the ocean. When faced with these works, I have no choice but to party. I cannot sit still. I have to get out. Art as exit is art for people who are moving. It's art that destroys itself, that disappears. It's art that is forgotten in the way that food is forgotten after it is eaten. Its only memory is the energy it gives us. Art must be a doorway, an entrance back into the world but the world at its most unreasonable (and hence most loving).

CF : **You have a background in punk music. What characteristics of this genre find their way into your work?**

BMJ : Punk for me is about two people standing in an alley behind a club sharing a beer in the middle of winter. When you take a drink, the cold can and the freezing wind combine to make your naked hand really cold. There are two of you, but only one has a pair of gloves, so that person gives one glove to the other person, and now each of you has a glove on, one left glove and one right glove, and it starts to feel as if you are the same person drinking a beer. I have tried in my way to keep that one glove on. ∎

Born 1980 in Alton, Illinois; lives and works in Los Angeles. Johnston holds degrees from Webster University (BFA, 2002) and Art Center College of Design (MFA, 2007). His work has been exhibited at Overduin and Kite, Los Angeles; Isabella Bortolozzi, Berlin; the International Project Space, Birmingham, England; Misako and Rosen, Tokyo; and Galerie 10m2, Sarajevo, Bosnia and Herzegovina. He has performed in clubs, squats, house parties, and yards throughout the United States and Europe.

From 2004 to 2005 Johnston hosted a weekly program on EFM radio in Sarajevo. His poems have appeared in *F.R. David, NOVEL,* and the *Journal of the Valkenberg Hermitage.*

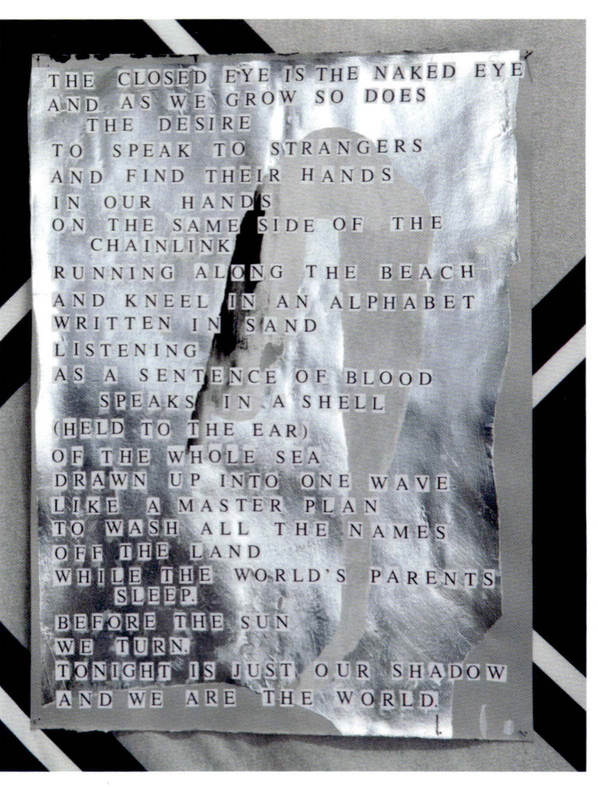

Psychic Curfew — cat. no. 81
Detail (right) and installation view (below)

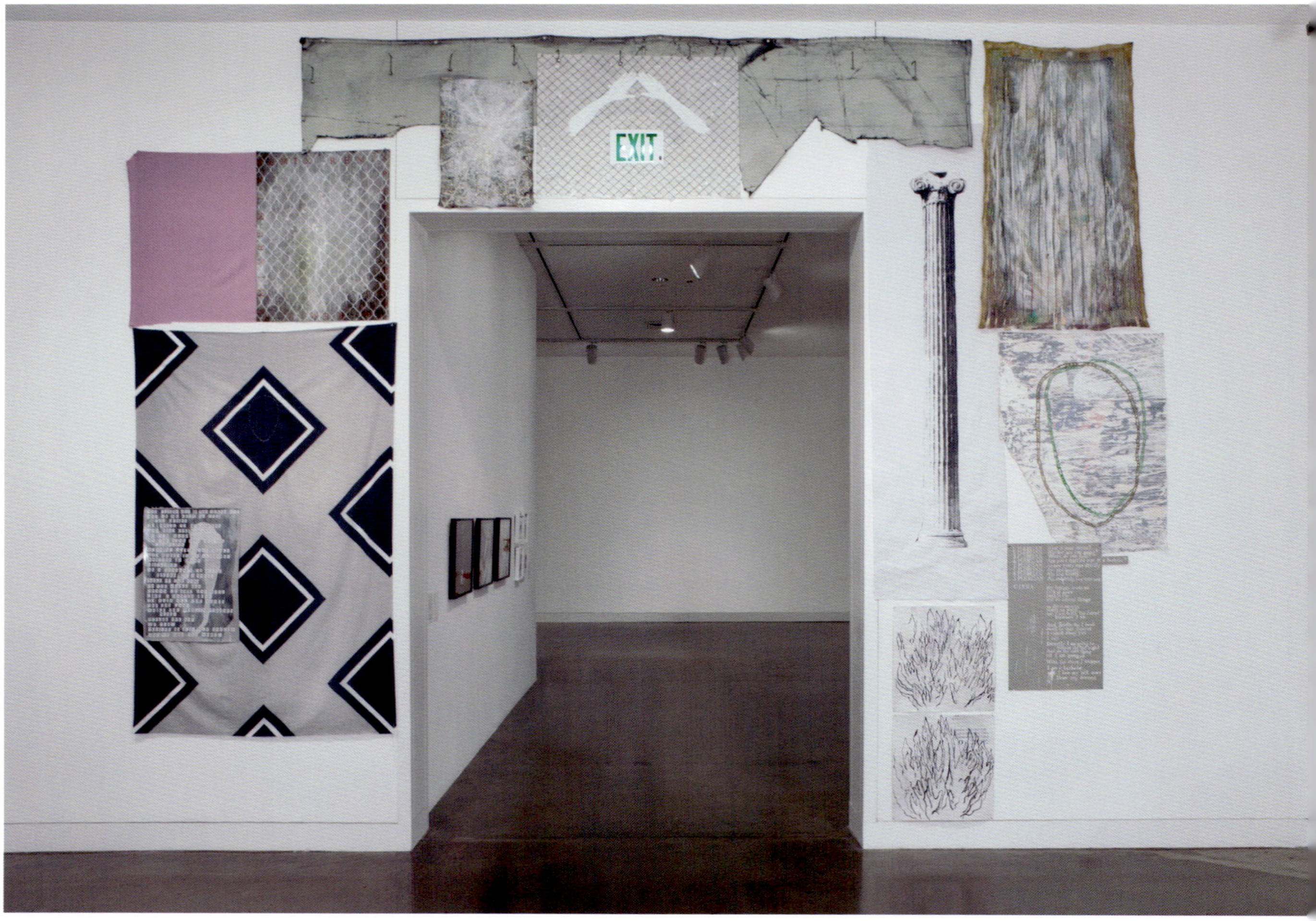

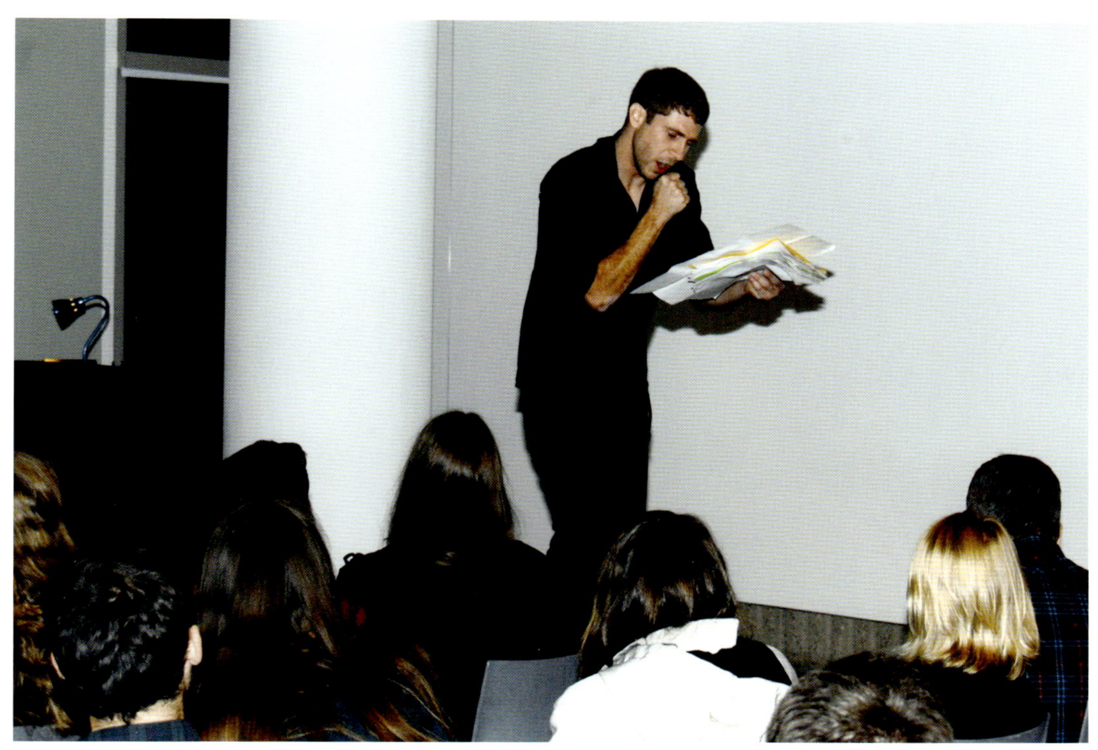

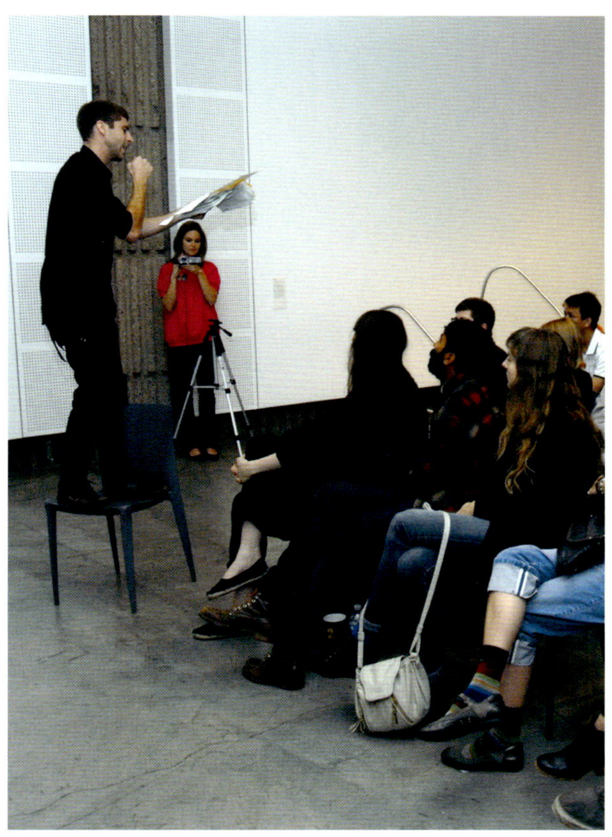

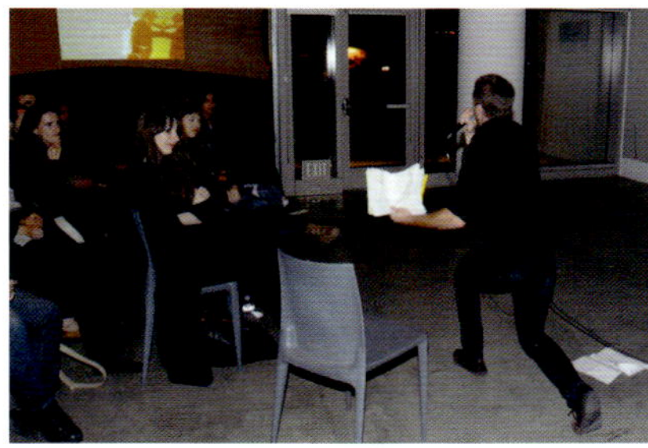

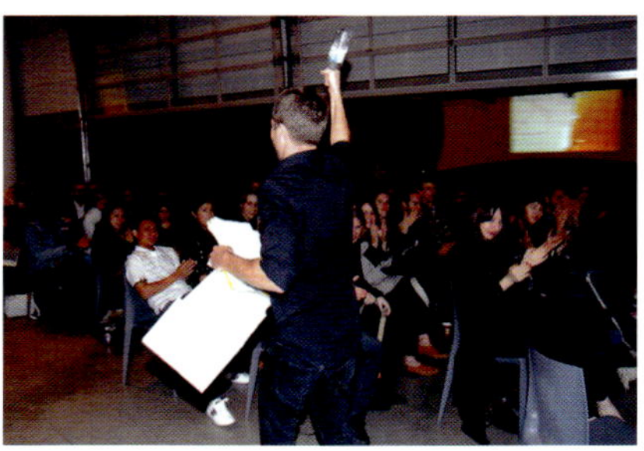

Performance, October 28, 2010 — 2010 California Biennial, Orange
County Museum of Art, Newport Beach, California

Vishal Jugdeo

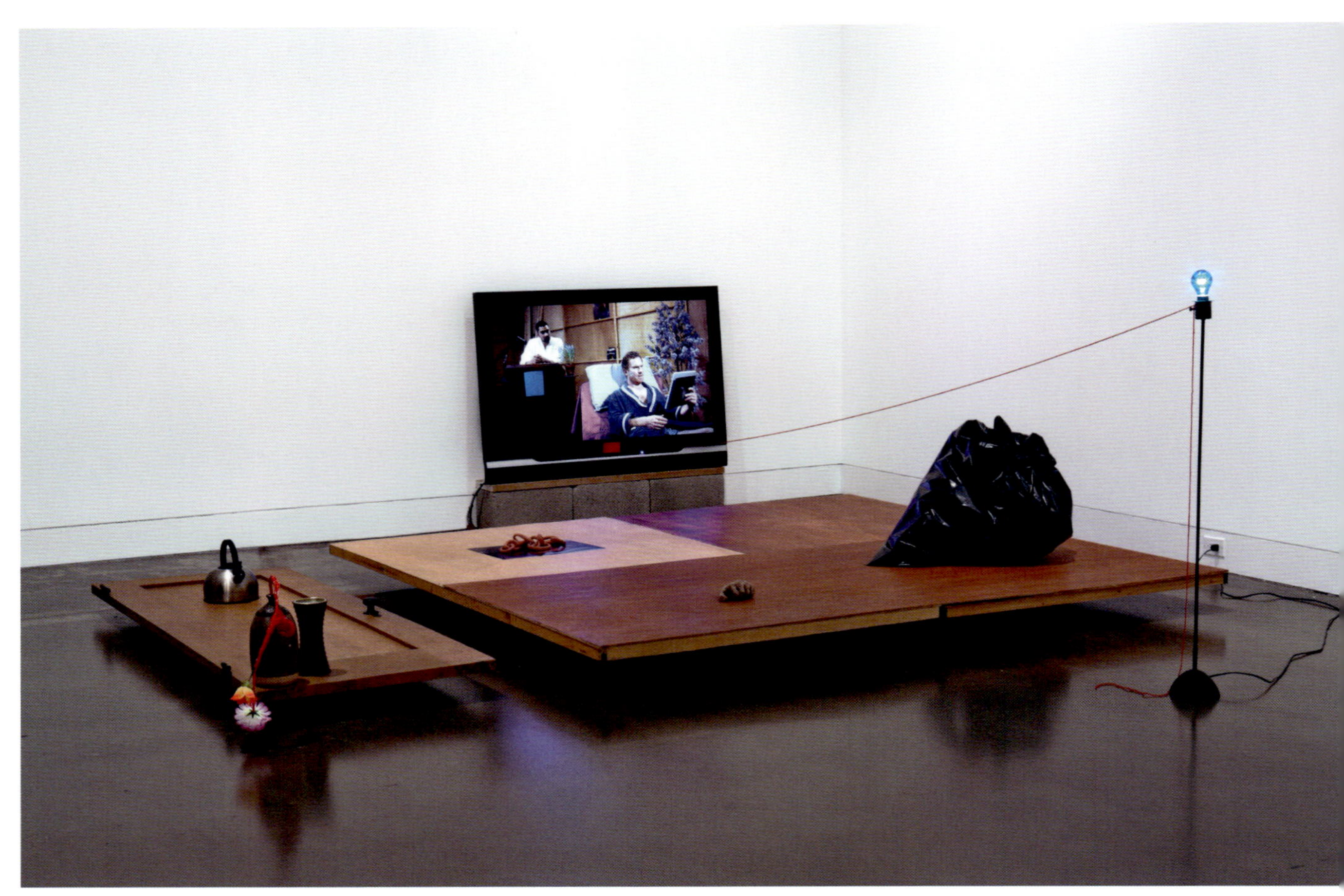

Thought Composition with Model of the World, 2010 — cat. no. 82

CF: **There is an obvious performative element in your work, but with it comes a strong aversion to prescribed roles. Why the aversion, and how does that play out in the performance?**

VJ: Any time I assign roles in the work, I consider them as provisional and transmutable. The aversion that you mention has to do with my resistance to thinking about relations in the world as fixed and unfree to transform. I engage performativity as a way of unsettling the order of things, embracing the inherent unpredictability and potential volatility of live situations. What attracts me to performance—and I think of most social activity as performance—is the fact that performers are in a continual process of reacting to the "alchemy in the air" at any given moment, whether they act spontaneously or with calculation. In the videos that I've exhibited recently, such as *Violent Broadcast* (2010), one way of thinking about the work is as a kind of sublimated power play, in which performers are cast in relation to one another both as characters in a fiction and in terms of positions of domination and submission. When I send the actors the scripts, sometimes only hours before filming, I don't provide information about the context or setting, just the words they have to say. And when they arrive at the shoot, they have to shape their performances around the situation that has been set up. As we film subsequent scenes, I change the sets, transposing new kinds of realities onto the work. The actors then have to interpret their roles on the fly according to the rules of decorum and rituals of power implied by the new situation, rather than as part of some larger narrative arc. I think that's why it's often difficult to pin down an exact sense of "character" in the work, because processes of identification are forever in a state of flux.

CF: **Since the props are seemingly static objects, are they also implicated in this state of flux? If not, what roles do the props play?**

VJ: I think of the props in the videos as overloaded vessels of signification that occupy leading rather than supporting roles. Objects are treated as physical manifestations of psychological or philosophical meanings. Their pivotal placement in the scenarios, especially as the dialogues touch on vast and complex ideas like injustice or intolerance, signals the dichotomy between the tangible reality of the characters' surroundings and a certain intangibility of the social order. When objects make their way into the installations, they seem to want to bear the weight of significance; they beg of a viewer, *please take me seriously, consider me something other than what I appear to be . . .*

CF: **Or "reappear to be," since objects from earlier works make guest appearances in other works . . .**

VJ: That's true. In some ways the practice encloses a hidden symbolic order, and I quite consciously cultivate a system of codes that operate only within the work. In part it's an attraction to private acts of communication, like the little ritualistic signals that lovers make for each other. I often adopt micro-gestures from other artists only temporarily, knowing that only they would be able to read them in the work. I'm interested in how those private forms of communication extend to the cultural or at least subcultural level. It's only through repetition that rituals or symbols become reinforced, and so the use and reuse of certain objects, images, and faces from project to project follow that logic. It's a personal cosmology of signs that is offered to the attentive viewer.

CF: **And it all comes together in the installations. What can you tell us about these stage sets/installations?**

VJ: Earlier on in my practice I discovered an impulse to create enclosures or containments, which I would build in the studio out of wall flats, carpeting, and whatever materials and objects were available. I would literally sit inside them to come up with ideas for artworks. I was influenced quite strongly by the phenomenological and psychological effects of Bruce Nauman's corridors and Dan Graham's time-delay chambers, so I started to place video cameras inside, which turned the constructions into seemingly live film sets. I exhibited the pieces as sculptural works, and I consider that series to be quite foundational to my practice. The staging of familiar architecture that began in those works spawned a methodology that I continue to use, in which each work begins as a very simple idea about a type of space.

CF: **I recently read an article about your work in which the idea of a collapse between the object and the subject was posited. Would you agree? If so, is this aspect integral to your work, and how do you see this collapse taking place?**

VJ: I think what you're talking about is my tendency to personify and anthropomorphize objects in the work, while simultaneously flattening or objectifying the subjects or characters. Yes, I'd agree with that observation. I do that. I'm not entirely sure why. I think sometimes we have artistic impulses that are not yet completed thoughts, even though they might get there someday. For the time being, I would guess that it has something to do with my interest in object-relations theory, which is a school of psychoanalytic thought that is all about the interpersonal. As I understand it, it proposed that all personal relationships are relationships to objects. I see artistic work as a practice of working through aspects of psychic life, in relation to material things and processes, and so naturally there is a collision of ideas around subjectivity and objectivity, however that manifests itself in the finished work. ∎

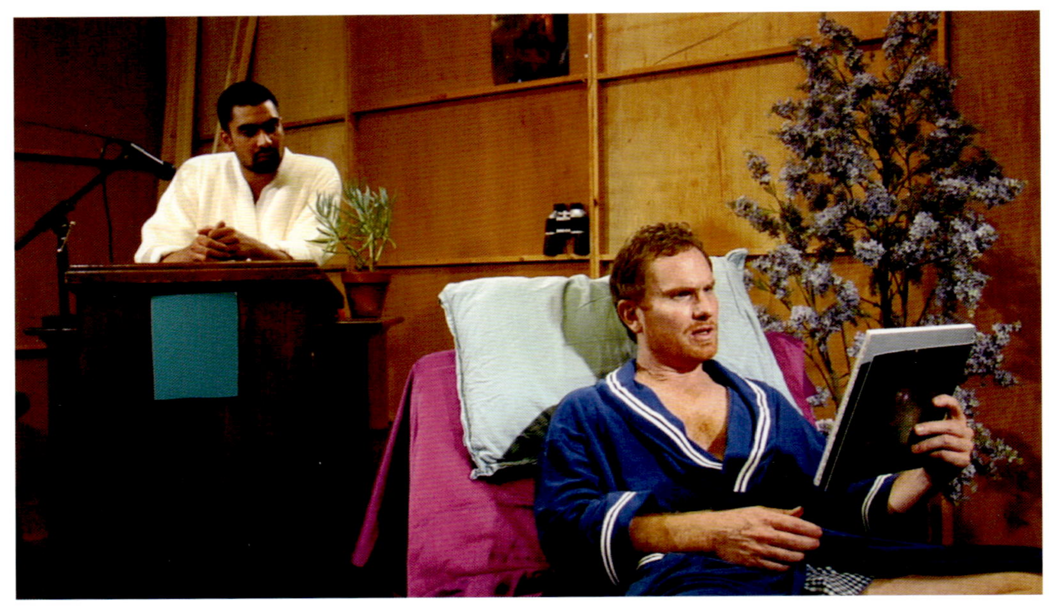

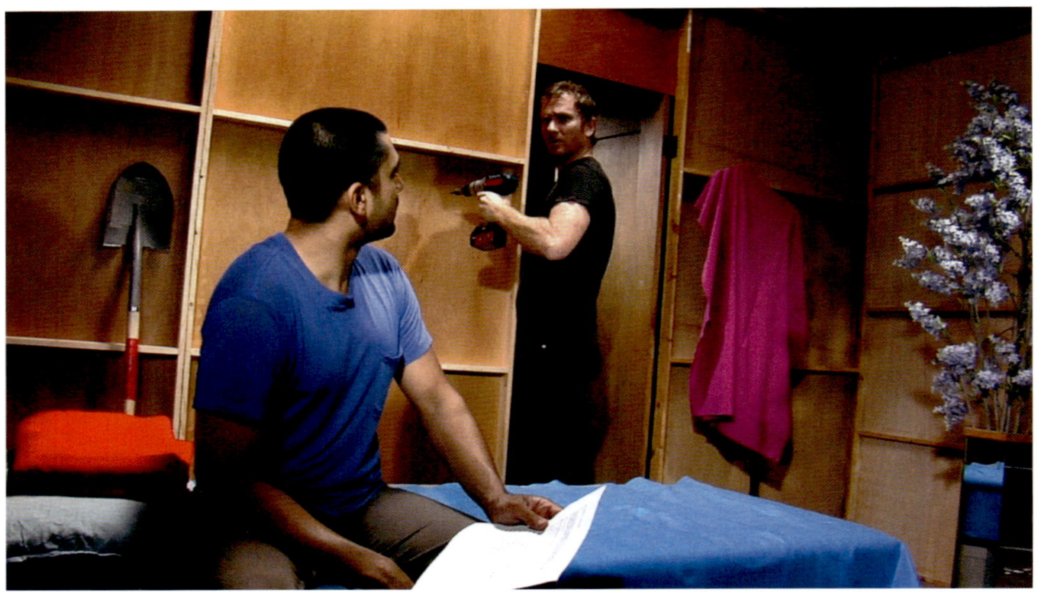

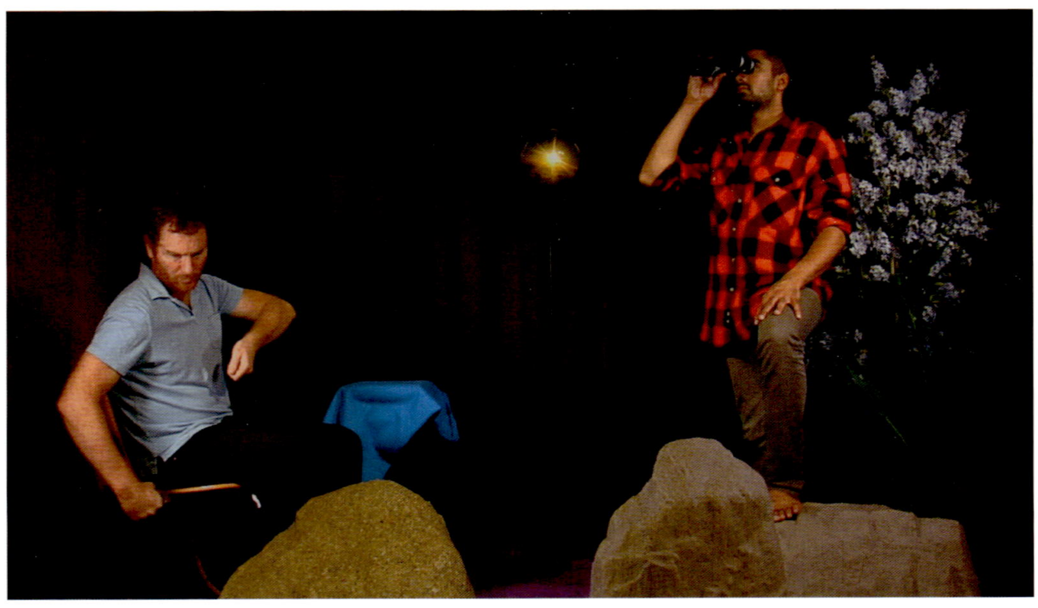

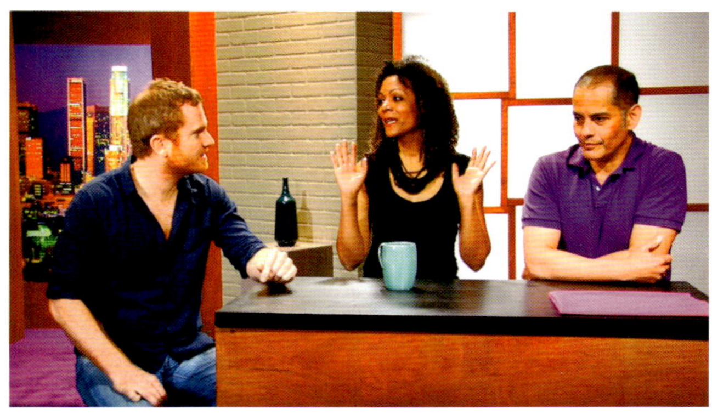

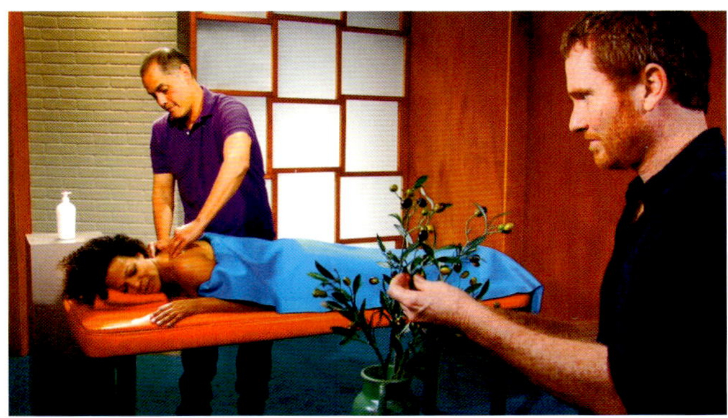

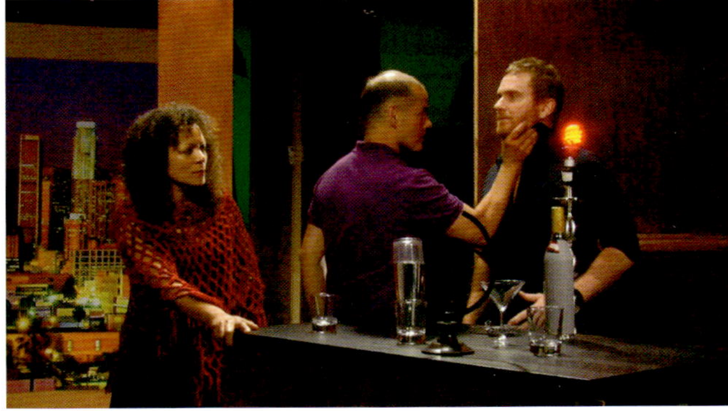

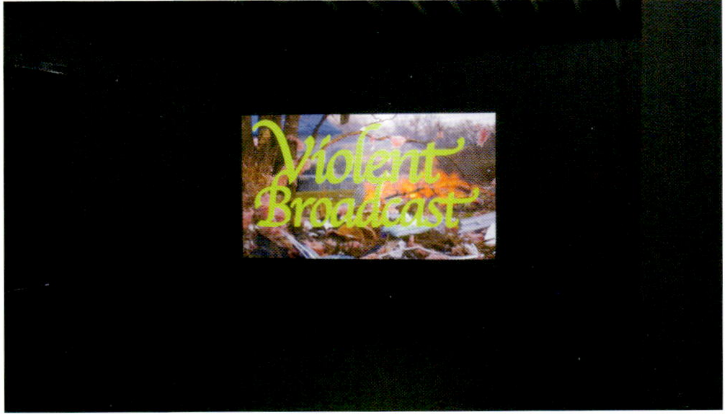

Above
***Violent Broadcast*, 2010**
HD video projection on custom screen, color, sound
Video: 8:00 min., 63 × 112 in. (160 × 284.5 cm) screen
Performers Cynthia Bond, Mark Espinoza, and William Wright;
director of photography: AJ Wedding
Courtesy of the artist
Stills and installation view, Las Cienegas Projects, Los Angeles

Opposite
Stills from ***Thought Composition with Model of the World*,
2010** — cat. no. 82

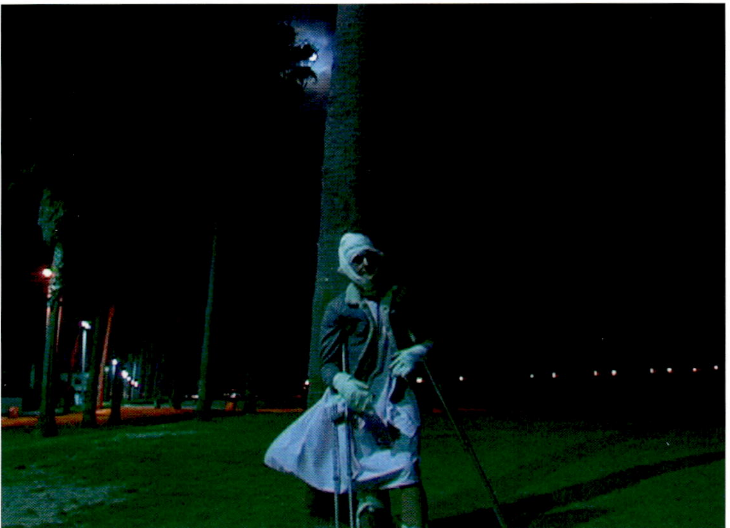

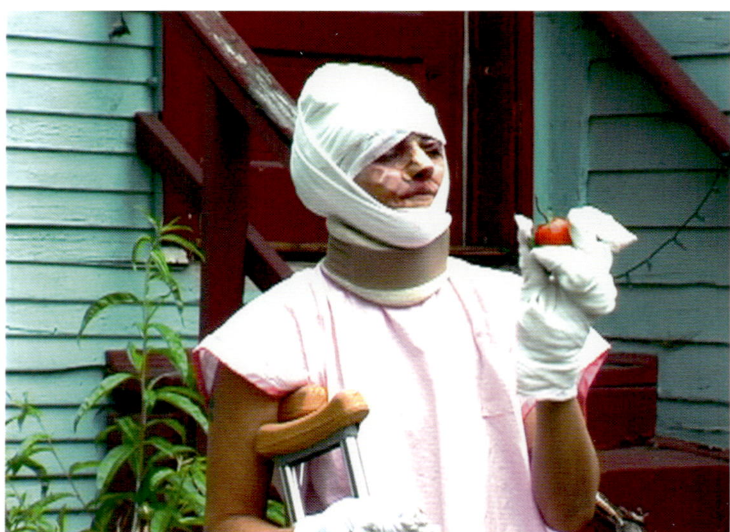

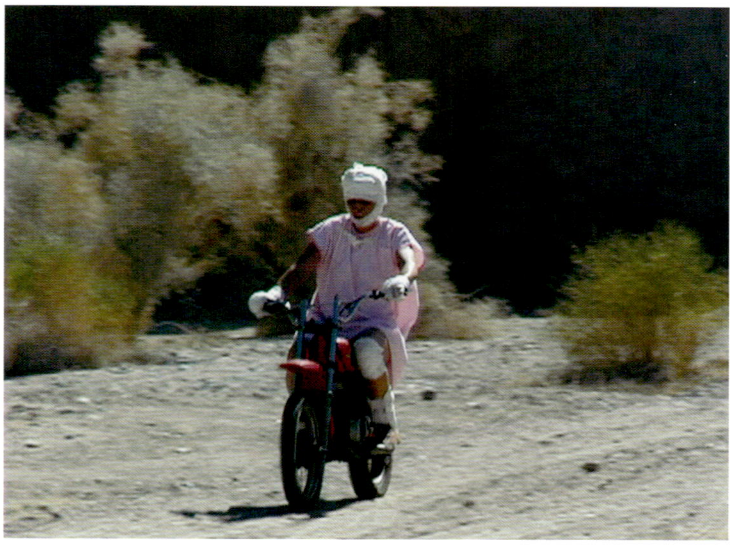

Stills from ***It's Cool, I'm Good,*** **2010** — cat. no. 83

GW: **Do you see yourself as portraying or constructing a "character" in your work, or do you understand what you're doing differently?**

SK: What people generally refer to as "character" in my work I see more as a "state of being," a metaphorical state, a representation or manifestation of issues, feelings, ideas, signs. In a literary sense, the word *character* is not so far off. In literature I think the symbolic has more play in terms of where it can reside, and "character" is one of those places. A person in a novel can commonly be read as a vessel for all kinds of meaning. In theater, performance, and moving pictures, it's much more difficult to maintain the conceptual construction in the foreground of the viewers' minds because a moving, talking person in time and space always appears to be just that. A person. Not a set of ideas.

I include things that might foil the seamlessness or believability of character, I try to blur the line between myself and character, and I do a lot with sound and editing to try and break the spell of full cinematic or theatrical fiction. In some respects, "character" in my work is an amplification of certain aspects of self, without ever really being about me per se.

The "character" in *It's Cool, I'm Good* is as much a Deleuzian desiring machine as it is a physicalized version of my own interiority doubled with a broader concern about trauma. We are a country traumatized by corrupted and nearly nonexistent promises of democracy and by our perpetration of trauma all over the world. Meanwhile, this "character" is based loosely on an ex-boyfriend of mine whom I nursed through a gruesome death from AIDS. And then from this base springs a "character" that is also a sign for the undisciplined (in the Foucaultian sense) citizen body exhibiting a kind of exuberance (albeit an ornery one) in the face of near destruction at the hands of the state. It is also an unruly fall guy for antidepressants—lonely and trying to go with the flow, hoping to get laid and find somewhere to plug in an excess of creative energy temporarily repressed by the effort it takes to make one's way in the world. And I'm all those guys.

GW: **In *It's Cool, I'm Good*, the protagonist changes the explanation of their injuries from scene to scene. This is a bit of a lowbrow reference, but in the most recent incarnation of the Batman franchise, the Joker does the same thing. How are the shifting explanations related to the concerns of the piece as a whole?**

SK: Funny you should mention the Joker. He never occurred to me as model for this protagonist, but I like that you offer the reference. He's a perfect parallel. The original Joker character was born out of trauma. He starts out as a chemical engineer who quits his job to become a stand-up comedian(!) but bombs at the comedy club. Then his wife and unborn child die in an accident. Then he falls into a vat of chemicals and is severely disfigured. The shock of his lousy luck makes him insane. I like to think it's the depth of his trauma that leads him to say, "My past? I always remember it differently. If I'm going to have a past, I prefer it to be multiple-choice! Hahahahaha . . . ."

In *It's Cool, I'm Good*, I'm trying to deflect the viewers' search for the "truth." In part because trauma reorganizes truth, but mainly because with this work I'm more interested in how we *cope* with what has happened and less concerned with how or even why it happened. I want to confound the question of what happened so I can steer away from sentimentality and keep us in the visceral experience of surviving. I'm often suspicious of too much story. I want to stay in the speed of the body. In this case certain mechanisms take over in what might be an effort to stay alive: incessant joking, flirting, ruminating, recounting facts, exploring, driving, walking, being. This is exuberance; this is something like a cross between will to live and will to power.

Changing the story over and over is also a way to portray the emotional armoring that can come with trauma (hence the title). Which is funny because I recently tried therapy for the first real time. I said to the therapist, "Look I can tell you all kinds of horror stories, but the telling doesn't seem to change my problems." I start in with the stories, and by the end of the session she's recommended a therapy called eye movement desensitization and reprocessing, a neurological approach developed during the first Gulf War to help veterans cope with PTSD. As the brain remembers the bad feelings, it starts digging up past traumas. And as the old source traumas emerge—the big, bad ones—eye movements neurologically transmit the memories to a different part of the brain so that you can recall what happened but you don't have to keep reliving the experience with the same level of fear and distress. Which is cool. I like my past to be multiple-choice too.

Another aspect of the post-trauma stage that interests me relates directly back to the issue of the Joker. His personal trauma shaped his social relationship to the world. It birthed a supervillain. I'm interested in the social aspect of what happens to us, how our personal experiences shape our responses to the world. We develop all kinds of neuroses, addictions, fears, phobias, antisocial behaviors. And doesn't that in turn impact what we do in the world, what kinds of projects we make, what kinds of organizations we form, how we steer our politics, how we fashion entire infrastructures? And if we take Foucault's position that madness is historically constituted, it makes so much sense that Joker in the 1990s doesn't suffer from "insanity" but from "supersanity." The protagonist in *It's Cool, I'm Good* is, in that respect, "superinjured," able to persevere beyond what's reasonable exactly because there is no other choice. A sort of punk-rock PTSD supervillain ex-comedian but with no special powers and no enemies.

GW: **Speaking of cinema, how do you understand or position your own work relative to the role that narrative plays in traditional filmmaking?**

SK: I come to narrative via reading and writing more so than watching, and yet it's the medium of film/video that allows me to privilege the experiential over the narrative arc. I do build story, particularly in my most recent work, braiding together strands for the viewer to follow. I want to provide some of the pleasure of story, but the pieces unpack more along psycho-emotional lines. The script is always punctuated by improvisation. Audio and visual information bear a significant load of meaning as well. Landscapes might function as double entendre.

In *It's Cool, I'm Good*, the desert is really the desert, replete with issues of water politics and sprawl, for example. But it is also a psychological space, in a Beckettian sense. Music and sound are integral as "texts" in their own right.

In live performance, you control almost everything with your body, timing especially and the rapport with the audience. I shoot and edit with the physical memory of what that's like. My live shows were driven in part by the desire to create an Artaudian catharsis and also maintain a Brechtian distance that would allow the audience to have autonomous, active consciousness. As a video maker, these concerns persist. The technology replaces the body, and I have to figure out how to make it "sweat." Vaudeville, stand-up, poetry, sermons, speeches, music all inform the way I'm trying to loosen up narrative structure. I'm getting permission from histories of experimental filmmaking, video art, and documentary at the same time that I'm stealing from Hollywood. Recently, I'm revisiting Marx Brothers' films and noticing a renegade disregard for convention. The films are surreal, almost druggy, because they were born on stage and then folded into film. Time, along with the fourth wall, is interrupted regularly for wordless physical skits, non sequitur speeches, songs, dances, and the magical moment when Groucho looks right at you and winks.

GW: **Do you consider humor to be a theme or more of a strategy? Is it the idea of humor that you're trying to get at, almost as a subject matter? Or is humor a device that you're deploying to get at something else, a formal strategy?**

SK: Right. Both. Especially in this most recent work, I'm trying to do both at the same time. Like a tattoo of a butt on a butt (as Beavis says to Butthead).

Humor has also been a central device in all the work I've made. I discovered its power in performance, specifically as a way to connect with the people. To establish camaraderie and give permission to laugh (because inevitably at some point the work also gets heavy). Once you're in, humor is freed up to start working on more complex levels as a strategy: upending expectations, disrupting norms, subverting meaning, interrupting hierarchy, critiquing the status quo. At its best, humor plays with lines of agreement while simultaneously relying on agreements: we laugh because we recognize. Freud says part of what gives us pleasure in humor is the experience of recognition.

In this recent work, I'm looking specifically at how humor functions as a survival mechanism and how it forms a language of its own, specifically in response to trauma. Here joking and humor are used likewise to mirror the way meaning is similarly upset by trauma. Trauma ruptures what we thought we knew.

Which leads me back to the earlier question about why my protagonist, like the Joker, keeps changing the story of the trauma. Kathy, the subject of my video *Kathy*, says that repeating stories of traumatic events can traumatize the listener. While the Joker can use this as a sadistic tool, I find ways to sidestep the direct retelling. I want to exorcise my demons just as much as the next guy, but I don't need to drag you down with me.

Boy, this is getting really unfunny. Which is exactly what Freud says will happen if you have to explain a joke. Part of a joke's pleasure is its innate economy, the compression of meaning. Which is why I really like fast shorties like: "What's brown and sticky? A stick." ∎

Born 1968 in San Francisco; lives and wor[ks] in Los Angeles. Kahn received degrees from San Francisco State University (BA, 1991) and Bard College (MFA, 2003). Her work has been shown at the Museum of Contemporary Art, the Getty Center, and the Hammer Museum in Los Angeles; the Sundance Film Festival; the Center for Ar[t] and Media (ZKM), Karlsruhe, Germany; P.S.1 Contemporary Art Center, Long Isla[nd] City, New York; Susanne Vielmetter Los Angeles Projects; and Elizabeth Dee Gall[ery] New York. She also participated in the 20[0] Whitney Biennial. She has received grant[s] from the California Community Foundatio[n,] the Durfee Foundation, and the Internatio[nal] Fund for US Artists, among others, and has been nominated for numerous award[s] and fellowships, including a Rockefeller Foundation fellowship. She teaches as adjunct faculty in new genres at UCLA, California Institute of the Arts, and Otis College of Art and Design.

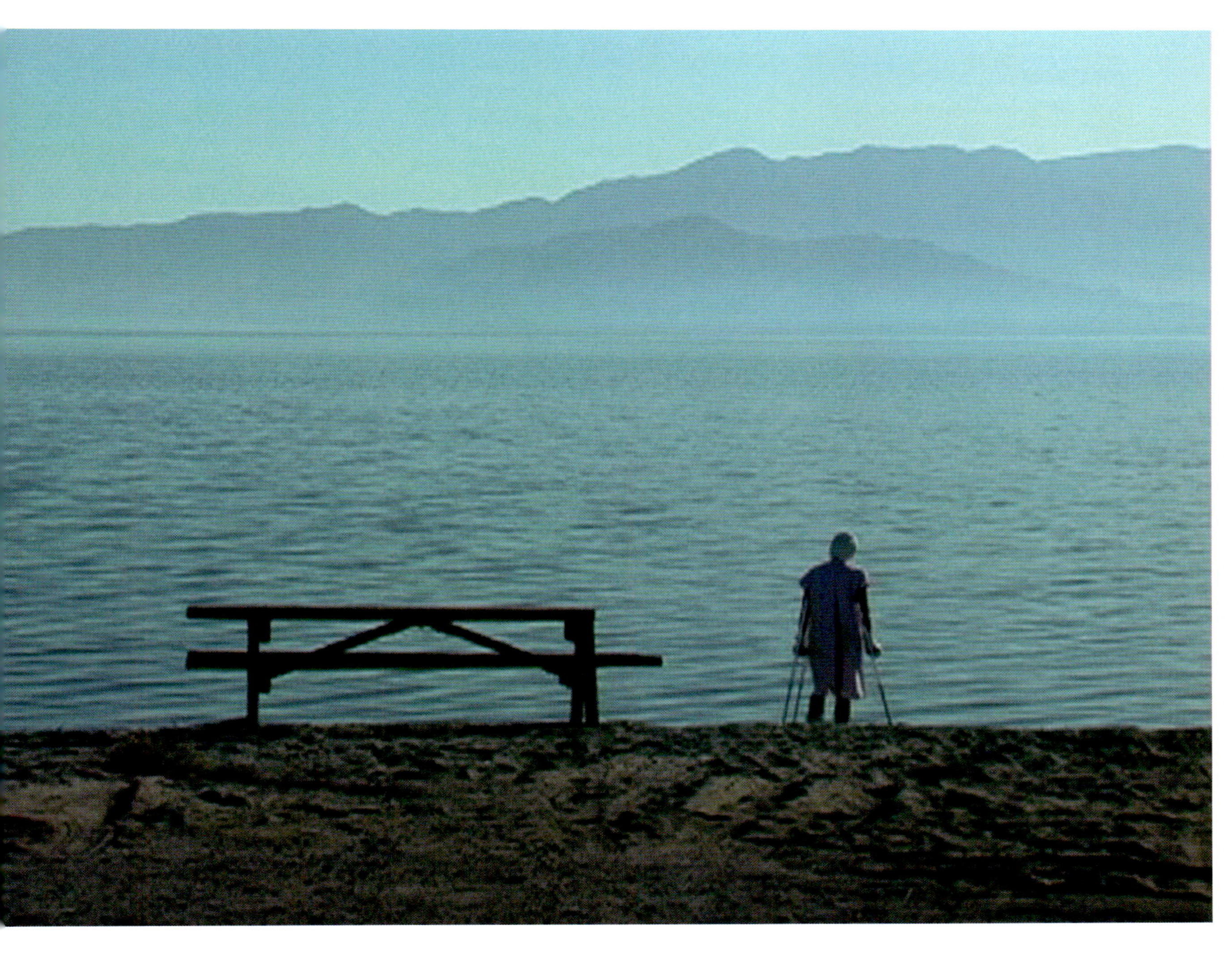

Still from **It's Cool, I'm Good**, 2010 — cat. no. 83

Andy Kolar

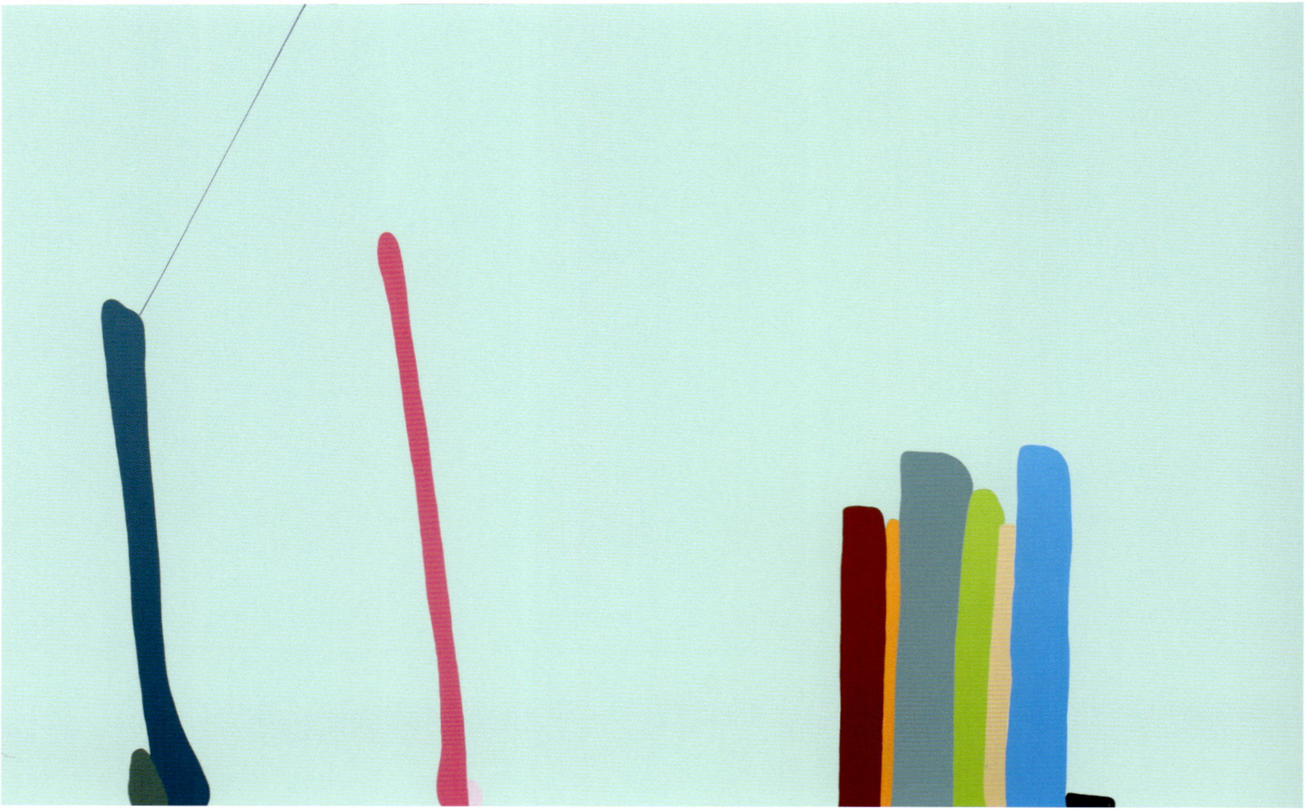

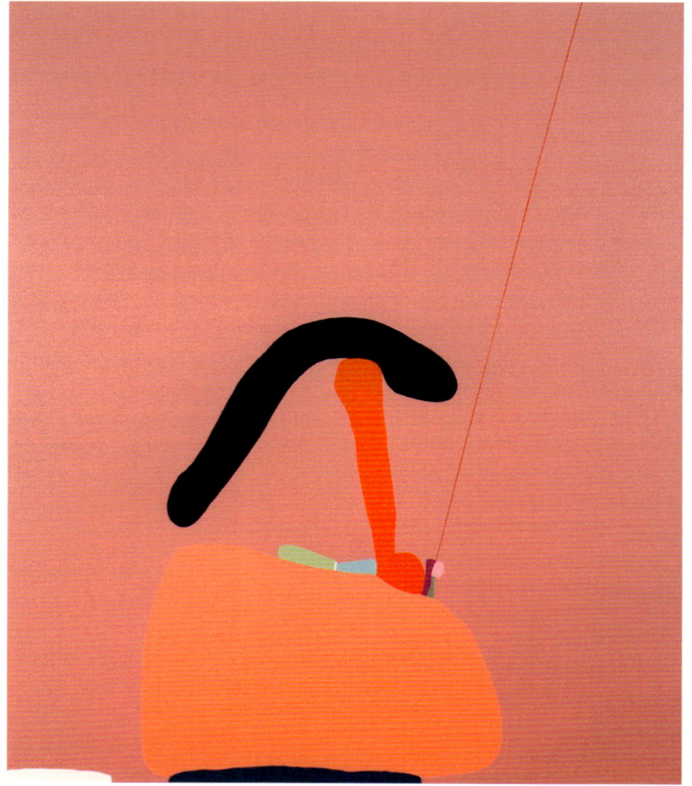

Above
Six Deep, **2009** — cat. no. 85
Finite, **2009** — cat. no. 84

Interview with Sarah Bancroft

SB: There is a certain tension in all of your work, with forms almost tumbling or touching, forms that seem to gravitate toward or repel one another in a corporeal fashion. Nonetheless, the compositions are abstract.

AK: I suppose so. I don't really think about being an "abstract painter" specifically. I make a lot of different work and really don't differentiate between the practices whether I am making paintings, sculpture, etc. I do work abstractly though, as I think that there is more potential in the work having a sort of vague quality. By this I mean that I find it difficult to work with images or with objects that already have imbued meanings or distinctions. I would rather make work that does not already require knowledge of a codified language of a specific image, text, or whatever, leaving the end result open to the interpretation of the viewer.

SB: The palette of your paintings is often a conscious response to work by other artists—some well known within the canon of Western art history, others not at all. Your *Mural* (2009), for instance, responded to Jackson Pollock's *Mural* (1943) in scale and title and as a source for select colors, although the two paintings operate very differently and look nothing alike. Can you speak about this process, how you are inspired by or push off other work?

AK: I began thinking about art in a different context a few years ago when I wasn't really thinking about making art but more about the experience that I had with it as a viewer. I wanted to continue to work abstractly but change the approach to working that I was utilizing to be somewhat more specific. I decided that I was going to take works that I viewed as important somehow or that I found interesting and remake them as abstract works.

Some of the works that I choose to respond to are abstract to begin with; some deal with imagery, and others are more conceptual pieces. Almost all of the pieces that I make are the same scale and use approximately the same colors as the work that I reference. I intentionally obscure the original referent so as to not cloud the intentions of my own work by giving the viewer a false mental image or context of the piece. I will scramble the original title or make my own title that vaguely refers to the piece.

SB: Can you talk about the large-scale painting that you are creating for the California Biennial?

AK: I had been thinking about the project for quite a while, since it was initially proposed. I was running the numbers of the wall size in my head when it struck me that one of the most famous paintings, *Guernica* (eleven feet, six inches by twenty-five feet, six inches), is almost exactly the size of the wall that I was given to make a mural on at OCMA. I realized that it would fit perfectly on the wall in the Pavilion, which is sixteen by twenty-three feet, eight inches. I had seen the painting in Madrid a little more than a year ago and so decided to make a "version" of *Guernica*.

SB: Yet it looks nothing like Pablo Picasso's *Guernica* and doesn't seem to borrow exclusively from that work's grisaille palette. *Guernica* functions as a history painting, an antiwar painting, a cathartic, visceral experience for the viewer as well. Is your painting a response to this particular painting or a response to the temper of our own times, just as *Guernica* was in its day?

AK: It does borrow partially from the palette of *Guernica*, although as a commissioned work this piece developed a little differently than the way that I normally work, so I had to bend my own rules a bit. I felt that I had to find a way to make the painting more complex. I decided to look more closely at colors associated with the cultural history of Spain and also the art historical and sociopolitical history of the painting. From there I came up with a palette that seemed to work.

My decision to use *Guernica* as a reference for the mural is not a direct response to the political climate that we happen to be in, nor am I trying to draw any relationships between the two points in history. I am interested in making a painting that responds to the referent in terms of it being a good fit for the space and in creating a challenge for the current project that I am engaged with in both scale and complexity.

SB: Do you see your work relating to the history of hard-edge painting in Southern California?

AK: I guess so in the lineage of abstract painting, but I would say that they were far more focused and formal, whereas I tend to embrace the odd and more nuanced aspects.

SB: I am always drawn to and curious about the red line in each of your paintings and works on paper. Can you tell me about this consistent presence in the work?

AK: The red line is like a mathematical constant, something that never changes throughout all the work. Often it points to an action that the title refers to.

SB: Like what? Can you give me an example?

AK: For instance, in *caída*, the new painting for the biennial, there is a form that looks like it's going to fall over. The red line is drawing attention to this imbalance. *Caída* means "fall off or out" or "downfall" in Spanish.

SB: Painting isn't dead.

AK: If painting died again, I didn't get the memo. ∎

Born 1981 in Spirit Lake, Iowa; lives and works in Los Angeles. Kolar is a graduate of Minnesota State University (BFA, 2004) and California State University, Long Beach (MFA, 2007). His work has been exhibited in solo and group exhibitions around Los Angeles and was included in the publication *New American Paintings* in December 2008. The catalog for his 2009 solo exhibition at Carl Berg Projects, Los Angeles, included an essay by Los Angeles critic and curator Christopher Miles.

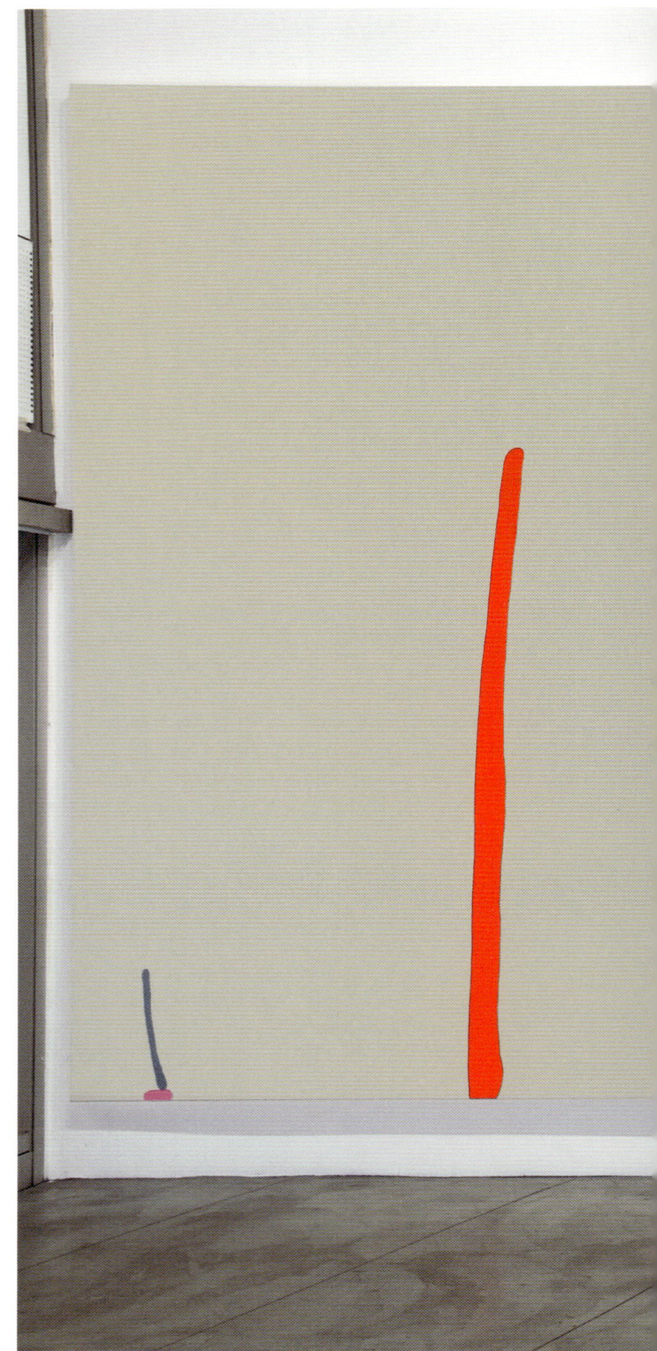

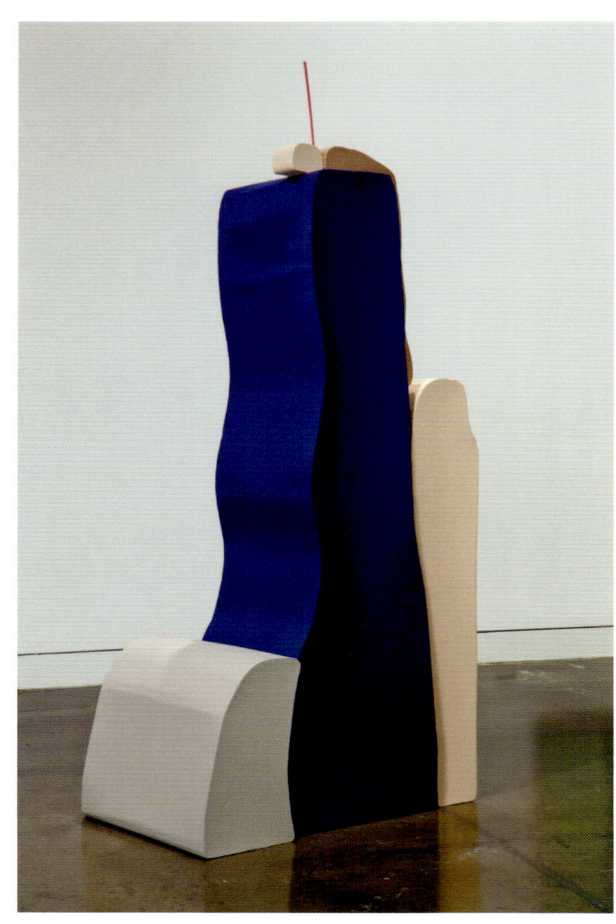

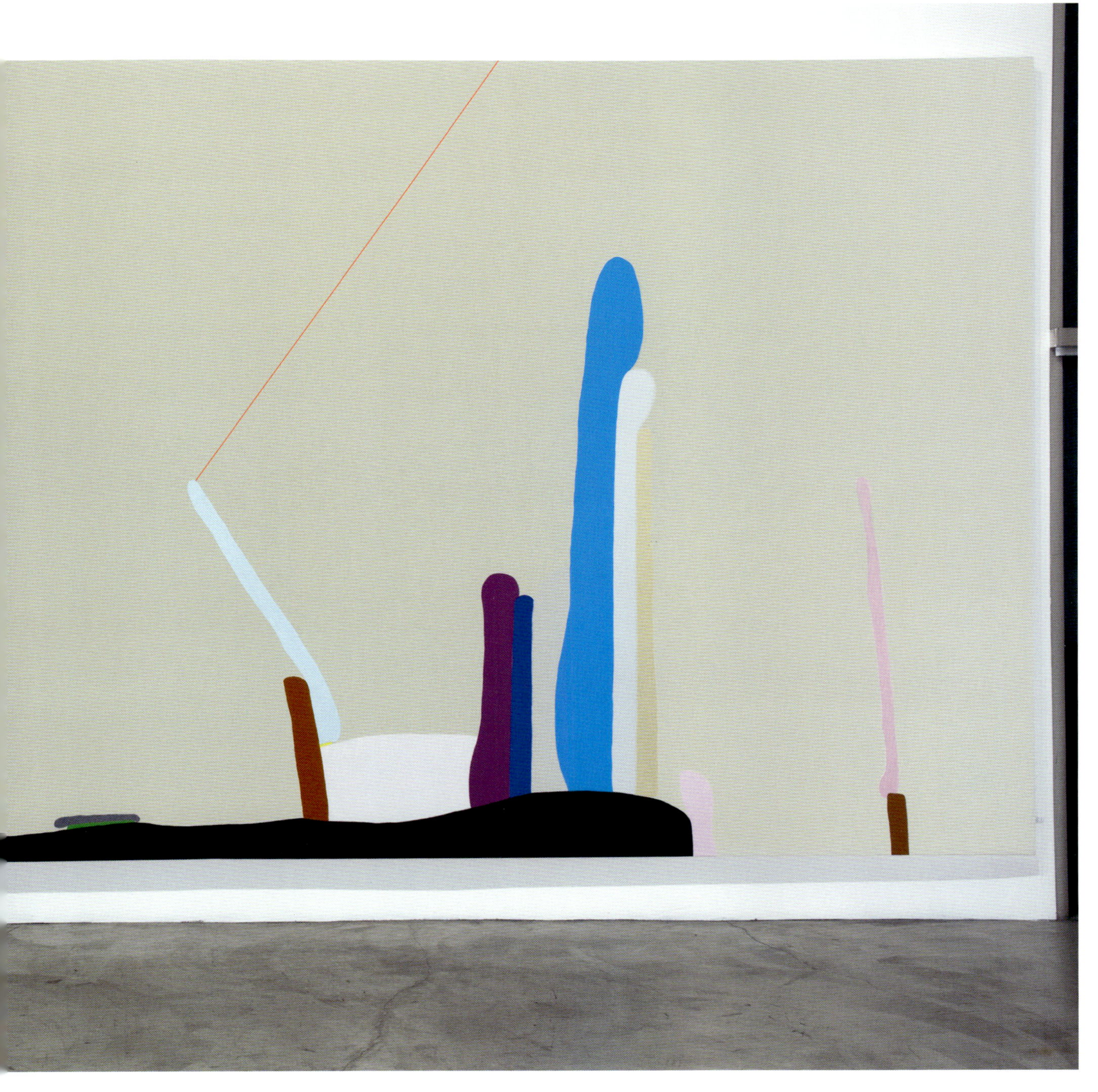

Jennifer Locke

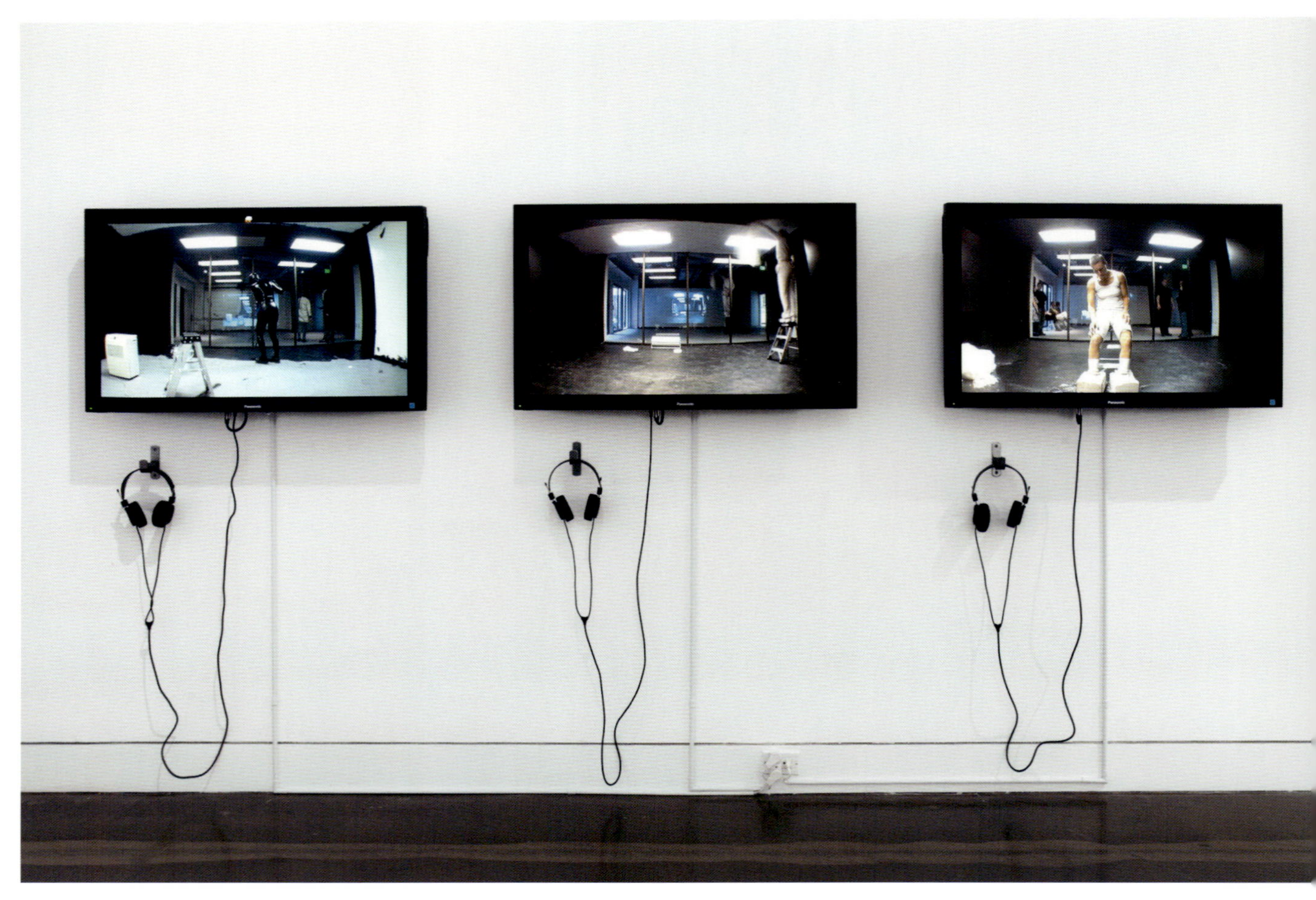

Left to right
***Black/White (Glue)*, 2009** — cat. no. 88
***Black/White (Ink)*, 2009** — cat. no. 89
***Black/White (Plaster)*, 2009** — cat. no. 90

Interview with Stacie Martinez

SM: **Describe your work in the biennial and how you prepare for such a physically demanding piece.**

JL: This piece is a video triptych of three live actions that I performed for the grand opening of the Marina Abramovic Institute. The opening took place over three days, for about four hours each day. This was interesting for me because I typically do performance pieces only once; I don't perform them over again. So I developed a series of three separate but interrelated actions that made sense for that context.

For the first action, I wore head-to-toe black latex, and I painted the ceiling, walls, and floor of the room black. I then took off the latex, poured five gallons of glue over my body, waited until it dried, then peeled it off in one piece. The entire action took almost four and a half hours. The second day, with the room still completely black, I wore a white sweat suit and covered the walls, ceiling, and floor with white butcher paper. I made a shallow plastic pool and filled it with black ink. I then jumped rope in the ink, splattering the walls, floor, and myself. I forgot to pack my mask, so I wound up inhaling a lot of the ink mist too. This action took almost three and a half hours. On the third day I removed all the paper so that the room was black again. I mixed forty pounds of dry plaster with water, poured it in boxes, and then put my feet into the boxes. When it dried, I had big plaster blocks on my feet. I then painted the walls and ceiling white again, dragging around my block feet, which made chalky drawings on the black floor. This took just over three hours.

To prepare for a live piece, I plan very carefully to ensure that the installation is just so and that I have every single finicky little thing that I could possibly need to carry it out. I don't rehearse, but I do go over my plan pretty obsessively beforehand. When the piece is happening, I'm generally so completely engrossed in it—partly because the tasks I give myself are so physically intense—that I'm really not thinking much about the audience. That part happens ahead of time.

SM: **Often, with performance art, the video captured is considered documentation of the action. But in your approach it plays a much more integral part; it's almost another performer. How does video work in your practice?**

JL: Well, to be clear, I actually don't think of myself as a "performance artist." My work is indeed very action-based, but I always think about the architecture in which the action takes place, the way the audience sees it, and how everything's oriented in relationship to the camera. The video camera is never in service to the action. It's more the other way around.

SM: **One thing that stands out about your work is that you establish strategic, structured systems of viewing. Can you talk a little more about this?**

JL: Yes, absolutely. In this piece the video shows the perspective of a camera mounted on the wall facing outward. The video shows me performing the action and, behind me, a glass wall through which you can see the audience. Behind the audience there's a projection of a live feed of this image, from the camera. The projected image is a repetition of itself—a hall of mirrors or a feedback loop. The audience could look back and forth between the live action and the projection, but they couldn't see both at the same time. They are part of the image too, so they have become subject matter.

I'm interested in viewing dynamics: how and how much the audience is shown, what is perceived as subject or object and how that shifts around . . . seeing and not seeing. For instance, the way the body in black latex disappears against the background as the room is painted black or the way the live video feed flattens and doubles the action . . . and the viewer in between. I'm always thinking about how to create barriers or filters to disrupt a straight view of the action. I often set up pieces in which it's in competition with its own representation. I also tend to orient the action toward the camera and away from the audience, so in order to view it frontally, they have to look at the projection. In a way, the audience's attention is almost secondary to the camera.

I never expect the viewer to stay for the full duration of the action—it's not a hostage situation. I'm fine with the piece being experienced partially, though I'm constantly surprised by some viewers' endurance. For this piece, there were a few people who stayed the full eleven hours.

SM: **So, out of curiosity, do you keep the peeled glue—you know, as a residue of the performance?**

JL: Ah, "residue." I'm not sure whether I like that word. I come from the tradition of addressing performance as sculpture, and "residue" always sounds like its unwanted leftovers. I'm actually starting to think that I use performance as a means to create video work and objects—almost like a live, condensed studio event. The video makes sense to me and just seems to work. I've kept the residual objects over the years too, but I've never been sure about my relationship to them. I'm thinking more about them recently. ∎

Born 1969 in Smithtown, New York; lives and works in San Francisco. Locke received her BFA (1991) and MFA (2006) from the San Francisco Art Institute. She has exhibited at the 1999 Venice Biennale; Air de Paris, Paris; the 2006 Havana Biennial; Art Basel, Basel, Switzerland; La Panadería, Mexico City; Palais des Beaux-Arts, Brussels; Canada gallery, New York; Yerba Buena Center for the Arts, San Francisco; and the Berkeley Art Museum. She has curated for Artists' Television Access and Queens Nails Annex, coproduced a cable access show, and sung in punk bands. Locke is an adjunct professor at Saint Mary's College of California, and she teaches at the San Francisco Art Institute.

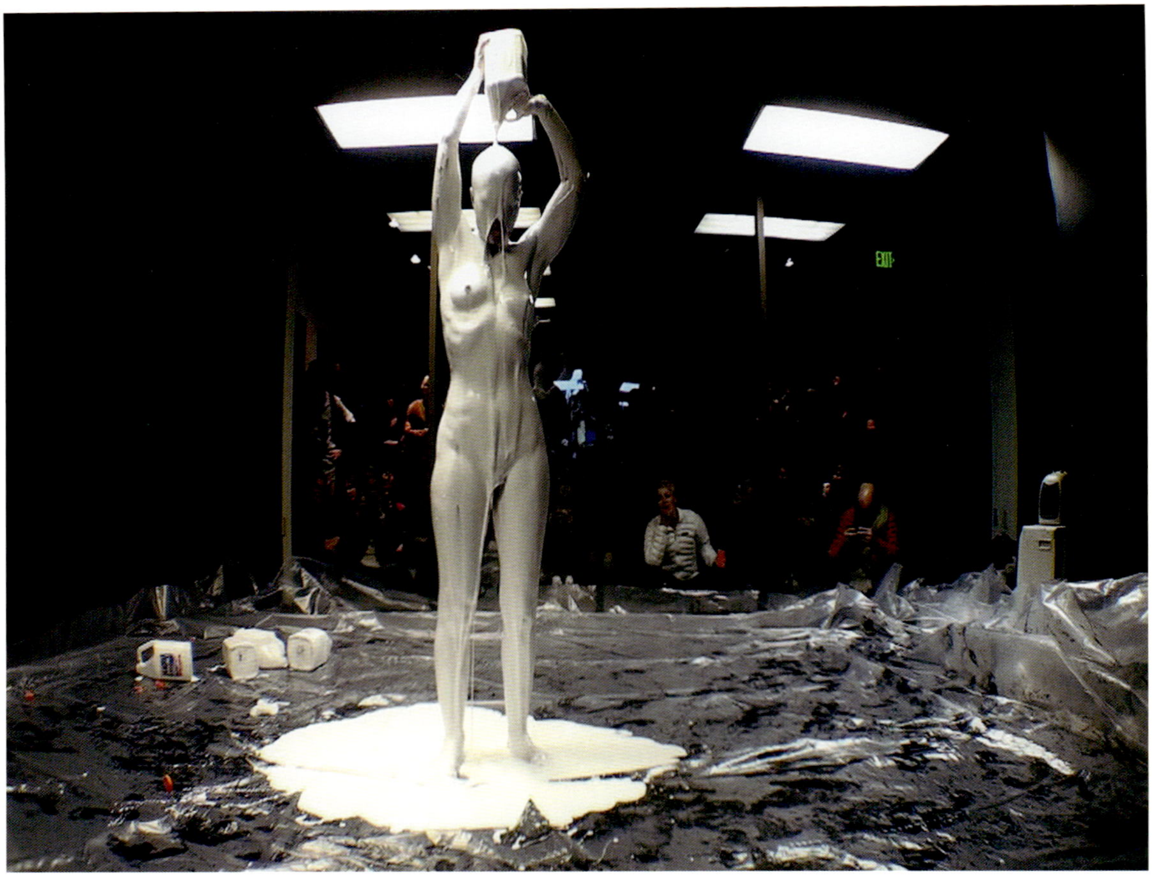

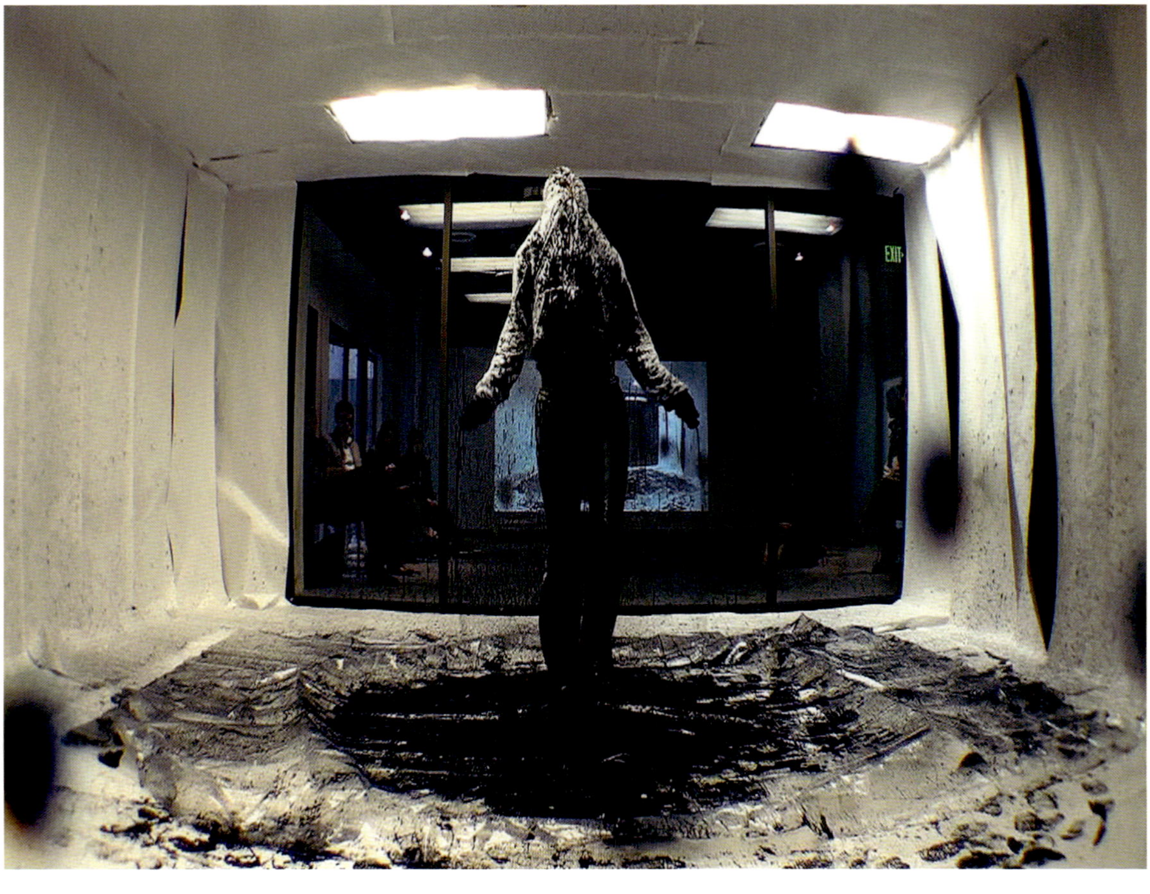

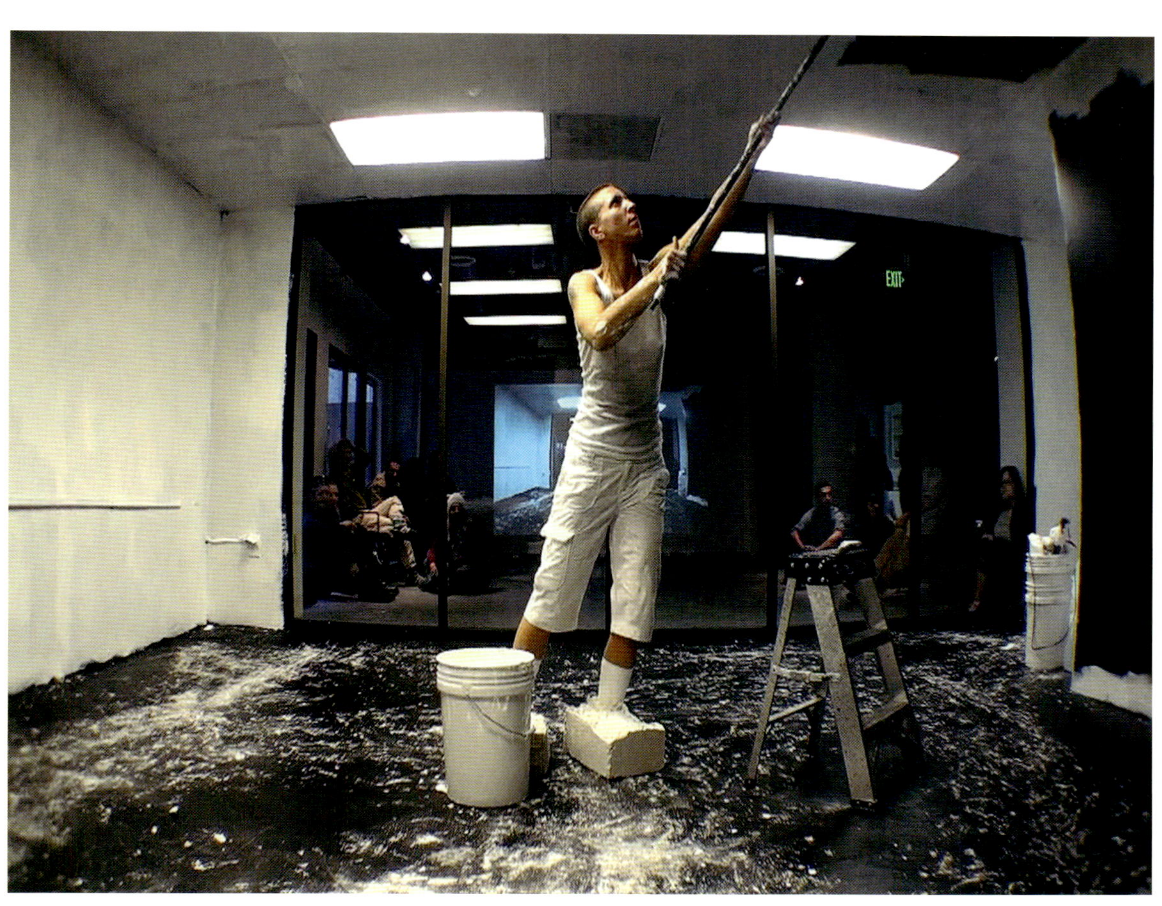

Opposite
***Black/White (Glue)*, 2009** — cat. no. 88
***Black/White (Ink)*, 2009** — cat. no. 89

Above
***Black/White (Plaster)*, 2009** — cat. no. 90

Los Angeles Urban Rangers

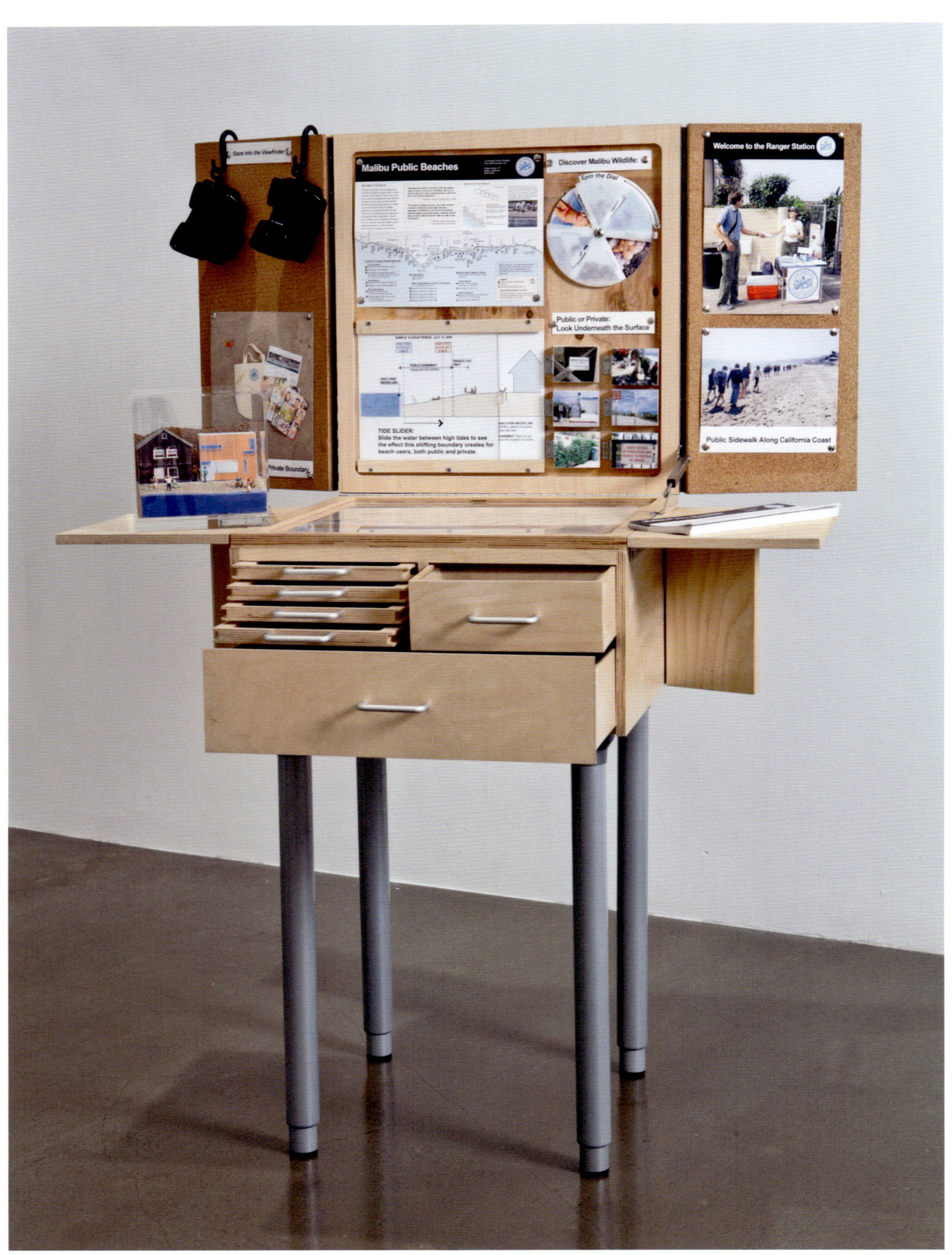

Portable Ranger Station, 2009–10 — cat. no. 92

Interview conducted by Chloë Flores with senior rangers Jenny Price, Emily Scott, and Therese Kelly

CF : Your project for the biennial is part of your Public Access 101 series, in which information and tours are provided to the public in locations in the city where public space may be contested, generally unknown, or underutilized. The biennial will kick off *Public Access 101: Downtown L.A.* First, what is your interest in expanding experience-based knowledge? Second, what makes this project different from the tours and programs already offered by the Los Angeles Conservatory or the Community Redevelopment Agency?

JP : Actually, this program won't be entirely about public access, but we're definitely interested in that, as any ranger would be. Los Angeles has a long history of privileging private spaces over public—probably more than any other major American city. And downtown—the city's center, historically, geographically, and in lots of other ways—has no major public park space. It's extraordinary and emblematic of L.A.'s problems with public space generally. The difference between us and some other programs, I think—which are great—is that we're really more about experiencing public spaces as public rather than talking about or explaining these issues around public space. Our *Malibu Public Beaches* project is a good example. We didn't emphasize the hugely contentious debates over whether people should use these public lands that are adjacent to private development—and that so often have been treated as private. We just named and treated them as public, which they are. We didn't emphasize the conflict. We just facilitated the use of these essential and well-loved public spaces. And the ranger figure is a great way to do that. Rangers are guardians of public lands.

ES : Our interest in expanding experience-based knowledge stems from a basic belief in the power of on-site observation and interaction to render meaningful insights into actual places. Which is not to say that the complexity of any given site is readily apparent upon first glance (which is certainly not the case), but much can be gleaned from creative, collective looking, and site-based experiences often form a strong starting point for investigating the contemporary urban landscape. We see ourselves largely as facilitators who aim to get people out into the city (and generally to familiar places within it) in order to provoke new questions and ways of engaging and imagining it. As you suggest, there are many examples of urban-focused programming by non-art groups in Los Angeles, and we take seriously the question of whether or not our work productively fills gaps in this constellation. One way our tours differ from those led by more straightforward entities is in their use of metaphor and performance to stress the unfixed, heterogeneous nature of places. I should add that while we have, to date, operated primarily in art and academic contexts (e.g., we were "born" within the 2004 exhibition *The GardeLAb Experiment* at Art Center College of Design and have since responded to various invitations by art and academic institutions to produce/share our work), we are increasingly inclined to "site" our work outside these spheres and to think about it in relation to non-art activities (e.g., public lands management, nonprofit environmental education, community planning) rather than first and foremost as art making.

TK : Certainly the types of things that we interpret and give guidance to are quite different from the itineraries of more traditional groups and tend to be open-ended or full of questions rather than answers. In addition to being site-based, there's also an interactive aspect that drives the experience so that, as Emily said, the collective looking or wondering becomes part of the experiential learning.

CF : Why has the group chosen the ranger model as a way to communicate the ideas and issues you're interested in?

JP : Well, we love the ranger character for lots of reasons. First of all, we want to take all that wonder and curiosity that folks bring with them to Yosemite and Yellowstone—and all that enthusiasm that a ranger exudes for how the world works—and bring it to the everyday places where we live. The ranger is also a guardian of nature, so we can interpret cities as places of nature—which they are. The ranger is wonderfully nonjudgmental and nonthreatening, and also is all about mobilizing folks to explore the world.

ES : There is an overlap between our central domain of interest (i.e., landscape systems) and that of the park ranger. Whereas rangers typically focus on places deemed "natural," however, our own work explores everyday built environments and the ways in which "nature" and "culture" are mutually produced. Initially, adopting the ranger persona was an experiment: to see how recontextualizing the lens and language of such a figure might help to rethink the city. Now, several years into the project, we are still discovering new facets of the character; for instance, how the ranger's "down-to-earth" and hospitable nature can be effective in disarming audiences and stimulating meaty exchanges, including about controversial spatial issues. We also like the ranger's connotations of public service and stewardship.

TK : I would just add that the ranger is a very recognizable figure who is also quite accessible, and I think these qualities enable participants to enter the work quite readily, without a great need for preface.

CF : Your projects call for your audience to actively engage in exploring notions of public and private space in Los Angeles and surrounding areas. Why is this participatory model an important aspect of your practice?

JP : This is absolutely central to our practice. We are less interested in telling people what to do and how to think about places, and incredibly interested in mobilizing people to explore and interpret and ask questions themselves. Like a lot of like-minded collectives in L.A. just now, we want to make it possible for folks to experience the often-invisible connections to people and nature that make places happen and to literally act out those connections.

ES : The subject of public space does not, in fact, cohere our work as a whole, although it is clearly a core theme in the Public Access 101 series that we are building upon during our residency with the 2010 California Biennial. I do think it's true, however, that all of our projects prioritize participation and specifically encourage people to become more participatory in the places around them, whether by way of small acts of discovery or active, civic involvement in spatial politics and planning. One way we do this is to foreground interactive exercises in our works. For example, we once invited people to an empty lot at the corner of Sunset and Alvarado to hike the site and then, around a campfire, informally discuss patterns of urban development in Los Angeles. In conjunction with a project on the Interstate Highway System, we developed a field kit and activity booklet for road trippers, meant in part to explode a "scenic viewpoint" mode of tourism. Our recent Malibu safaris largely hinged upon group exercises such as a no-kill access way hunt, trailblazing the public-private boundary hike, and public easement potluck.

TK: The participatory aspect is essential to what I'd call "site activation." And by that I mean that the content of our work and explorations is conveyed through the actual medium of the participants. Hollywood Boulevard becomes a trail only when people are actually hiking it; the beaches in Malibu become public only when they are embodied by the public. By inviting people to activate a site, we engage them in a networked view of our everyday environment: we make the world, and the world makes us. Our urban habitat is nature, and we are a part of that nature.

So I wouldn't actually call them "audience," as you do. They are equally the performers. Also, we're not limited to public space as a topic or even to Los Angeles as a site. Public space is one of many invisible systems and hidden infrastructures that we have looked at, but the interpretive model is broad enough that we've been able to research and engage a diverse set of trajectories of the everyday (waste systems of the L.A. County Fair and mating rituals on Hollywood Boulevard, among others). And while we are based in L.A.—and certainly founded on a sense of looking and uncovering that is grounded in L.A.—the interpretive framework is portable enough that we have given programs in such places as New York, Stockholm, the Netherlands, and the U.S. interstates.

CF: **Much of your practice involves remapping a city's urban and surrounding spaces (placing your group art historically in line with other artist groups, such as the Situationist International). Can you talk a little about the map as a tool for exploration and as point of entry into your work?**

ES: Maps can be a concise tool for reframing information or representing interpretive overlays. They also possess a very different temporality than events and so for us have often served as a residue of our programming, not to mention a means to disseminate it to broader audiences over time. Of course, producing maps is also part of our mimicry of the National Park Service and its fabulous-looking guides, with their unmistakable black band, Helvetica font, geological diagrams, wildlife photographs, etc. I actually think the Situationist International reference is rather remote, as that group developed a specific mode of mapping based on their concepts of the *dérive* and psychogeography, which were part and parcel of their critique of postwar urbanism in Paris. Ours, by contrast, is more generally about recontextualization. (Incidentally, we were once asked to perform a *dérive* in Hollywood in connection with a one-day event at LACE and can highly recommend hitting Hollywood Boulevard with a fistful of Situationist manifestos and trail mix in hand.)

TK: Maps help our project immensely by giving us a medium to literally make visual many of the invisible or overlooked

systems and infrastructures at play in our urban landscape. They complement our guided hikes and, as Emily said, exist beyond the project as an "event" by continuing to facilitate individual exploration and wonder. I think maps are a unique medium in that they are not only a tool for documenting space but also have the ability to create new spatial relationships that may not have existed before. In this sense, I think the Situationist reference is relevant: By juxtaposing nonadjacent sections of Paris, *The Naked City* made spatial that group's practice of wandering. Likewise I think our maps contextualize our urban hikes. Unlike those of the Situationists, however, our maps aren't fictionalized. Maps inherently convey a sense of authority of fact, and we try very hard to ensure accuracy of the information depicted on our maps. Also, the maps are not stand-alones; they are always part of a guide that includes an informative frame, diagrams, and additional resources.

Maps and guides are just one of our tools to facilitate exploration. We also use interpretive field kits, specimen collecting, questionnaires, activity books, props, and of course guided hikes.

CF: **You are one of two artist collectives invited to be in this year's biennial as part of the residency program. How does your practice function within the residency format as opposed to being invited to participate in a thematic exhibition that already places your work in a broader contemporary art historical context?**

JP: Well, a couple of things. First, our practice is emphatically place-based. We really insist on being specific about the places we interpret and explore—and it's a lot more effective to do that if you're actually on the ground, in the place itself. And also, we emphasize interaction and experience. The residency program—as opposed to a static exhibition inside a museum space—allows us to contribute a project that's both place-based and experiential. Although, in general, any museum itself is a space that's more than worthy of exploration—in which case, here we come with our hats!

ES: This is the second residency we've undertaken, the first being at the Museum de Paviljoens in Almere, the Netherlands, in 2008. Because a majority of our labor is devoted to researching specific sites and developing related programming and tools, the residency format is rather ideal. Residencies (whether at a local art institution or in a distant national park) afford a group such as ours the time and funding to focus our attention on new work and the (often slow) collaborative process necessary to achieve it.

TK: I'm grateful to have the opportunity to work in residency. It's a great match for the type of work we do because it moves the conversation away from object making and gives us a temporal and spatial moment to interpret. It really becomes a catalyst for our collaborative efforts.

CF: **Anything else to add?**

JP: We want people to have a lot of fun. It's very important to our practice. And we like wearing the hats. You would too. ∎

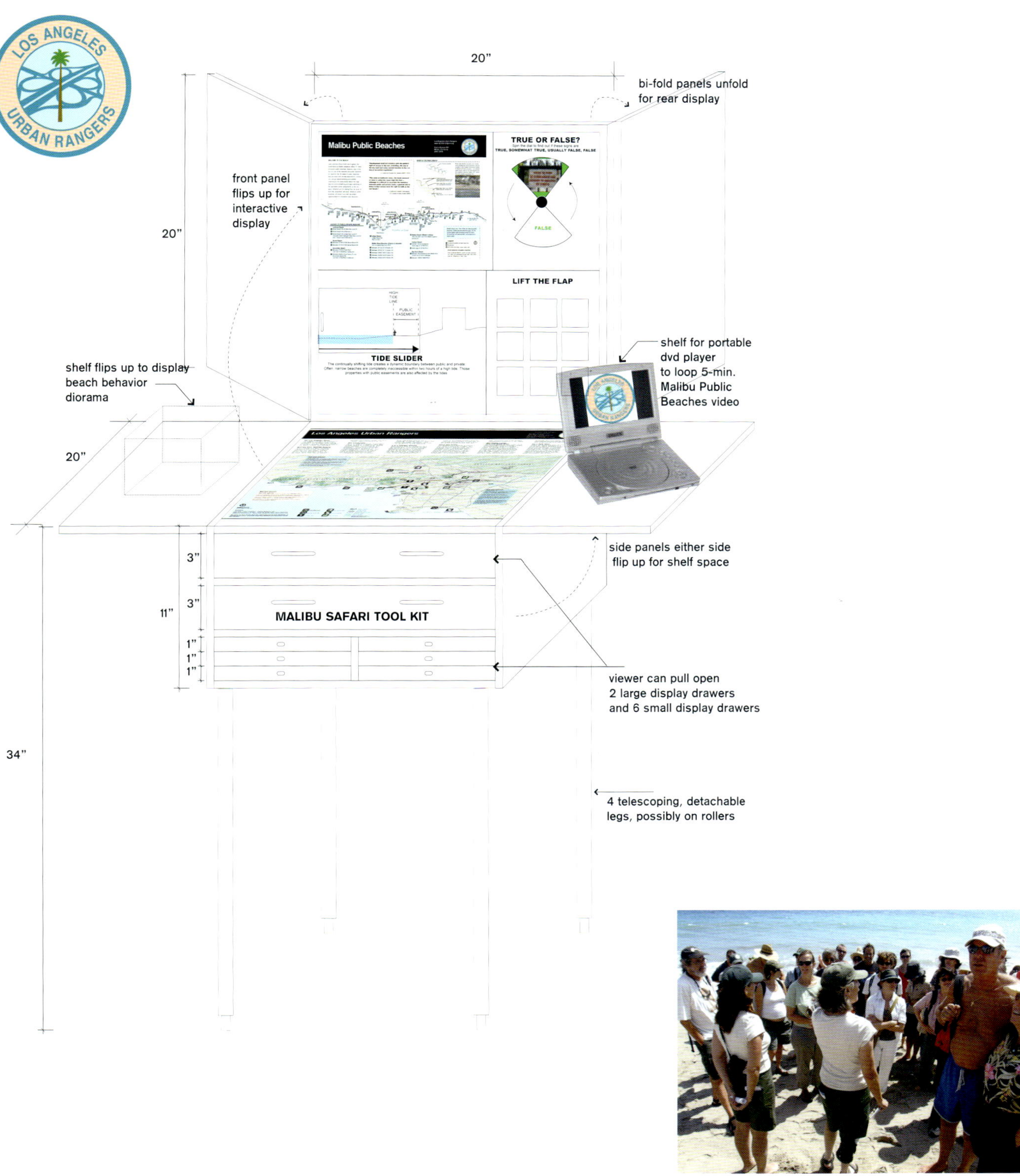

Above
Los Angeles Urban Rangers Official Logo, 2004
Portable Ranger Station (diagram), August 2009

Right
Public Access 101: Malibu Public Beaches, 2007–10 — cat. no. 91

Los Angeles Urban Rangers (LAUR), founded in 2004, is an interdisciplinary collective including artists, writers, architects, and geographers. The Rangers are Nicholas Bauch (b. 1978, Rochester, Minnesota); Sara Daleiden (b. 1975, Waukesha, Wisconsin); Therese Kelly (b. 1972, Pittsburgh); Ron Milam (b. 1975, Torrance, California); Jenny Price (b. 1960, St. Louis); Emily Scott (b. 1971, Bluffton, Indiana); and Sara Wookey (b. 1972, Columbus, Ohio).

Tom Mueske

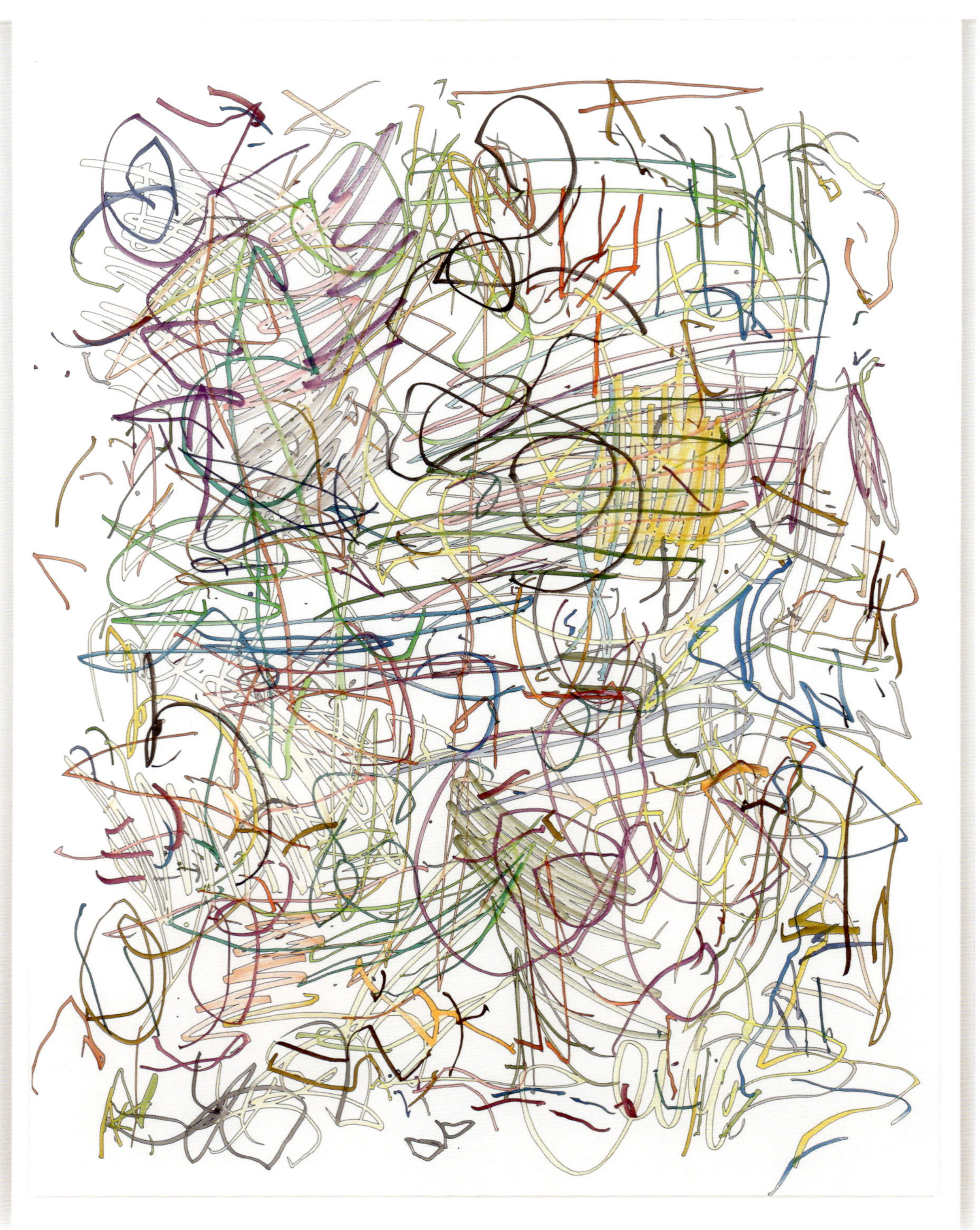

Untitled, 2010 — cat. no. 101

Interview with Grant Wahlquist

GW: Your previous work was largely executed with paint, but you recently transitioned to making drawings almost exclusively. What brought about this shift in medium? Is there something about the practice of drawing that is more conducive to creating the sort of pictures you're interested in? Communicating a specific idea or experience to the viewer?

TM: I started making works on paper because of the immediacy of drawing. I feel that drawing is more personal and universal than other media. Everyone can relate to the technical facility needed to make a drawing—it's not mysterious. Drawing with ink on paper is unforgiving and vulnerable. Works on paper are also less aggressive objects than paintings or sculpture. These sensitive qualities that drawings possess are communicated quietly. They are provocative.

GW: You initially approach a piece by making marks with colored markers and then outlining them, which creates a striking push-pull between the formal and the informal or accidental. How are the initial marks made to create this quality? Is the idea of the accidental something of interest to you? What function does it serve?

TM: When I begin the drawings with colored markers, I attempt to perform gestures that are sincere and genuine. I often make marks with my wrong hand or behind my back. This removes any expectations of what is "good" or "bad" that I might bring to the work. I then begin the labor-intensive process of outlining the marks with black ink. The outline preserves, modifies, and reiterates the original act and ultimately transforms it.

I am interested in accidental and inadvertent moments at the studio. When you try to create art, all you are doing is wasting time making decorative ornaments. I am very aware of this paradox. The function of working in an unpremeditated manner is to be unrestricted and give myself honest opportunities to make art. Simultaneously it is imperative to have strict parameters. Without order there is no chaos.

GW: There's obviously a visual similarity between your work and that of artists who can loosely be thought of as modern. Is there an intentional engagement with the traditions of modernism going on? If so, what traditions? Abstract expressionism? Minimalism? Or is the idea of "engaging with a tradition," inasmuch as it involves notions of influence/reference/relevance, something you're intentionally seeking to avoid?

TM: I attempt to create work that relates to both the provisional nature of contemporary art and the historic tradition of abstraction. I do that through my choice of materials and process. I wouldn't say that there is an intentional engagement, rather a natural disposition to minimal ideas. I don't consider myself an abstract artist—I illustrate abstraction. I avoid representation in favor of pure labor that promotes a visual experience. I think of myself more as a literalist. I make works on cotton with ink—there's nothing abstracted.

The idea of "engaging with a tradition" is something that is unavoidable. It's not just a problem specific to abstract art. Instead it's a condition that all contemporary artists must face, regardless of media. The process of negotiating and sorting through the discount bins of art history is vital to the process of making relevant work.

GW: I was thinking the other day about the dearth of criticism in major art publications dealing with abstraction. Even when you do see it, it involves some sort of sociopolitical contextualization. Nobody seems to strictly engage with the work itself. Is there something about emphatically abstract work that makes it inherently difficult to write or speak about today?

TM: Artists and writers have a hard time engaging abstract work because no one knows what it means. All abstract work made today is derivative, in some way, of an earlier period. It's unavoidable. It's also impossible to articulate a visual experience with an object that exerts a life force.

When inherently abstract work is topically contextualized, the work doesn't change, but the press release does. This again is a problem not just with abstract art but with all art today. It's equally difficult to convey the experience involved with a conceptual project as it is with abstract art—if you want to talk about the work and not just the theory.

GW: I noticed a copy of a Richard Tuttle catalog in your studio. I once went to see Tuttle's work with a date, who remarked that it seemed really dumb, like something anybody could do—yet Tuttle is so cerebral to me, so formal. Do you consider yourself a formalist? And in what sense?

TM: Historically a formalist deemphasizes content in artwork. Roberta Smith suggests that we confuse "content" with "subject matter," and abstraction always has content, though it lacks subject. I don't think one can create or destroy content—it's always there. Not having an opinion is still an opinion. I think art is a form of pure decision making, and every decision made has its own connotations. Nonobjective work is an analytical reaction to something external or internal. I like to think of what I do as risky conservatism. ∎

Born 1981 in Worthington, Minnesota; lives and works in Los Angeles. Mueske attended the University of Northern Iowa (BFA, 2005) and the San Francisco Art Institute (MFA, 2007), where he received a Graduate Fellowship Award. His work has been exhibited at the San Jose Institute of Contemporary Art; the Jones Center for Contemporary Art, Austin, Texas; and the Center on Contemporary Art, Seattle. His work was the subject of solo exhibitions at the University of Northern Iowa, Cedar Falls, in 2010, and at Haines Gallery, San Francisco, in 2008.

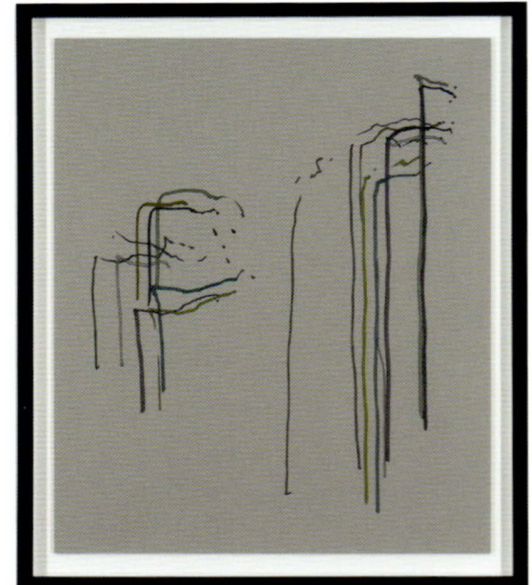

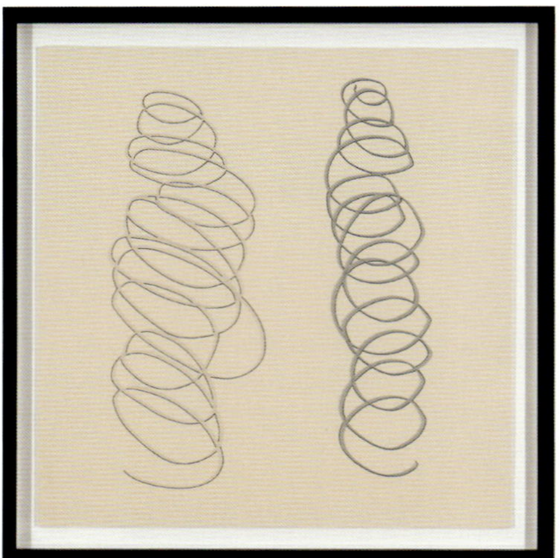

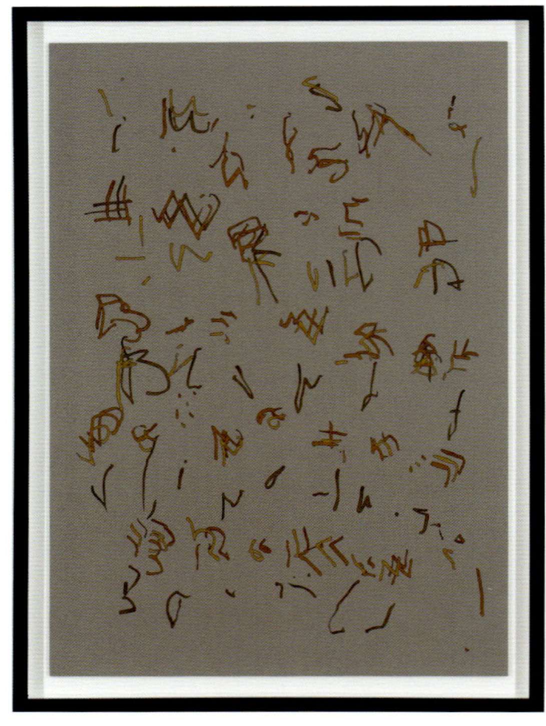

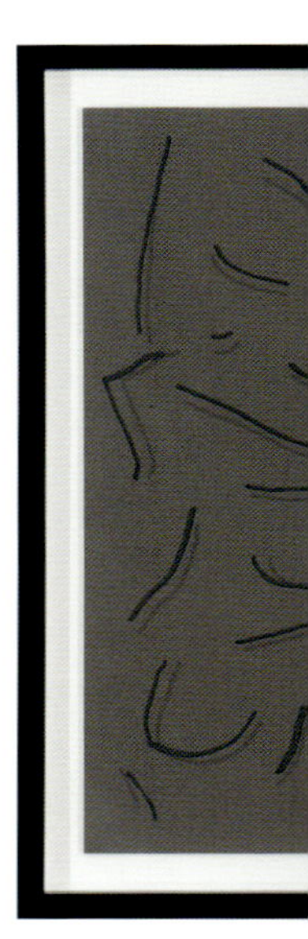

Analytics VII, **2010** — cat. no. 100
Analytics VI, **2010** — cat. no. 99
Analytics V, **2010** — cat. no. 98
Analytics IV, **2010** — cat. no. 97
Analytics III, **2010** — cat. no. 96
Analytics II, **2010** — cat. no. 95
Analytics I, **2010** — cat. no. 94

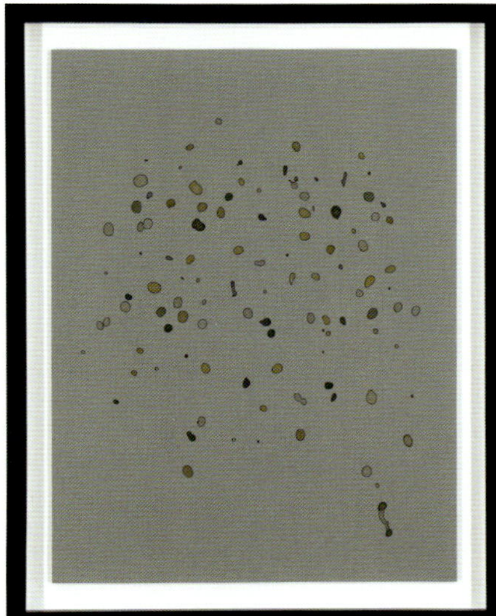

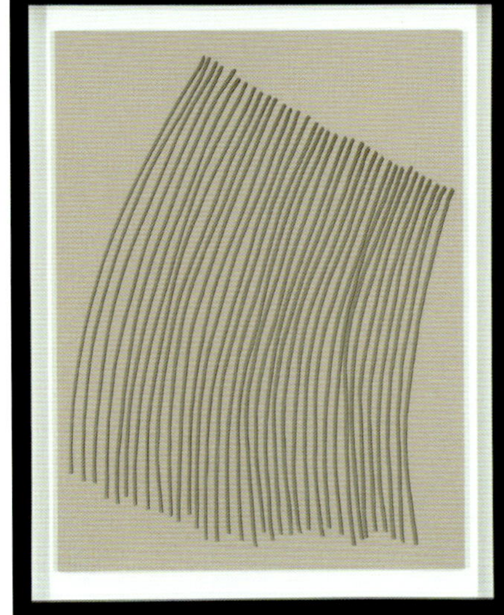

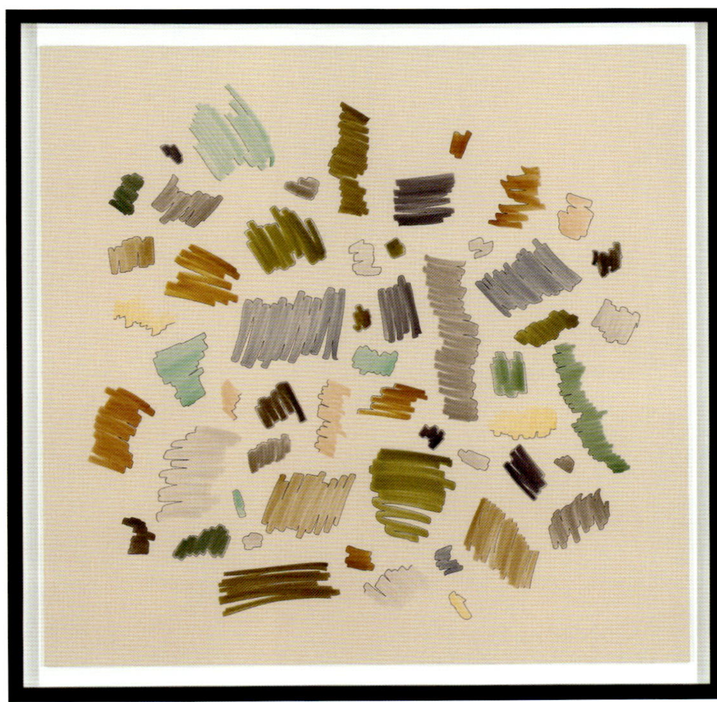

Tucker Nichols

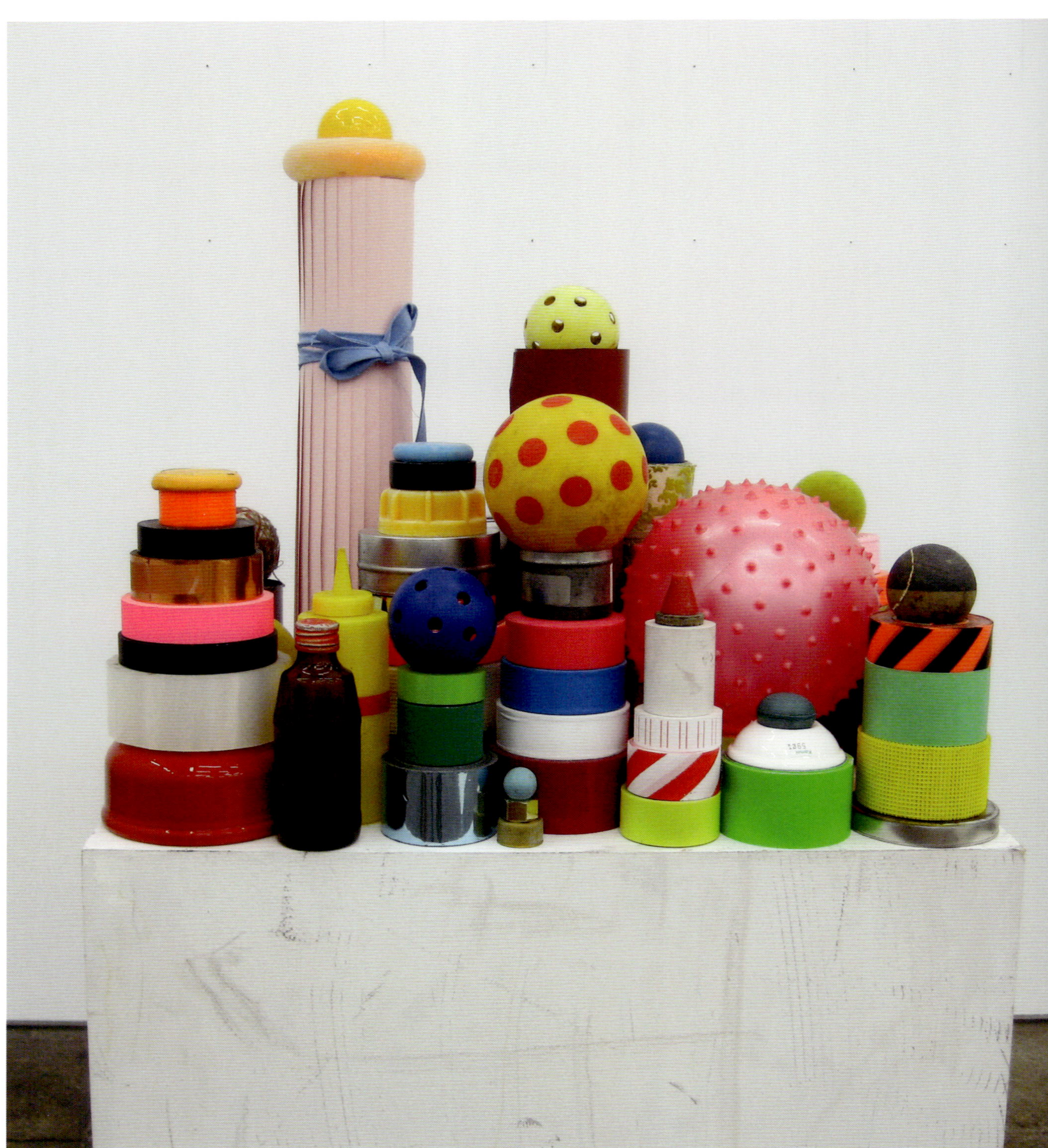

Untitled, 2010 — cat. no. 102

SB: **There's a certain comic whimsy and simple wisdom throughout your work. The drawings as well as the text-based works often involve subtle institutional critique, tempered with humor. People can walk by without getting it, or it can hit a mental target and deliver its message immediately. Talk to me. What's going on here?**

TN: I can't really say anything about the effect of what I make on other people or really what any of it means. I'm aware of a viewing public to an extent, but at the end of the day the only audience I can trust is me. The world feels really big and absurd to me; it's impossible to take it all in, and yet that's exactly what we're trying to do. I feel it when I read the paper or when I get lost on the Internet or drive by a giant shopping mall. The only response that feels right to me is the things I end up making. Maybe I prefer low-tech, handmade responses because they feel more human. But I can't describe what I like about what I make any more than I can describe why I like certain music. And I make plenty of work that I really don't like at all. My batting average is pretty low, all told.

SB: **You came out of a background in Chinese history and philosophy. Relevant?**

TN: Not particularly, although I still think about Chinese painting, and I like to look at great examples. I still get chills. One thing I've taken away from studying that world is that traditionally there was very little distinction between artists, scholars, poets, collectors, and even government officials. They were often all the same people. I find the boundaries we operate within today to be pretty arbitrary. Today's art world is a strange ecosystem. I suppose some rules make sense, but it could use a good flushing.

SB: **A large part of your practice now is creating work for reproduction in magazines, journals, and newspapers—** *McSweeney's* **and the** *New York Times***, for instance. How is the work in, say, the** *New York Times* **distinct from works produced in a residency or as part of your studio practice, if at all?**

TN: Of course the format is different in print, and the audience is much more varied than in a gallery or a museum. But the practice of making the work is really the same for me. The printed page is just another exhibition space. Working in different media forces me to think about new projects as if for the first time. I've made drawings for fancy underwear designs too. I just needed to know what it would feel like. It felt really good actually.

SB: **Yes, I saw those polka-dot-ish underpants at your residency space at the Headlands. I thought: Wow, the pattern on that pair of ladies' underwear looks just like something he'd make. I guess that's why he strung them up on the wall in here! Wrong.**

TN: Even though I'm drawn to the same forms—text, buildings, stripes, monuments, and so on—when I change the format, the whole experience of making the thing changes for me. There's a big difference between a line drawing framed in a gallery and a pair of panties made from my printed lines on an otherwise naked body. I want to know more about why the differences feel so pronounced.

SB: **If there were a brilliantly misguided or misinformed character creating banners for OCMA, whom would he be hoping to reach? What would he be hoping to do or achieve in Orange County during the biennial?**

TN: When I came down to visit the museum, I was struck by the surrounding environment. I've never been to a museum that's so close to a big mall; it feels like it's surrounded on all sides. Before I got a good look at the galleries, I walked to the mall to get a quick cup of tea. It was bustling with people and strollers and all kinds of social activity, and I got lost in it. I was totally spun around, and I think I kept walking by the same fountain. By the time I found my way back to the museum, it was closed. I sat outside on the lawn and drank my tea and thought about what I wanted to do for the show. It felt kind of perfect, actually.

I like to use vague alter egos as a way of guiding decisions for work I'm making, particularly when it's designed for a particular place. Orange County is a place I don't know very well, so the idea of making signage here is appealing. I'm picturing someone who was assigned to paint new signs at the mall and got the address wrong. I found the text for these banners here in California; they relate back to ideas I have about living in California, about the dreams that brought us all here and the reality of what this place is actually like. I love living here; it's a land where anything is possible, but it's a really weird place.

SB: **So that explains the banner pieces, at least to some extent. Can you speak more particularly about the huddle of objects on the scraped-up pedestal?**

TN: I've been collecting tape and balls and bottles for many years now. They populate my life, and I always have some combination of them around. The trunk of my car has at least five balls in it for improvised bocce games with my brother, and the tape comes from all over: a stationery store in Bangkok, a roll of electrical tape washed up on the beach. One day in my studio I collected a pile of these things—this time all the really colorful ones—and just started playing around and piling them up. What would an arrangement like this be for? A proposal for a city of the future by an architect who didn't know CAD? A description of life undersea for someone who'd never been snorkeling? A mass of improvised trophies? In the end it feels just as hopeful and just as futile as many of my deepest feelings and ideas. It's satisfying to make something that contains both optimism and failure for some reason. Again, very Californian somehow. ∎

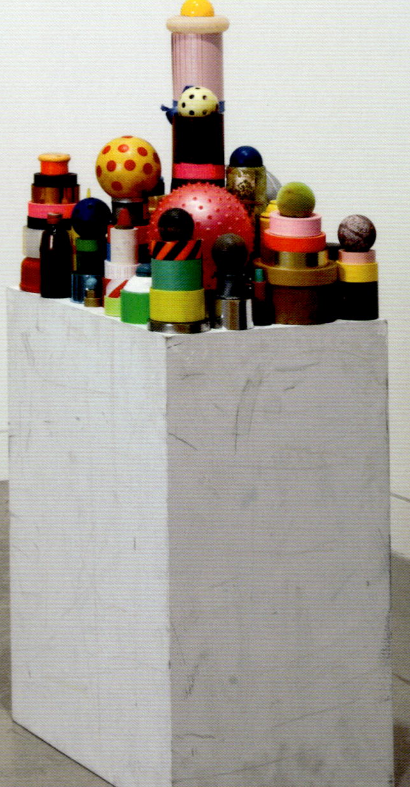
SHAPE
UP &
SAVE

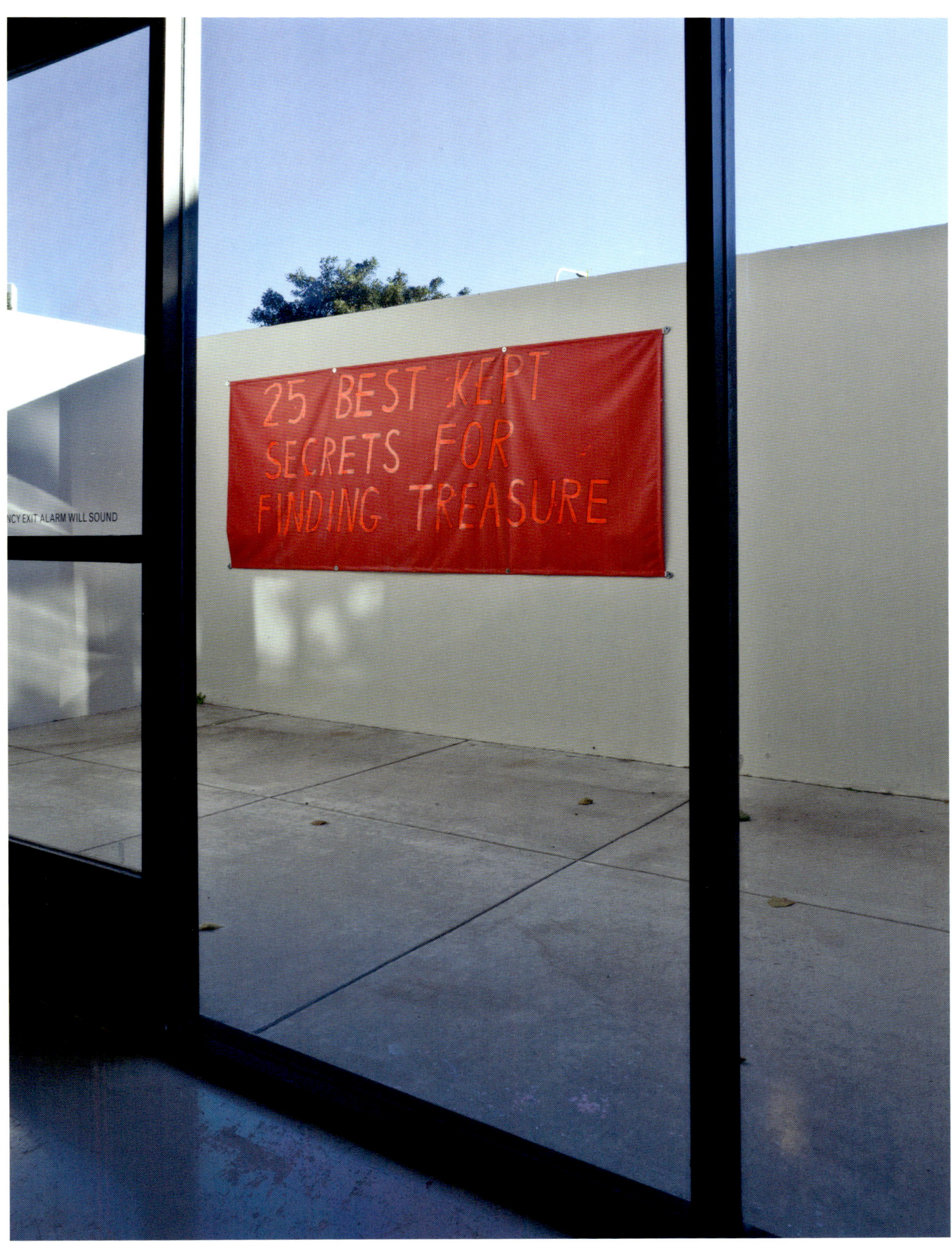

Untitled, 2010 — cat. no. 103
Untitled, 2010 — cat. no. 102

Untitled, 2010 — cat. no. 104

Camilo Ontiveros

On April 23, 2010, in the State of Arizona, law SB 1070 was passed.
A portion of the law states:

> FOR ANY LAWFUL CONTACT MADE BY A LAW ENFORCEMENT OFFICIAL OR AGENCY OF THIS STATE OR A COUNTY, CITY, TOWN OR OTHER POLITICAL SUBDIVISION OF THIS STATE WHERE REASONABLE SUSPICION EXISTS THAT THE PERSON IS AN ALIEN WHO IS UNLAWFULLY PRESENT IN THE UNITED STATES, A REASONABLE ATTEMPT SHALL BE MADE, WHEN PRACTICABLE, TO DETERMINE THE IMMIGRATION STATUS OF THE PERSON. THE PERSON'S IMMIGRATION STATUS SHALL BE VERIFIED WITH THE FEDERAL GOVERNMENT PURSUANT TO 8 UNITED STATES CODE SECTION 1373(C).

In response to this anti-immigration policy, my project for the 2010 California Biennial is the following OCMA Biennial law:

> WHERE REASONABLE SUSPICION EXISTS THAT A PERSON ENTERING THE MUSEUM IS AN ALIEN WHO IS UNLAWFULLY PRESENT IN THE UNITED STATES, A REASONABLE ATTEMPT SHALL BE MADE, WHEN PRACTICABLE, TO GRANT THIS PERSON FREE ACCESS TO THE MUSEUM DURING THE COURSE OF THE CALIFORNIA BIENNIAL.

> —Camilo Ontiveros

After considerable discussion among the staff and Board of Trustees, the Museum determined that it could not accommodate Camilo Ontiveros's request to grant free access to the museum during the course of the 2010 California Biennial as described in the artist's proposal. In so doing, the Museum would be placed in the position of discriminating on the basis of race or nationality. In addition to being contrary to the Museum's mission, values, and established policy, such practices are illegal in the State of California. Passed in 1959, the Unruh Civil Rights Act reads:

> ALL PERSONS WITHIN THE JURISDICTION OF THIS STATE ARE FREE AND EQUAL, AND NO MATTER WHAT THEIR SEX, RACE, COLOR, RELIGION, ANCESTRY, NATIONAL ORIGIN, DISABILITY, MEDICAL CONDITION, MARITAL STATUS, OR SEXUAL ORIENTATION ARE ENTITLED TO THE FULL AND EQUAL ACCOMMODATIONS, ADVANTAGES, FACILITIES, PRIVILEGES, OR SERVICES IN ALL BUSINESS ESTABLISHMENTS OF EVERY KIND WHATSOEVER.

> —Orange County Museum of Art

Free Entry (California Biennial Law), 2010 — cat. no. 105

**Interview conducted by Grant Wahlquist with
Camilo Ontiveros and Sarah Bancroft**

GW: It would be helpful to begin with a description of your project for the biennial, *Free Entry* (2010). And subsequently I was wondering if you could elaborate on why you chose the biennial in particular as a platform to respond to the controversy surrounding Arizona's immigration law SB 1070. I know that some other proposals were initially being pursued. How and why did the two of you ultimately decide to move ahead with *Free Entry*?

CO: My purpose in this project is to create a law that mirrors the absurdity of the Arizona law and questions its effect. What does this law mean within a society and its systems? What is the notion of the "alien" that it creates? *Free Entry* is not entirely about mirroring the Arizona law or turning it on its head. The project does not rely on its performance in the museum and whether it can happen or not. Rather, it highlights the racism that is permitted to occur in this "legal" system of governance, and it questions how people of color are treated within governmental structures. What this law brings to immigrant communities is fear. It criminalizes people, especially of Hispanic descent, and oppresses communities. It calls people "aliens," grouping them according to their so-called illegality rather than valuing their contribution to society.

While SB 1070 brings the aesthetics of citizenship and the formation of the "alien" to the forefront, the racism within American governance extends far beyond this one law. We see it exercised in the fence along the U.S.-Mexico border; we see it in treaties such as NAFTA, which put people in Mexico out of jobs because they cannot compete with American corporations and are forced to migrate in order to bring food to their families; we see it in the exploitation of undocumented labor; we see it in ICE raids that tear families apart. The fight against SB 1070 is just one among many in the struggle for immigration reform and human rights.

SB: Camilo presented several proposals for the biennial during a long studio visit. The fourth or fifth was a proposal for a museum admissions policy tentatively titled "free entry." He suggested that the museum admissions desk identify visitors who appear "Hispanic" and give them free entry to the museum. I immediately thought of Daniel J. Martinez's admissions tags reading "I can't imagine ever wanting to be white" for the 1993 Whitney Biennial as well as Michael Asher's admissions policy performed as part of this year's Whitney Biennial. Nonetheless, Camilo and I decided to include another project in the biennial, a project that he had first suggested during our initial studio visit. The more I thought about this selection, however, the more *Free Entry* was tugging at the worried seam of my choice, gnawing at me. The admissions policy simply had an urgency and a pertinence that couldn't be ignored. The museum administration was also on board with exploring this proposal, which was heartening. Camilo was in Mexico working on the original selection when I called to ask him to pursue *Free Entry* instead. He had come to the same conclusion independently, so we were in total agreement. The process was very simple, although it took place over a few months: Camilo provided an official project proposal,

and it went to our legal counsel for review and was presented at a board meeting for approval because of the legal implications. (This is quite unusual, as the board normally has no decision-making power in the curatorial process.) That was one of the most exhilarating board meetings I've attended, as people were fully engaged on both sides of the debate. There were strong questions and discussions about the work, not only from a legal standpoint but also regarding whether or not this was "art," a "performance piece," or a political statement. The power of the proposal and the process was demonstrated in that meeting.

At the board meeting, it was decided in no uncertain terms that the project could not proceed as written because it was legally untenable. This did not come as a surprise. Although we were given the green light to develop a "performance" in the spirit of the proposal that did not discriminate, Camilo ultimately determined that unless the project was realized to the letter of the proposal, it could not happen as an active admissions policy. He would not compromise on the details. This was neither a crisis nor an impasse, as the process of the proposal working its way through legal considerations and museum bureaucracy is the locus of the project.

GW: I'm very much interested in your creating a "law" that mirrors, inside the museum, a "real" law outside the museum. There seems to be an investigation of certain binaries: inside/outside, political/aesthetic, etc. Is that part of your intention? Or does abstracting the proposal from a concrete political situation move too far away from what would otherwise be a very specific engagement?

CO: The inside cannot exist without the outside, and politics cannot exist without aesthetics. *Free Entry* turns the language of the law on its head. It removes the Arizona law from the so-called field of politics to the field of aesthetics and, in doing so, reveals the mutual determination of politics and aesthetics. I'm working with the language, decontextualizing and recontextualizing the language of law. Everything we do in art is political, just as everything we do in politics is artistic.

GW: Did you both initially plan that the project would actually be executed, or did you foresee this problem? Either way, once it was clear that your proposal would not actually be executed, how did things change? For instance, how do you understand the relationship of your negotiations and conversations with the museum to the piece as a whole, Camilo? How did becoming a much more integral part of the piece work for you, Sarah? It's an interesting power shift—whereas the biennial involves the selection of work, in a way this piece reverses the flow and claims the museum.

CO: When I proposed the project and I was told that *Free Entry* would not happen because the museum thought that it was "unconstitutional" and that it would discriminate, I understood their response because it was one of the issues that I intended to bring up in the piece. It is important that an institution like the Orange Country Museum of Art take a political position in relation to SB 1070. This is especially true for a cultural institution in a place like Orange Country with a large right-wing Republican population and where anti-immigrant groups like the Minuteman

Project originated. OCMA is taking a position in relation to the Arizona law. All cultural institutions should do the same.

SB : Camilo presented a means to explore the legal and aesthetic concerns and limitations of the law, and I provided the forum. I'm really part of the system—the museum is the system—that Camilo has used to make his point.

The proposal was problematic, and I certainly knew that it was unlikely to be instituted precisely as written (although inside the museum we explored ways to randomize free entry in a fashion that was not discriminatory). Camilo and I never discussed a backup plan should the proposal "fail"; the success or failure of the proposal was never the motivating force for including this project. If it weren't going to be enacted as an admissions policy, we discussed posting Camilo's proposed biennial law as text on the wall, and he suggested including the museum's official response for declining the proposal on legal grounds as well. It's essentially shorthand for the whole process.

GW : **Gilles Deleuze and Félix Guattari once wrote, "Each failure is a masterpiece, a branch of the rhizome."[1] They made the statement in the context of literature, but it obviously has wider ramifications. The proposal was unable to be executed, but in the process it became something else that is arguably more interesting. Has the process of dealing with *Free Entry* changed how you understand a "successful" project?**

SB : I've been thinking a lot about exquisite failure. There must be room for failure, lapses, lacunae, and unpredictability when it comes to process. A good curator needs to get out of the way and let the work do the work. Moreover, the "failure" of *Free Entry* on constitutional grounds is also its success. It's okay not to know how something—a concept, a proposal—will work out. The reification of an idea is amorphous, and that's the strength of Camilo's practice. The reification of an idea has no bounds, no "route" to success or failure; it just is.

CO : To think about success and failure in a project predetermines its outcome. In my practice I leave the outcome open to change, and I accept that how it develops comes out of the many steps of the process. My process is dialogical. I often see myself as the middleman who presents a platform upon which things happen. With regard to *Free Entry*, this project has not ended. Any struggle is a process whose evolution gives life to the struggle. ■

Notes

1. Gilles Deleuze and Félix Guattari, *Kafka: Toward a Minor Literature* (Minneapolis: University of Minnesota Press, 1986), 39.

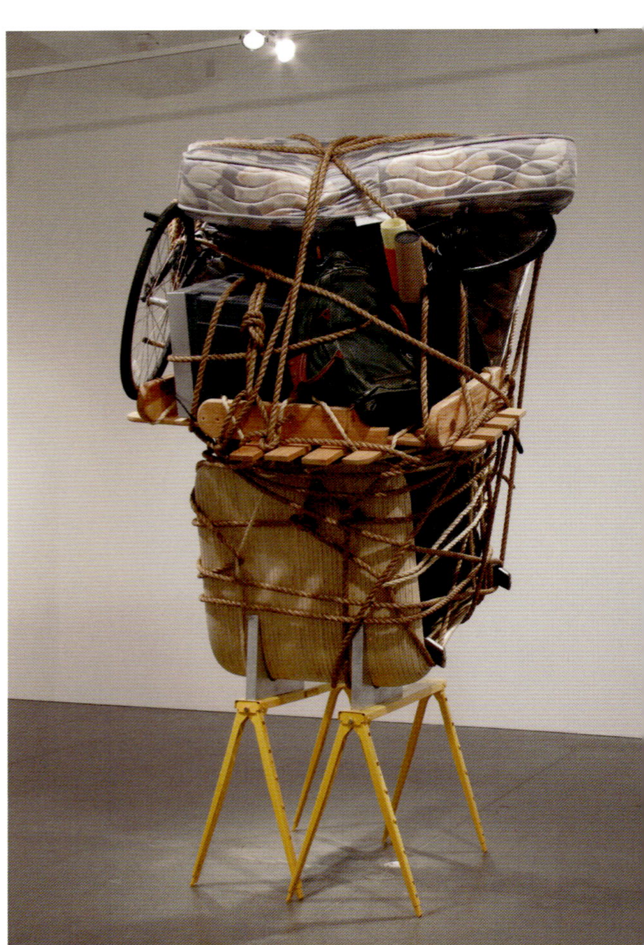

Born 1978, Rosario, Sinaloa, Mexico; lives and works in Los Angeles and Tepic, Nayarit, Mexico. Ontiveros graduated from the University of California, San Diego (BA, 2006), and the University of California, Los Angeles (MFA, 2009). He is cofounder of Lui Velazquez in Tijuana and of Salon Proceso, an art space in South Central Los Angeles. He has participated in exhibitions at Steve Turner Contemporary, Los Angeles; the Armory Center for the Arts, Pasadena, California; ARCO Madrid; LACE, Los Angeles; the National Museum of Mexican Art, Chicago; CECUT, Tijuana; Centro de la Imagen, Mexico City; and the Lab, San Francisco.

Temporary Storage, 2009
Personal belongings, 400 feet of rope, sawhorse, aluminum bases, and wooden sculpture
192 × 72 × 72 in. (487.7 × 182.9 × 182.9 cm)
Courtesy of the artist and Steve Turner Contemporary, Los Angeles
Installation view, Wight Gallery, University of California, Los Angeles

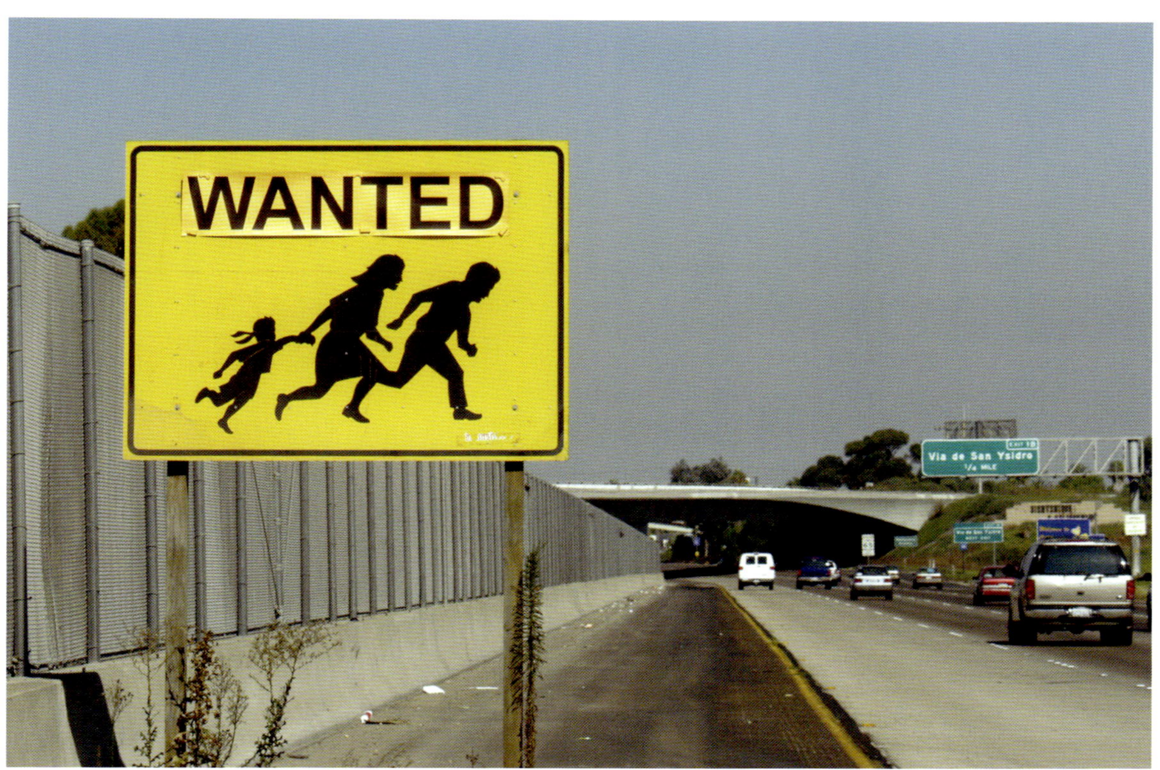

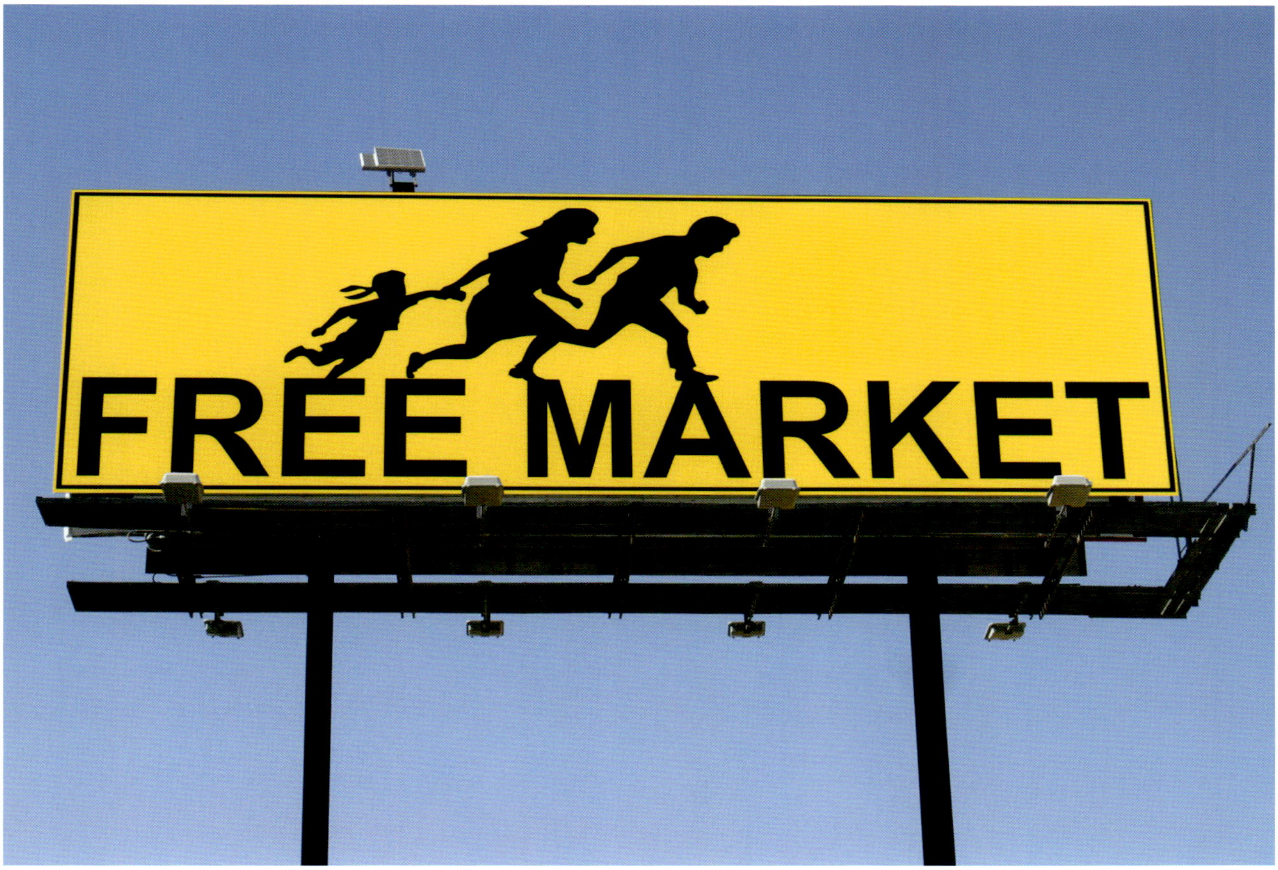

Top
***WANTED*, 2005**
From the project CAUTION
Freeway sign intervention
Courtesy of the artist and Steve Turner Contemporary, Los Angeles

Bottom
***FREE MARKET*, 2010**
From the project CAUTION
Billboard mock-up
Courtesy of the artist and Steve Turner Contemporary, Los Angeles

Nikki Pressley

Practice
Drawing, sculpture, installation, video, text, sound

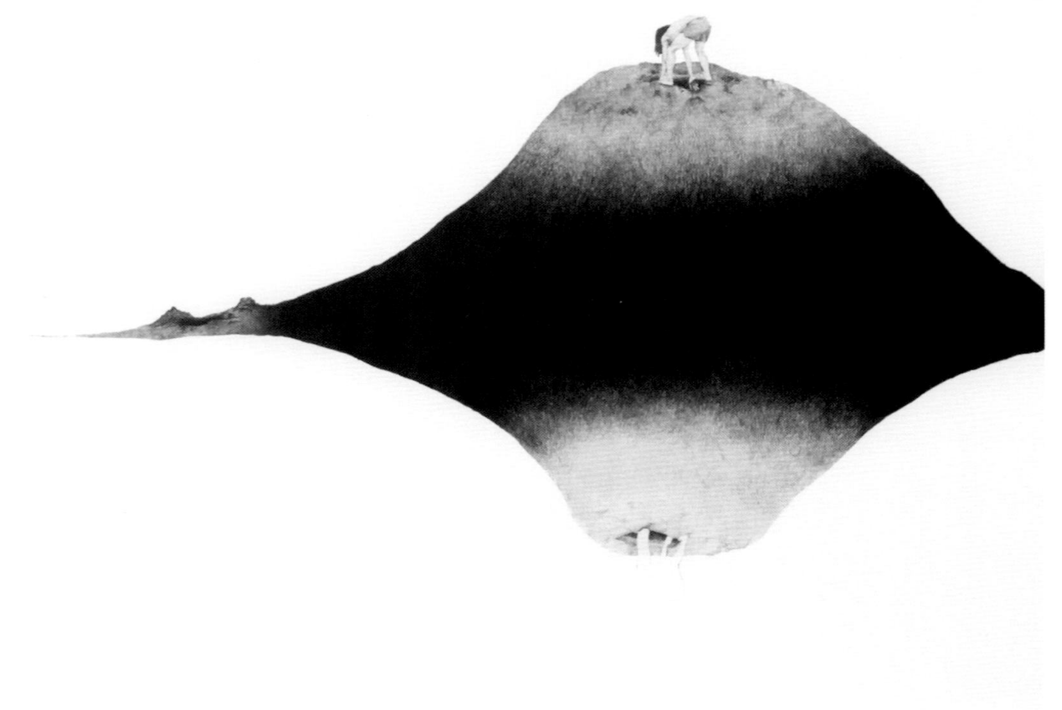

Requiem, **2010** — cat. no. 106

Interview with Grant Wahlquist

GW: Much of your work involves investigation of the history of various cultures. What is it about history as subject that attracts you? What sort of posture do you assume toward received histories?

NP: For me, history is a starting point for exploring community, society, and self. It is a crucial link to our present and future realities, a link that can be misrepresented and marginalized. I view history as a series of fluid narratives, some of which never see the light of day. It's these narratives and the linking and relinking that can occur that make history interesting, malleable, and relevant. I am very interested in the moments, personally and collectively, when history and memory intersect—the slipperiness of memory coupled with the unstable nature of histories— and how we locate ourselves within them and then derive meaning from the two.

I understand the term *received histories* to refer to the accepted or mainstream narratives of history. I believe that these histories should be viewed with a critical eye. The presentation of historical narratives is contentious ground, usually resulting in those with power having the final written word, making text and language all the more fascinating subjects to explore. What makes the past fascinating is that we constantly have the opportunity to recover histories and memories in ways that can be generative and transgressive in our present. By becoming involved in that process, we become timekeepers, shifting authority from more centralized structures of power.

GW: Could you tell me about your drawing *Word* (2010), which will appear in the biennial? How was the piece executed? What are the sources of the text, and why were they of interest to you?

NP: *Word* is a fifty-by-thirty-eight-inch graphite drawing with embossing. The work utilizes both sides of the paper and will be presented in a double-sided frame. The "front" of the drawing is a biblical text translated into the Gullah language. The Gullah people are direct descendants of slaves and reside in and around the Sea Islands, off the coast of South Carolina and Georgia. Their dialect is a hybrid of West African and English, which became a functional necessity for slaves arriving from West Africa and also a form of agency, an attempt to retain as much of their indigenous culture as possible. The Gullah people, like many colonial slaves at the time, adopted Christianity and have translated the New Testament into the Gullah dialect. The passage used, John 1:1, is a common Christian passage used to establish the deity and humanity of Christ, initiating the idea of the Trinity. The other text that is embossed into the paper is the beginning of an oral tale of Anansi the spider, a popular character in the African diasporic tradition. The embossed text takes on a ghostly quality, pointing to the elusive nature of traditions that pass information orally. The text itself and its treatment simultaneously represent an attempt at agency within a foreign system and the adoption of the language of that system for the purpose of survival. The pairing of the more rigid nature of the assimilated biblical text with the fluidity of an oral narrative points to a collision within culture that has direct effects on personal meaning and memory.

GW: The list of materials used in your untitled drawing of 2010, another work shown in the biennial, is quite interesting. Why did you select these particular materials for the drawing, and how do they inform the concerns of the piece?

NP: I am very interested in medieval manuscripts as early tools of communication and possibly even advertising. The issue of illiteracy is an interesting focal point for me, as many in medieval congregations had to rely upon visual language and aesthetics in order to comprehend the narratives and then locate their beliefs. The ash was from my own accumulation from months of incense burning and became a symbol of a reverent and meditative practice. The dirt destabilizes the gold, which represents ornamentation, illumination, and preciousness or value. It will be an agent of the degradation of that material over time, documented within the space of the frame. The natural materials symbolize the residue of a more private practice juxtaposed with the more symbolic and iconic reading attributed to the gold leaf.

GW: Your previous works were photorealistic drawings of protest images. The works to be shown in the biennial all deal with religious tradition in some way. On one level, there seems to be a turning "inward"—away from the political and toward the spiritual. Can you talk about what prompted this turn? What common concerns or strategies link this body of work with what came before?

NP: I think this "inward" turn was prompted by many factors. I was coming from a place of critically thinking about contemporary strategies and intentions of resistance and agency. I had spent so much time perceiving these historical movements on a macro level that the personal and more communal aspect became lost. At some point I began to see a parallel between cultural histories and religious practice. Both utilize particular icons (literal and figurative) and language in order to perpetuate themselves through generations. Collective memory is an important aspect of both, creating cohesiveness, shared understanding, and experience. I am interested in how the personal creation of meaning affects how we relate to and buy into a collective experience. Both bodies of work deal with a deep yearning for space, for belonging, for a language of your own to negotiate the world. ∎

Born 1982 in Greenville, South Carolina; lives and works in Los Angeles. A graduate of Furman University (BA, 2004) and California Institute of the Arts (MFA, 2008), Pressley has had solo exhibitions at Las Cienegas Projects, Los Angeles, and Mint Gallery, Valencia, California. She has participated in group exhibitions at the Torrance Art Museum, Torrance, California, and at Remy's, Coma Art Space, and Avenue 50 in Los Angeles. She is a contributor to the *Liberator Magazine*.

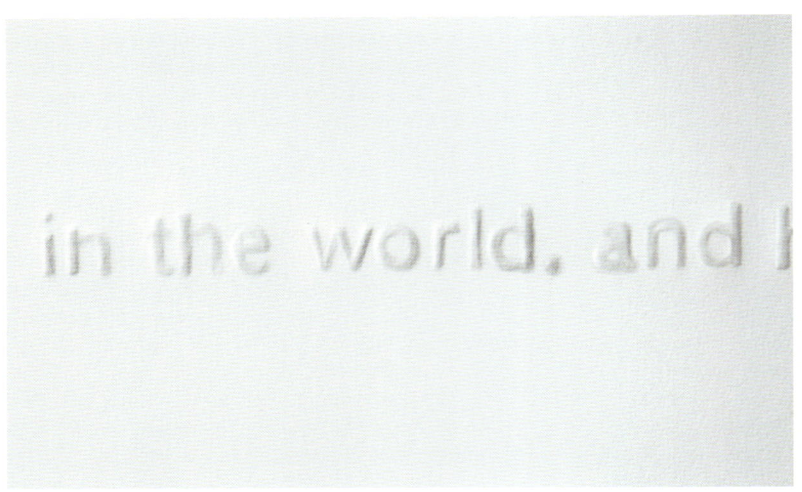

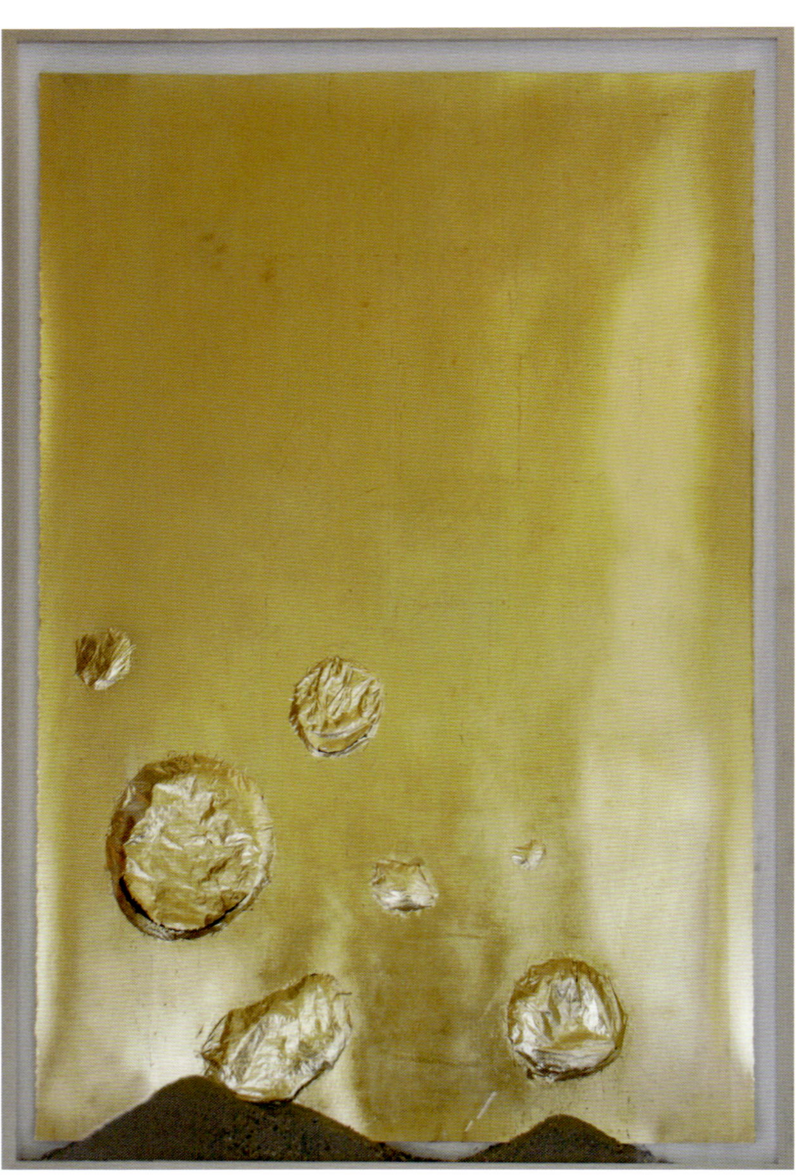

Above
***Word*, 2010** — cat. no. 108 (detail of back with embossed text)
Untitled, 2010 — cat. no. 107

Opposite
***Word*, 2010** — cat. no. 108 (front)

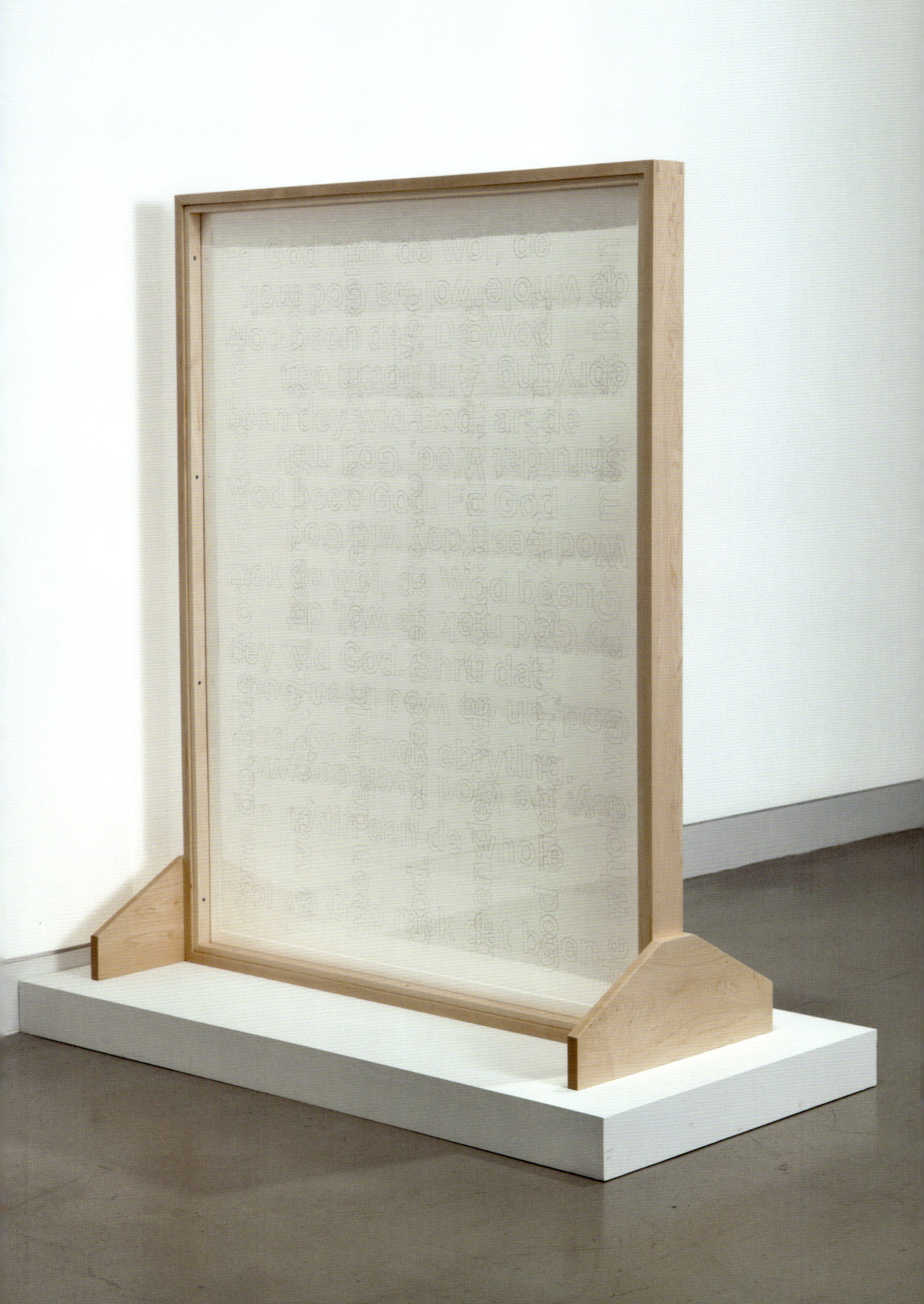

Andy Ralph

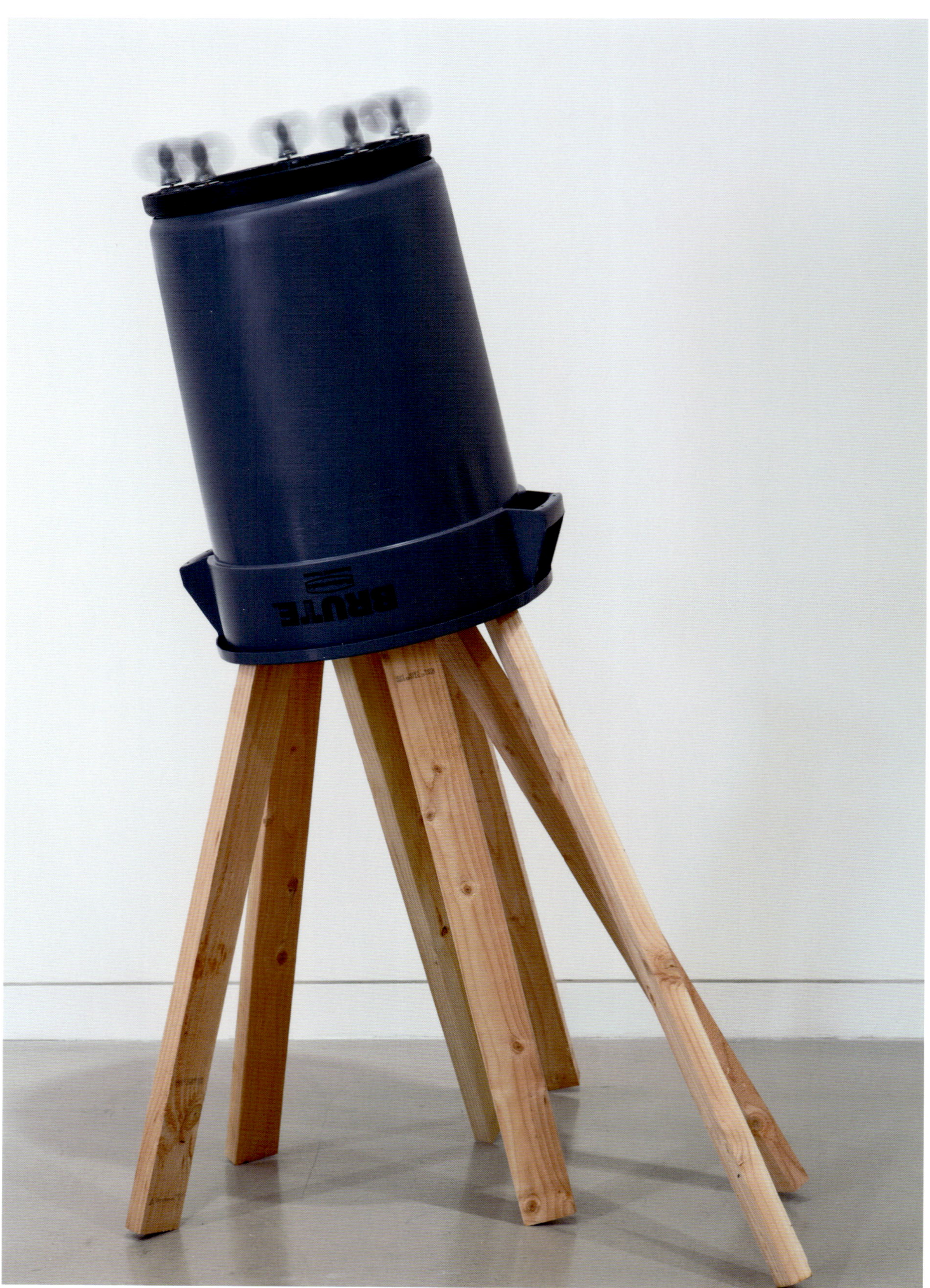

***Trash Clan**, 2010* (detail) — cat. no. 110

GW : **Can you tell me about the two works you'll be exhibiting in the biennial, *Trash Clan* and *Reclining Lawn Chair*? I'm particularly interested in the process of their creation and the materials used.**

AR : *Reclining Lawn Chair* was made specifically for the California Biennial. Early this year I made two similar Lawn Chairs for a group exhibition at the Museum of Contemporary Art in San Diego. I'm glad for the opportunity to have made another chair for this show, even though it's a bit physically taxing. I'm pretty sure my current tendonitis of the elbow and wrist is directly related to all of the aluminum pipe I needed to bend by hand using a conduit bender for this piece.

Both pieces in the biennial take on animal/monster–like qualities, maybe referencing jellyfishes or ghosts . . . slow moving, almost clumsy. Drunken jellyfish ghosts perhaps. *Trash Clan* and *Reclining Lawn Chair* are both scenes frozen in time. Yet *Trash Clan* has an actual kinetic element that references life just a little bit more. The process of getting the casters to spin for the length of the exhibition makes me like the piece even more. It was a labored process, all of it just to achieve a certain detail. And the experience of figuring out how I will accomplish these details is always priceless.

GW : **You previously made what I'd like to describe as non-functional tools—rubber screws, lead hammers, etc. What concerns connect these two bodies of work? Notions of utility and the unexpected seem to be important.**

AR : The previous works were similar in that there was an intensive research process of figuring out how to handle the materials and execute them. Thematically, I think the main connection was the idea of grabbing onto objects that are already very involved in my life. They were things I use all the time. I wanted to impose a strange sort of fictionality on top of them. It's very important to me in general to use immediate materials that people are already familiar with. There shouldn't be any guesswork to figure out what it is. At the same time I want them to be humorous, to twist what are considered base objects into something strange. In terms of differences, the new works have a kinetic quality, either referencing movement or having parts that actually move.

GW : **There's a consistent thread in your work of selecting particular objects with domestic associations (although not always) and translating them into other materials. I'm curious—how do you choose the initial object or figure? What makes an object a ripe subject for such translation?**

AR : There really isn't any one idea or theme. For me, the final product is more interesting than whatever the initial object is. I have an idea, and the objects that I shape into the final piece are just the first things that come to mind to facilitate the idea. Obviously they are things that are or were once in my life, but they're not homages or interrogations. For example, I grew up with the kind of lawn chairs I'm currently working with, but I'm not necessarily interested

in their nostalgic qualities; it's more about the process of manipulating found material.

GW : **You'll be exhibiting sculpture in the biennial, but you also make drawings. How do these two aspects of your practice relate to each other? What sort of impulses drive you to draw, as opposed to make an object?**

AR : I wish I could say that the drawings I make are plans for what I ultimately build, but I don't think of them that way at all. I'm usually drawing at the same time that I'm making sculpture. Like two parallel streams, sharing a similar visual vocabulary and color palette. I do, however, make actual plans for the sculptures. These are usually done on the move. Scribbled out on whatever I can find at the time: scratch paper, cardboard, Home Depot receipts, parking tickets. When I make finished drawings, I'm very conscious of the composition and design qualities. They're finished works in and of themselves, with their own perspective and color. The act of making a finished drawing is much more immediate than making a sculpture as well. No research is needed. I pick what paper I want to use; grab the appropriate pencils, pens, and markers; and pause from the time-consuming nature of my sculptural practice and make something instantaneous and quick.

GW : **I'm impressed by the variety of materials that you use and the technical know-how involved in your work. Do you usually work with materials that you already have some experience with, or is the process of experimentation important to you?**

AR : The material choice is always based on the idea. There's also the practical issue: I want to achieve a certain quality or detail and need to figure out how to get it there. That's where the research and experimentation come in, which are really enjoyable to me. I enjoy driving around to different businesses, meeting different craftsmen and learning about their interests, which are sometimes obscure. The majority of the time I get funny looks right away, followed by, "Why in the hell would you want to do that?" But eventually I do find the person who is excited about my idea and wants to help. For example, Derrick Chaney was a vital part of this trash can piece. He designed and fabricated the circuit board that dictates the movement of the casters. So the process for me becomes a very social one, and with the right help I can pull off almost anything. ∎

Born 1982 in Lake Arrowhead, California; lives and works in San Diego. Ralph received his BA in visual arts from Point Loma Nazarene University in 2004. His work has been presented in exhibitions at the Society of Arts and Crafts, Boston; Aqua Art Wynwood, Miami; Castle House Gallery, Poulsbo, Washington; Phantom Gallery, Long Beach, California; Spacecraft Gallery, Luis De Jesus Seminal Projects, San Diego; and the Museum of Contemporary Art San Diego.

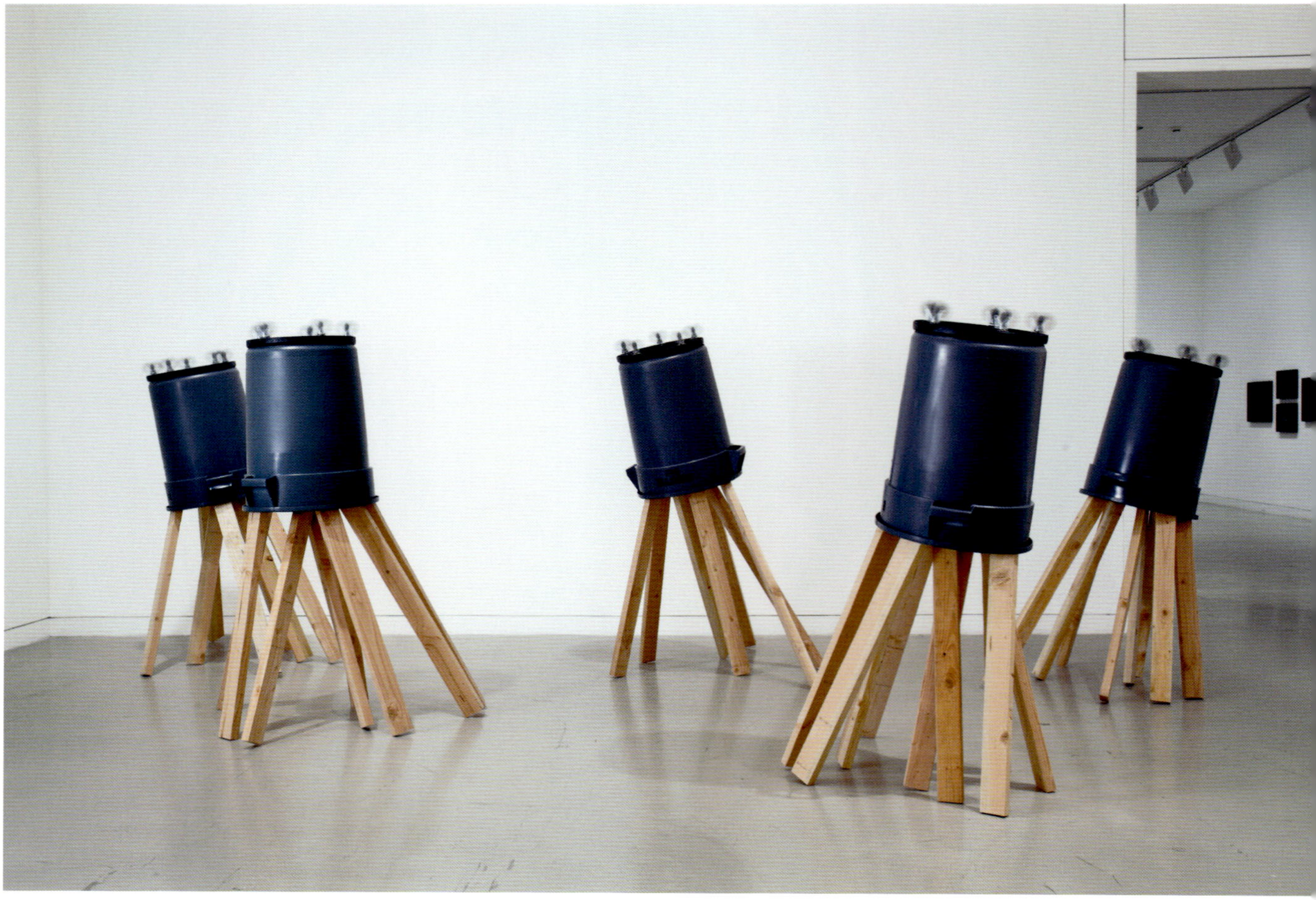

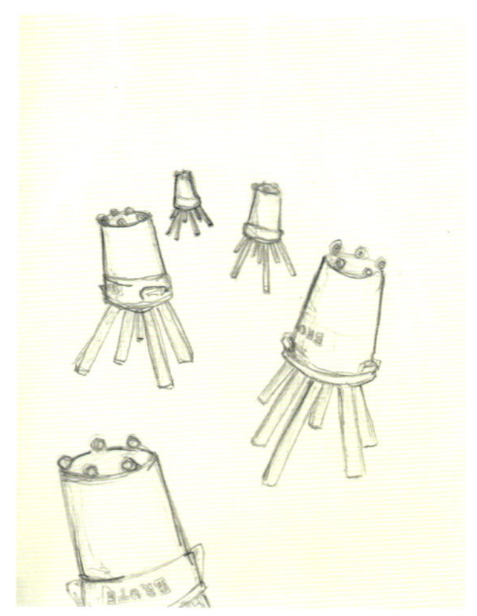

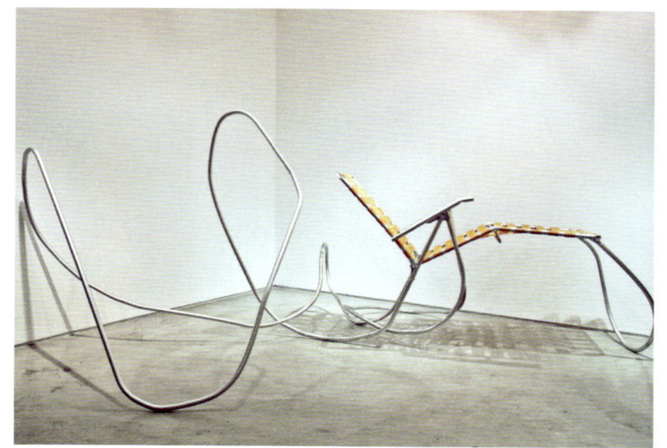

Above
Trash Clan, **2010** — cat. no. 110

Trash Clan Drawing, **2010**
Pencil on paper
8 × 5 in. (20.3 × 12.7 cm)
Courtesy of the artist

Right and opposite
Reclining Lawn Chair, **2010** — cat. no. 109
Installation view, Space/Jayme, San Diego

148

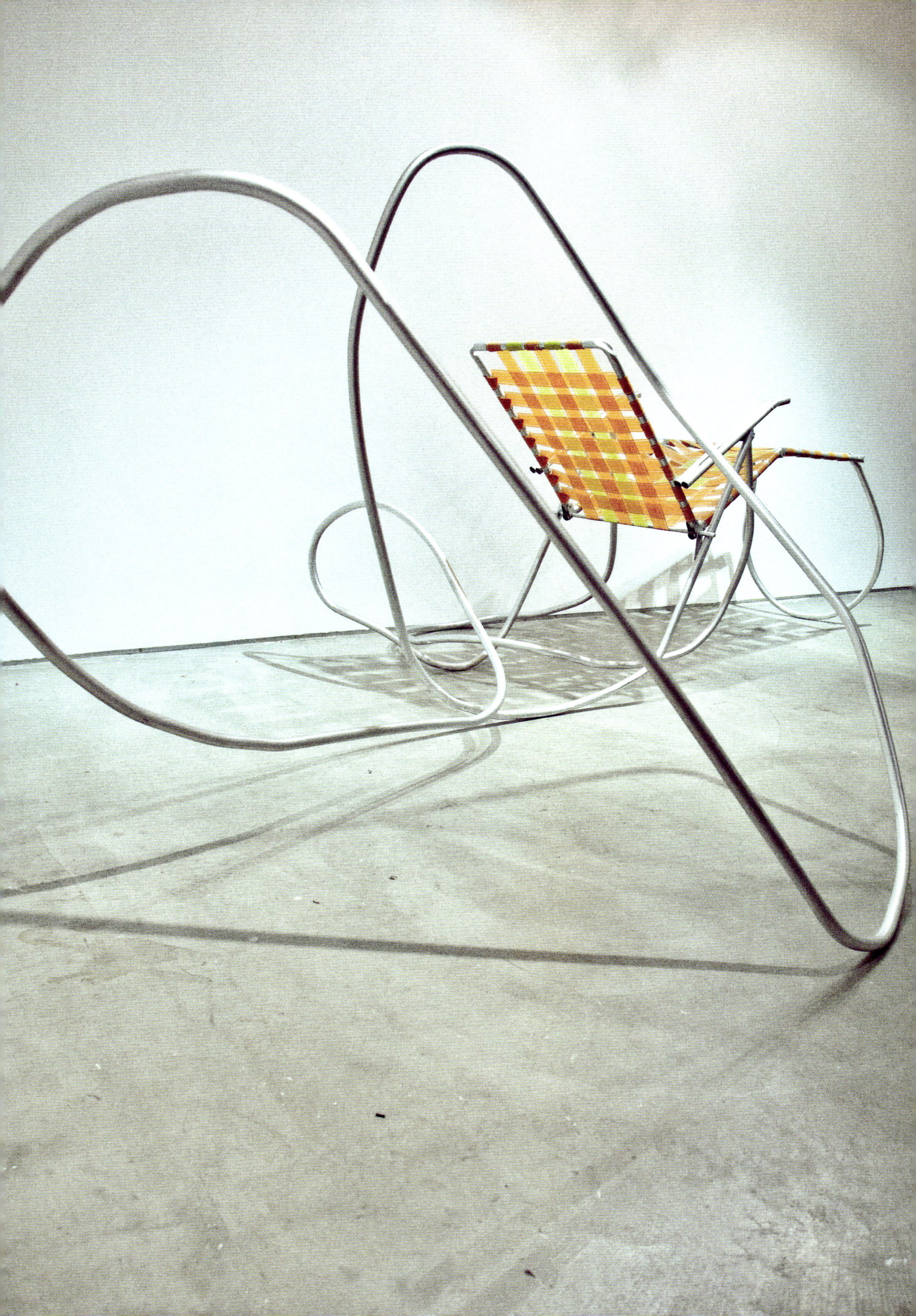

Will Rogan

Practice
Sculpture, photography

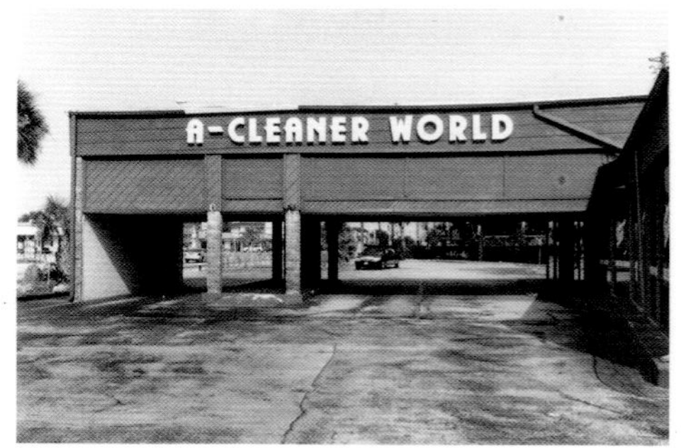

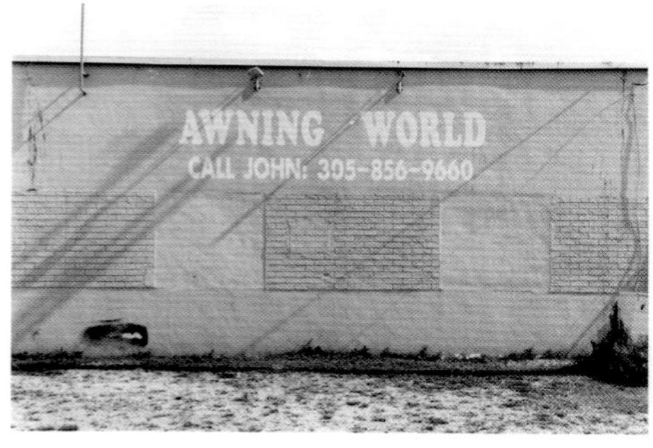

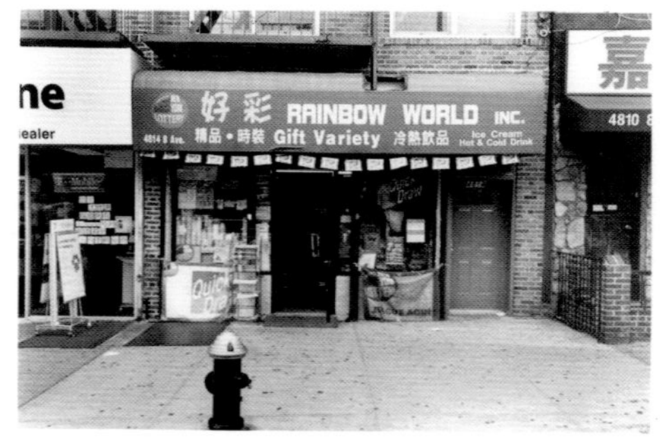

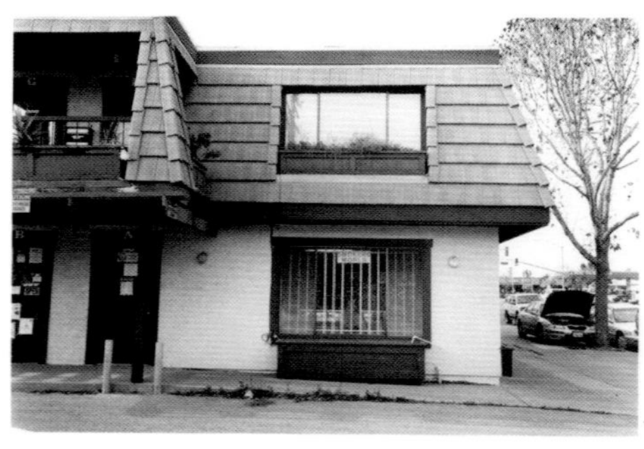

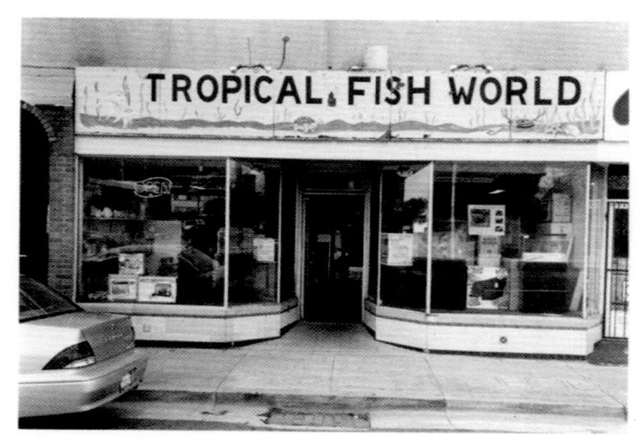

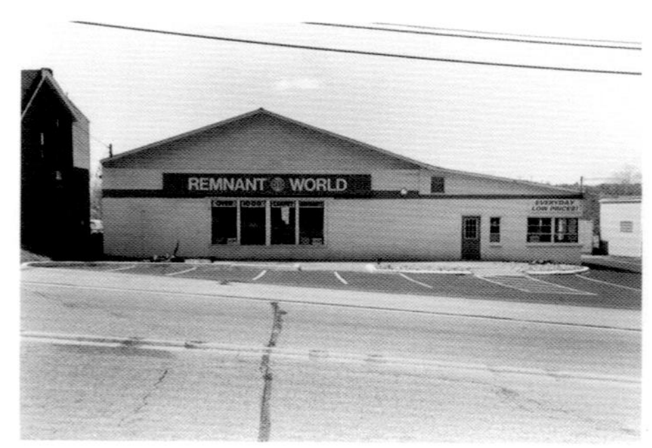

KM : **Your work has encompassed photography, installation, sculpture, video, and artist's books. It seems that your artistic practice revels in the odd, often unnoticed peculiarities of everyday objects and life. Could you please comment on this?**

WR : I think that feels accurate because that's where I start— I begin with things that I notice are already there. My process is all about having a kind of focus or mindfulness. I spend a lot of my life noticing things; it is a huge part of how I occupy my time.

KM : **The Other Worlds photographs included in the California Biennial seem to reveal this process of focused looking, in this case, at mundane signage in the urban landscape. How did this series begin?**

WR : That body of work began in winter 2008. It started because I saw a shop sign four blocks from my house that made me laugh: Vacuum World. I found this funny because of its potential for multiple readings. At first it just made me laugh, but then I began to think about other shop signs that had the same lazy approach to naming: Remnant World, Popcorn World, et cetera—a world for everything.

KM : **Were you thinking of any other artists—for example, Ed Ruscha's early conceptual artist's books on different themes?**

WR : Yes, exactly, I was thinking about Ed Ruscha's books, most particularly his *Every Building on the Sunset Strip*, and also Hans-Peter Feldmann's Bilder books. This series of photos was originally intended for a book form, but it never made it into one.

KM : **You worked in the art library at the San Francisco Art Institute, which has an incredible repository of art books. It seems that this has influenced your practice significantly.**

WR : Working in an art library has definitely influenced me. Not just the place but the people who work there, in particular the archivist, Jeff Gunderson. That library is full of gems, and he is the protector and organizer of them. When I worked there, I collected a file of material—photographs of artists that I found in books that the library was getting rid of. I am currently making a body of work with this material called Mediums. Part of the project will be specifically for the San Francisco Art Institute Library, returning the images to their original source.

KM : **How does your involvement in editing/publishing *Thing*—a multiple or book that resides in an object— relate to the rest of your artistic practice?**

WR : It's a different working mode and way of thinking. I'm very interested in objects and people's relationships to objects—how we are affected by them and how they affect us. Every object has narrative potential. *Thing is* a collaborative project, and for that reason I tend to keep it separate, but there definitely are parallels to some of the work I end up making.

KM : **Your artistic production, no matter the medium, is characterized by an incredibly droll, deadpan wit. In closing, can you please comment on this?**

WR : When something makes me laugh, that is a strong emotion for me. As with all humor, there is also something disturbing or convoluted about it. Humor is just one way into something more complex for me; maybe that is why I seem deadpan or droll. Because by the time I am done making the work, whatever it may be, I am done laughing and am interested in something else in the work. This is the only way I can stay engaged. It can't be funny the whole way through for me. I would get bored. ∎

Born 1975 in Highland Park, Illinois; lives and works in Albany, California. The father of Anina and Amelia, Rogan is a graduate of the San Francisco Art Institute (BFA, 1999) and the University of California, Berkeley (MFA, 2006). He attended the Skowhegan School of Painting and Sculpture in 1998 and received a MacArthur Media Arts Fellowship in 2004. His work has been shown at Altman Siegel Gallery, San Francisco; Laurel Gitlen Gallery/ Small A Projects, New York; Jack Hanley Gallery, San Francisco; the San Francisco Museum of Modern Art; the Oakland Museum of California; Mori Art Museum, Tokyo; the Seattle Art Museum; and CCA Wattis Institute for Contemporary Arts, San Francisco.

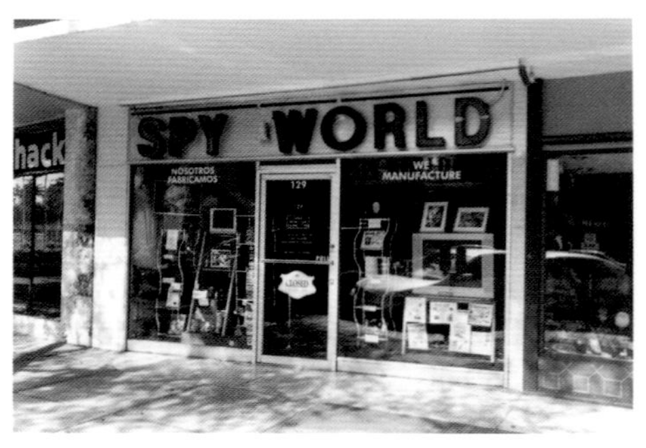

SPY WORLD
NOSOTROS FABRICAMOS
129
WE MANUFACTURE

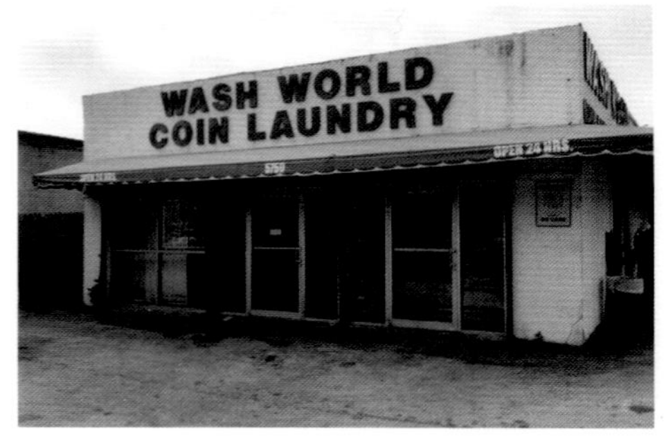

WASH WORLD
COIN LAUNDRY
OPEN 24 HRS.

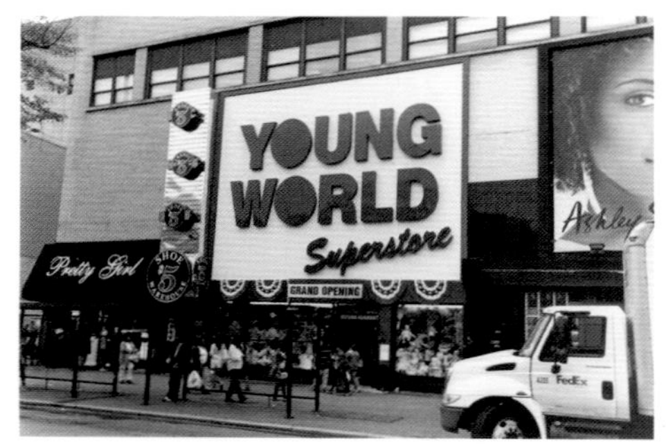

YOUNG
WORLD
Superstore
Pretty Girl
GRAND OPENING
Ashley
FedEx

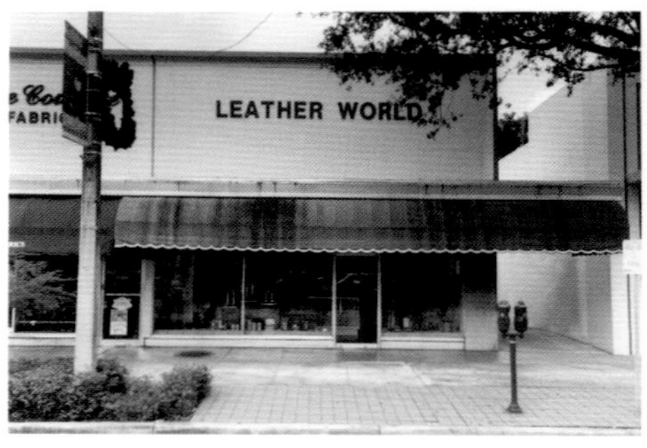

LEATHER WORLD
FABRIC

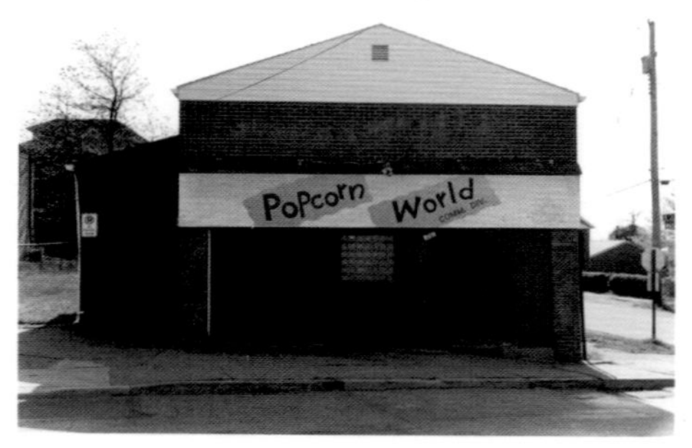

Popcorn World

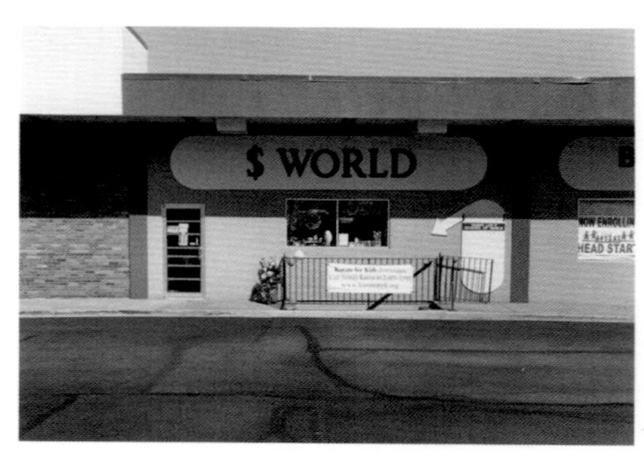

$ WORLD
NOW ENROLLING
HEAD START

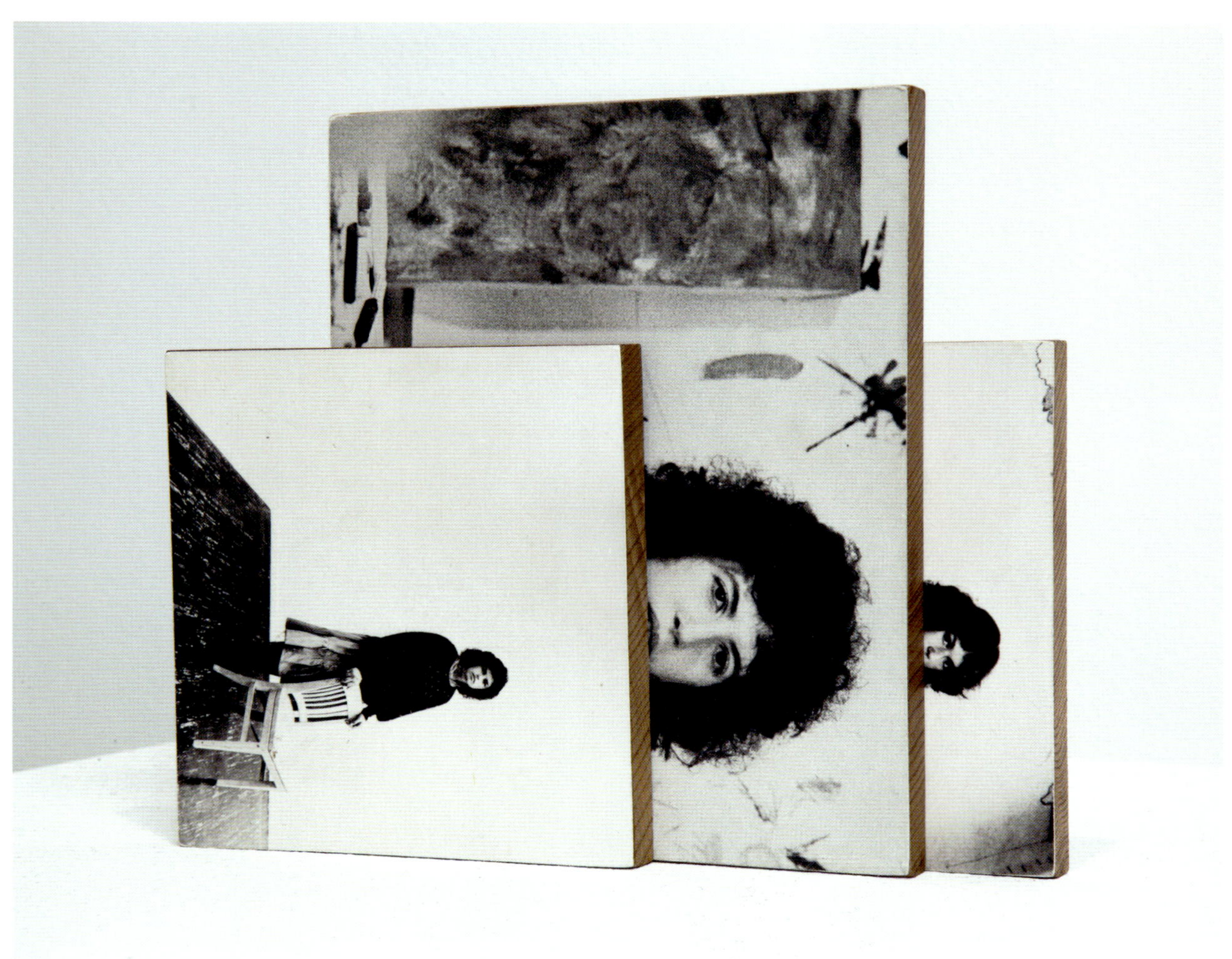

Page 150 clockwise from top left
Untitled, 2009
From the series Other Worlds
Cat. nos. — 111, 117, 112, 113, 114, 118

Opposite, left column
Untitled, 2009
From the series Other Worlds
Gelatin silver print
8 × 10 in. (20.3 × 25.4 cm)
Miller Meigs Collection; courtesy of Laurel Gitlen, New York

Untitled, 2009
From the series Other Worlds
Gelatin silver print
8 × 10 in. (20.3 × 25.4 cm)
Miller Meigs Collection; courtesy of Laurel Gitlen, New York

Untitled, 2009
From the series Other Worlds
Gelatin silver print
8 × 10 in. (20.3 × 25.4 cm)
Miller Meigs Collection; courtesy of Laurel Gitlen, New York

Opposite, right column
Untitled, 2009
From the series Other Worlds
Cat. nos. — 119, 116, 115

Above
Mediums 3, **2010** — cat. no. 120

153

Paul Schiek

Practice
Photography, sculpture, installation,
artists' books (founder of TBW Books)

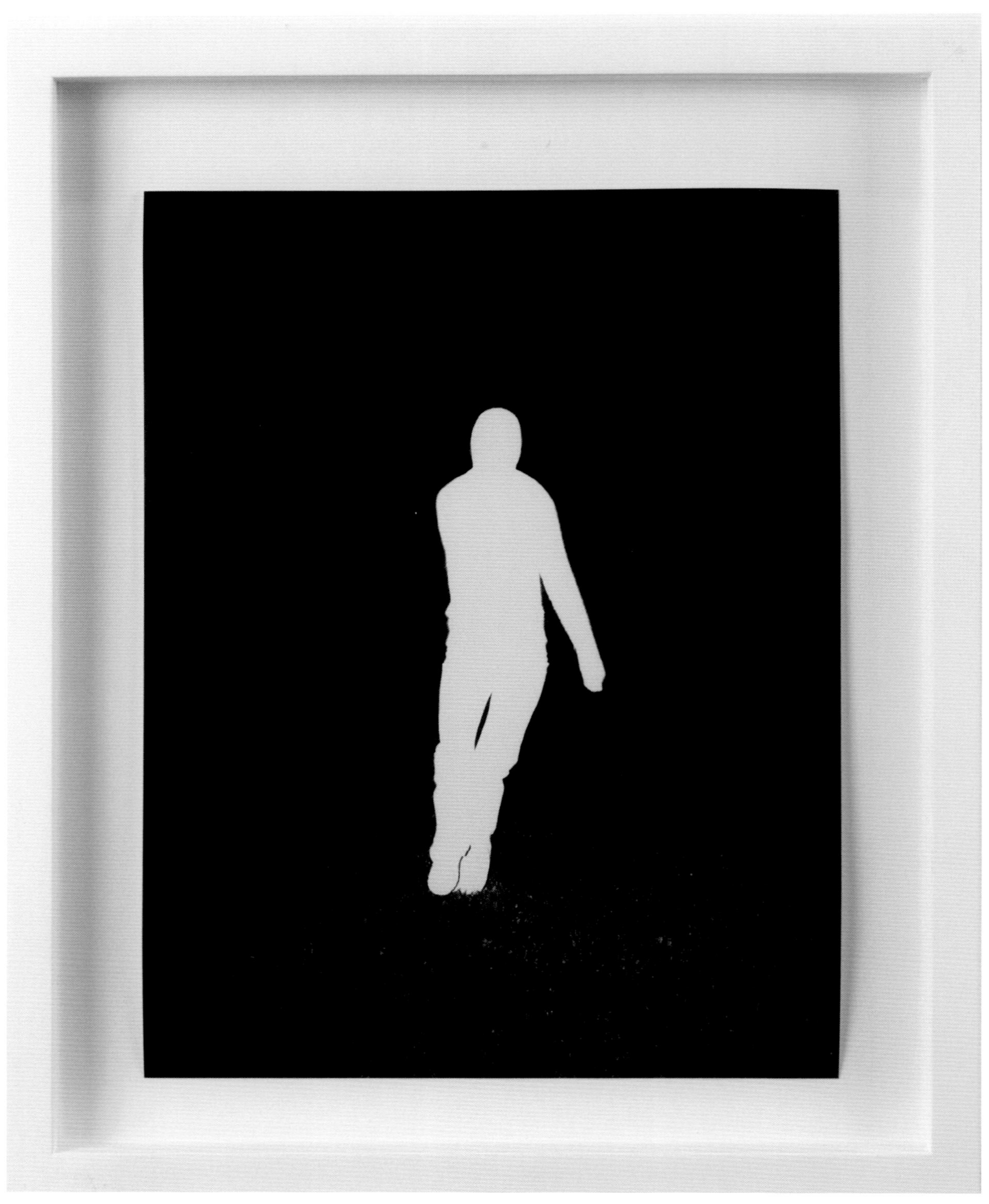

a single perfect moment, **2007** — cat. no. 123

SB : **Until recently your practice was heavily based in photography, in addition to the artists' books that you make and distribute through TBW Books. Can you explain the shift in your practice?**

PS : The shift is hopefully a natural progression. Even when I was being trained as a photographer, I was thinking in terms of being an artist at large. So I was looking at sculpture, painting, installation, and most notably music as references for my work. I'm not bored with photography; it's the exact opposite: I'm overly stimulated by it. I love it so much, but I look at so much of it that I'm not sure how I can add anything in a world where everything is photographed. I've started thinking of my photos in terms of objects. I always made them hoping that I would show them in books, and that has me thinking of photos more sculpturally. For instance, I started altering many of my images by cutting them. I have also been collecting lawn sculptures that I remember seeing in the Midwest, where I grew up. I alter them slightly and display them in my work. Many of the lawn sculptures that I remember were religious figurines or racially charged figurines. Almost everything in my work is rooted in my life as a boy growing up in the American Midwest, in Wisconsin to be exact.

SB : **Can you tell me about the sculpture and the photographs that you will be presenting in the biennial?**

PS : The sculpture is one that I found while I was back in Wisconsin in 2009. It's a generic ceramic sculpture that you paint yourself. This particular one is probably twenty years old and is the classic "man and woman embracing" type, with the inscription "to have and to hold." Whoever owned this one painted the woman white, with blue eyes and blond hair, and the man black. I thought about this sculpture in the context of the black "lawn jockeys" that were so common where I lived. Growing up, there was no dialogue around this sort of imagery. It just was. In some way my attraction to these sculptures is to try to understand why my neighbors had them, what function they served. When I shipped the sculpture home, the figures' legs broke off in transit. At first I was upset, but it forced me to lay them down, rather than show them standing up like they would be in someone's garden, and it just made the sculpture into something entirely different and better in my opinion. So I started to buy other sculptures—Virgin Marys, lawn jockeys, etc.—anything dealing with racial stereotypes or religious imagery. I bought one from a woman who told me "this cute little guy lost his legs," so I laid him down as well. A natural theme started to emerge. In some way I'm letting these sculptures rest after years of exhaustion. Obviously it's more complex than all that, but that is the departure point.

The sculpture in the show acts as the bridge between two of the photos. One photo is a solid dark silhouette of a man, and the other is of a woman completely overcome by light. The tension between light and dark and all that historically comes with it (specifically in Western Christian thought) is a huge theme in my work. With the photo of the man, I cut a hole in the center where his hands were. He's sort of reaching into the sky, and I thought it was a good photo but better if I just cut a hole in it. I seem to always be photographing hands or people grabbing each other or holding onto something. In all honesty I think that comes from a work ethic that believes in hands—I was never told that I could get through life with my smarts—I was going to have to work with my hands. I'm fascinated by hands and by labor. The other photo is titled *a single perfect moment,* and it looks as if the figure has been cut out of the photo, but it's actually a woman dressed in white completely illuminated by a flash of light. I shot a lot of photos at night and was always excited by how the flash would light up a scene for a split second and then it was immediately dark again, and for that second, even though everything in the dark at that point in my life was no good, that moment looked perfect.

SB : **Tell me about TBW Books and the artists' books that you produce and distribute. How does creating artists' books with photographers complement or counterbalance your art practice?**

PS : When I was finishing art school, I wanted to make a book instead of having a show at a gallery. I didn't believe anyone would come to a show of mine, and I wanted to show my friends all over the country what I had made, so I made a book—five hundred copies—and gave them to everyone I could. The book, *good by angels*, to this day holds a huge place in my heart. After that, I just spent every penny I made building a company that publishes books. It's now in its fifth year, and I have published about fifteen titles. I sell them as subscriptions to eliminate distributors. It's been about the hardest undertaking in my life but one that I am very proud of. I am fascinated by mechanization and factories and assembly lines. I sort of created my own little factory, but instead of being forced to work there, I can choose to work there. It's also about job security on some level. I have never felt that I am owed an art career. I have many guilt issues about calling myself an artist. And I feel like if I can call my mom and tell her, "Today I packaged and shipped three hundred orders and built a new shelving unit in the office," then I'm all good.

SB : **What do you want the people who encounter your work in the biennial or a gallery to take away?**

PS : Questions, not answers. I'm not interested in art that gives you answers. ■

Born 1977 in Fond du Lac, Wisconsin; lives and works in Oakland, California. Schiek is a graduate of the California College of the Arts (BFA, 2005). He has had solo exhibitions at Stephen Wirtz Gallery, San Francisco; Thomas Erben Gallery, New York; and Newspace Center for Photography, Portland, Oregon. His work was shown in *Bay Area Now 5* at the Yerba Buena Center for the Arts, San Francisco, and was included in the book *Shoot: Photography of the Moment* (Rizzoli, 2009). Schiek is the founder of TBW Books, a publishing imprint that has produced books of his images and those of other photographers.

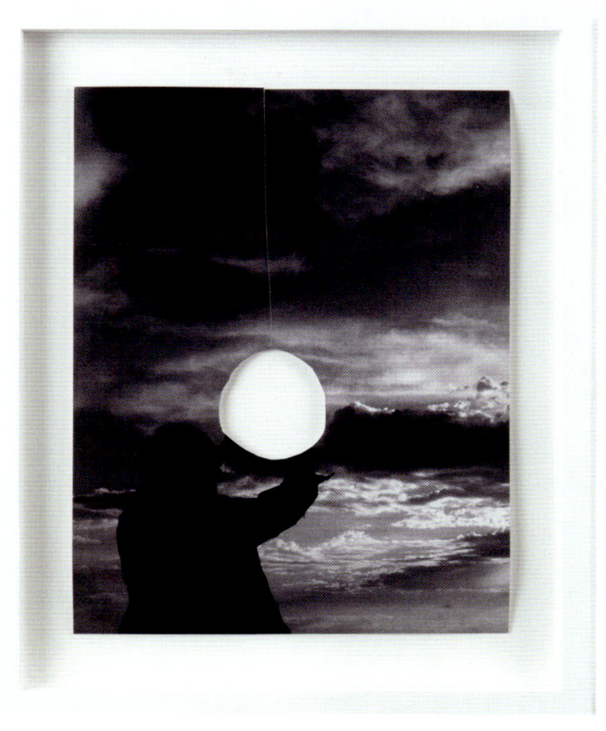

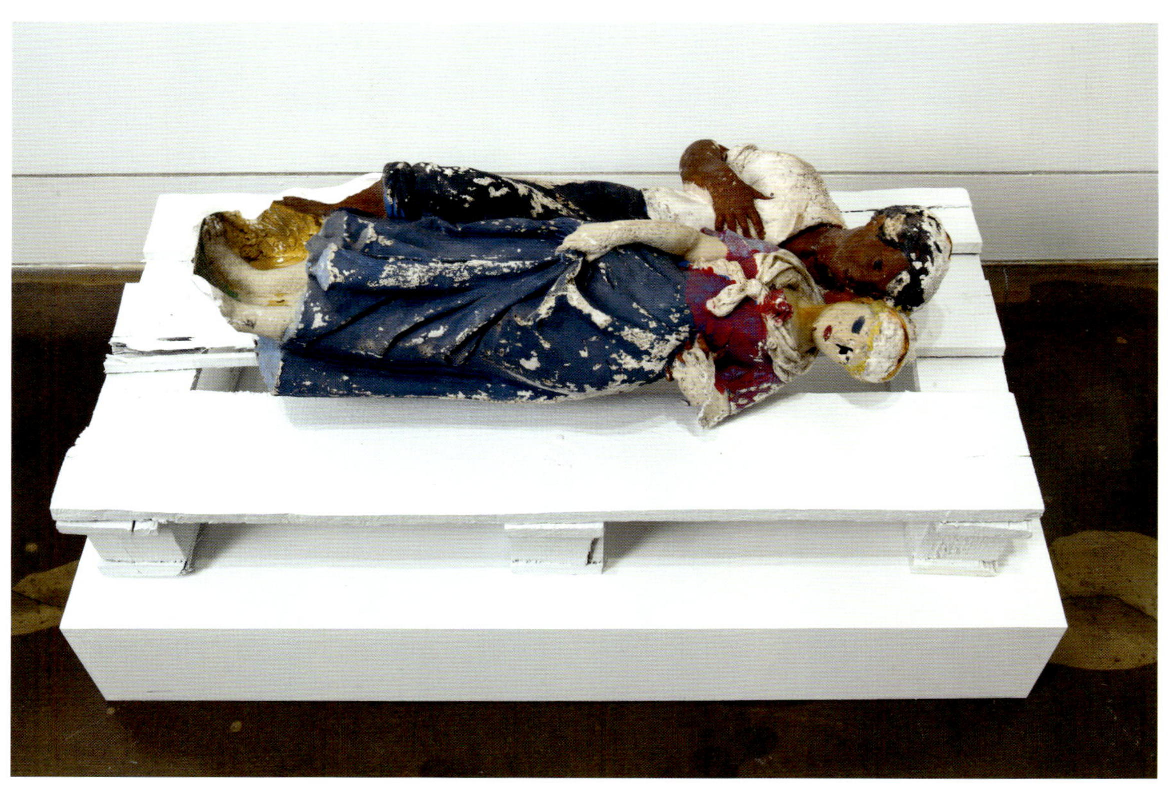

Taravat Talepasand

Practice
Painting, drawing, mixed media, sculpture

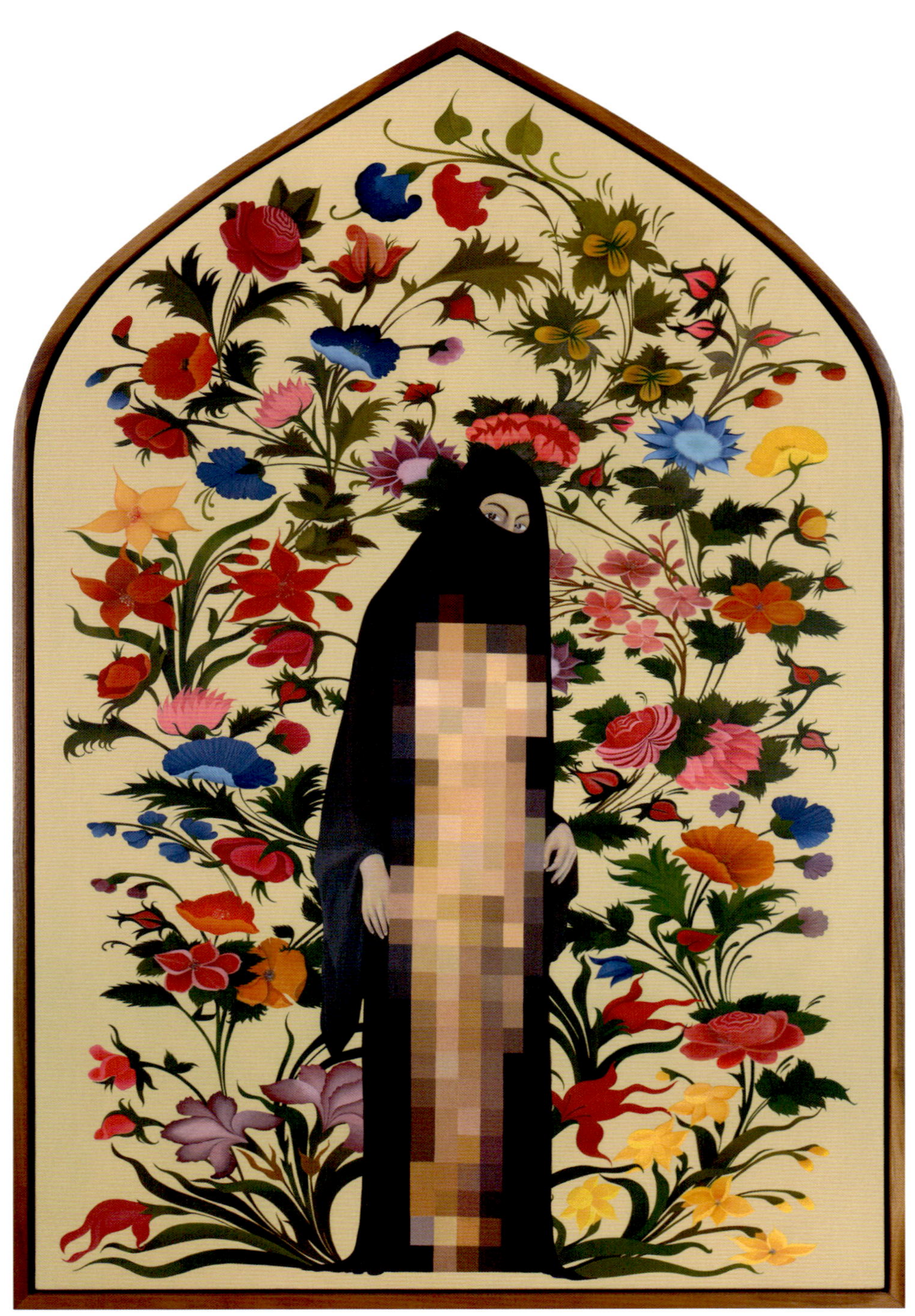

***The Censored Garden*, 2008** — cat. no. 126

Born 1979 in Eugene, Oregon, to Iranian parents during the Iranian Revolution; lives and works in San Francisco. Talepasand is a graduate of the Rhode Island School of Design (BFA, 2001) and the San Francisco Art Institute (MFA, 2006). She is the recipient of the 2010 Richard C. Diebenkorn Fellowship and has exhibited at the Yerba Buena Center for the Arts, the de Young Museum, and Marx & Zavattero in Francisco; Leila Taghinia-Milani Gallery and Plane Space in New Charlie James, Los Angeles; gale sans titre, Brussels; the di Rosa Preserve, Napa, California; and th 2003 Oregon Biennial. Talepasan featured in the book *Different Sar New Perspectives in Contemporar Iranian Art* (2009) and in the film on the Ocean Floor* (2010).

AB: **When we spoke recently, you mentioned two words that are central to your work: *andarooni* and *birooni*.**

TT: *Andarooni birooni*, literally meaning "insider outsider," is a term that Iranians use to describe that divide and contrast between self and other. There are two distinct sides of a person who is displaced from their culture; when I'm in Iran, I realize how American I am, while in America I am perceived differently. Proud of both nationalities, I find myself playing with conflicting traditions.

In the drawing *Hafez, September 9, 1978* (2009), I found that moment when my mother was on the edge of being an insider outsider. The date reflects nine months before my birth and the rise of the regime. Preparing to leave Iran with crossed arms protecting my life, we moved our traditions to the United States. *Hafez* literally means "memory," and while many assume that the title refers to the poet Hafez, it's actually the shrine of Omar Khayyam that stands behind my mother like a phallic erect structure. I am a product of Iran that has been displaced by my mother's choice of being *andarooni birooni*. My mother's stance and gaze are direct, of a time and moment when leaving Iran meant splitting oneself. I transcend this duality by transgressing tradition.

AB: **In your earlier work you explored personal identity through the tradition of Persian miniature painting. More recently, you've been examining Iranian pop culture, politics, and the Green movement. How is your work *Angel of Iran (Dirty 50cc)* (1982–2010) both a reflection and a subversion of contemporary Iranian culture?**

TT: Traditional Persian miniature painting is a type of storytelling. I was trained in Iran but was always trying to modernize the tradition of Persian painting. Rather than depending on the past, I had become more interested in the present and future. My choice of painting with egg tempera is my way of connecting to the history of painting, while the content deals with the now. Tremendous changes are happening culturally, and the best way to follow that is through media, politics, and popular culture. Living outside Iran, I found my way into Iranian pop culture through the Internet. Following the lives of Iranian youth and their struggle has been my obsession.

Angel of Iran (Dirty 50cc) is an exact replica of a "Basij" motorcycle. Basij-e Mostaz'afin, literally "mobilization of the oppressed," is an Iranian volunteer militia of young boys created by the order of Ayatollah Khomeini. The Basij cruise around the streets and police society for anything that disrupts the Islamic code. They are a cultural fear creating fear. Mud-flap Iranian girls spray-painted on the back of trucks, opium flowers, and the distinct color of green are present and associated with male Iranian culture. Recently, "badly veiled" women who are not modestly dressed have been called a "corrupt minority" by Iranian clerics: "Drug traffickers are hanged, terrorists executed and robbers are punished for their crimes. Shall we let badly veiled women be free in the society and corrupt our youth?" The Basij are a part of this cultural campaign. The motorcycle is a subversion of that fear and is specific to female insurgency.

AB: **Tell me about your recent drawing *Hey Haji* (2010), which is included in the biennial.**

TT: Every culture has its derogatory slurs, and in *Hey Haji* I am presenting myself as the Towel Head: towel head, sand nigras, camel jockey—all derogatory terms for Arabs. And I am presenting myself as Haji Firooz—a blackface troubadour who ushers in the Persian New Year, my Iranian "Santa Claus." The towel symbolizes Persians who are mistaken for Arabs, while the painted blackface suggests oil as a suffocating resource and refers to a direct conflict between Iranian tradition and American racism. Both cultures disseminate a caricature for tradition.

AB: **One reading of your large-scale painting *Censored Garden* (2008) is that the pixilated figure references the censoring of the female body by strict Islamic dress codes. But you've told me that the central figure is actually an image you found on a pornographic website of a woman with her head and face covered but her body fully revealed. Can you tell me more about the work and your decision ultimately to pixilate the figure in your own representation?**

TT: I had found the perfect marriage between beauty and ugliness, desire and censorship, tradition and innovation. Since the veil conceals the body, it also elicits a heightened sexual response for many men. I have been researching and collecting pornographic images of Middle Eastern women; this is from a specific collection of a woman in a black burka revealing her fake tits and olive skin. Shocked and fascinated, I combined a specific Esfahani floral motif within an arabesque frame, assuming a window frame or doorway into a garden. This is my way of attracting the viewer to something that is taboo. The decorative elements and the figure contradict each other. The pixilation lends itself to the censorship of the female figure that is found in both American and Iranian culture. Pornography is close to nonexistent in Iran in comparison to the West, where nothing is left to the imagination. However, the law strictly enforces restrictions for both sides.

AB: **You've recently been included in a number of exhibitions, as well as a film, centered on Iranian women artists.**

TT: I am in the recent film *Pearls on the Ocean Floor* by Robert Adanto, a documentary on the lives of Iranian female artists around the world who primarily make work that describes their personal reflections on Iran. Strong opinions are expressed about the ongoing changes in Iran, both past and present, creating a community of *andarooni birooni* women. My process of working involves a lot of learning and living. I've always expressed myself through drawing and painting, but now it's a lifestyle, in a way spiritual. Fascinated with culture and its fast changes, I have translated my ideas into other forms of art, working with a variety of mediums that maintain the conversation between East and West. I will always be a meticulous painter and drawer, but don't be surprised if you come across Taravat porcelain booby burka sculptures . . .

"I am the corrupt minority." ∎

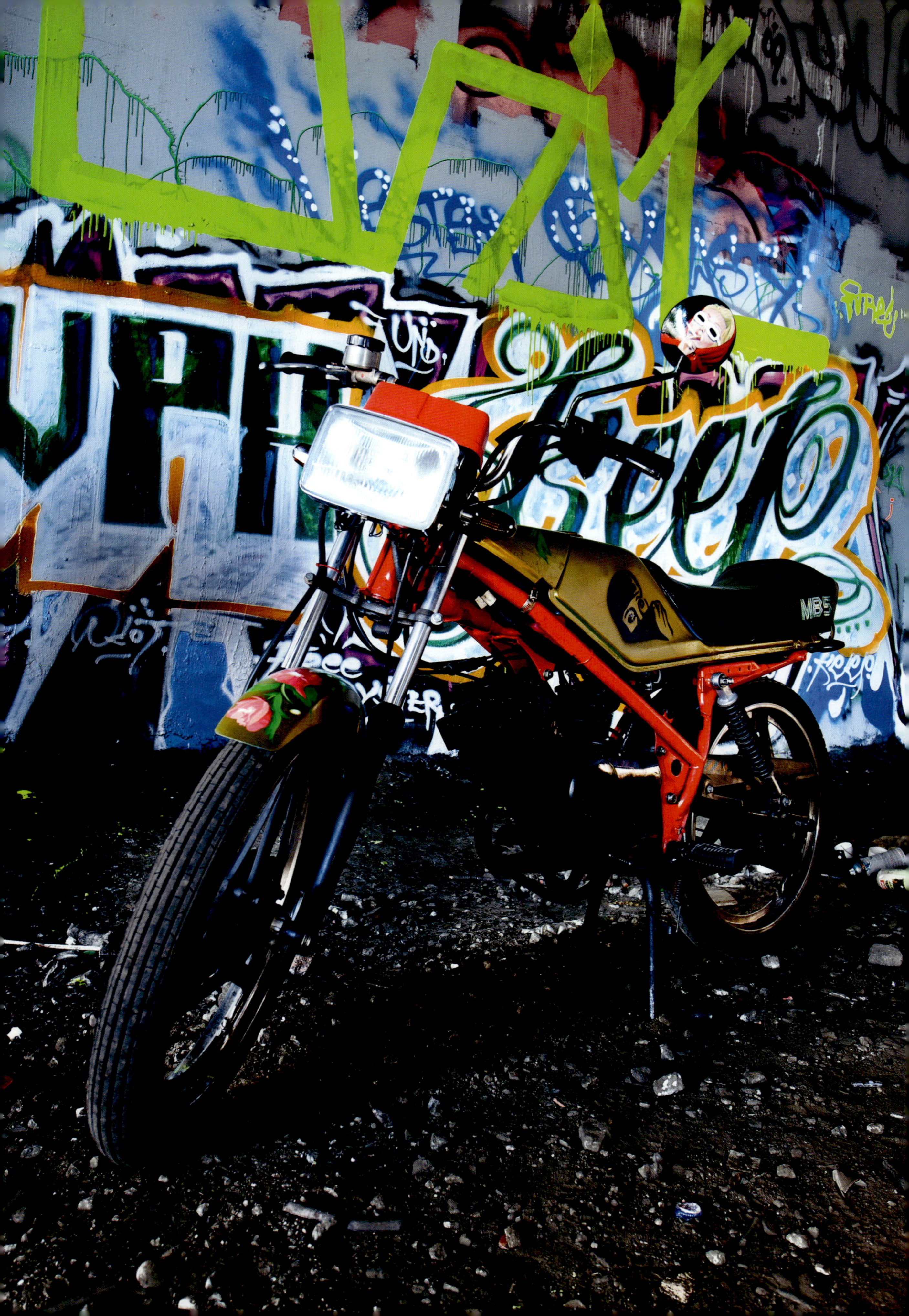

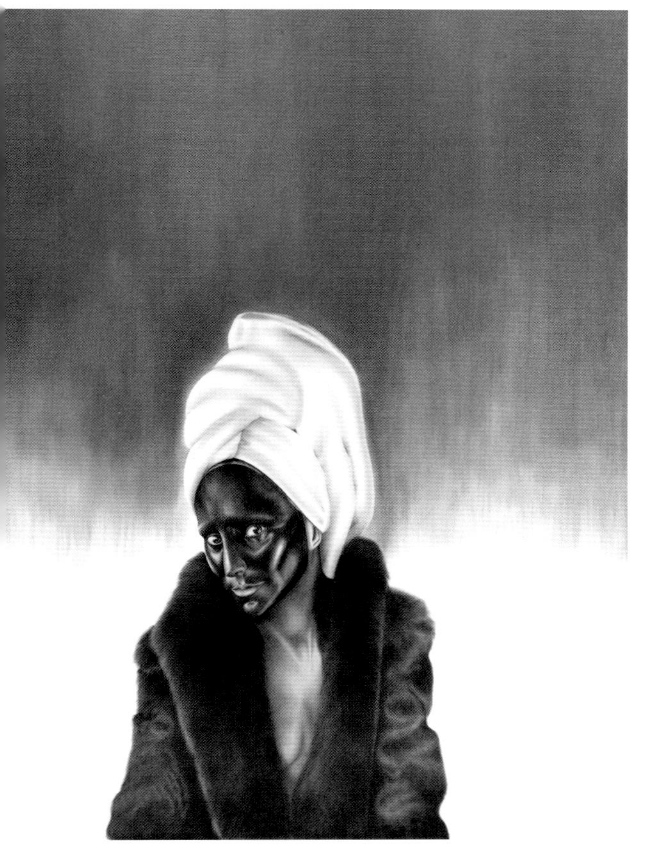

Angel of Iran (Dirty 50cc), **1982–2010** — cat. no. 125

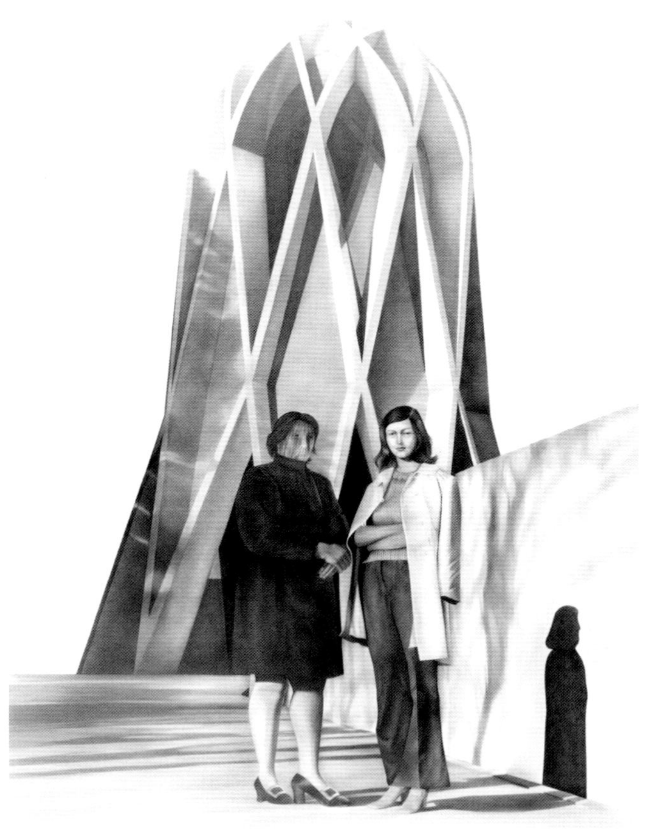

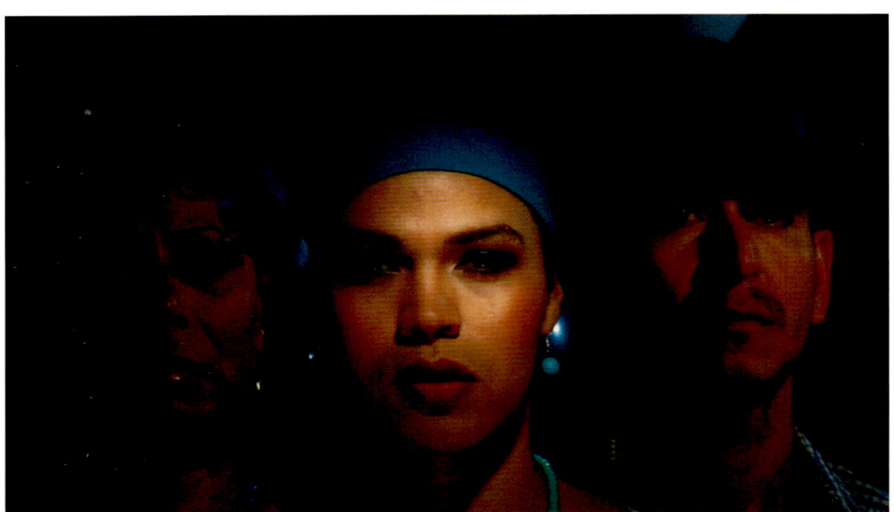

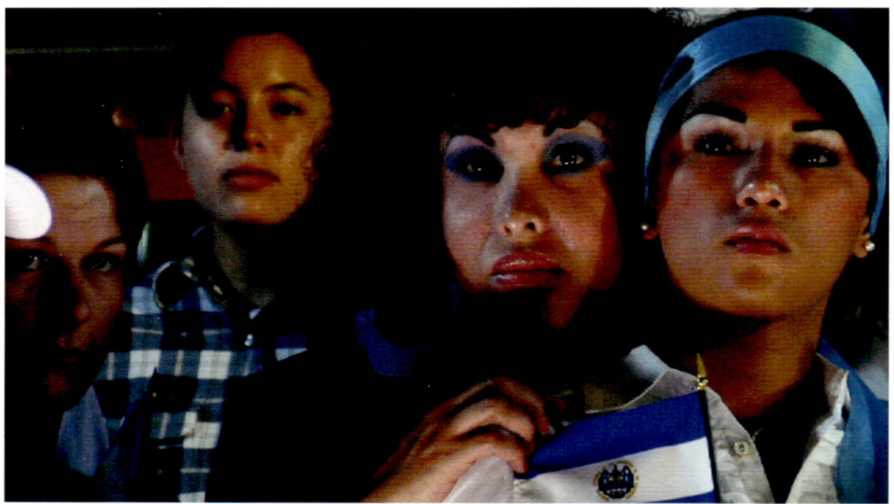

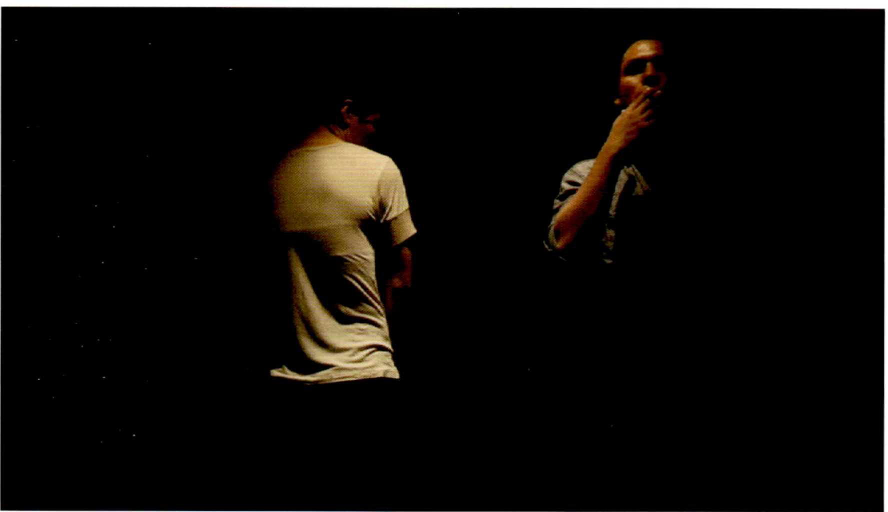

Stills from **Damelo Todo (Give Me Everything)**, 2010 — cat. no. 128

CF : **Can you briefly describe your work for the biennial?**

WT : *Damelo Todo (Give Me Everything)* (2010) is a projected video installation that hovers between performance, document, and social event. I feel most comfortable talking about it in terms of the conditions of its production. I was throwing a party/performance night at a bar called Silver Platter for two years, and *Damelo Todo* is basically the culmination of that lived experience, in both subject and style. I'm currently working on a larger documentary called *WILDNESS* (the name of the party that I threw in collaboration with DJs Total Freedom & NGUZUNGUZU), which involves crossover characters. I draw a lot of inspiration from my queer nightlife, which is very much about creating environments that are both nurturing and fantastical—and I see the need for both in my community. So *Damelo Todo* is about that effort, both on screen and beyond the frame.

CF : **Much of your recent work deals with the idea of the voice as a metaphor and as the medium through which themes of language, identity, and gender politics are explored. Can you talk a little about this?**

WT : Right now my practice revolves around two major concepts. The first is "the voice as cock," which comes from something my voice teacher, Juliana Snapper, used to say before a live performance: "Remember! Your voice is a cock!" I guess that's like picturing the audience in their underwear. The first time she said it, my whole world changed. Understanding the voice in terms of power, penetration, and object was so transformative. The second concept is a performance technique I call "full body quotation," which is about embodying the word, not only through text but through everything that contributes to its meaning—i.e., the voice as that thing outside of language. I have always connected to this idea of voice as someone who grew up with a split-immigrant-racial identity, in which many of my formative familial and cultural identifications excluded language. There is also a layer of *Damelo Todo* that is about re-creating this experience. The film is not subtitled, so it privileges a bilingual viewer. And for the rest of us—your point of entry is whatever you bring to it.

CF : **You mentioned voice, and in a previous conversation you talked about the voice as a metaphor for community representation, one that provides a voice to underrepresented and underprivileged communities. This concept definitely extends across the scope of your work. But in the wake of providing a voice, you've built a stronger community. Do you consider this community organizing central to your work? If so, what's its role in your artistic practice?**

WT : I feel very oppositional to the idea of "underprivileged" and "underrepresented" at the moment. Who is under whom? I don't consider myself to be a community organizer at the moment either, because I'm deep in the throes of editing a documentary about "my community"—and I believe that as soon as you start to create a representation of others, you inherently set yourself apart. It's simply impossible to be both on the outside observing and on the inside experiencing. The process of making the film

WILDNESS has been about trying to inhabit that limbo for as long as possible. I hope I can survive—meaning, I hope that afterward I can still access that feeling of being a part of this thing that I am trying to represent. Does that make sense? I don't mean to be so abstract about it, but I really think that for an artist, filmmaker, activist, or whatever—if your practice depends on social relationships—the whole idea of "speaking for others" is a very tricky, flawed, and doomed path. But I kind of like that! I don't believe *WILDNESS* is about a community, but rather the film calls into being a community that doesn't actually exist . . . so maybe after the film comes out, that community will form? That would be dreamy! But not likely.

CF : **For *Damelo Todo*, you've chosen to use film as a format for your artistic expression. Why?**

WT : Every audience and every format has conventions. I used to think (very naively) that visual art was outside those conventions because it was so deconstructive, but we all know that being unconventional, transgressive, or whatnot is the convention in the visual arts. My approach to making *Damelo Todo* and *WILDNESS* is about really considering the limits of any given format/audience. To oversimplify it, it's often a tension between trying to clarify something versus trying to complicate it. Art asks questions; documentary gives answers. Again, I'm oversimplifying, but I like the challenge of what those two basic tenets imply about audience. I think there is a narrower audience for the visual arts because ambiguity and codedness can be uncomfortable for a lot of people. So you reach a lot more people when you try to find a common language. I feel resistant to the category of "experimental documentary" because that would imply that "experimental" is a style. Or at least in the film world, people think experimental is a style—basically, anything that isn't straightforward storytelling. But for me "experimental" implies that you are challenging not only form but everything about how meaning is circulated as well. So for me, right now, making *WILDNESS* as a rather straightforward documentary feels experimental because there's a necessity both to clarify meaning and to circulate widely. I want as many people as possible to see the important "ambiguity of being" that is shared by transgender and immigrant communities. ∎

Born 1982 in Worcester, Massachusetts; lives and works in Los Angeles. Tsang is a graduate of the School of the Art Institute of Chicago (BFA, 2004) and the University of California, Los Angeles (MFA, 2010). His work has been presented at REDCAT, Los Angeles; Art in General, New York; the Kitchen, New York; Sala de Arte Publico Siqueiros, Mexico City; Impakt Festival, Utrecht, the Netherlands; and the International Short Film Festival in Oberhausen, Germany. Tsang's recent projects *Damelo Todo (Give Me Everything)* and *WILDNESS* are centered on Wildness, the party/performance night that he co-organized with DJs Total Freedom and NGUZUNGUZU for two years at the Silver Platter in Los Angeles. Tsang's short film *Shape of a Right Statement* was included in *Artforum's* "Best of 2008: Film."

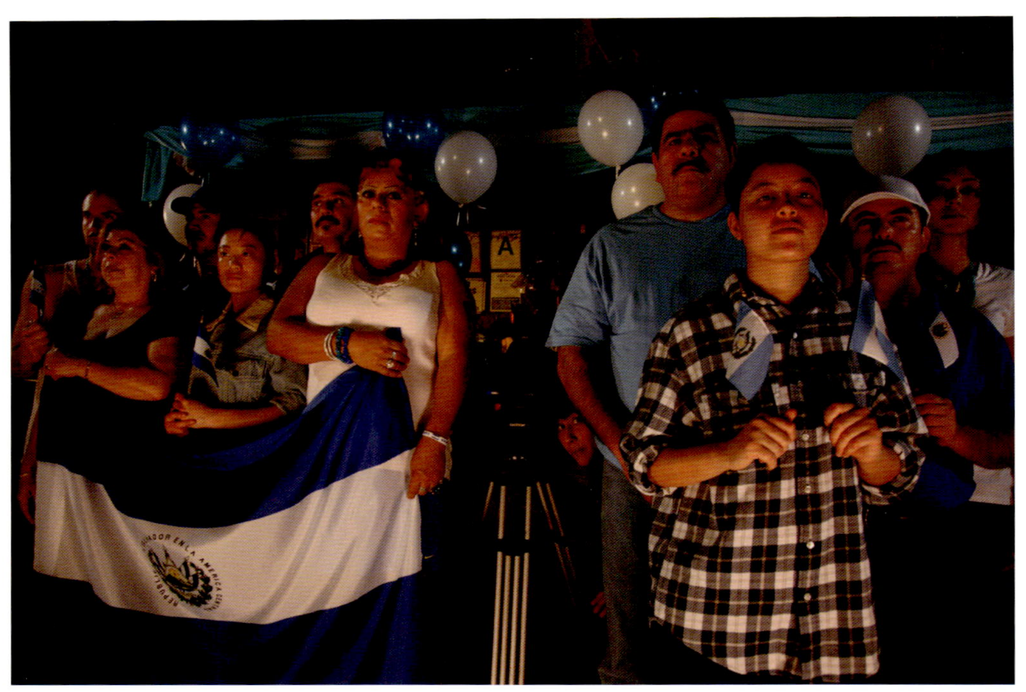

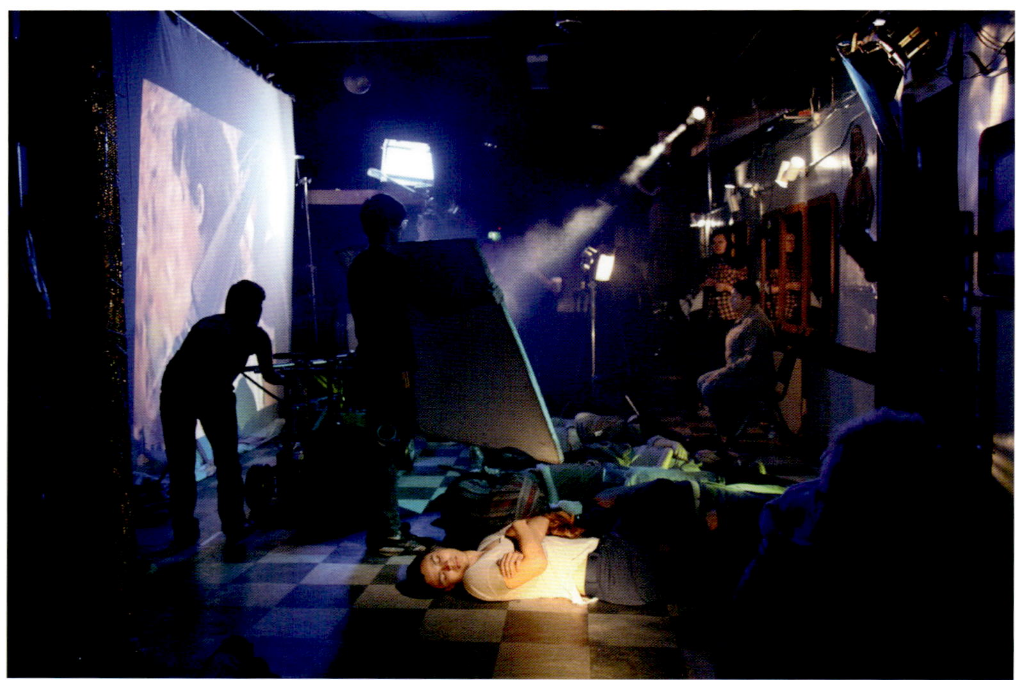

Production stills from **_Damelo Todo (Give Me Everything)_**, 2010
Courtesy of the artist

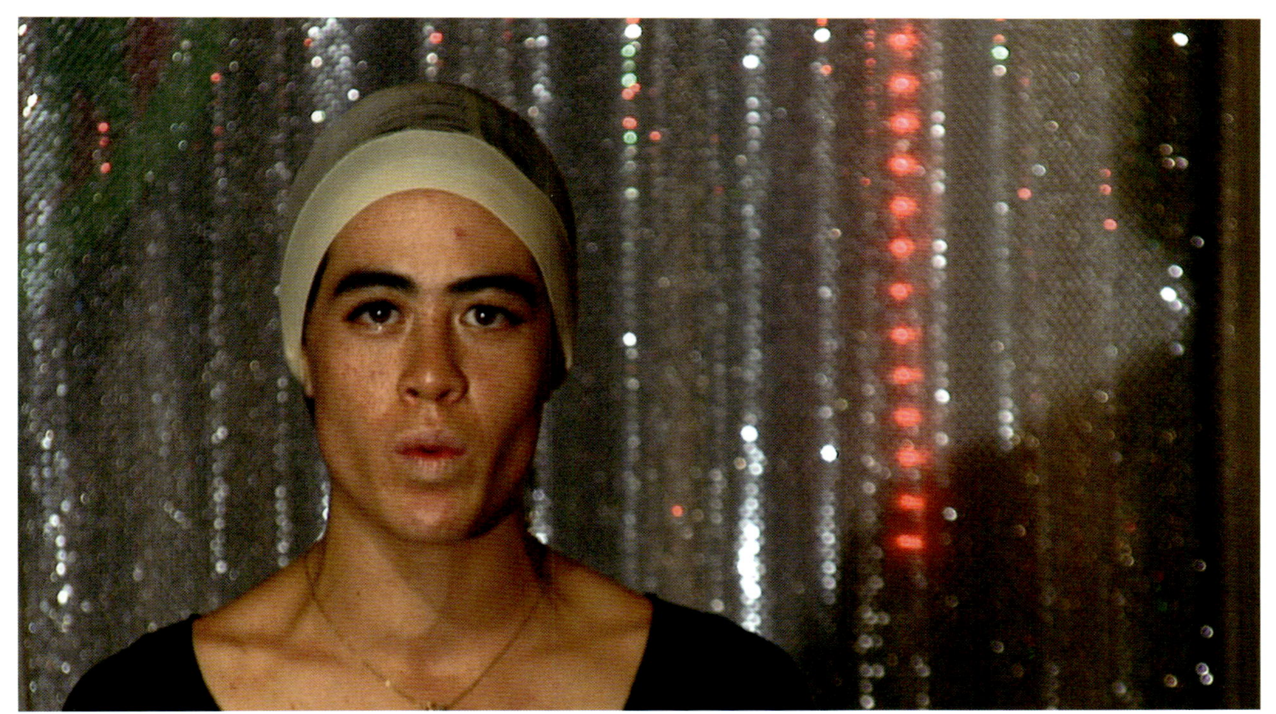

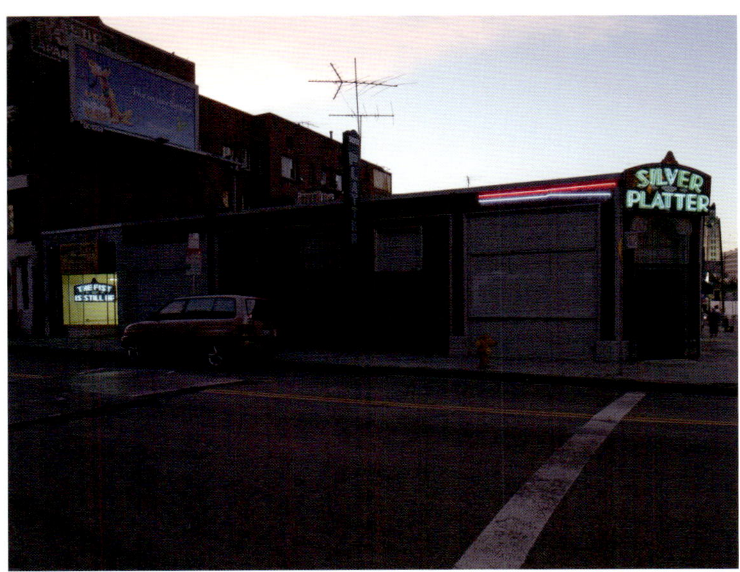

SILVER PLATTER

Top
Still from **The Shape of a Right Statement**, 2006
Single-channel video
Courtesy of the artist

Bottom
"STILL" lightbox, 2009
Digital C-print
Courtesy of the artist

Zlatan Vukosavljevic

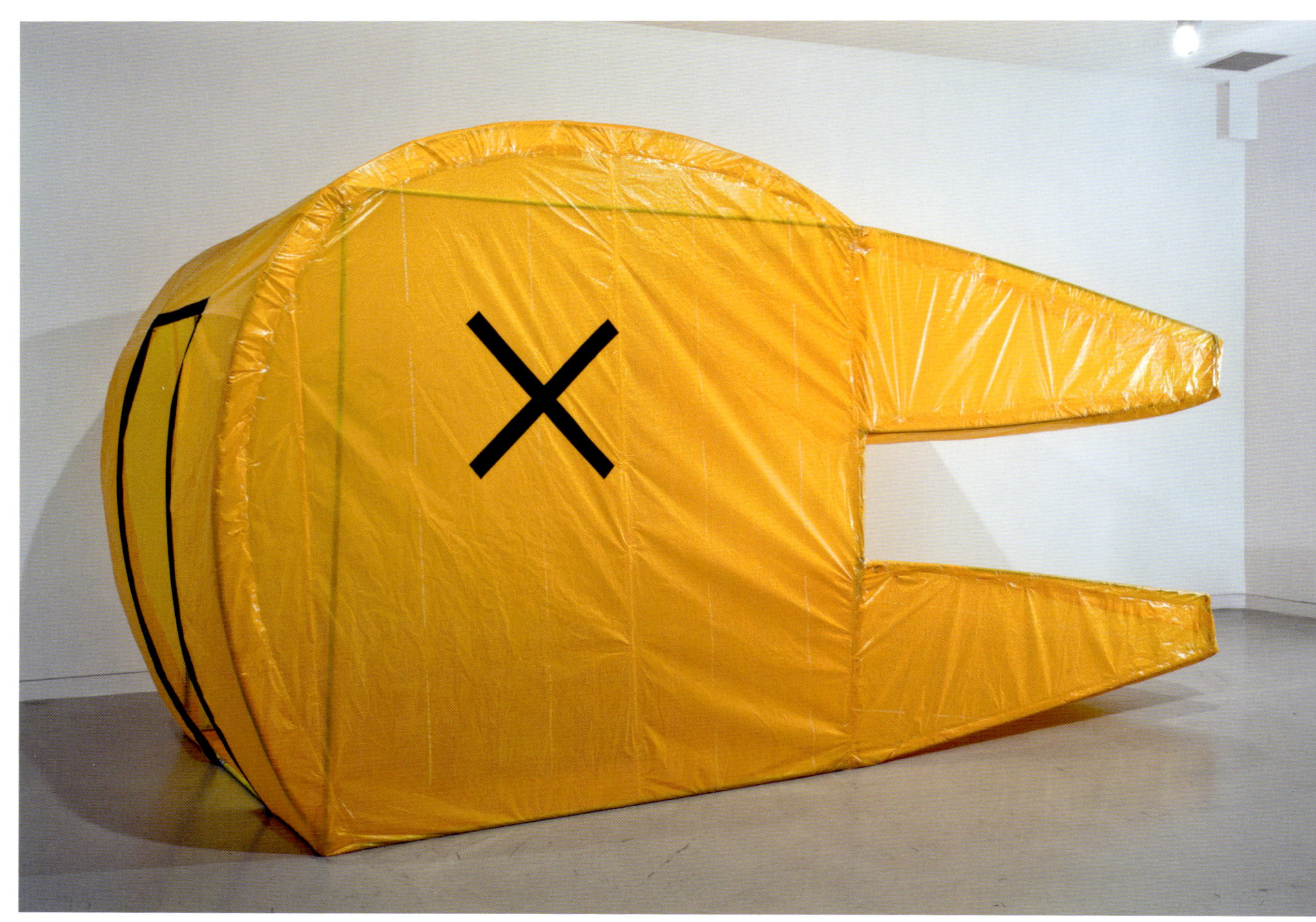

DuckBunny Chamber, **2010** — cat. no. 129

Interview with Chloë Flores

CF : Much of your work centers on creating structures that rearticulate space for social experiences; however, this experience is dependent upon participatory action from the audience. How do you invite the viewer to participate?

ZV : The way I work is something akin to experimental science, in which, through experimentation, one's ideas emerge. What interests me about this process is that the experimental shape that comes out of this technique is a life-size model that has to be open for participation. I want the design of this model to be continually altered, but there isn't a prescribed scenario. I work off the sensation that "something's missing." The participant, or collaborator (as I like to think), fills in that void, bringing in a new element (or the missing part) to complete the process or continue the experiment. I start with barriers to organize and mediate the path of direction and think about how the viewer would respond to the space. The barriers are later transformed into the walls of the chamber. The yellow glowing structure with a cute camouflage design has a single opening, similar to a trap.

CF : What is the desired effect of these structures? That's to say, what kind of experience are you trying to convey, transmit, or produce?

ZV : As I mentioned, the experiment continues once someone enters the structure. There they are alone, as the space is suitable for only one person and isolated for the moment from the other objects or artworks around it. There is a slipper monument in the center, which invites one to slip into some kind of ritual, relaxation, or guru-driven transformation. The yellow translucent walls do not protect you; instead, they act as an extension of the body, an extra layer of protection. The chamber itself is based on my studies of fortifications, specifically the one-man bunker and its function of seizing and holding the space. We don't live in these structures—they are there only for special times, troubled times, dark times. The yellow translucent chamber has the same elements associated with a one-man bunker: that of waiting, watching, anticipation, and considering your next move. In this sense it embodies anthropomorphic characteristics. Visually the exterior of the bunker looks like a head, and the gun slits look like eyes.

CF : You've talked about social architecture and your interest in utopian ideas from the 1960s. How do these utopian ideas play out in your work?

ZV : Modernist architects such as Le Corbusier worked with utopian ideas of collective living in small modules (*modulor* is the exact word) within huge city blocks. I am trying to transform the module as an instrument of possible control and constraint, somewhat similar to the street barricades made during the student revolts of 1968—a spontaneous invention by the students, who tilted cars on their side to form barricades. This action opposed preconceived ideas of revolutionary strategy and its organizing principles.

CF : You definitely pull from your architectural background, not only with the language that you use to describe your practice and artwork but also in the way that you reference materials to create interconnectivity between people and a space—how the design of a space plays into the way that we think about ourselves and our community and how it affects the way we act. Can you talk about your interest in these phenomena?

ZV : It all stems from original ancient enclosures, the demarcation of land, which has been through many transformations over time. From stone ramparts and fortifications to the transparent glass architecture of modernism. Through its evolution, if we call it that, we have lost something—our need for protection. The transparency of materials anticipates the transparency of political and social relations that we hear so much about today. Walter Benjamin talked about this in relation to film and architecture. Foil, the material I use for *DuckBunny Chamber* (2010), is a step back from total transparency; it's opaque, bringing into question the boundaries of protection in a time of total transparency.

CF : You've talked about your work's connection with the 1960s, specifically placing it within the art historical trajectory established in the 1960s with minimalist sculpture and the relationship of the body, the object, and the space; most of these objects, however, were not made to physically interact with, or walk into, for that matter. Which artists from this period are you referencing, and what is it about their work that intersects with what you are doing?

ZV : Some of the Carl Andre sculptures were originally made to walk onto. In an interview from 1969, Andre says something like, "it's most important to be able to stand in the middle of the sculpture." He is referring to his steel or aluminum plates installed on the floor. Today most minimal sculptures in exhibitions are protected by ropes, guards, or taped lines of demarcation, so we don't have the opportunity to experience what it is like to stand in the middle of the artwork. I hope that my chamber, with its aluminum plate and slippers in the center, will bring that option back. ∎

Born 1958 in Požarevac, Serbia; lives and works in San Diego. Vukosavljevic studied architecture in Belgrade, Yugoslavia, and has been an artist in residence at the MAK Center for Art and Architecture, Los Angeles, and at Quartier 21 in the MuseumsQuartier, Vienna. He collaborated with Los Angeles–based artist Jason Rhoades at the Kunsthaus Graz in Austria and, together with Franz West and Heimo Zobernig, created the installation *Studiolo* during the Venice Biennale in 2005. *Studiolo* was included in the New Festival at the Centre Georges Pompidou, Paris, in 2009 and in the exhibition *The New Décor*, curated by Ralph Rugoff, at Hayward Gallery, London, in 2010.

This page
DuckBunny Chamber, 2010 (details) — cat. no. 129

Opposite clockwise from top
Protection Stage, 2010
Isolation panels, tape, aluminum, wool, fluorescent lights, metal
tubes, sandbags, wire, and wooden structure
Panels: 96 × 120 × 1 in. (243.8 × 304.8 × 2.5 cm) each;
wooden structure: 96 × 96 × 108 in. (243.8 × 243.8 × 274.3 cm)
Courtesy of the artist

Smoke Signals, 2006
Graphite and paper on paper
12 × 10 in. (30.5 × 25.4 cm)
Courtesy of the artist

Star Bunny, 2010
Plexiglas, cotton, wire, tape, and metal tubes
108 × 108 × 108 in. (274.3 × 274.3 × 274.3 cm)
Courtesy of the artist

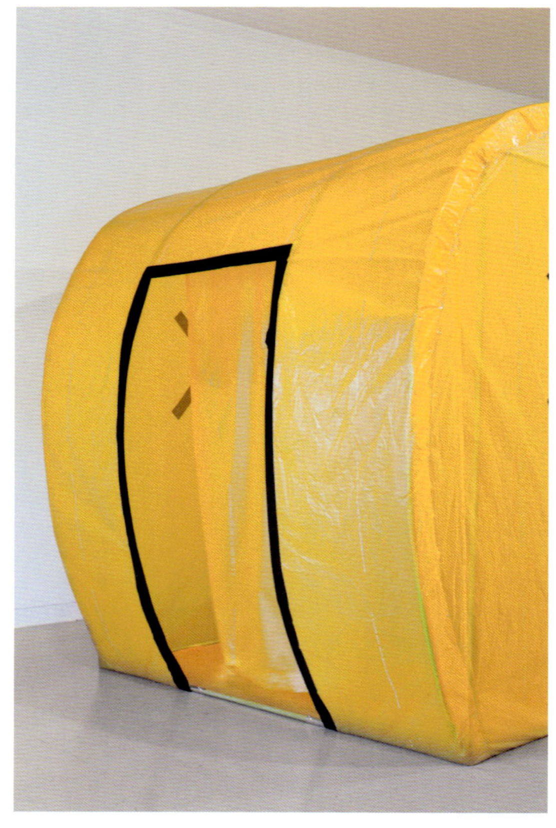

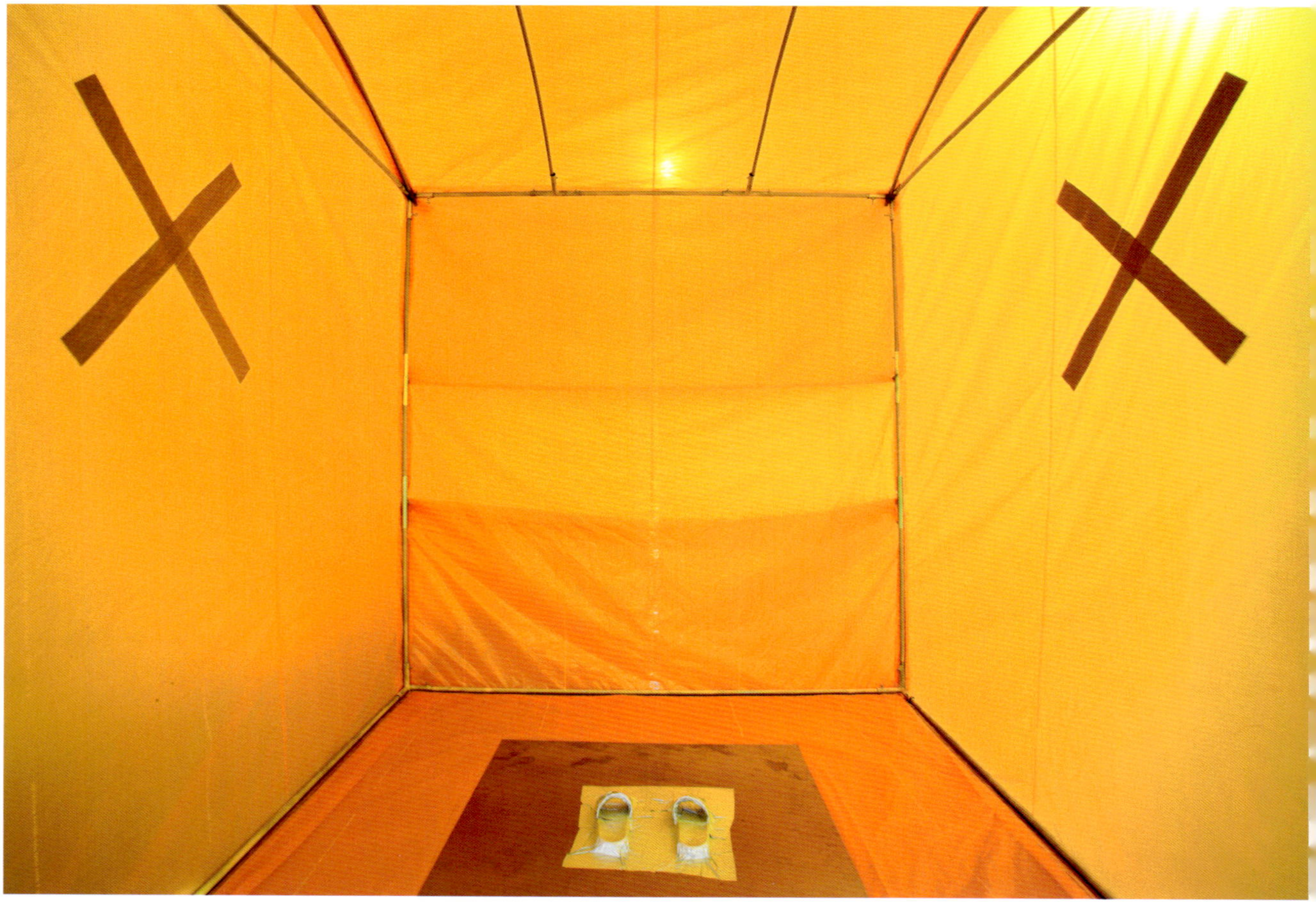

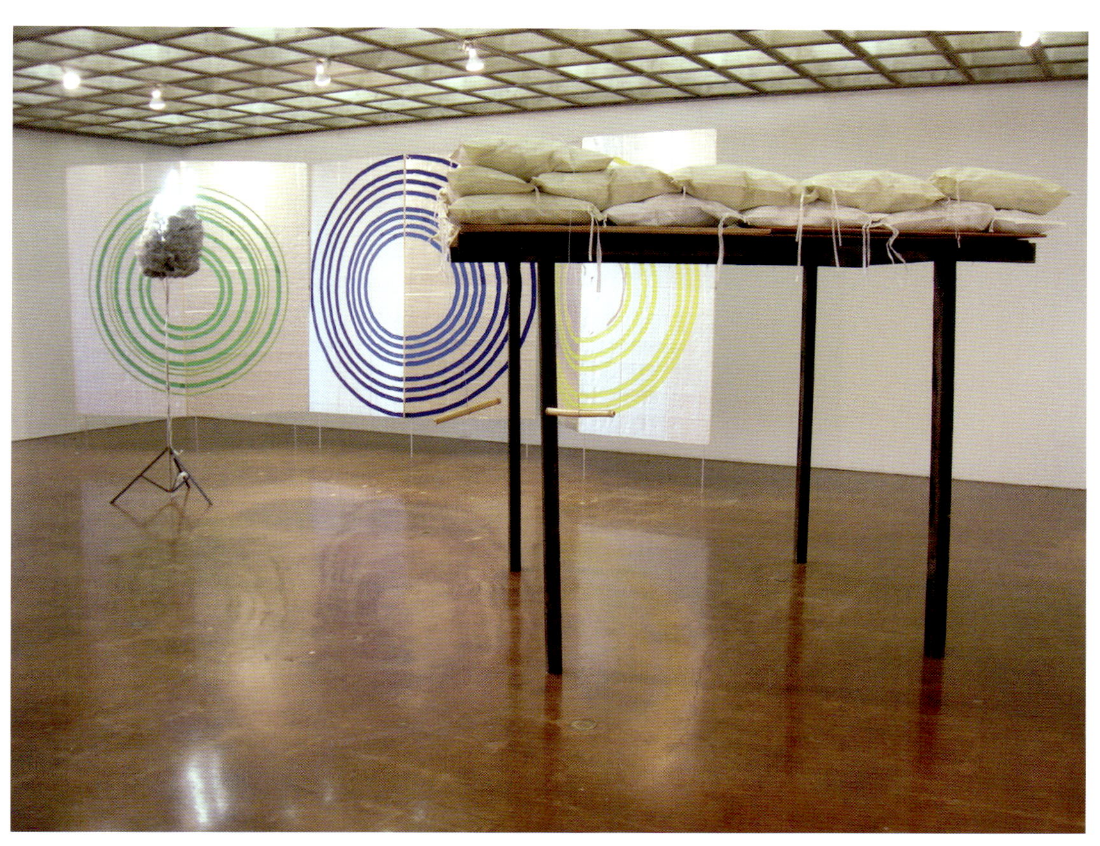

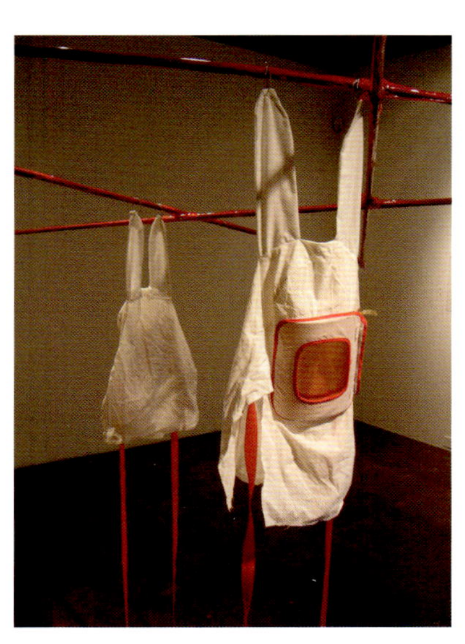

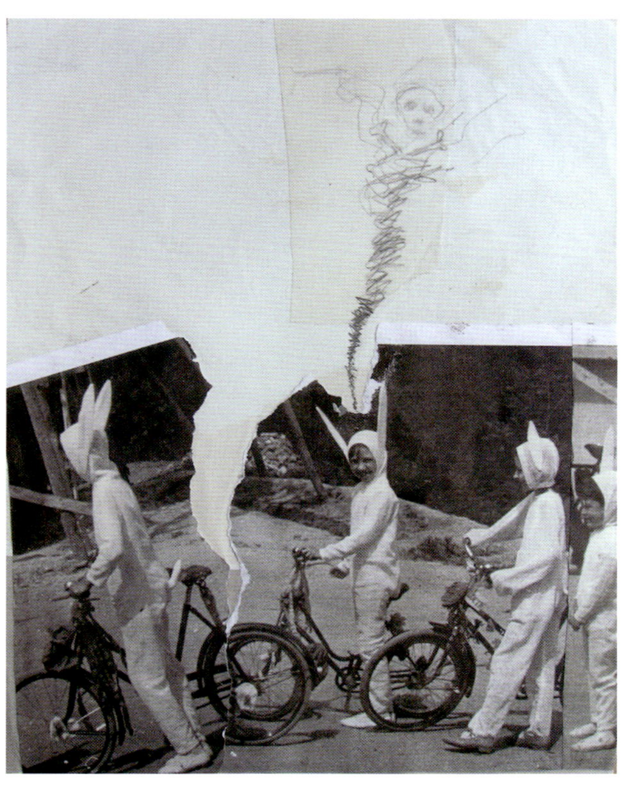

Nina Waisman

Practice
Installation, interactive media, sound,
performance, video, two-dimensional works,
sculpture

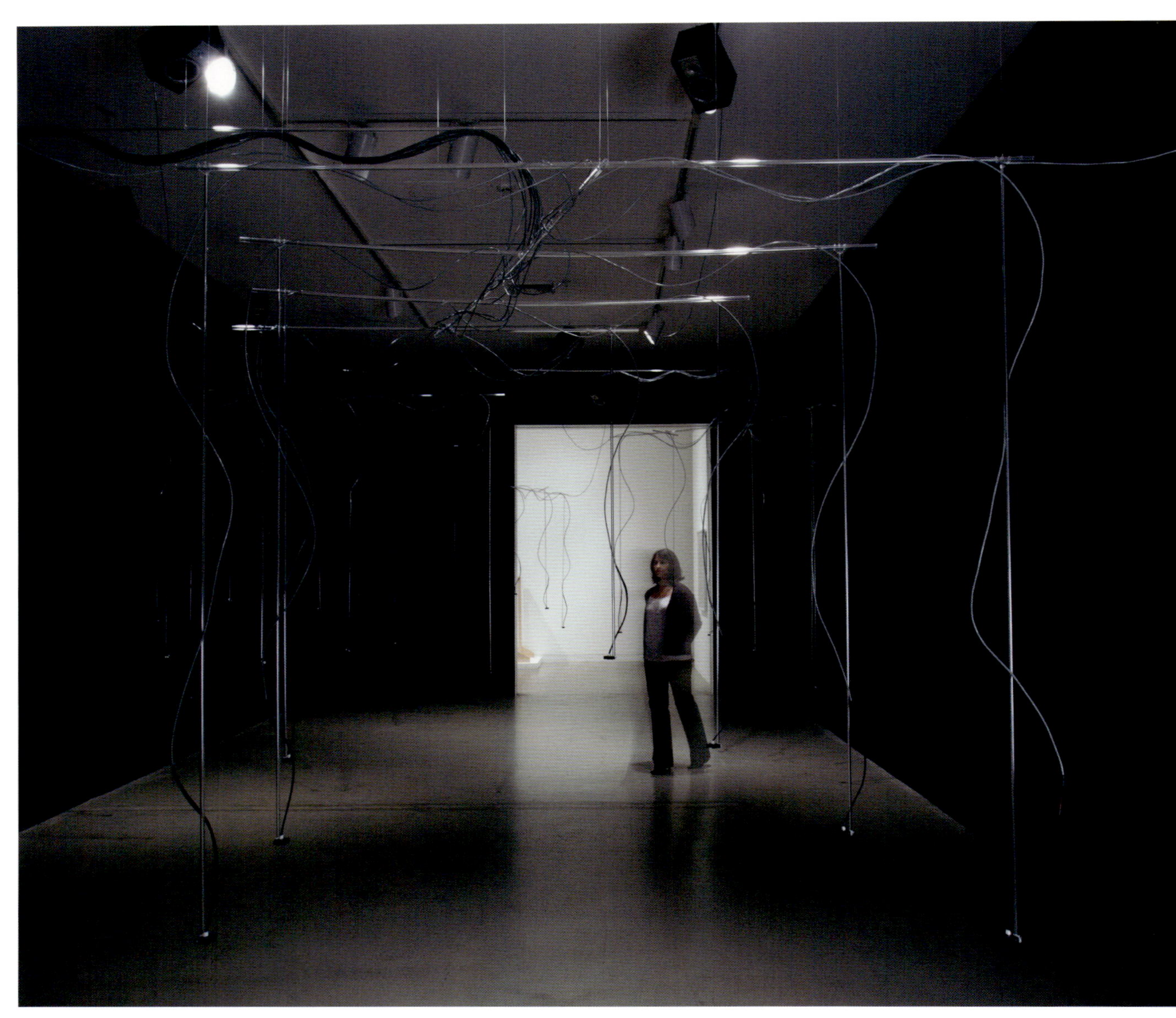

Between Bodies/Tijuana, 2008–10 — cat. no. 130

Born in Salt Lake City, Utah; lives and
works in San Diego. Waisman is a
graduate of Harvard University (BA),
Art Center College of Design (BFA,
2004), and the University of California,
San Diego (MFA, 2008). In addition,
she trained as a classical dancer at the
School of American Ballet, New York.
She has collaborated with the *particle
group* and CUBO, and her work h
been presented at the House of W
Cultures, Berlin; CECUT, Tijuana;
Museum of Image and Sound, São
Paulo, Brazil; the San Diego Muse
of Art; Luxe/Stephan Stoyanov Ga
New York; LACE, Los Angeles; and
Arts Exchange, Los Angeles.

CF : **Originally conceived for the Centro Cultural Tijuana in Mexico, *Between Bodies* has been resited for the California Biennial at the Orange County Museum of Art. What role do these public spaces play in the contextual framing of this artwork?**

NW : There is much that binds Orange County and Tijuana! Mass media's portrayal of Tijuana, through a lens focused sensationally on drug-cartel crimes, suggests that the U.S.'s only connection to Tijuana today is through fear. Yet many OC residents and their employees have family living in Tijuana. Many low-priced electronics enjoyed in Orange County are made by people earning ten dollars a day in Tijuana's maquiladoras; families working in these maquiladoras cannot afford to eat properly or rent a home with a roof. Some U.S.-based companies making electronics in Tijuana dump toxic by-products there, poisoning water, land, and residents. Technologies enabling keyboard-punched orders for Tijuana-produced goods further obscure the links between our lives and the Tijuana residents fulfilling those orders.

Between Bodies offers a tech-altered *dérive* through Tijuana—technology connects museum visitors' gestures to richly varied everyday sound gestures in Tijuana, to lives not portrayed by mass media. The sensing body's role as theremin, tuning a city, is enhanced—as visitors pass through the museum, naturally (or unnaturally) moving toward and away from sensors, Tijuana's sounds are mixed, shifted in pitch, volume, speed.

Sounds of labor—of bodily gestures possibly engaged in by many visitors—open the piece, creating a common denominator of bodily and sonic experiences heard throughout Tijuana but also most anywhere in the world. A gestural dialogue is set up between museum visitors and *Tijuanenses,* one that might open the city to those who know it only through sensational reporting. The piece ends with sound gestures connected to surveillance, similarly heard worldwide. In between, visitors interact with a range of broadly recognizable yet localizing sound gestures. For *Tijuanenses*, this experience triggers layers of personal experience and history. For nonresidents, a virtual tour may be produced but complicated by concrete bodily dialogues (discussed further below).

CF : **In recent art history—and in contemporary art practices, for that matter—there is an inclination toward participatory artwork. As much of your work is interactive, requiring an active viewer to complete the piece, it's possible to look at your artwork through this lens. How do you see the role that an active audience plays in relation to your work?**

NW : Art (and non-art) reception is always participatory—perception of objective matter is actively shaped by perceivers' physiological and cultural histories. As a former dancer, I'm interested in how we think through our whole bodies—not just our eyes—thus many of my works bring such body-based thinking to the surface. The spaces I create, though teched out to varying degrees, are often odd exaggerations of everyday interactions that I'd like to raise experiential questions about.

Consider this dictionary definition: "transducer, n. a device that is actuated by power from one system and supplies power usually in another form to a second system." I'm thinking of the body as a vast system of transducers, triggered by powers (physical, social, technological) in its environment. In the case of *Between Bodies*, sited in Orange County, a visitor's encounter with a city (Tijuana) and some of its people is technologically enhanced by binding the visitor's and Tijuana's everyday gestural spaces, linking in turn—should one care to consider them—two distinct yet interdependent ecologies. On the first level, sound waves, entering the visitor's body in response to its motions, can be transduced into curiosity, pleasure, displeasure. A desire for control can be transduced with the comprehension that sound can be manipulated. There might be an erotic, empathetic, or exploitative power transduced by one body's manipulation of another body. Each "transducer" in the museum can become a watched performer, as others in the room look to see who or what is making sound: sonic energy converts here into social dynamics built around exhibitionist energies and/or fears.

But transduction here ideally is not a one-way street. To explore the sound of another body (or system) can lead one to listen to its rhythms, its pitch, and to become attuned to them. A bodily dialogue may be generated.

CF : **This relationship (among audience, artwork, movement, and space) is mediated through technology. Why use technology to facilitate this interaction?**

NW : Well, neurologists have found that simply hearing the sound of another body performing an action can lead us to experience this action in the brain and muscles. We don't enact the gesture, but nerve clusters for producing it fire, and muscles are primed to act. Neurologists link this "mirroring" to a survival-driven need for empathic skills—when I hear you do something, I experience your state and can sense how we might next interact.

Meanwhile, Rodolfo Llinás, an NYU neuroscientist, explains that random, learned gestural skills—walking, typing, etc.—play together in our brains when we don't move. Llinás's research concludes that the overlaying of these gestural tapes is the source of creative thought: new logics arise from interference between replayed memories of our motor-based actions. A new tech gesture, then, is not a small thing!

So hearing sounds of recorded bodies performing actions can lead listeners to "mirror" the heard gestures. These mirrored gestures, overlaid with whatever gestural tapes are already playing in a listener's brain, can lead to new, affiliated logics. Adding to this everyday, gestural pileup, visitors to my installations employ tech-controlling gestures to manipulate sounds heard in the space. This logic-forming, gesturally mashed-up medium interests me, given our increasing use of mediated sound, physical computing devices, and surveillance systems (policing borders and behaviors everywhere). My work asks experientially: how might tech-inflected gestures shape the logic of relationships facilitated by technology? ∎

Sounds from the streets of Tijuana include:

Border gates (pedestrian entrance into Tijuana)

Taxi drivers calling for fares on Revolución

Wind chimes for sale near Revolución

Filing devalued coins into pricier tourist mementos on Revolución

Bike-horn used to advertise sweet ices to passers-by on Revolución

Street musicians playing Fara-Fara for market-goers near Revolución

Making tortillas in a corner restaurant on the way to 5 Y 10

Die-cutting cardboard for packaging in Colonia Chilpancingo

Typing online reports of toxic manufacturing practices in Chilpancingo-based factories (these factories produce consumer items for the US market)

Pushcart salesman calling for ice cream sales in residential streets of Colonia Chilpancingo

Raking up street rubble to prevent it being thrown by cars at pedestrians in Los Laureles

Hammering repairs on improvisational housing in Los Laureles

Jump-roping girls on the street of Los Laureles

Boys and men digging a ditch along the street in Los Laureles

Children riding tricycles and bikes in circles outside their homes in Los Laureles

Norteño music played in a street market in ejido Maclovio Rojas

Car-mounted advertising playing through the streets of Maclovio Rojas

Telecommunicating via dial-up (volunteers in community-run government offices in Maclovio Rojas seeking basic services and constitutionally granted title to community land, in the face of global corporations' attempts to privately acquire this land)

Ice cream truck heard throughout the streets of Maclovio Rojas

Children working in the market in Maclovio Rojas

Bike bells advertising push-cart sales

Roosters raised for cockfights

Military helicopters

Police sirens

Footsteps

Wind

Birds

The I-5

Recorded sounds used in ***Between Bodies/Tijuana,***
2008–10 — cat. no. 130

Below
***Space Shifter/Rhythm Machine 2.0*, 2010**
Site-specific mixed media, computer, software, electronics, audio equipment
With Pure Data programming by Marius Schebella
Dimensions variable
Courtesy of the artist
Installation view, Stephan Stoyanov/Luxe Gallery, New York

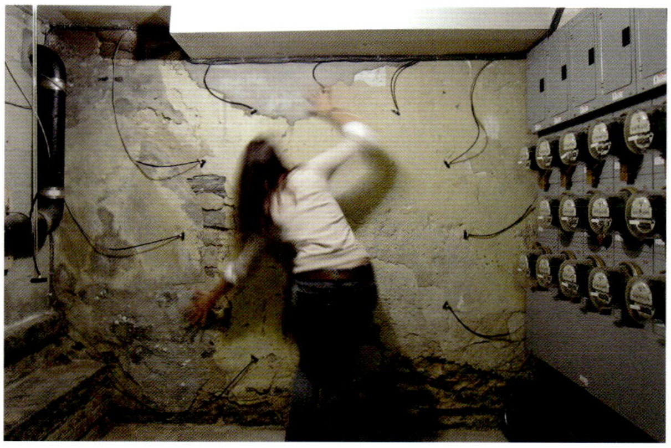

CUBO collective (Giacomo Castagnola, Camilo Ontiveros, Nina Waisman, and Felipe Zuñiga)
***mediawomb*, 2009**
Computer, software, electronics, audio equipment, sensors, wire, speakers, recycled cardboard egg crates, and wood
With Pure Data programming by Marius Schebella
Dimensions variable
Courtesy of the artists
Installation in CALIT2 lobby at the University of California, San Diego

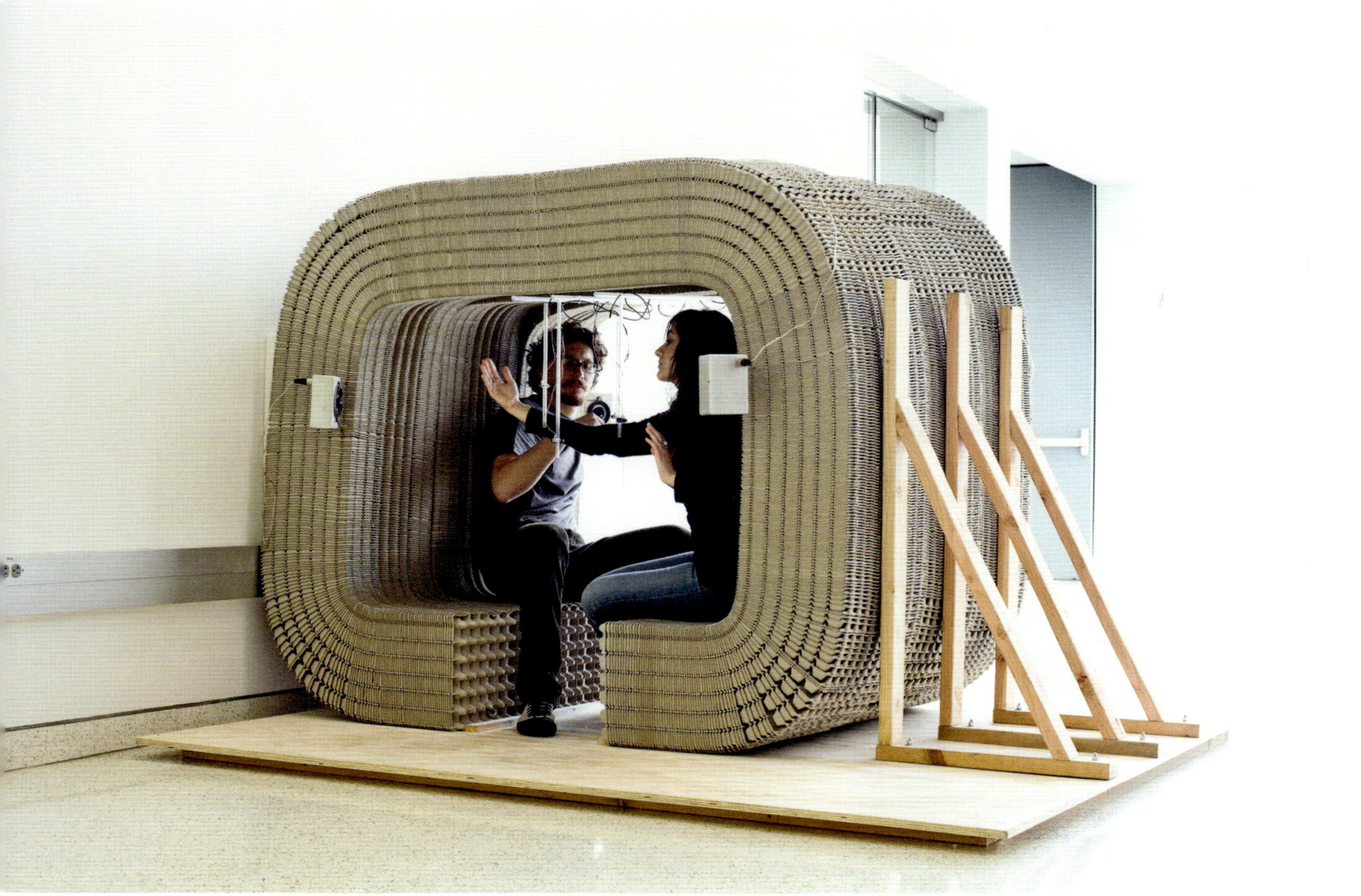

Flora Wiegmann

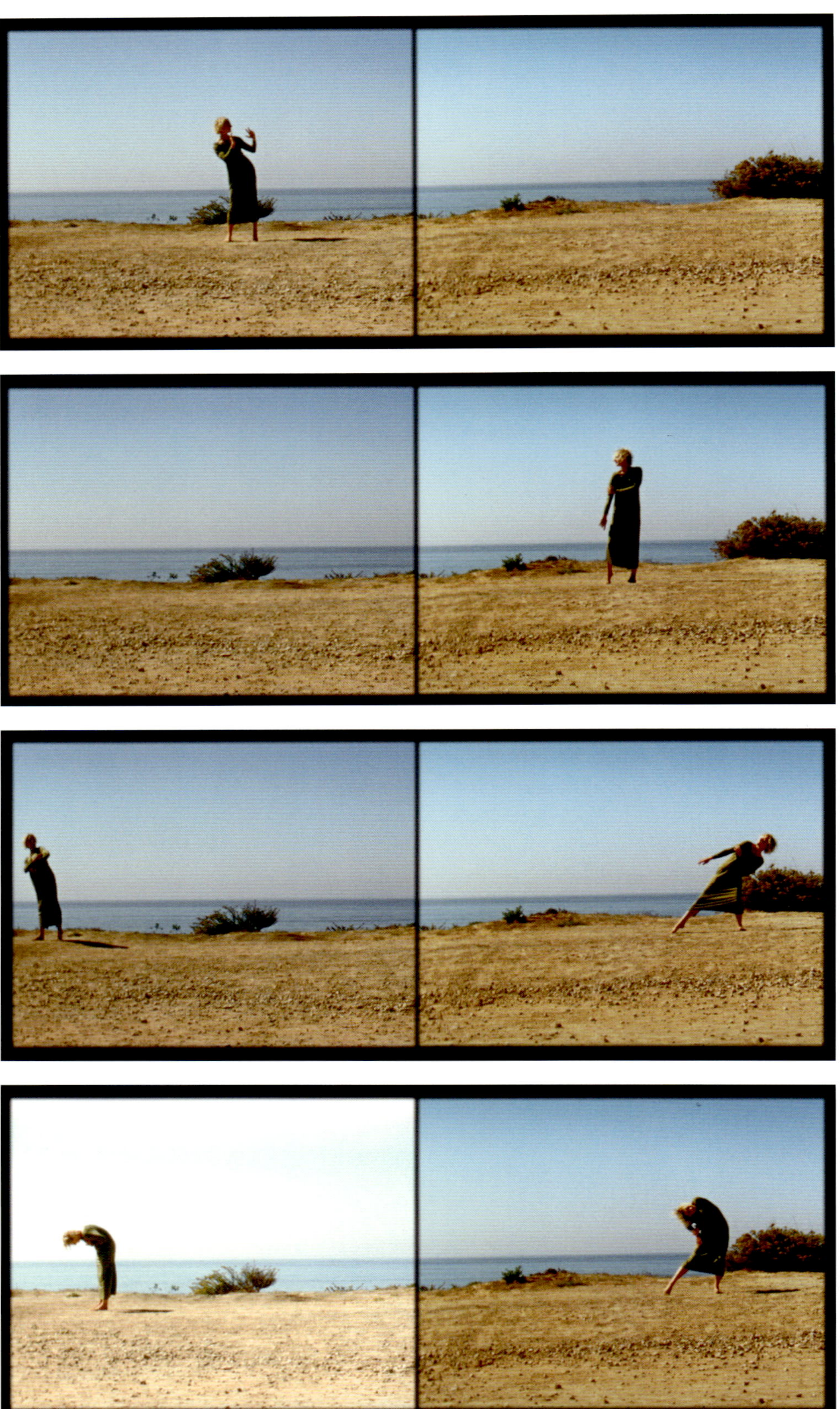

Stills from *Wandering (Still)*, **2010** — cat. no. 132

Interview with Chloë Flores

CF: **Your project for the biennial, *Wandering (Still)* and *(Detail)*, involves thirteen performances. What is the inspiration for this work?**

FW: Late last year I began researching a modern dance pioneer who worked in Germany in the early part of the twentieth century, Mary Wigman—originally spelled Wiegmann, so it's quite possible that I'm related to her. Her technique and choreographic process piqued my interest because she utilized improvisation to translate things like emotion, subconscious drives, and the supernatural into movement. Dance was her language, and she was an extremely expressive and dramatic communicator. Her work also highlighted the changing roles of a choreographer as soloist, as a leader of a group, and as a member of a group, all the while celebrating each dancer as an individual and artist, not as a Wigman replica.

The motivation for *Wandering (Still)* and *(Detail)* comes out of two photographic images from *Wandering*, part of Wigman's *Scenes from a Dance Drama* (1924). The contrasting images look as if they might illustrate two different dances. I liked that disjunction and wondered how the dance eventually traveled through one moment to reach the other. Utilizing these images and textual descriptions of the actual dance, I'm reanimating these moments with my own choreographic choices (the present), while conjuring up the methods of Wigman (the past).

In the film I dance each role of *Wandering*; therefore I attempt to embody various women with distinct histories, muscle memories, and physical patterning (again, the celebration of the individual dancer). The live performances extend into real space, without the limits of specific choreography. I will attempt to embody one character per performance to see if I can let go of my own habits to take on someone else's, demonstrating a lineage through movement from 1924 to now.

Lastly, I would just add that in this climate, in which re-performance of historical work (by its author or someone else) is popular, that is not my particular goal. I am trying to leave behind the idea of authentic reconstruction to emphasize a contemporary form. Disintegration of information through time, memory, and context disallows for a perfect redo and opens up the doors to appropriation and translation concurrently.

CF: **Interpreting the gestural habits of a dancer through a visual image is working under the assumption that one could read the body as a text—a text that is based in a language of movement. Can you talk a little about this in relation to this project?**

FW: One can get a lot of information by looking at a body. Each person's history of movement is recorded and contained in the body as a physical translation of something experiential. It exists then as ephemera within the body, which can be read from the outside, so body as text is certainly an appropriate term. Body language is exactly that; mannerisms or postures convey unspoken information, whether purposefully communicated (gestures) or not (involuntary or habitual action). In addition, the bodily experience of the beholder interprets what is being seen. So we are all forming our own interpretation, based on how we inhabit the world. While I embody the gestures and postures of thirteen different women, I'm participating in the same process.

CF: **You've described your work as being "place-specific"— as responding to and considering the context of a site, its architecture, and the social environment in which the performance takes place. When that context is a museum setting, how do you see your work operating in relation to the other static art objects in the space that you are inhabiting?**

FW: It's rare for me to make dances that can be transported from site to site. I begin with specific conceptual structures for each project; therefore, aspects of the hosting space are integral and nontransferable. I think it differs from the term *site-specific*, which I link to a more social-historical-collaborative *process* with a site. Instead I focus on the body in that particular space. In turn, my work is often made on site, so the architecture and other objects sharing the space influence the movement. I refrain from literally referencing artworks, but since it's all happening in the same place, viewers will naturally make visual connections to whatever else is around.

CF: **So in a way you're embodying the movement, and the movement is embodying the specific place. Why is this methodology important to your body of work?**

FW: I've formed my way of working out of a discomfort with performance as spectacle. I attempt to subvert this idea by leaving out at least some of the elements that create a domineering scene, a flash, or something that calls out, "Ta-da!" at the end. Instead I tend to work with a more subdued sensibility to which "embodying the space" is much more applicable than "taking over a space." Again, the idea sharing is key to my work, as is specificity in the use of time. Past performances have ranged from five minutes to two weeks in duration. Of course, no one person will see a long-term work in its entirety, but he/she could visit on a few different days or might witness only thirty seconds passing through the room. That's why I often improvise, preventing any one moment from being precious or unmissable. I want an audience to be in control of their viewership, be it how long they might stay to watch or where they choose to place themselves in relation to the performing bodies.

Because a large percentage of people who come in contact with my work may not have prior experience with dance, or may feel that they don't have the tools to understand it, I hope to present work that might encourage a phenomenological reading, which validates both the viewer's bodily experience of the performance and my own. ∎

Born 1976 in Lincoln, Nebraska; lives and works in Los Angeles. Wiegmann is a graduate of Columbia College, Chicago (BA, 1998), and the University of California, Los Angeles (MFA, 2007). She has collaborated with artists Felicia Ballos, Fritz Haeg, Drew Heitzler, Amy Granat, Silke Otto-Knapp, Alix Lambert, Margo Victor, and Andrea Zittel. Her projects have been presented at the ICA, Philadelphia; the Whitney Museum of American Art, New York; the Los Angeles County Museum of Art; Los Angeles Contemporary Exhibitions; the Kitchen, New York; Highways Performance Space, Los Angeles; Art2102, Los Angeles; Art Basel, Miami; the Banff Centre, Banff, Canada; and Le 102, Grenoble, France.

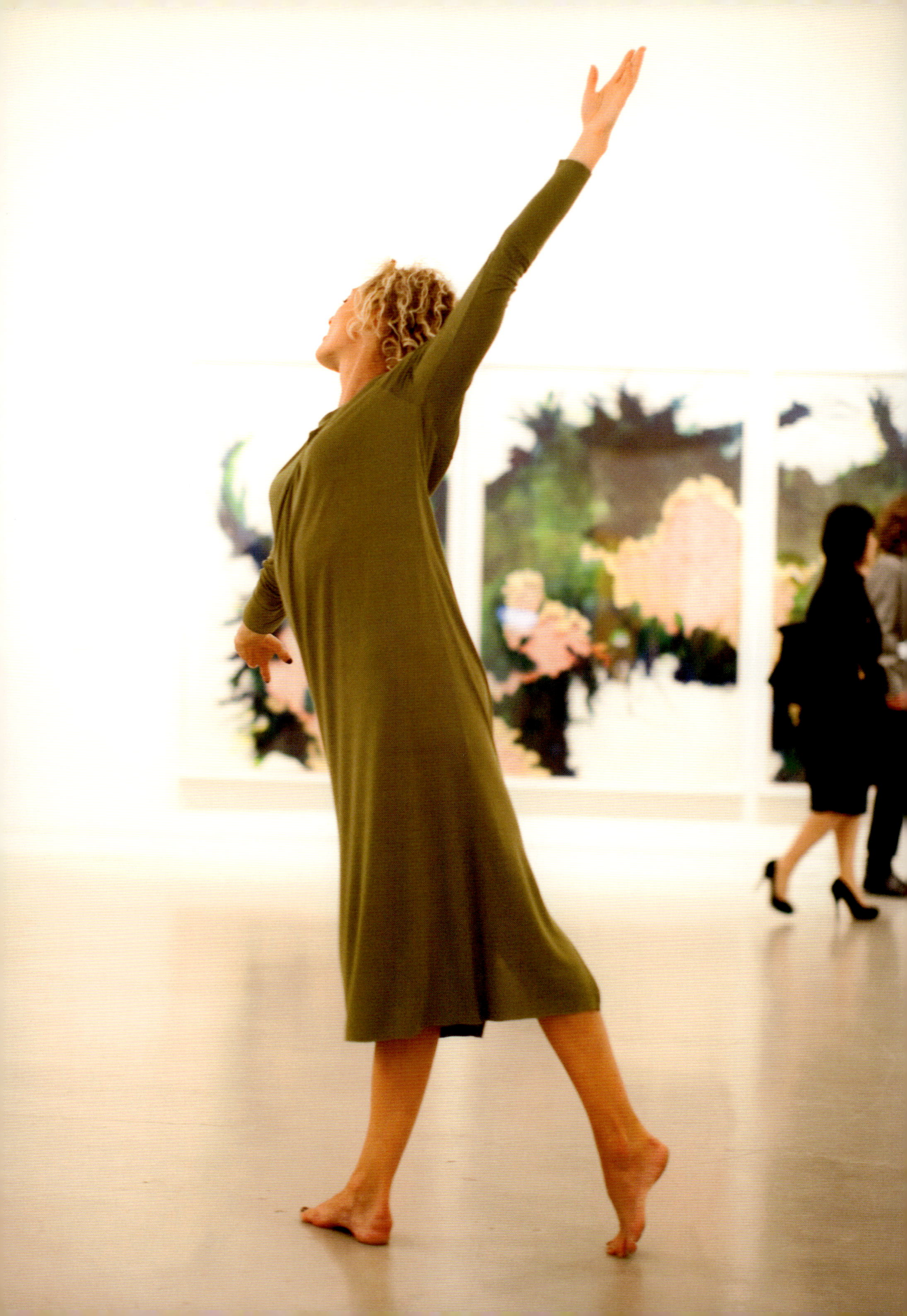

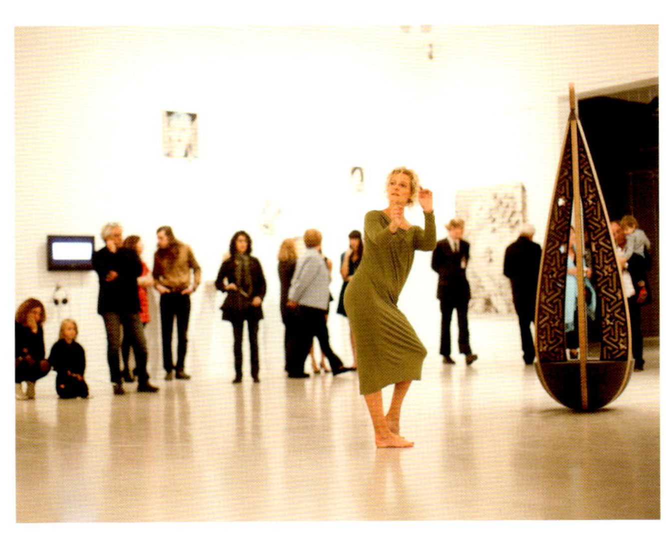

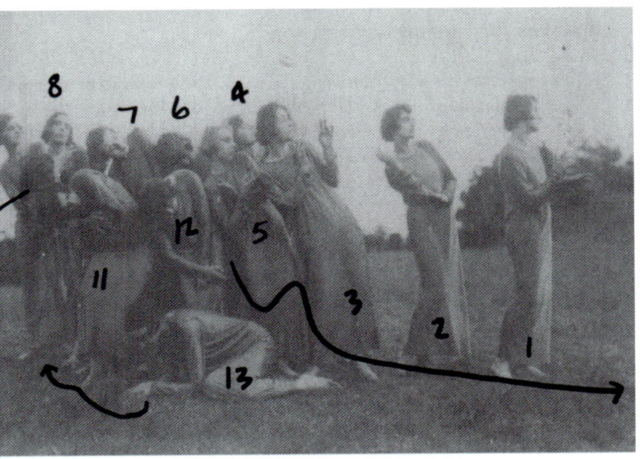

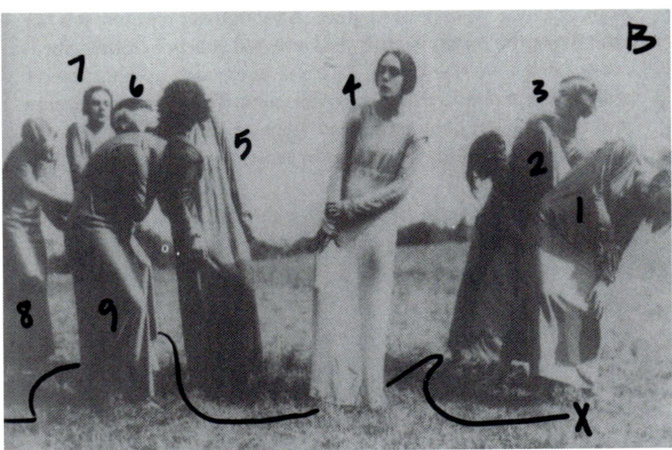

<u>Above and opposite</u>
***Wandering (Detail)*, 2010** — cat. no. 131
Performance during the 2010 California Biennial

<u>Below</u>
***Spatial Study for Wandering (Wigman Image A and B)*, 2010**
Courtesy of the artist

Allison Wiese

Practice
Sculpture, installation, architectural intervention, sound, performance, two-dimensional works

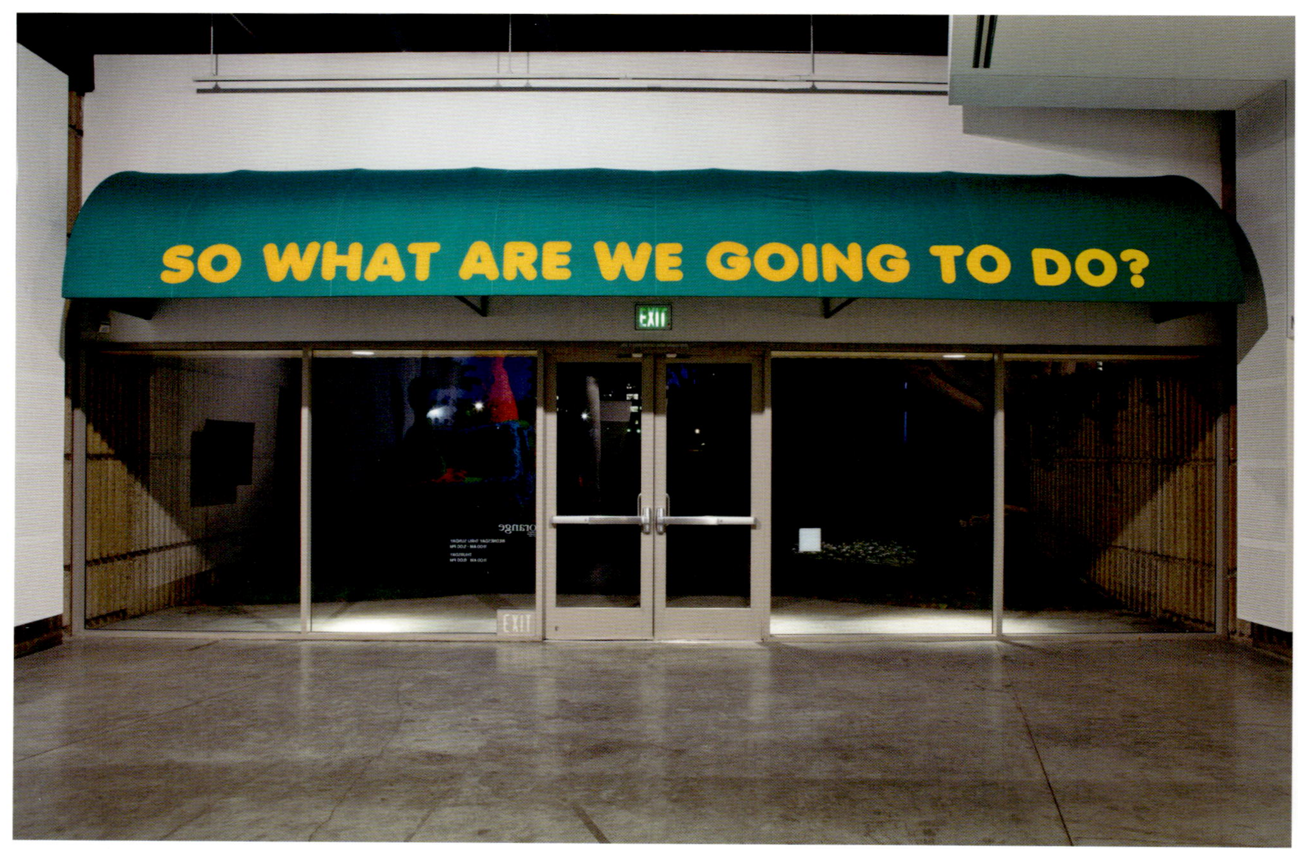

Untitled (Awning), **2010** — cat. no. 133

Interview with Chloë Flores

CF : **An aspect of your work involves removing everyday objects from their original context (for example, moving out-of-season California Valencia oranges to a Houston gallery space). Why is this displacement an important component of your work?**

AW : Displacement is a nice way to talk about it: the actual journey may not always be obvious to everyone who encounters the work (most folks don't know from where and in what seasons different oranges are harvested), but the ordinariness of the objects still begs thought about their life outside an art context and maybe about the boundary of the frame around them. Conjecture over the source of the produce on the floor is part of my work just as is conjecture over the original meanings of the texts I use. I'm interested in the often-irritating friction between the dumb and literal reading and the further-flung contexts that are equally a real part of understanding something.

CF : **Why displace an existing object rather than fabricating it?**

AW : I like to make meaning with the ready-to-hand. And real stuff is often the most efficient for me to work with, in both pragmatic and poetic terms. It's also the funny tension between the literal and the figurative implicit in sculpture that motivates me. Lately I've been thinking a lot about the conventions of the grade school commodity map and the road movie as vehicles to examine hyperbolic representations of scale and place. A cornucopian pile of oranges may seem heroic one minute and pragmatic the next, alternately pure synecdoche and nothing but by-product.

CF : **Some of your works deal with signage: blinking lights conveying a message via Morse code on a mobile advertising sign, pickup lines on theater marquees, quotes and slogans printed on road signs or displayed in neon lights. In these projects language is displaced, playing with and against our preconceived ideas about it and how it is displayed. What's your interest in the role of language and how it's displayed in relation to ideologies?**

AW : My recent work finds its vocabulary within a certain vein of populist Americana. I'm often restating texts (ranging from Ben Franklin's *Poor Richard's Almanac* to the aforementioned authorless pickup lines) that originate in particular historical discourses within new contexts. I'm interested (with a simultaneous and perverse kind of hopelessness and optimism) in replumbing the social and political landscape of the recent past as a way of both querying the lingering presence and viability of certain American myths and pointing to truths about the present.

I like the format of commercial signage (sandwich boards, marquees, and flashing car-lot signs) because of its vernacular quality—it's what's around anyway. And it's talking to you. But signage of this kind normally accommodates only certain tones. Using it as a platform for the sorts of communication I'm interested in satisfyingly undermines something at the same time that it opens up weird and improbable possibilities.

Many of my projects are invested in some kind of collision between the small, incidental, improvisational, or personal and the public, large, or half-official. I think the signage I've used acts as an interface between these two scales. For example, pickup lines insinuated (licitly and illicitly) onto the marquees of single-screen movie theaters in towns that I was ostensibly forming a meaningful relationship with as an artist-in-residence cast me in the earnest, if ridiculous, role of attempted seducer of entire cities.

CF : **For the biennial you are placing an awning within the museum context and, in doing so, referencing the non-literal signs of the built environment around us. That is to say, this displaced everyday object calls attention to the ways in which we inhabit and experience interior and exterior space. What is your interest in architectural intervention? And more specifically, can you speak about this concept in relation to this project?**

AW : I've always been attracted to the friction that institutions (and their architectural manifestations) can provide. A recent untitled project involved installing a redwood gazebo inside the galleries of the Museum of Contemporary Art San Diego in an act of architectural turducken. It's a rustic Californian do-it-yourself yard project trapped in the craw of a protomodernist house turned postmodern museum. Gazebos are all about prospect and site, and so is the MCA San Diego, albeit in very different ways.

Sculptors have always had a real tussle/make-out session with material going on in a way that painters (whose medium is naturally about an illusion of one further remove) are less likely to. I guess I handle buildings as yet another part of that wrestling match. It's a sort of quixotic ignoring of scale. I also really like the maple syrup bottles shaped like little log cabins. I think expansively about the space and time through which ideas and objects travel, and I guess I try to treat buildings and spaces the same way that I do other materials. Of course they're not quite the same as the other functional or mundane stuff that I'm attracted to—they house us. And they sometimes have meanings and histories that we're less apt to ignore.

Awnings are a funny case—they're ostensibly all about functionality (as shade/shelter) but pretty transparently serve as announcements, whether they're acting as commercial signage or not. They kidnap entire buildings, and they seem to vibrate between a weird optimism and an insincerity of some sort that I find fascinating. ∎

Born 1969 in New York; lives and works in San Diego. Wiese is a graduate of Brown University (BA, 1992) and the University of California, San Diego (MFA, 2000). Her work has been exhibited at Machine Project, Los Angeles; the Museum of Contemporary Art San Diego; and Socrates Sculpture Park, Long Island City, New York. She is the recipient of a 2007 Louis Comfort Tiffany Award and has received grants from Art Matters, Creative Capital, and the Cultural Arts Council of Houston.

Wiese is a fellow of the MacDowell Colony, an alumna of the Skowhegan School of Painting, and was a Core Fellow of the Museum of Fine Arts, Houston, from 2001 to 2003.

Untitled, 2010
Redwood
108 × 96 × 108 in. (274.3 × 243.8 × 274.3 cm)
Courtesy of the artist
Installation view, Museum of Contemporary Art San Diego

Untitled, 2005
Valencia oranges and cartons
72 × 108 × 108 in. (182.9 × 274.3 × 274.3 cm)
Courtesy of the artist

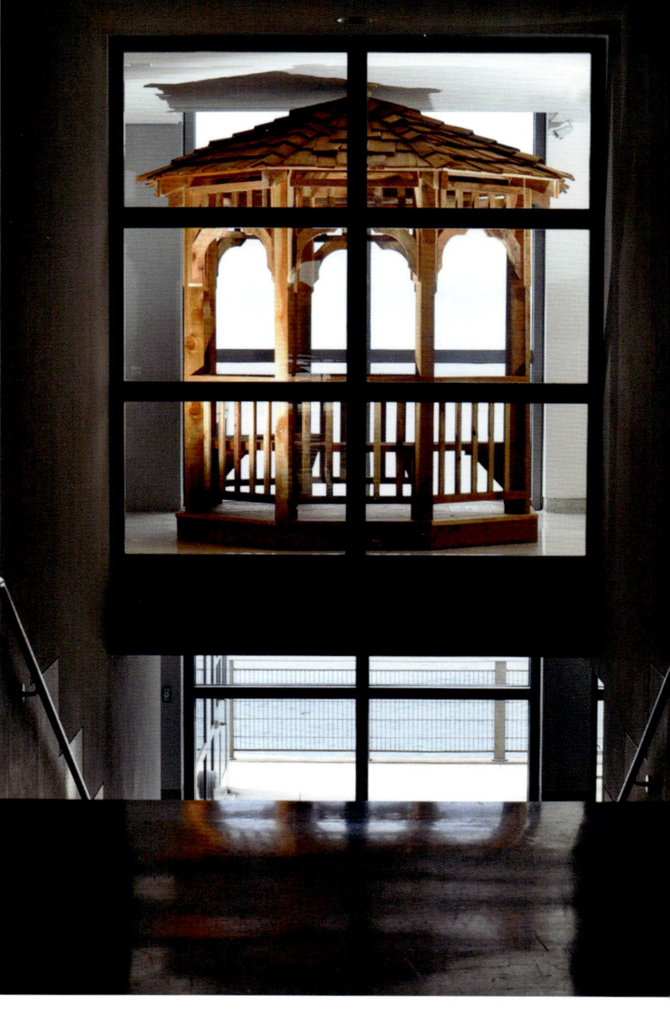

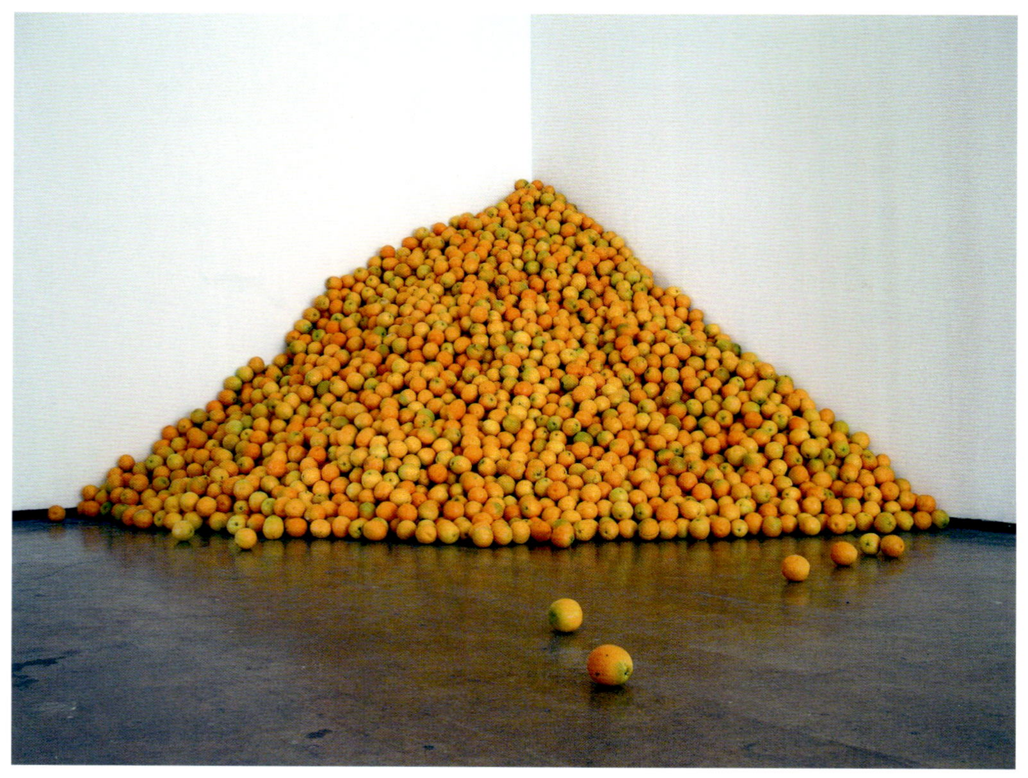

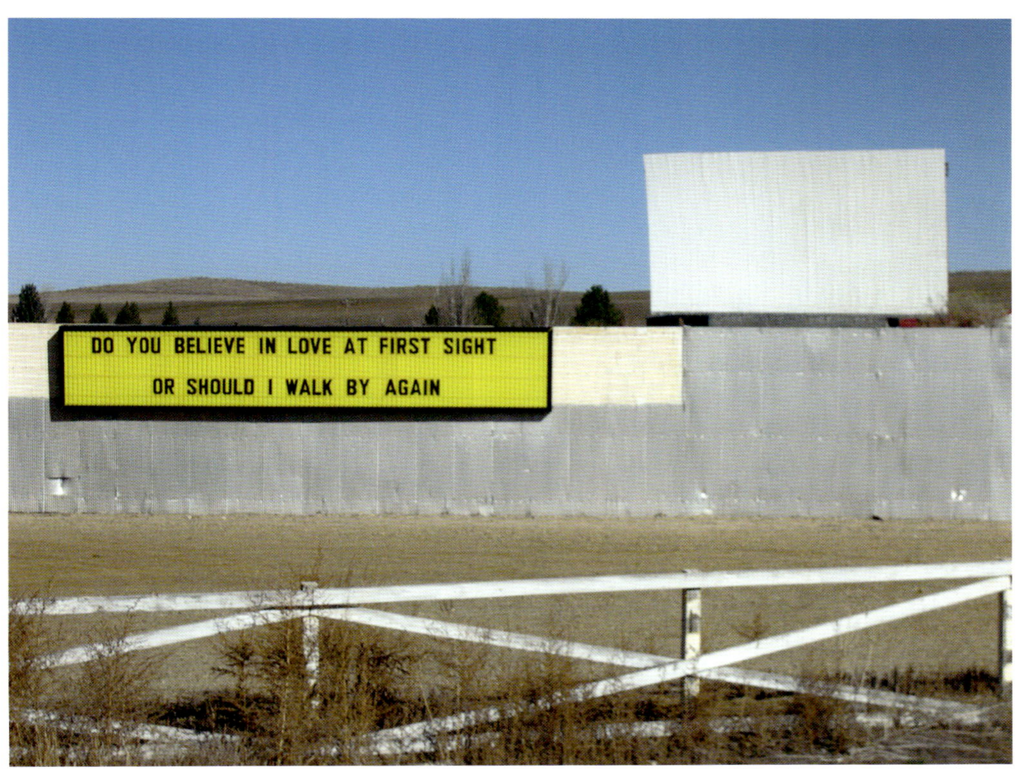

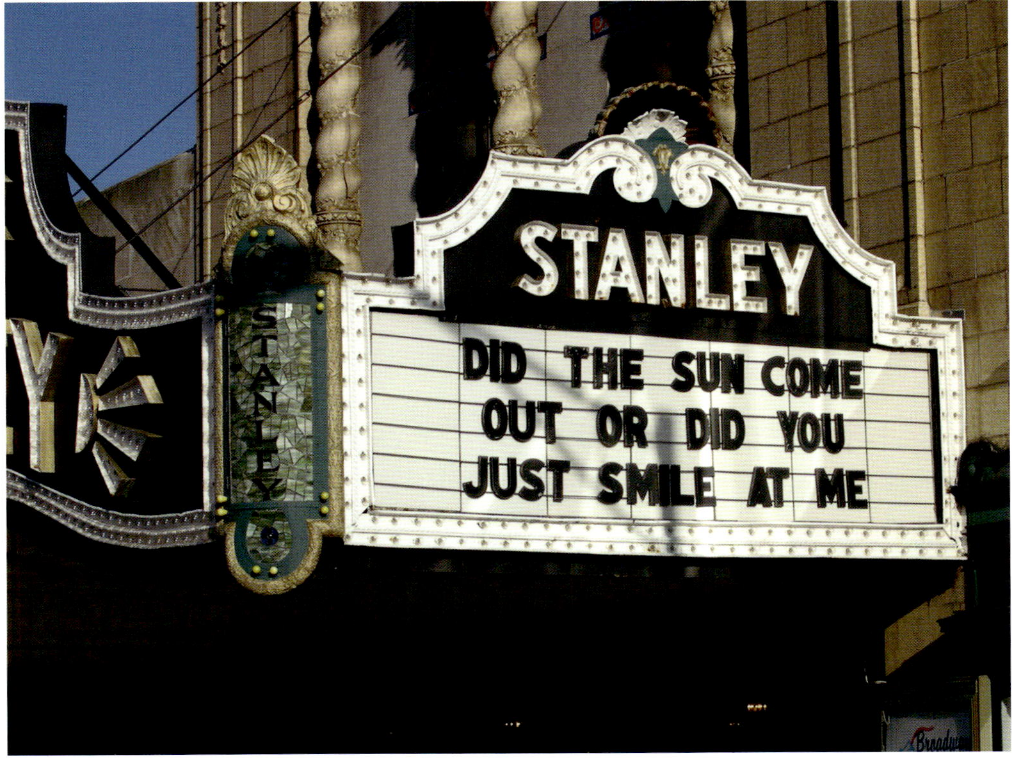

Sheridan Line, 2004
Marquee text at the Sky Line Drive-In Theater, Sheridan, Wyoming
Courtesy of the artist

Utica Speed Seduction: Pick-Up Line (For Mark), 2004
Marquee text on the Stanley Movie Theater, Utica, New York
Courtesy of the artist

Lisa Williamson

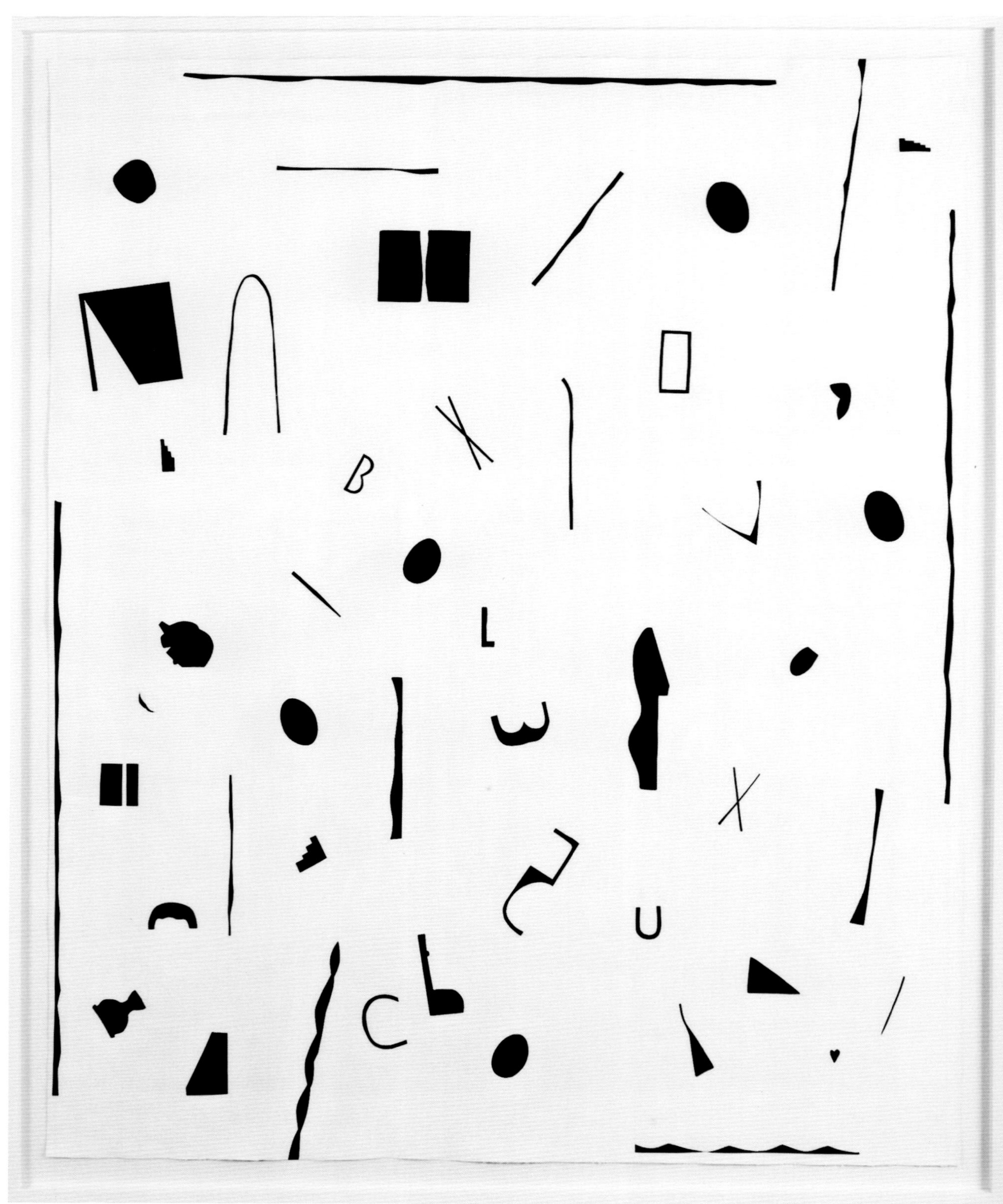

As a Beer Mat and Cutting Board, 2010 — cat. no. 134

Interview with Grant Wahlquist

GW: **A fair amount of your previous work was done in video, but you recently began making paintings. What brought about this leap between media, and how is it reflective of your concerns more broadly? Do you think of yourself as a painter?**

LW: I was making videos, often in the form of vignettes, one subject rolling onto the next, or in some cases a whole set of subjects collapsed on top of one another. But at the same time I've always been making things—objects or texts or drawings—whatever fits the larger project in mind. To me there isn't much difference between the videos I've made and the objects I've made. I think what links all the works together are these jumps, attempting to organize and relate a whole series of contents through the forms that work best. Painting is interesting and remains totally relevant because of its absolute value as art. Its parameters are so complete. I definitely don't consider myself a painter—I have too much respect for its history and makers—but painting seems like such an articulate form to work with, or at least to borrow from.

GW: **Your project for the biennial involves a collection of works in various media. Can you describe the process behind the work? How do you understand the relationships among the media involved?**

LW: The work that I am showing in the biennial jumps between forms, but there is an inherent logic or sensibility that travels throughout. What is visible is the attempt to think through material, to form connections that are both simple and also sometimes more long-winded or obtuse. My work circles around art itself—how to carve out a language that is relevant and shape-shifty and self-generative. As a subject, art is so completely weird and tangential and huge. Anni Albers wrote really beautifully about the need for parameters in art, to define limits as a means for development. This is something I think about a lot in the studio—how to pull in the reins and make some sense in the end. Things tend to develop in parallel, and the attempt to define some sort of outline for each group of works takes a lot of sorting through and editing down.

GW: **There is a sense in which your work references minimalism. There seems to be an investigation of minimalism's emphasis on both the formal and the material that's very sophisticated. What is it about the legacy of minimalism that interests you?**

LW: While some of the most recent work has a very strong material or formal presence, I wouldn't specifically align my work with minimalism. A lot of art histories can be seen in my work. Instead of masking influence, I'm trying to better understand and work through influence. Many of the objects I've incorporated into recent projects are "base"—the surfaces are smooth, space is considered, and the objects are definitely specific. But I started to work with more "base" forms as a way to start over or to clear my head, to drop everything down to the lowest common denominator as a means to move forward. I love the minimalists—some of the most far-out and expansive thinking can be located behind work of this time. John McCracken relates his beautiful planks to alien life and time travel;

Jo Baer has managed to shift from hard-edge painting to metaphoric figuration (which is a really wild jump); and while Sol LeWitt orbited around structure, he also had a great sense of humor. This is all amazing to me—that so much strangeness and personality can lurk beneath even the subtlest forms.

GW: **Your practice seems as much about the leaps that occur "in between" the discrete objects that make up an installation. What happens when your work is shown in the context of other artists' work, as it will be in the biennial?**

LW: Group shows are obviously difficult. The main concern is that your work is sort of amputated from its original context. Choosing what to exhibit is dependent on the type of physical space that I have access to. If I am in the corner of a room, just knowing that there are in fact two walls that meet gives me enough ground to start organizing my thoughts. Showing works together initially is important to me. Once a group has existed in proximity, I'm okay with individual pieces then going out into the world. But setting the scene and defining the relationships that exist among the works is definitely a part of the work itself. Otherwise it just feels like a stutter or an incomplete sentence.

GW: **In our previous conversations, I was struck by your repeated use of the word *optimism*. What is it about your practice in particular, but also art making in general, that strikes you as optimistic?**

LW: Opting to make work and to be an artist is a bold move at any time. You are putting a lot of energy and belief into a path that is convoluted by nature. To me, optimism is embedded in the decision to be an artist from day one. You are trying very literally to "work" it out, to materialize meaning, and while there is a lot of history to look at, you are claiming a position in the end. This is difficult and somewhat daunting. Working through such an immense and open space is inspiring, and in terms of the work I make, I feel that some of this "optimism," belief, or enthusiasm carries through. Or at least I'd like to think so. ∎

Born 1977 in Champaign-Urbana, Illinois; lives and works in Los Angeles. Williamson is a graduate of Arizona State University (BFA, 2000) and the University of Southern California (MFA, 2008). She has been the subject of solo exhibitions at Unosunove Arte Contemporanea, Rome, and Small A Projects, New York. Her work has been presented in group exhibitions at Layr Wuestenhagen, Vienna; David Kordansky Gallery, Los Angeles; Shane Campbell Gallery, Chicago; Renwick Gallery, New York; White Columns, New York; Invisible Exports, New York; CCA Andratx Kunsthalle, Mallorca, Spain; and ACME, Los Angeles.

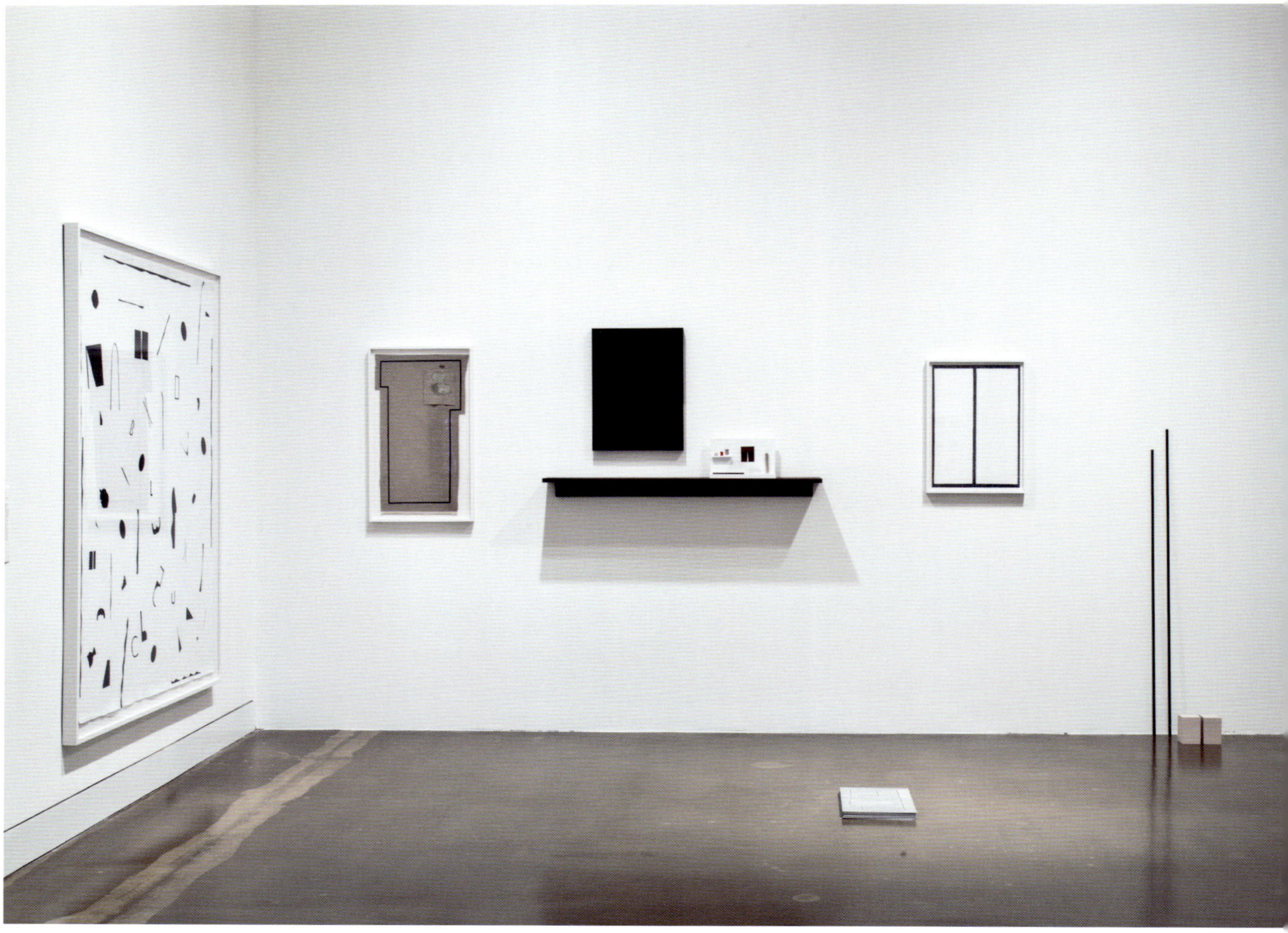

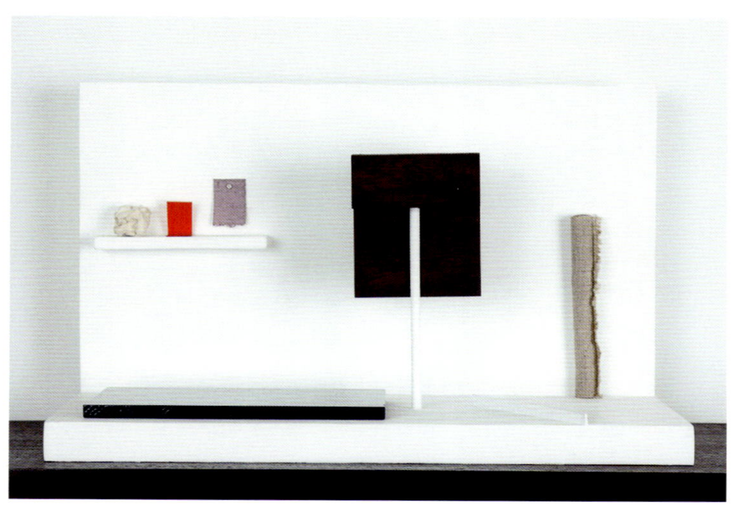

Installation view — cat. nos. 134, 139, 138, 135, 136, 137
***Shelf Painting/A Model Situation Has Five Parts*, 2010**
(detail) — cat. no. 138

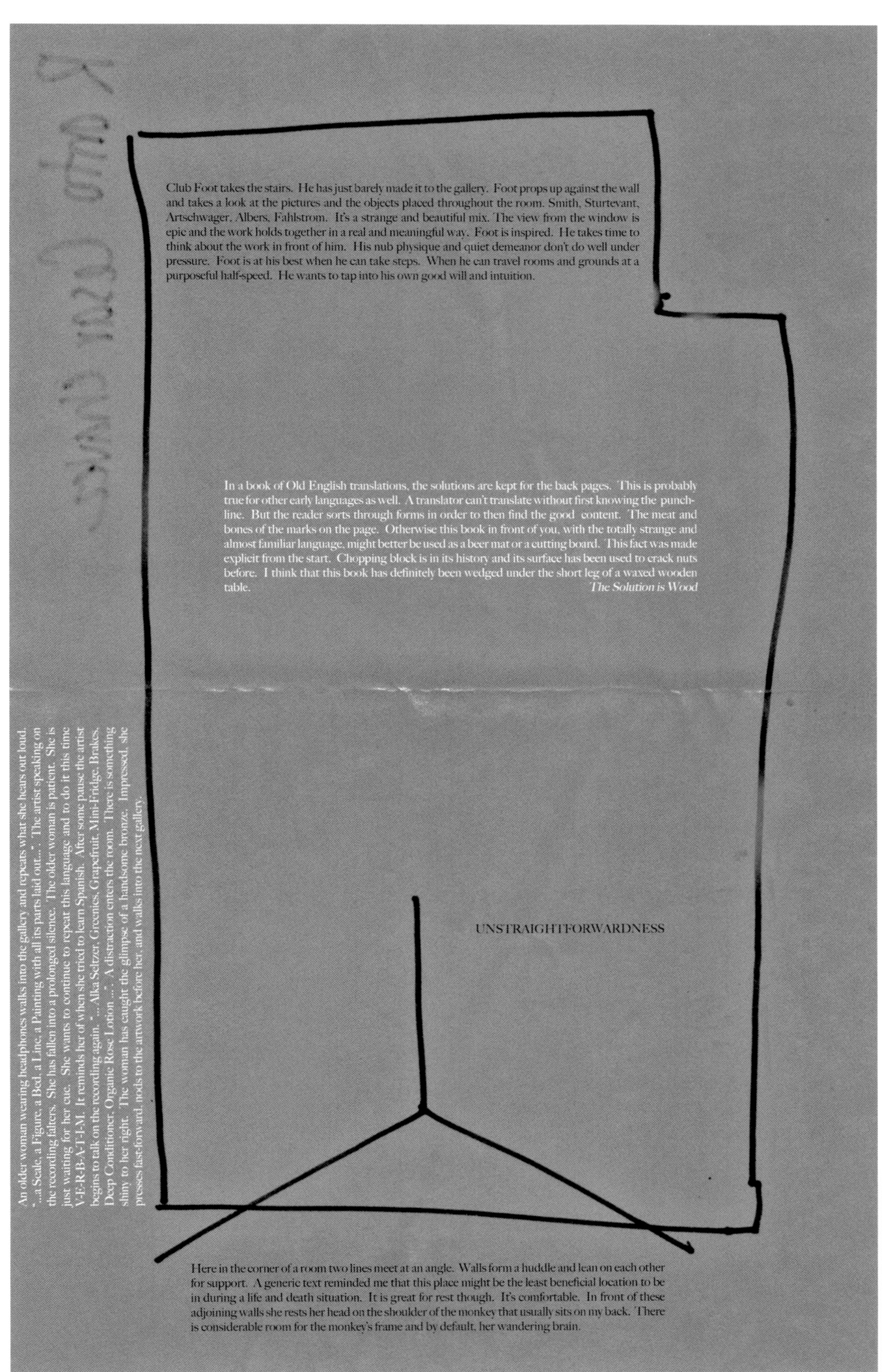

Club Foot takes the stairs. He has just barely made it to the gallery. Foot props up against the wall and takes a look at the pictures and the objects placed throughout the room. Smith, Sturtevant, Artschwager, Albers, Fahlstrom. It's a strange and beautiful mix. The view from the window is epic and the work holds together in a real and meaningful way. Foot is inspired. He takes time to think about the work in front of him. His nub physique and quiet demeanor don't do well under pressure. Foot is at his best when he can take steps. When he can travel rooms and grounds at a purposeful half-speed. He wants to tap into his own good will and intuition.

In a book of Old English translations, the solutions are kept for the back pages. This is probably true for other early languages as well. A translator can't translate without first knowing the punch-line. But the reader sorts through forms in order to then find the good content. The meat and bones of the marks on the page. Otherwise this book in front of you, with the totally strange and almost familiar language, might better be used as a beer mat or a cutting board. This fact was made explicit from the start. Chopping block is in its history and its surface has been used to crack nuts before. I think that this book has definitely been wedged under the short leg of a waxed wooden table.

The Solution is Wood

An older woman wearing headphones walks into the gallery and repeats what she hears out loud. "...a Scale. a Figure. a Bed. a Line. a Painting with all its parts laid out." The artist speaking on the recording falters. She has fallen into a prolonged silence. The older woman is patient. She is just waiting for her cue. She wants to continue to repeat this language and to do it this time VE-R-B-A-T-I-M. It reminds her of when she tried to learn Spanish. After some pause the artist begins to talk on the recording again. "...Alka Seltzer. Greenies. Grapefruit. Mini-Fridge. Brakes. Deep Conditioner. Organic Rose Lotion..." A distraction enters the room. There is something shiny to her right. The woman has caught the glimpse of a handsome bronze. Impressed, she presses fast-forward. nods to the artwork before her, and walks into the next gallery.

UNSTRAIGHTFORWARDNESS

Here in the corner of a room two lines meet at an angle. Walls form a huddle and lean on each other for support. A generic text reminded me that this place might be the least beneficial location to be in during a life and death situation. It is great for rest though. It's comfortable. In front of these adjoining walls she rests her head on the shoulder of the monkey that usually sits on my back. There is considerable room for the monkey's frame and by default, her wandering brain.

Diagram, 2010 — cat. no. 135

David Wilson

Practice
Drawing, site-specific gatherings and performance

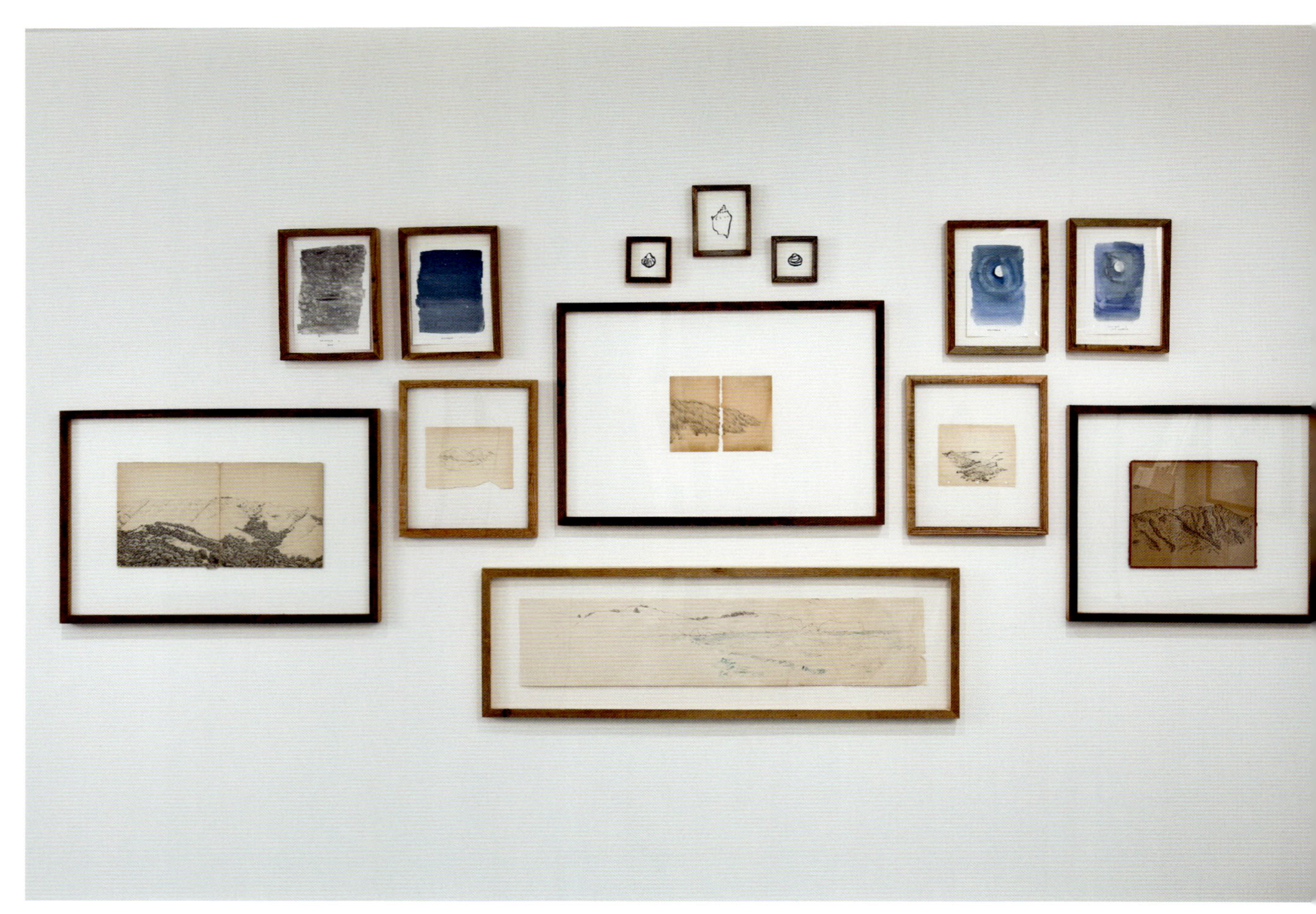

Installation view
Top row: 149, 150, 152, 154, 153, 147, 148
Middle row: 146, 143, 144, 145, 140
Bottom: 142

Born 1982 in Framingham,
Massachusetts; lives and works in
Berkeley. A graduate of Wesleyan
University (BA, 2005), Wilson has
shown his work at the Berkeley Art
Museum, Eleanor Harwood Gallery,
Triple Base, Tartine, and Baer-Ridgway
Exhibitions in San Francisco and at
Hatch Gallery in Oakland. He organizes

gatherings and performances of a
more adventurous and spirited na
under the name Ribbons, and in
recognition of these efforts, he wa
awarded a 2009 GOLDIE award fro
the *San Francisco Bay Guardian* an
2009 Alternative Exposure Grant f
Southern Exposure.

Interview with Anna Brouwer

AB: Your practice of going out and surveying a site and re-cording its features, its flora, invites associations with nineteenth-century exploration of the American West. How has your artistic practice developed as a result of moving to the West Coast?

DW: I grew up in the suburbs. If you didn't have a good imagi-nation, you'd be pretty bored. I think my interest in explo-ration comes from a long journey of play, stemming from my earliest moments of hunting around my backyard for fort spots. Coming to the West Coast was in large part an act of wonder, and since I got here, I've been treating it like my big backyard. The hills, the ocean, the forest—they all make me want to be here.

I think this is completely in line with the early waves of explorers. They were marking the path and sharing this country's wonders. Now, as I explore the landscape where I live, this marking and sharing come through sitting in a place and drawing. Leading up to my departure from the East Coast, I made a drawing at a local orchard every month for six months. Sitting in the harvest, sitting in the snow, sitting in the bloom. This taught me a deep lesson of observation: drawing from the place allowed me to wed my bodily experience with my experience of attention and mental translation into a true sense document. Drawing is how I know a place.

AB: How did you start having gatherings at specific sites? You've mentioned that it came less from a desire to make art that is performative, or a deliberate associa-tion with the history of "happenings," and more from your experience in getting together with friends to play music.

DW: The instinct to bring people to the spots where I spend time exploring and making drawings came out of a simple excitement for sharing these place discoveries with the people I love. Being involved in a music community and playing in bands made the idea of setting up a perfor-mance-based show a natural first point of reference.

Over time, the ideas for these gatherings have opened up, and I now think of performance in the service of broader experiences. At times in the service of exuberance, as in a Lucky Dragons touch-based sound performance planned to connect a group of people with the sunset hour atop a hill during an overnight occupation of Angel Island. Or at times in the service of tribute and healing, as in a tape recording of an old friend's voice singing traditional can-torial prayer songs to a group of people silently sitting amidst a memorial structure.

I think a lot about how prime experiences create the deep-est memories. In my drawing practice, I seek that as an individual, returning to places over and over, creating a bond. I see these gatherings as opportunities to create an experience that is held together by a group of people and that forms a memory bond between people and a site. It's a powerful feeling.

AB: You create detailed invitations and maps for the gath-erings, but these can also be used to find the site after the event has taken place. Can you talk more about this as it relates to your project for the biennial?

DW: I like celebrating the journey. I create maps and drawing directions to help people find sites but also because the act of finding is a central part of the experience. When you're anticipating an arrival, your awareness is piqued, and you process space in a very physical way. Following these maps is meaningful whether the journey happens in the context of a gathering or just as a lone wander.

For the biennial, I will be arriving at the area of the mu-seum as a first-time visitor and using my first impressions and first wanders to create a set of walking directions. I'm excited about being unfamiliar and trying to find a place that calls to me. I'll be sharing my foot trail with museum visitors and inviting people to take the walk on their own time. I imagine that I might be leading people to a place that they are already familiar with, but perhaps in my out-sider's way of getting there, it might be experienced anew.

AB: You summed up your work by saying, "We love friend-ships." This is a great way to talk about events that inspire people to take active and creative roles within a temporary community.

DW: Yes, these group projects are the perfect answer to my quiet drawing practice. The exchange and celebration that come between people working toward a common vision is the brightest constellation of all. It is really important to fill your life with inspirations, and being connected to the peo-ple who take your world and broaden it is an ultimate joy.

I just helped plan a large group residency and retreat at a beautiful property in Ukiah. About forty artists came together to create a camp over a week, which was then shared and lived within for a long weekend by one hun-dred or so friends. We created an outdoor kitchen as a collaboration between a crew of furniture designers and builders and Chez Panisse chef Jerome Waag. We cooked a pig underground for twenty-four hours and then had a pretty serious dance party to celebrate with Lucky Drag-ons and Sorcerer and a bunch of other performers. It was quite the time.

AB: You use the name Ribbons on your publications, your website, and also on your invitations.

DW: Ribbons was formed as net for catching friends in collab-orative efforts. Five years ago my friend Frank Lyon and I hatched a handful of outdoor gatherings. At the time Rib-bons became most associated with these gatherings, and that still feels appropriate since, although Frank moved to New York three years ago, these projects remain rooted in collaboration.

With projects that are about bringing people together, there is an inherent socialness to the process. Each event is a unique constellation of people working together, so when it comes time to send out an invitation, even if it is an idea that began in my mind, letting the invitation come from Ribbons keeps it from feeling like one person claim-ing an idea and reflects the broader spirit of community. Ribbons is a way of letting go of authorship and sharing the experience with a fluid sense of involvement. It's the name to use when it's not just me. ■

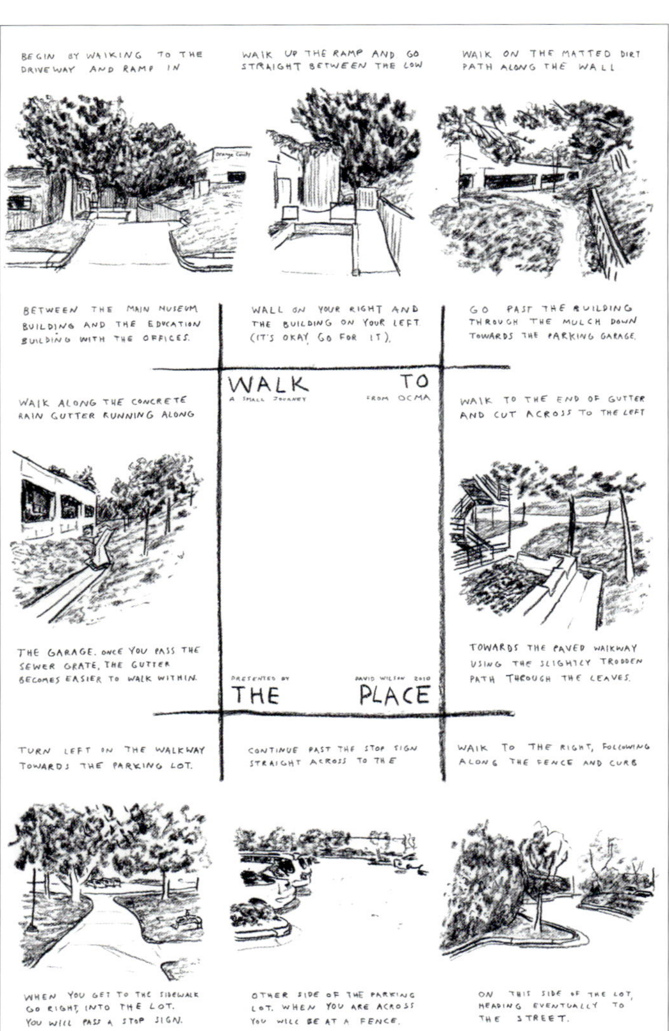

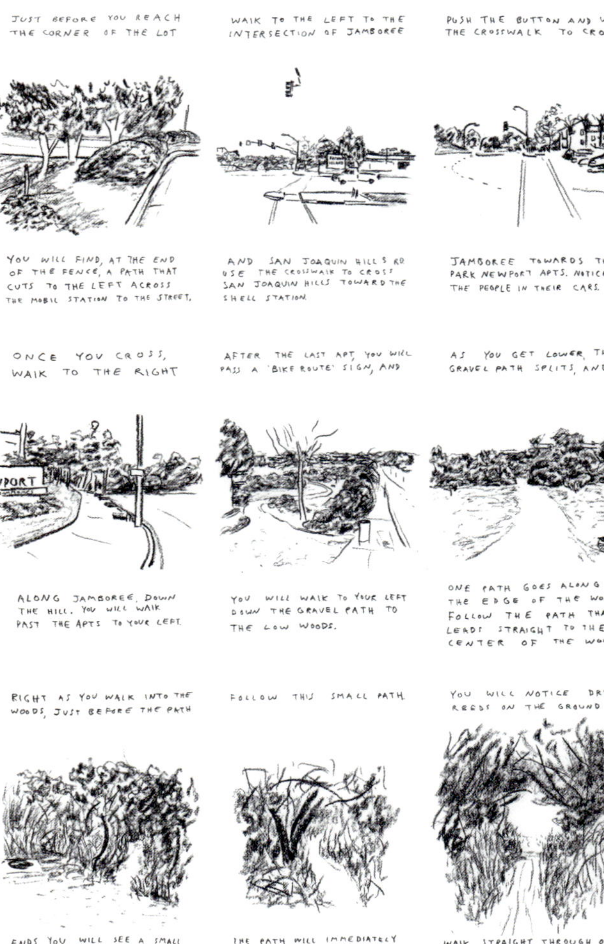

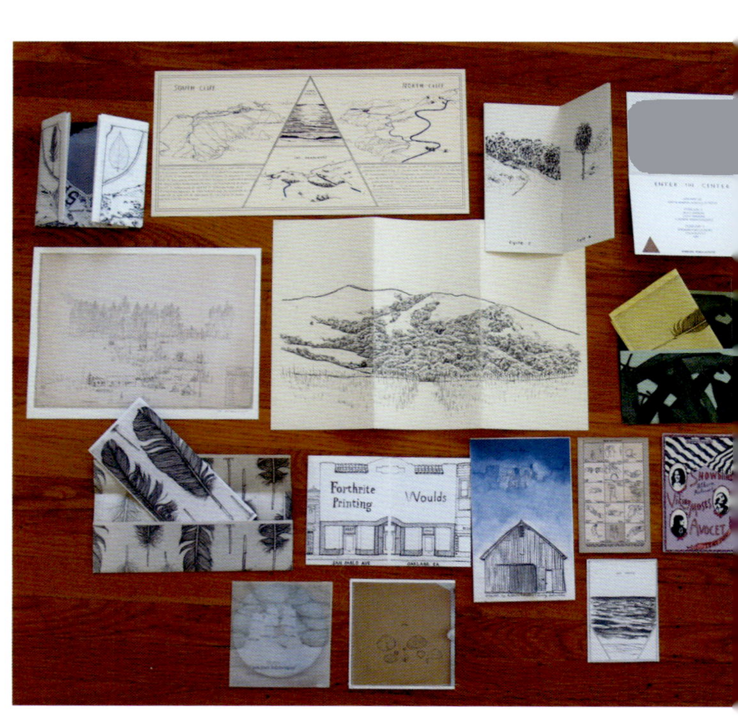

Above
***Walk to the Place (Takeaway Map)*, 2010** — cat. no. 156

Right
***Ribbons Invitation Collection*, 2005–10**
Print ephemera
Dimensions variable
Courtesy of the artist

Opposite
***Walk to the Place Gathering*, October 23, 2010**
Newport Beach, California

***Lucky Dragons performing at Ribbons Angel Island
Gathering*, 2008**
Tiburon, California
Courtesy of the artist

***Memorial Fort Gathering*, 2009**
Richmond, California
Courtesy of the artist

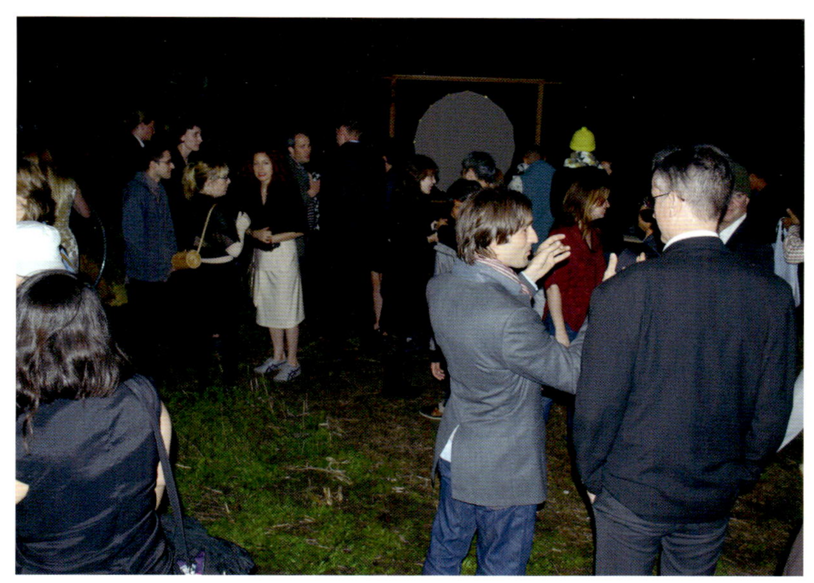

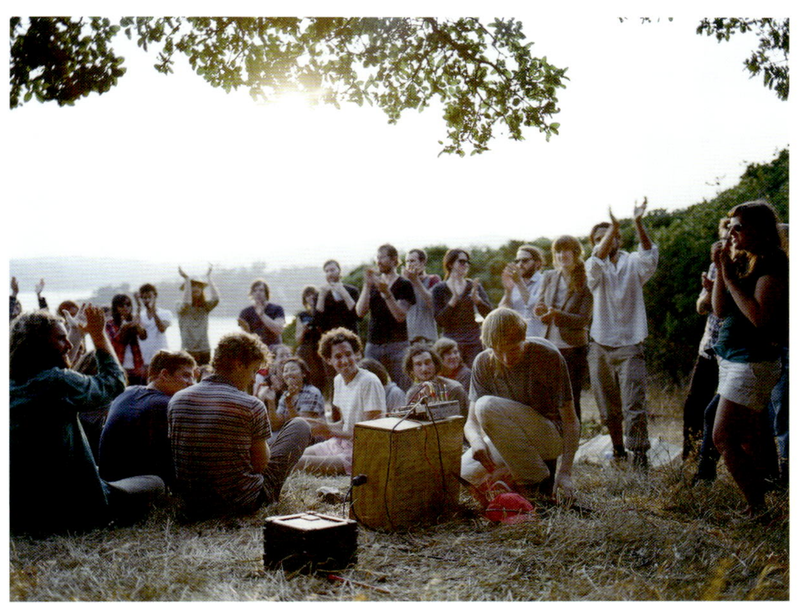

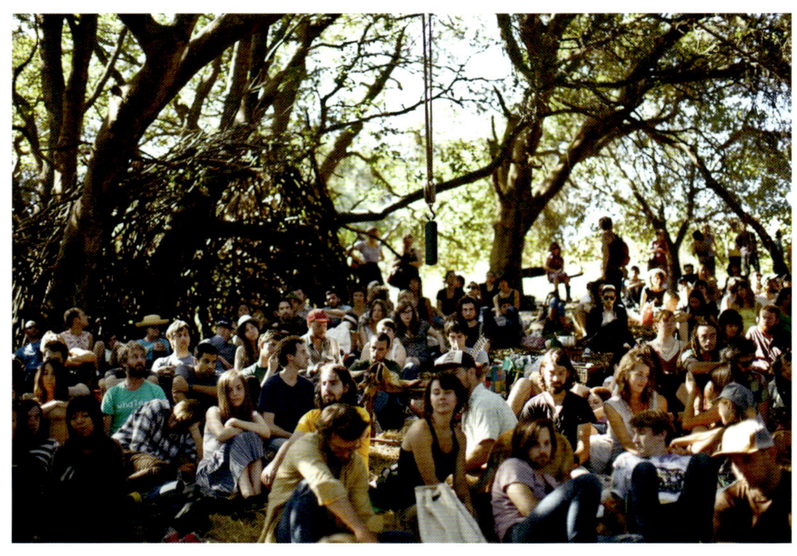

Patrick Wilson

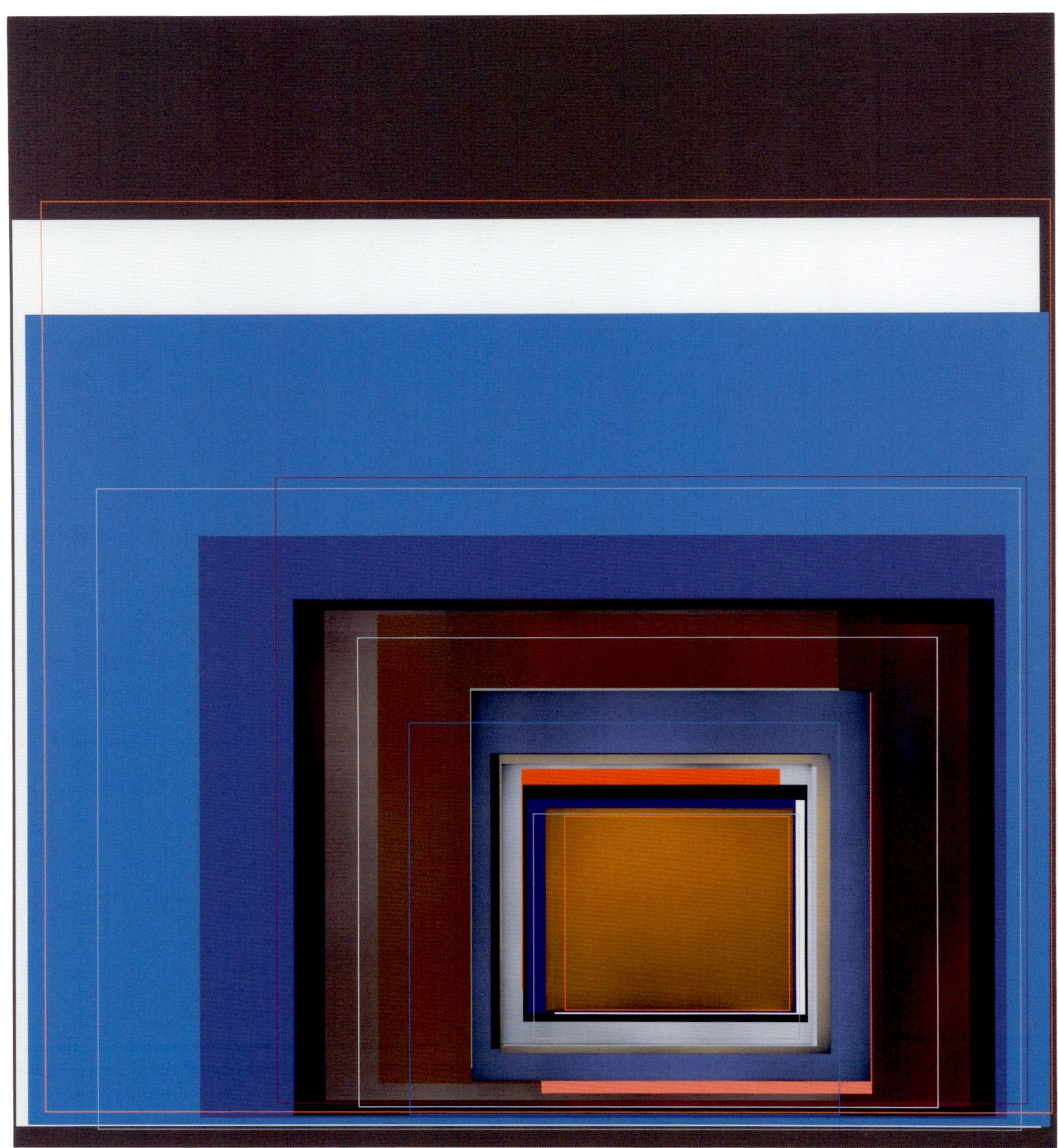

Insomniac, **2010** — cat. no. 157

Interview with Stacie Martinez

PW: Every morning when I walk into the studio, I feel lucky. There is nowhere I would rather be. The four new paintings in the 2010 California Biennial are made with the hope that they're worth looking at, that they're worth spending some time with, and that they will be of some positive value to the person standing in front of them. *Insomniac*, *Shape to the Unseen, Romeo,* and *Juliet* are a snapshot of my obsession with painting. While they don't indicate the entire range of possibilities, they do stand in nicely for much of what I believe in.

SM: **Tell me about your painting technique: where you start, how you arrive at the end.**

PW: My technique is pretty straightforward. I move color around in controlled areas using a combination of drywall blades, rollers, and masking tape. The paintings are acrylic on canvas, over panel. They're composed with a precise calibration of light, space, color, structure, texture—my visual alphabet. The language is abstraction. I often begin with a very simple sketch meant to establish the ground rules—basic colors or structural relationships. The process quickly becomes intuitive as I respond shape by shape, color by color, to what I see. By remaining open to abrupt changes of direction and intent along the way, I'm able to keep the geometry from becoming too rigid or predictable.

Over the last ten years or so, my work has gradually evolved from somewhat minimal to something more frenetic and full of energy. With the increased amount of information, I often have to walk the line between dissonance and harmony, but I think that kind of tension helps to keep the paintings from feeling sort of sleepy. I'm never quite sure where I'm headed, as one thing leads to the next, but knowing when a painting is finished is often as simple as a sudden rush of adrenaline.

SM: **When we spoke, you said that, unfashionable as it might be, you were in "pursuit of beauty." I wouldn't agree that it's "unfashionable," but "beauty" *is* difficult to define—it's a subjective, abstract concept with art historical heft. How do you know when you've achieved it in your paintings?**

PW: Defining beauty is a task reserved for a much larger discussion and seems in many ways to be futile—the words serving as an incomplete and empty substitute for the real thing—always dancing around it, but never really being *it*. I'm not ready to take a stand and say with absolute authority what beauty is because the concept is not only subjective but also very loaded. I do know what my understanding of beauty is, and it has nothing to do with political posturing, cultural variation, or art-world banter; it's something far more universal, and it's undeniable— the ocean, a flying bird, a perfect tree, a tender embrace. That is the kind of beauty that I pursue with my paintings: the type that makes me feel ecstatic, the type that words don't stick to.

It sounds simple, and maybe a bit trite, but I believe that there is nothing more difficult to achieve, and nothing more meaningful when it happens. If a painting achieves

beauty, I just know—there really isn't another way to say it. And when a painting fails to achieve beauty, hopefully at the very least it can still bring great joy and pleasure. To be able to add an object to the world capable of causing those types of feelings is what drives me.

SM: **Your process seems very intuitive and personal. How would you suggest that a viewer approach your work?**

PW: My paintings are experiential. People should approach them with open eyes and uncluttered brains.

A really didactic sort of academic conceptualism is all around us in the art world. It's everywhere—museums, galleries, nonprofits, art schools. . . . It's what we've become accustomed to seeing. To me, the truly visual has been systematically devalued, and as a result, we have become aesthetically malnourished. I think people often have a hard time trusting themselves to simply stand in front of an object and let that act become something. It's messy, intuitive—there's no right or wrong. Instead many feel more comfortable trying to understand art or attempting to connect the dots. That way of thinking can quickly become a dead end.

I've always been more responsive to art that is than to art that's about. My paintings are nonobjective. They're born, no doubt, from countless bits of information—from all the things in my life. But I have no interest in trying to illustrate those ideas, or in preaching to the viewer and casting my ideals upon them. The paintings are intended to be experienced, which in itself will probably mean something entirely different to each person. I think that's amazing! Fresh.

SM: **The idea of "duration" is something one would be more likely to associate with video or performance art, and yet it is an important aspect of your work. Tell me about this.**

PW: Now, maybe more than ever, it's critical that we all take a step back and slow down. We are a culture obsessed with speed, technology, efficiency. We need to get there quickly, have instant access, text, tweet, multitask. We don't have time for anything with more information than 140 characters. This way of living has led to a fussy, agitated state of mind in which many have an unwillingness or, worse yet, a compromised ability to sit still and look at an artwork for an extended period of time. I think this has taken a lot of the joy and meaning away from our lives. My paintings require time to unfold, and it's not accidental. The really important stuff—the surprises, the hidden connections, the pleasure, the beauty—all have their own pace. ■

Born 1970 in Redding, California; lives and works in Los Angeles. Wilson is a graduate of the University of California, Davis (BA, 1993), and Claremont Graduate School (MFA, 1995). He has had solo exhibitions at Marx & Zavattero, San Francisco; Susanne Vielmetter Los Angeles Projects; and Curator's Office, Washington, D.C. His work has been shown at the Blaffer Gallery, University of Houston; the Riverside Art Museum, Riverside, California; and the Hirshhorn Museum and Sculpture Garden, Washington, D.C., and is in the collections of the Hirshhorn Museum and Sculpture Garden, the Los Angeles County Museum of Art, the San Jose Museum of Art, and other institutions.

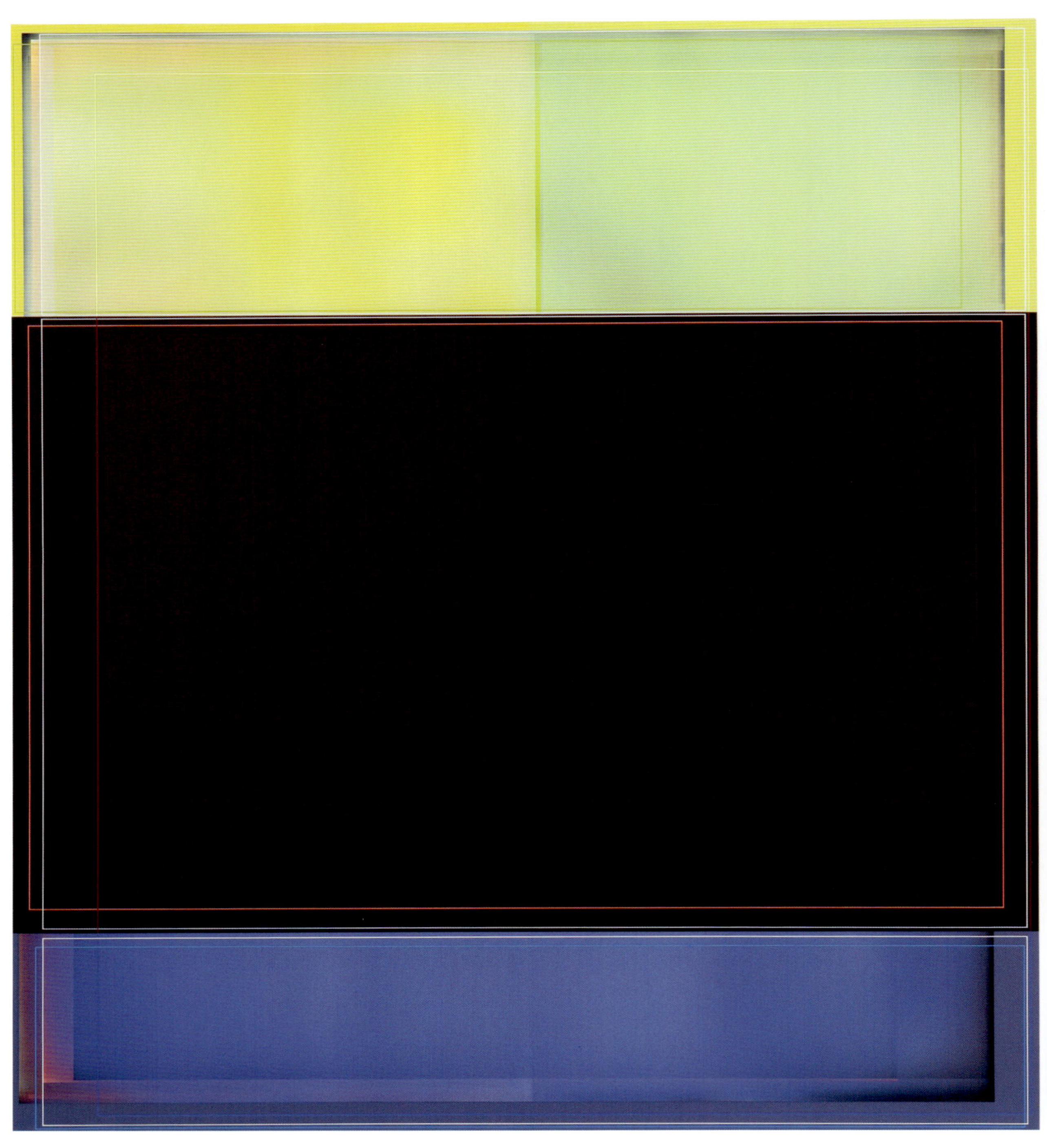

Shape to the Unseen, 2010 — cat. no. 160

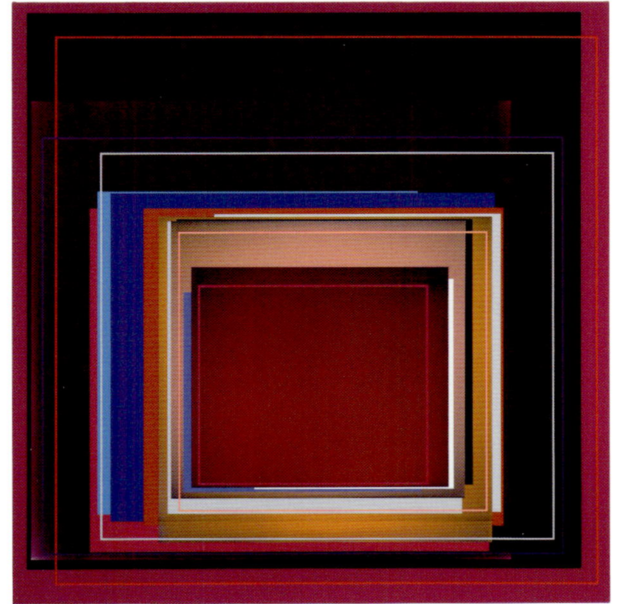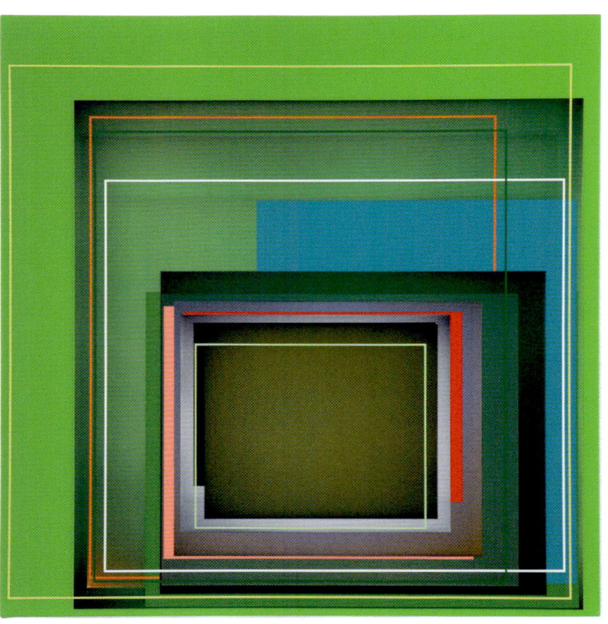

From left
Romeo, 2010 — cat. no. 159
Juliet, 2010 — cat. no. 158

John Zurier

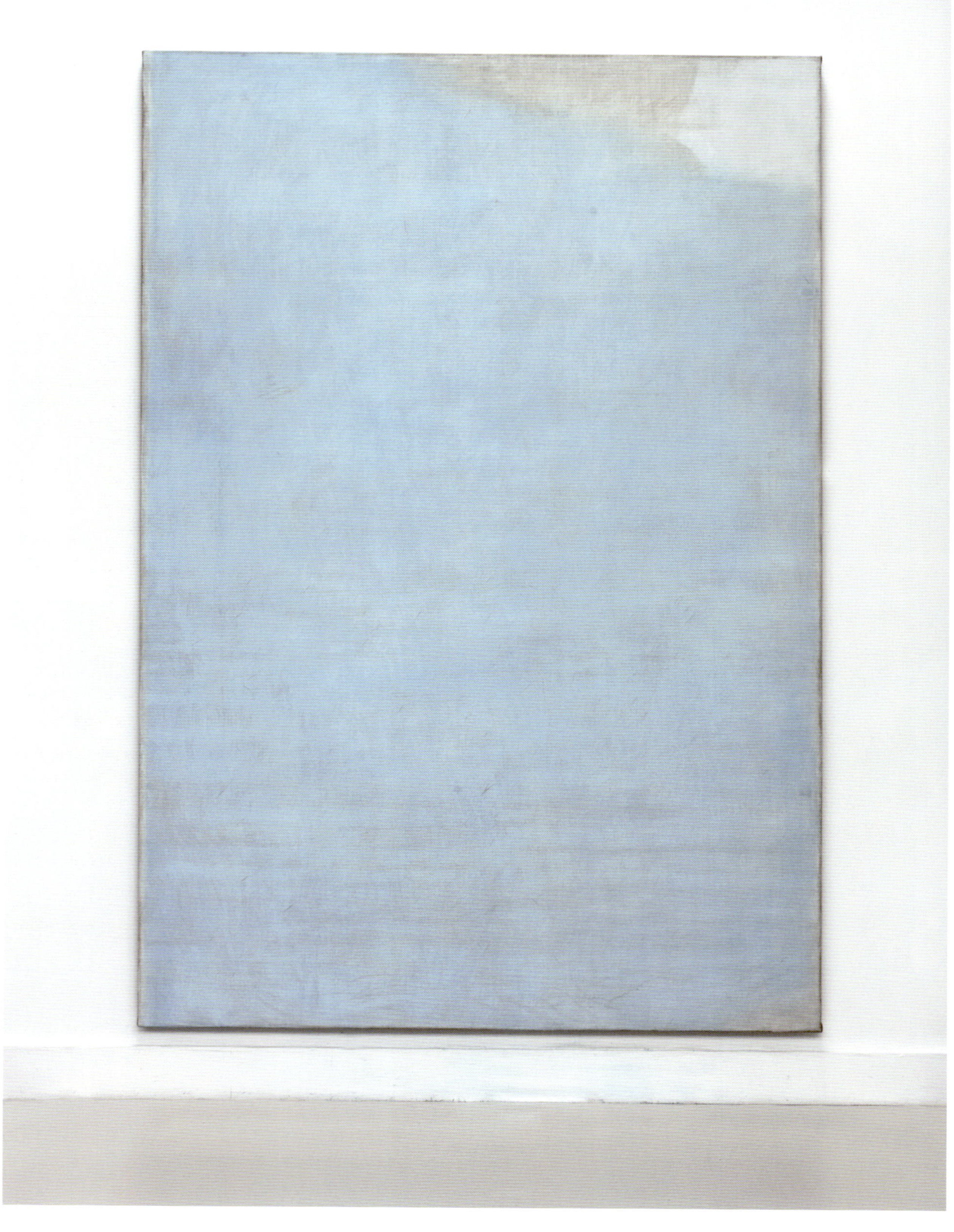

The Future of Ice, **2010** — cat. no. 162

Interview with Karen Moss

KM: **The title of one of your paintings, *Muuratsalo 3*, refers to the island of Muuratsalo in Finland. Did this visit to the Finnish landscape inspire your new series of paintings?**

JZ: Yes, I visited Finland and Muuratsalo with some friends in August 2007. We spent an afternoon at architect Alvar Aalto's summer home, looking at the house and swimming in the lake. Aalto was also a painter, and he had a little studio there. The Muuratsalo series was inspired by that day. I loved the way the light fell on the white walls, the birch trees, the rocks, and water. Coming from California, I had never seen summer light like that. It was bright and cold and clear but also weak, without strong contrasts, which I like very much.

Color is always the main thing in my work: it carries the content of the painting, and since it is also tied to our experience in time, our sense of interior time, it evokes associative memories. The less contrast paintings have, the more suggestive they become. I'm a spontaneous painter, and it was only after I painted the first of these paintings that I recognized the source.

KM: **Tell me about the new process that you used to make the painting you have just finished, *The Future of Ice*.**

JZ: It was made with distemper, which is a tempera paint made with dry pigments mixed into a glue solution. It is the same material I used for the Night series paintings, but it is applied differently. The Muuratsalo paintings were made with oil paint on a white ground, and though this painting relates to them, it has no ground layer. The color is painted right on top of the raw linen so it soaks into it and interacts with the color of the linen. I'm interested in how the light and blue color are absorbed into the thin surface of the painting.

KM: **It reminds me of pastel and actually appears very much like a Tiepolo trompe l'oeil cloud painting in a cupola . . .**

JZ: The Tiepolo association is very apt. His blue skies are infinite but not otherworldly…. I like that you saw this link to Tiepolo even though I wasn't aware of it. I was thinking about Matisse. At the end of July I saw his *Bathers by the River* and also Cézanne's blue Bather at MoMA. Seeing these two paintings helped me finish this painting. It's not that I took the blue color from them, but I realized that the color had to be more specific. That's what I mean when I say that color is the main element of my paintings. The color needs to be exactly right; it can't be simply close enough.

KM: **I am intrigued that all your paintings in the biennial are blue—having seen your other work, I know that you also use other colors. Why blue?**

JZ: It fills a psychic need that I can't explain. But I know it has to do with the range of emotion of blue. For the past couple of years I have found myself drawn to blues not just in nature, but also when looking at paintings in museums. I saw a painting by the Swedish painter Torsten Andersson, *The Sky between Us*. It is a very light blue, and I was think-

ing of this painting when I made my first Muuratsalo painting. And there are two paintings, both Depositions from the Cross—Gerard David in the Frick, and the Rogier van der Weyden in the Prado—in which, for me, Mary's grief is expressed and felt through the blue. In both paintings the blue goes from the deepest blue to the faintest light blue as if the color is traveling through the painting like a scent. The airiness and tenderness, the way the blue mirrors feeling, in these two paintings were in my mind when I started both the Muuratsalo and the Night paintings.

KM: **Did your move to this new studio with larger windows and more space affect your painting?**

JZ: Yes, I'm sure the different space and light have influenced the paintings. I have always—well, mostly—worked in natural light, in daylight. And this studio has beautiful soft, indirect, bright light.

KM: **What about the two smaller deep blue paintings from your Night series: when did you make these, what process did you use, and what are their specific referents?**

JZ: I started the series in 2006 and finished the last one just a few months ago. These paintings were inspired by some indigo textiles that I saw in Japan. I was also looking at Italian fifteenth-century tempera paintings as well as traditional Japanese painting and ceramics. Around this time I started becoming very interested in Japanese aesthetics, with its emphasis on elegance, emptiness, the transience of things, and mystery. I made the paintings with very thin layers of distemper. I am not systematic by nature, and each one of them is so different, but they all start with my drawing the folds of the linen, and at the very end I make the horizontal scrapings.

KM: **The horizontal lines make the paintings look like fabric with a warp and a weft . . .**

JZ: Yes, that's true, but I'm also interested in the layers and transparency and the sense of light and depth.

KM: **I think it is interesting that you are working simultaneously in so many ways; you are so clearly not a "minimalist" painter.**

JZ: The polemics of minimalism don't interest me, because I don't really think it is relevant to painting, because there is no room for ambiguity.

KM: **Yes, minimalism is all about culture, and your work seems to be about nature?**

JZ: Yes, maybe it is about the culture of nature. ∎

Born 1956 in Santa Monica, California; lives and works in Berkeley. Zurier received both his BA (1979) and MFA (1984) from the University of California, Berkeley. One-person exhibitions include shows at Peter Blum Gallery, New York; Gallery Paule Anglim, San Francisco; Larry Becker Contemporary Art, Philadelphia; and Galeria Javier López, Madrid. His work has also been shown at the Berkeley Art Museum; the Seventh Gwangju Biennale, Gwangju, South Korea; Hunter College Art Gallery, New York; and the Oakland Museum of California. Zurier participated in the 2002 Whitney Biennial. He is eminent adjunct professor at California College of the Arts in San Francisco and the recipient of a 2010 John Simon Guggenheim Fellowship.

Installation Map

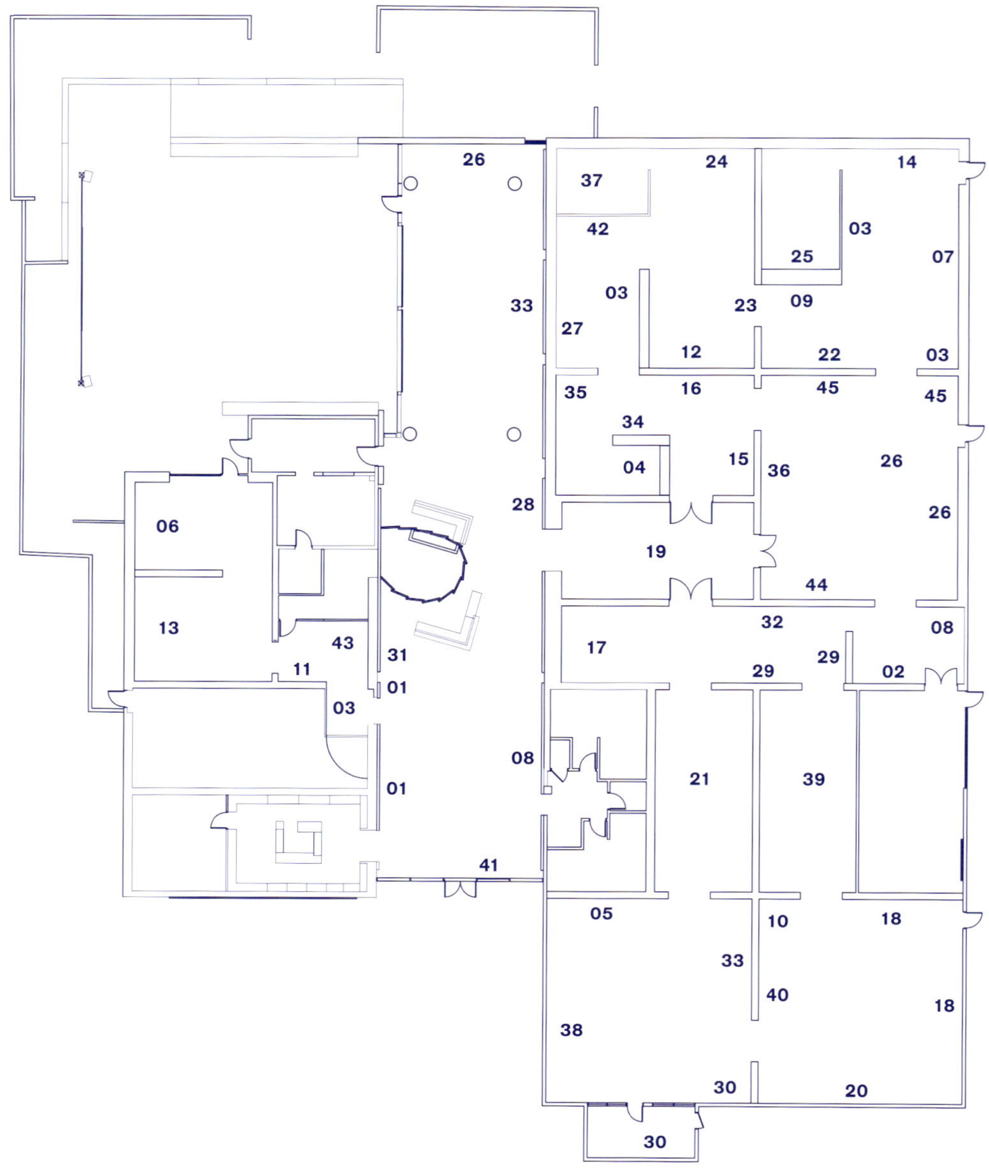

01	**David Adey**	16	**Katy Grannan**	30	**Tucker Nichols**
02	**Agitprop**	17	**Alexandra Grant**	31	**Camilo Ontiveros**
03	**Gil Blank**	18	**Sherin Guirguis**	32	**Nikki Pressley**
04	**Nate Boyce**	19	**Drew Heitzler**	33	**Andy Ralph**
05	**Luke Butler**	20	**Violet Hopkins**	34	**Will Rogan**
06	**Juan Capistran**	21	**Alex Israel**	35	**Paul Schiek**
07	**Zoe Crosher**	22	**Glenna Jennings**	36	**Taravat Talepasand**
08	**Brian Dick**	23	**Barry Macgregor**	37	**Wu Tsang**
09	**Dru Donovan**		**Johnston**	38	**Zlatan Vukosavljevic**
10	**Mari Eastman**	24	**Vishal Jugdeo**	39	**Nina Waisman**
11	**Electronic Disturbance**	25	**Stanya Kahn**	40	**Flora Wiegmann**
	Theater/b.a.n.g. lab	26	**Andy Kolar**	41	**Allison Wiese**
12	**Carlee Fernandez**	27	**Jennifer Locke**	42	**Lisa Williamson**
13	**Finishing School**	28	**Los Angeles Urban**	43	**David Wilson**
14	**Eve Fowler**		**Rangers**	44	**Patrick Wilson**
15	**Rebecca Goldfarb**	29	**Tom Mueske**	45	**John Zurier**

David Adey

1. *Pump*, 2007–10
   Horse respirator, football, and drywall screws
   Dimensions variable
   Courtesy of the artist and Luis De Jesus
   Los Angeles

2. *Flock*, 2010
   Ceramic figurines, neon, wiring, and
   electronics
   Dimensions variable; lambs: 7 × 3 × 7 in.
   (17.8 × 7.6 × 17.8 cm) each
   Courtesy of the artist and Luis De Jesus
   Los Angeles

Agitprop

3. *The Third Party*, 2010
   Mobile interview cart: plywood, fabric,
   foam, amplifier, and microphones
   42 × 72 × 30 in. (106.7 × 182.9 × 76.2 cm)
   Courtesy of Agitprop

Gil Blank

4. *No Title*, No Date
   C-print mounted in acrylic resin artist's
   frame
   50 ⅜ × 54 ⅛ × 2 ¼ in. (128 × 137.5 × 5.1 cm)
   Courtesy of the artist and LaMontagne
   Gallery, Boston

5. *No Title*, No Date
   C-print mounted in acrylic resin artist's
   frame
   23 ½ × 31 ¼ × 2 in. (59.7 × 79.4 × 5.1 cm)
   Courtesy of the artist and LaMontagne
   Gallery, Boston

6. *Wiederholungszwang I.ii.1–I.ii.12*,
   No Date
   Laser-etched graphite blocks
   Dimensions variable, blocks: 5 × 7 ¼ × 2
   in. (12.7 × 18.4 × 5.1 cm) each
   Courtesy of the artist and LaMontagne
   Gallery, Boston

7. *Wiederholungszwang I.ii.13–I.ii.24*,
   No Date
   Laser-etched graphite blocks
   Dimensions variable, blocks: 5 × 7 ¼ × 2
   in. (12.7 × 18.4 × 5.1 cm) each
   Courtesy of the artist and LaMontagne
   Gallery, Boston

8. *Wiederholungszwang I.ii.25–I.ii.36*,
   No Date
   Laser-etched graphite blocks
   Dimensions variable, blocks: 5 × 7 ¼ × 2
   in. (12.7 × 18.4 × 5.1 cm) each
   Courtesy of the artist and LaMontagne
   Gallery, Boston

Nate Boyce

9. *Interlaced Increments*, 2010
   Three-channel video, color; CRT monitors
   Variable durations, looped
   Courtesy of the artist

10. *Parallel Series II (Zoom, Rotation,
    Collision)*, 2010
    Single-channel digital video, color, sound
    2:45 min.
    Courtesy of the artist

Luke Butler

11. *Captain X*, 2008
    Acrylic on canvas
    18 × 22 in. (45.7 × 55.9 cm)
    Collection of ArtNow International,
    San Francisco

12. *Captain XIII*, 2009
    Acrylic on canvas
    16 × 19 in. (40.6 × 48.3 cm)
    Collection of Arnd F. Stockhausen

13. *Landing Party II*, 2009
    Acrylic on canvas
    26 × 32 in. (66 × 81.3 cm)
    Courtesy of the artist and Silverman
    Gallery, San Francisco

14. *Captain, Crew IV*, 2010
    Acrylic on canvas
    18 × 20 in. (45.7 × 50.8 cm)
    Courtesy of the artist and Silverman
    Gallery, San Francisco

15. *Spock*, 2010
    Acrylic on canvas
    16 × 18 in. (40.6 × 45.7 cm)
    Collection of Christopher Kronner

16. *Vic Tayback*, 2010
    Acrylic on canvas
    19 × 23 in. (48.3 × 58.4 cm)
    Courtesy of the artist and Silverman
    Gallery, San Francisco

Juan Capistran

17. *This Machine Kills Fascists or Labor
    Sets You Free (Love Is the Message)*,
    2010
    Mixed-media installation with sound
    144 × 120 × 120 in. (365.8 × 304.8 × 304.8 cm)
    Courtesy of the artist

Zoe Crosher

18. *Like Miko Smiling for Christopher Williams*, 2008
From the Reconsidered Archive of Michelle duBois
Black-and-white fiber print with custom frame
Edition 1/10
19 ¾ × 23 ¾ in. (50.2 × 60.3 cm)
Collection of Siri Kaur

19. *Looking Another Way*, 2008
Polaroid and ink
4 ⅛ × 3 ½ in. (10.5 × 8.9 cm)
Courtesy of the artist and DCKT Contemporary, New York

20. *Super Foto* (Me), 2009
Light-jet print with glossy lamination mounted on aluminum
Edition 1/5
30 × 20 in. (76.2 × 50.8 cm)
Courtesy of the artist and Eleanor Harwood Gallery, San Francisco

21. *Final Image from the Disappearing of Michelle duBois*, 2010
Pigmented ink on Museo Silver Rag
35 × 22 in. (88.9 × 55.9 cm)
Courtesy of the artist and Aperture Foundation, New York

22. *Her Fantasy Film Shoot on the Beach*, 2010
From the Unveiling of Michelle duBois
Digital C-print
Edition of 5
40 × 30 in. (101.6 × 76.2 cm)
Courtesy of the artist and Emma Gray HQ, Los Angeles

23. *Kodak Color Film*, 2010
From the Unveiling of Michelle duBois
Digital C-print
Edition of 5
50 × 37 1/2 in. (127 × 95.3 cm)
Courtesy of the artist and Emma Gray HQ, Los Angeles

24. *Mock Mock-up*, 2010
In collaboration with Juliette Bellocq
From the Unveiling of Michelle duBois
Four ink-jet prints
Edition of 3
24 × 120 in. (61 × 304.8 cm) each
Courtesy of the artist

25. *The Vanishing of Michelle duBois*, 2010
For Aperture Editions, from the Unraveling of Michelle duBois
Pigmented ink on Museo Silver Rag
30 × 22 ½ in. (76.2 × 57.2 cm)
Courtesy of the artist and Aperture Foundation, New York

Brian Dick

26. *The Nationwide Museum Mascot Project Presents: OCMAscot*, 2010
In collaboration with Christen Sperry-Garcia
Recycled cardboard, newspaper, and tissue paper; piñata work by Piñata World, El Monte, California
Dimensions variable
Courtesy of the artist and Luis De Jesus Los Angeles

27. *The Nationwide Museum Mascot Project's Piñata Cozy with Glowfitti Room*, 2010
In collaboration with Christen Sperry-Garcia
Piñata cozy: recycled cardboard, newspaper, and tissue paper; piñata work by Piñata World, El Monte, California; glow room: plywood, acrylic resin, phosphorus power, and cardboard; Econoline van courtesy of the Orange County Museum of Art
Dimensions variable
Courtesy of the artist and Luis De Jesus Los Angeles

Dru Donovan

28. Untitled, 2008
Ink-jet print
20 × 25 in. (50.8 × 63.5 cm)
Courtesy of the artist

29. Untitled, 2008
Ink-jet print
20 × 25 in. (50.8 × 63.5 cm)
Courtesy of the artist

30. Untitled, 2008
Ink-jet print
20 × 25 in. (50.8 × 63.5 cm)
Courtesy of the artist

31. *Untitled 5*, 2010
From the series Lifting Water
Photograph
7 × 5 ½ in. (17.8 × 14 cm)
Courtesy of the artist

32. *Untitled 6*, 2010
From the series Lifting Water
Photograph
5 ½ × 7 in. (14 × 17.8 cm)
Courtesy of the artist

33. *Untitled 17*, 2010
From the series Lifting Water
Photograph
5 ½ × 7 in. (14 × 17.8 cm)
Courtesy of the artist

34. *Untitled 20*, 2010
From the series Lifting Water
Photograph
7 × 5 ½ in. (17.8 × 14 cm)
Courtesy of the artist

Mari Eastman

35. *Carved portrait of a woman*, 1995–2010
Wood and fluorescent tape
13 × 6 ½ × 4 in. (33 × 16.5 × 10.2 cm)
Courtesy of the artist and Cherry and Martin, Los Angeles

36. *Standing figure with black hair*, 1995–2010
Wood and glitter
11 ½ × 3 ½ × 1 ¾ in. (29.2 × 8.9 × 4.4 cm)
Courtesy of the artist and Cherry and Martin, Los Angeles

37. *Model #01*, Anne, 2010
Flashe, oil stick, oil, and glitter on canvas
14 × 12 in. (35.6 × 30.5 cm)
Courtesy of the artist and Cherry and Martin, Los Angeles

38. *Model #02*, Carolina, 2010
Flashe, oil stick, oil, and glitter on canvas
18 × 14 in. (45.7 × 35.6 cm)
Courtesy of the artist and Cherry and Martin, Los Angeles

39. *Model #03*, Odile, 2010
Flashe, oil stick, tie-dyed canvas, and pushpins on canvas
22 × 20 in. (55.9 × 50.8 cm)
Courtesy of the artist and Cherry and Martin, Los Angeles

40. *Moonscape with Fo-Dog*, 2010
Flashe, oil stick, ink, correction fluid, spray paint, acrylic, and glitter on canvas with painted canvas fringe
68 × 46 in. (172.7 × 116.8 cm)
Courtesy of the artist and Cherry and Martin, Los Angeles

41. *Triangles*, 2010
Prismacolor, oil stick, and oil on canvas
20 × 16 in. (50.8 × 40.6 cm)
Courtesy of the artist and Cherry and Martin, Los Angeles

Electronic Disturbance Theater/ b.a.n.g. lab

42. *The Transborder Immigrant Tool (TBT)*, 2007–present
i335 Motorola phones, walkingtools.net software, images, poetry, and audio
Dimensions variable
Courtesy of Electronic Disturbance Theater/b.a.n.g. lab

Carlee Fernandez

43. *Life after Death*, 2010
    Taxidermy leopard, taxidermy lobster,
    taxidermy rabbit, pants, blouse, cape,
    socks, fingerless gloves, hat, sandals,
    bronze rifle, bronze handgun, bronze wine
    bottle, and wool mat
    8 ½ × 152 ¼ × 112 in. (21.6 × 386.7 ×
    284.5 cm)
    Courtesy of the artist and ACME.,
    Los Angeles

Finishing School

44. *54*, 2010–11
    Mixed-media installation: production set,
    banner, film trailer, and website
    Dimensions variable
    Courtesy of the artists
    The Orange County Museum of Art
    presentation of *54* was realized in part
    through a 2010 California Biennial
    residency supported by the Nimoy
    Foundation.

Eve Fowler

45. *Two Friends at Home*, 2009
    C-print
    20 × 24 in. (50.8 × 61 cm)
    Courtesy of the artist and Horton Gallery,
    New York

46. *Woman from Behind in Hotel Room
    Naked*, 2009
    C-print
    14 × 11 in. (35.6 × 27.9 cm)
    Courtesy of the artist and Horton Gallery,
    New York

47. *Woman Seated Naked*, 2009
    C-print
    Edition 1/3
    16 × 20 in. (40.6 × 50.8 cm)
    Courtesy of the artist and Horton Gallery,
    New York

48. *Woman Sleeping*, 2009
    C-print
    20 × 16 in. (50.8 × 40.6 cm)
    Courtesy of the artist and Horton Gallery,
    New York

49. *Woman Standing Shirtless in a Doorway*,
    2009
    C-print
    14 × 11 in. (35.6 × 27.9 cm)
    Courtesy of the artist and Horton Gallery,
    New York

50. *Woman Waiting*, 2009
    C-print
    24 × 20 in. (61 × 50.8 cm)
    Courtesy of the artist and Horton Gallery,
    New York

51. *A Single Image Is Not Splendor*, 2010
    C-print
    30 × 40 in. (76.2 × 101.6 cm)
    Courtesy of the artist and Horton Gallery,
    New York

52. *The Sophie Horowitz Story, Sarah
    Schulman, 1984, the Naiad Press Inc.
    "We all knew Laura Wolfe. She was part
    of a group known as Women Against
    Bad Things . . .* (see p. 70–72 for full
    title), 2010
    Books and photocopies
    Dimensions variable
    Courtesy of the artist and Horton Gallery,
    New York

Rebecca Goldfarb

53. *Traveling through Darkness: Some
    Sense of the World Turned On When
    Flaneur and Collector Meet for the
    Second Time*, 2010
    Flashlights, wax, cardboard boxes, and
    poplar wood
    130 × 201 × 16 in. (330.2 × 510.5 × 40.6 cm)
    Courtesy of the artist and Baer Ridgway
    Exhibitions, San Francisco

Katy Grannan

54. *Anonymous, Los Angeles*, 2008/printed
    2008
    Archival pigment print on cotton rag
    paper mounted on Plexiglas
    Edition 1/3, signed and numbered verso
    in ink
    39 × 29 in. (99.1 × 73.7 cm)
    Courtesy of the artist; Fraenkel Gallery,
    San Francisco; and Salon 94, New York

55. *Anonymous, Los Angeles*, 2008/printed
    2009
    Archival pigment print on cotton rag
    paper mounted on Plexiglas
    Edition 3/3, signed and numbered verso
    in ink
    39 × 29 in. (99.1 × 73.7 cm)
    Courtesy of the artist; Fraenkel Gallery,
    San Francisco; and Salon 94, New York

56. *Anonymous, Los Angeles*, 2008/printed
    2009
    Archival pigment print on cotton rag
    paper mounted on Plexiglas
    Edition 1/3, signed and numbered verso
    in ink
    39 × 29 in. (99.1 × 73.7 cm)
    Courtesy of the artist; Fraenkel Gallery,
    San Francisco; and Salon 94, New York

Alexandra Grant

57. *First Portal (mind) (after Michael
    Joyce's "Six Portals," 2007)*, 2008
    Crayon, acrylic, felt-tipped marker,
    graphite, gouache, watercolor, and
    colored ink wash on heavy rolled paper
    114 ⅜ × 80 in. (290.5 × 203.2 cm)
    Los Angeles County Museum of Art,
    Partial gift of Honor Fraser and purchased
    with funds from the Acquisition
    Committee for Contemporary Works on
    Paper

58. *Second Portal (eye) (after Michael
    Joyce's "Six Portals," 2007)*, 2008
    Mixed media on paper
    115 ⅞ × 80 in. (294.3 × 203.2 cm)
    Collection of Scott London; courtesy of
    Honor Fraser Gallery, Los Angeles

59. *Fourth Portal (tongue) (after Michael
    Joyce's "Six Portals," 2007)*, 2008
    Mixed media on paper
    117 ¼ × 80 in. (297.8 × 203.2 cm)
    Collection of JoAnne Colonna and James
    Acheson; courtesy of Honor Fraser
    Gallery, Los Angeles

Sherin Guirguis

60. *Bein El-Qasrein*, 2010
    Walnut, plywood, and lead
    96 in. (243.8 cm) high, 29 1/2 in. (79.4 cm)
    diameter
    Courtesy of the artist
    This sculpture was realized in part
    through a 2010 California Biennial
    residency supported by the Nimoy
    Foundation.

61. *Untitled (Dome)*, 2010
    Mixed media on paper
    Triptych, panels: 96 × 51 in. (243.8 × 129.5
    cm) each
    Courtesy of the artist

Drew Heitzler

62. ***OCMA Stack*, 2010**
Ink-jet prints on watercolor paper
2 ¼ × 16 ¼ × 12 ¼ in. (5.7 × 41.3 × 31.1 cm)
Courtesy of the artist; Blum & Poe, Los
Angeles; and Renwick Gallery, New York

63. ***There's Always Money in the Banana
Stand*, 2010**
Ink-jet prints on watercolor paper
Dimensions variable
Courtesy of the artist; Blum & Poe, Los
Angeles; and Renwick Gallery, New York

Violet Hopkins

64. ***Crown Gold*, 2008**
Pencil on paper mounted on metal
3 ¼ × 3 ¼ in. (8.3 × 8.3 cm)
Collection of Jennifer and Manfred
Simchowitz, Los Angeles

65. ***Black Narcissus*, 2010**
Pencil and acrylic ink on paper
80 × 80 in. (203.2 × 203.2 cm)
Courtesy of the artist and Foxy
Production, New York

66. ***Inkblot 44*, 2010**
Ink on paper
19 × 25 in. (48.3 × 63.5 cm)
Courtesy of the artist and Foxy
Production, New York

67. ***Inkblot 52*, 2010**
Ink on paper
8 × 10 in. (20.3 × 25.4 cm)
Courtesy of the artist and Foxy
Production, New York

68. ***Inkblot 81*, 2010**
Ink on paper
19 × 25 in. (48.3 × 63.5 cm)
Courtesy of the artist and Foxy
Production, New York

69. ***Inkblot 93*, 2010**
Ink on paper
19 × 25 in. (48.3 × 63.5 cm)
Courtesy of the artist and Foxy
Production, New York

70. ***Inkblot 107*, 2010**
Ink on paper
12 × 18 in. (30.5 × 45.7 cm)
Courtesy of the artist and Foxy
Production, New York

71. ***Inkblot 109*, 2010**
Ink on paper
12 × 19 in. (30.5 × 48.3 cm)
Courtesy of the artist and Foxy
Production, New York

72. ***Sing Swan Song*, 2010**
Pencil on paper mounted on metal
3 ½ × 3 ½ in. (8.9 × 8.9 cm)
Courtesy of the artist and Foxy
Production, New York

Alex Israel

73. ***Property*, 2010**
Rented cinema props
Dimensions variable
Courtesy of the artist
This installation was realized with the
generous support of the San Diego
Jewish Community Foundation.

Includes the following works:

A. ***Bookend*, 2010**
Plaster
8 ¼ × 4 ¼ × 2 in. (21 × 10.8 × 5.1 cm)

B. ***Storyteller*, 2010**
Chrome, wood, and upholstery
44 × 19 ½ × 21 in. (111.8 × 49.5 × 53.3 cm)

C. ***Sex*, 2010**
Cardboard and videocassettes
10 × 15 ½ × 12 ¼ in. (25.4 × 39.4 × 31.1 cm)

D. ***Dreams*, 2010**
Tin
3 × 9 × 3 in. (7.6 × 22.9 × 7.6 cm)

E. ***Time*, 2010**
Plastic
4 × 8 × 2 in. (10.2 × 20.3 × 5.1 cm)

F. ***Desire*, 2010**
Glass and dog biscuits
14 × 7 ¾ × 7 ¾ in. (35.6 × 19.7 × 19.7 cm)

G. ***Desire*, 2010**
Ceramic
11 × 8 × 9 ½ in. (27.9 × 20.3 × 24.1 cm)

H. ***Forever*, 2010**
Velvet and brass
1 ½ × 2 × 2 ¼ in. (3.8 × 5.1 × 5.7 cm)

I. ***Remember*, 2010**
Resin
36 × 13 × 29 in. (91.4 × 33 × 73.7 cm)

J. ***Bookend*, 2010**
Plaster
8 ¼ × 4 ¼ × 2 in. (21 × 10.8 × 5.1 cm)

K. ***Island*, 2010**
Wood
30 ½ × 24 × 24 in. (77.5 × 61 × 61 cm)

L. ***Pedestal*, 2010**
Fiberglass
31 ¾ × 10 ½ × 10 ¾ in. (80.6 × 26.7 × 27.3 cm)

M. ***Diana*, 2010**
Plaster
23 ½ × 16 ¾ × 8 ¾ in. (59.7 × 42.5 × 22.2 cm)

N. ***Venus*, 2010**
Fiberglass
15 × 27 ¾ × 18 in. (38.1 × 70.5 × 45.7 cm)

O. ***Infinity*, 2010**
Mirrored glass and metal
81 × 85 × 35 ½ in. (205.7 × 215.9 × 90.2 cm)

P. ***Pacific*, 2010**
Poly-cotton fabric and polyfill
86 × 86 in. (218.4 × 218.4 cm)

Q. ***Osiris*, 2010**
Fiberglass
62 × 19 × 27 ½ in. (157.5 × 48.3 × 69.9 cm)

R. ***Infinity*, 2010**
Mirrored glass and metal
81 × 85 × 35 ½ in. (205.7 × 215.9 × 90.2 cm)

S. ***Magic*, 2010**
Felt
5 ½ × 11 × 8 in. (14 × 27.9 × 20.3 cm)

T. ***Stump*, 2010**
Wood
20 × 13 ½ × 13 ½ in. (50.8 × 34.3 × 34.3 cm)

Glenna Jennings

74. ***Ellie*, 2007**
From the series Inheritance
Archival pigment print
37 × 47 in. (94 × 119.4 cm)
Courtesy of the artist and Luis De Jesus
Los Angeles

75. ***Fang*, 2007**
From the series Inheritance
Archival pigment print
37 × 47 in. (94 × 119.4 cm)
Courtesy of the artist and Luis De Jesus
Los Angeles

76. ***Gradual transition from one world to
another*, 2008**
From the series Raskolnikov
Archival pigment print
20 × 30 in. (50.8 × 76.2 cm)
Courtesy of the artist and Luis De Jesus
Los Angeles

77. ***Only to live, to live, and live!* 2008**
From the series Raskolnikov
Archival pigment print
16 × 20 in. (40.6 × 50.8 cm)
Courtesy of the artist and Luis De Jesus
Los Angeles

78. *She forgot what was important and fastened on little things*, 2008
From the series Raskolnikov
Digital pigment print
20 × 29 ½ in. (50.8 × 74.9 cm)
Museum of Contemporary Art San Diego,
Museum purchase

79. *crossing sides*, 2010
From the series Likely Stories and other
sides
Archival ink-jet transparency, wood,
Plexiglas, acetate, motor, fluorescent
lights, and vinyl text
30 × 45 × 3 n. (76.2 × 114.3 × 7.6 cm)
Courtesy of the artist and Luis De Jesus
Los Angeles

80. *in bathroom*, 2010
From the series Likely Stories and other
sides
Archival inkjet transparency, wood,
Plexiglas, fluorescent lights, and vinyl text
12 × 20 × 2 ¼ in. (30.5 × 50.8 × 5.7 cm)
Courtesy of the artist and Luis De Jesus
Los Angeles

Barry Macgregor Johnston

81. *Psychic Curfew*, 2010
Mixed-media installation
Dimensions variable
Courtesy of the artist and Overduin and
Kite, Los Angeles

Vishal Jugdeo

82. *Thought Composition with Model of the World*, 2010
Mixed-media sculpture: wood, cinderblocks,
unfired clay and self-hardening clay, duct
tape, door, kettle, garbage bag, silk flowers,
paper, plasma flat-screen TV, speakers, HD
video players and synchronizer, and stereo
receiver; high-definition video, four-channel
sound; video written, directed, and edited
by Vishal Jugdeo; performers Vishal Jugdeo
and William Wright; director of photography
AJ Wedding
Video: 8:35 min.; installation: 144 × 144 in.
(365.8 × 365.8 cm), variable
Courtesy of the artist and Thomas Solomon
Gallery, Los Angeles

Stanya Kahn

83. *It's Cool, I'm Good*, 2010
Video, color, 5.1 surround sound
35:02 min.
Courtesy of the artist and Susanne
Vielmetter Los Angeles Projects

Andy Kolar

84. *Finite*, 2009
Oil on canvas
51 × 45 in. (129.5 × 144.3 cm)
Collection of Crowell & Moring LLP, Irvine,
California

85. *Six Deep*, 2009
Oil on canvas
81 × 132 in. (205.7 × 335.3 cm)
Courtesy of the artist and Carl Berg
Projects, Los Angeles

86. *caída*, 2010
Oil on canvas
135 × 276 in. (342.9 × 701 cm)
Courtesy of the artist
This painting was realized through a 2010
California Biennial residency supported
by the Nimoy Foundation.

87. *Tallie*, 2010
Acrylic paint on cardboard
75 × 34 ¾ × 26 in. (190.5 × 88.3 × 66 cm)
Courtesy of the artist and Carl Berg
Projects, Los Angeles

Jennifer Locke

88. *Black/White (Glue)*, 2009
Live sculptural action culminating in
a looping video triptych
264:27 min.
Courtesy of the artist

89. *Black/White (Ink)*, 2009
Live sculptural action culminating in
a looping video triptych
205:52 min.
Courtesy of the artist

90. *Black/White (Plaster)*, 2009
Live sculptural action culminating in
a looping video triptych
188:29 min.
Courtesy of the artist

Los Angeles Urban Rangers

91. *Public Access 101: Malibu Public Beaches*, 2007–10
Video, color, sound
5:00 min.
Courtesy of Los Angeles Urban Rangers

92. *Portable Ranger Station*, 2009–10
Mixed media with ephemera
14 × 20 × 20 in. (35.6 × 50.8 × 50.8 cm)
folded; 53 ¾ × 38 ½ × 22 in. (136.5 × 97.8
× 55.9 cm) unfolded
Courtesy of Los Angeles Urban Rangers

93. *Public Access 101: Downtown L.A.*, 2011
An urban hike designed to facilitate
exploration and understanding of one of
America's most forgotten downtowns.
This event was conducted on January
29, 2011, as part of a California Biennial
residency supported by the Nimoy
Foundation.

Tom Mueske

94. *Analytics I*, 2010
Marker and ink on museum board
25 × 26 in. (63.5 × 66 cm)
Courtesy of the artist and Haines Gallery,
San Francisco

95. *Analytics II*, 2010
Marker and ink on museum board
17 × 13 in. (43.2 × 33 cm)
Courtesy of the artist and Haines Gallery,
San Francisco

96. *Analytics III*, 2010
Marker and ink on museum board
17 × 13 in. (43.2 × 33 cm)
Courtesy of the artist and Haines Gallery,
San Francisco

97. *Analytics IV*, 2010
Marker and ink on museum board
17 × 13 in. (43.2 × 33 cm)
Courtesy of the artist and Haines Gallery,
San Francisco

98. *Analytics V*, 2010
Marker and ink on museum board
27 × 19 ½ in. (68.6 × 48.9 cm)
Courtesy of the artist and Haines Gallery,
San Francisco

99. *Analytics VI*, 2010
Marker and ink on museum board
18 × 17 ¾ in. (45.7 × 45.1 cm)
Courtesy of the artist and Haines Gallery,
San Francisco

100. *Analytics VII*, 2010
Marker and ink on museum board
21 × 17 ¾ in. (53.3 × 45.1 cm)
Courtesy of the artist and Haines Gallery,
San Francisco

101. **Untitled**, 2010
Marker and ink on museum board
40 × 32 in. (101.6 × 81.3 cm)
Courtesy of the artist and Haines Gallery,
San Francisco

Tucker Nichols

102. Untitled, 2010
Mixed media on pedestal
50 × 24 × 16 in. (127 × 61 × 40.6 cm)
Courtesy of the artist and ZieherSmith
Gallery, New York

103. Untitled, 2010
Enamel on vinyl banner
120 × 48 in. (304.8 × 121.9 cm)
Courtesy of the artist and ZieherSmith
Gallery, New York

104. Untitled, 2010
Enamel on vinyl banner
48 × 120 in. (121.9 × 304.8 cm)
Courtesy of the artist and ZieherSmith
Gallery, New York

Camilo Ontiveros

105. *Free Entry (California Biennial Law)*,
2010
Wall text (artist's project proposal and
the Orange County Museum of Art's
response)
Dimensions variable
Courtesy of the artist

Nikki Pressley

106. *Requiem*, **2010**
Graphite on paper
44 × 30 in. (111.8 × 76.2 cm)
Courtesy of the artist

107. Untitled, 2010
Acrylic base coat, gold leaf, dirt, and ash
on paper
44 × 30 in. (111.8 × 76.2 cm)
Courtesy of the artist

108. *Word*, **2010**
Graphite and embossing on paper
50 × 38 in. (127 × 96.5 cm)
Courtesy of the artist

Andy Ralph

109. *Reclining Lawn Chair*, **2010**
One-inch aluminum pipe, aluminum
hardware, and lawn chair webbing
55 ½ × 139 × 87 in. (141 × 353.1 × 221 cm)
Courtesy of the artist and Luis De Jesus
Los Angeles

110. *Trash Clan*, **2010**
32-gallon Brute trash cans, Rubbermaid
Brute dollies, Douglas fir two-by-fours,
astable-DC motor control boards, DC
gear head motors, II.IV Li-Polymer
batteries, universal smart chargers
Five parts: 67 ½ × 52 ½ in. (171.5 × 133.4
cm), 67 ¼ × 49 in. (170.8 × 124.5 cm), 70
× 49 in. (177.8 × 124.5 cm), 66 ½ × 43 in.
(168.9 × 109.2 cm), 66 × 39 ½ in.
(167.6 × 100.3 cm)
Courtesy of the artist and Luis De Jesus
Los Angeles

Will Rogan

111. Untitled, 2009
From the series Other Worlds
Gelatin silver print
8 × 10 in. (20.3 × 25.4 cm)
Miller Meigs Collection, Corvallis,
Oregon; courtesy of Laurel Gitlen,
New York

112. Untitled, 2009
From the series Other Worlds
Gelatin silver print
8 × 10 in. (20.3 × 25.4 cm)
Miller Meigs Collection, Corvallis,
Oregon; courtesy of Laurel Gitlen,
New York

113. Untitled, 2009
From the series Other Worlds
Gelatin silver print
8 × 10 in. (20.3 × 25.4 cm)
Miller Meigs Collection, Corvallis,
Oregon; courtesy of Laurel Gitlen,
New York

114. Untitled, 2009
From the series Other Worlds
Gelatin silver print
8 × 10 in. (20.3 × 25.4 cm)
Miller Meigs Collection, Corvallis,
Oregon; courtesy of Laurel Gitlen,
New York

115. Untitled, 2009
From the series Other Worlds
Gelatin silver print
8 × 10 in. (20.3 × 25.4 cm)
Miller Meigs Collection, Corvallis,
Oregon; courtesy of Laurel Gitlen,
New York

116. Untitled, 2009
From the series Other Worlds
Gelatin silver print
8 × 10 in. (20.3 × 25.4 cm)
Miller Meigs Collection, Corvallis,
Oregon; courtesy of Laurel Gitlen,
New York

117. Untitled, 2009
From the series Other Worlds
Gelatin silver print
8 × 10 in. (20.3 × 25.4 cm)
Courtesy of the artist; Laurel Gitlen, New
York; and Altman Siegel, San Francisco

118. Untitled, 2009
From the series Other Worlds
Gelatin silver print
8 × 10 in. (20.3 × 25.4 cm)
Courtesy of the artist; Laurel Gitlen, New
York; and Altman Siegel, San Francisco

119. Untitled, 2009
From the series Other Worlds
Gelatin silver print
8 × 10 in. (20.3 × 25.4 cm)
Courtesy of the artist; Laurel Gitlen, New
York; and Altman Siegel, San Francisco

120. *Mediums 3*, **2010**
Wood, oil paint, and book pages
Dimensions variable, as shown: 5 ¼ ×
6 ¾ × 1 ¾ in. (13.3 × 17.1 × 4.4 cm)
Courtesy of the artist; Laurel Gitlen, New
York; and Altman Siegel, San Francisco

Paul Schiek

121. *see you in the next one (have a good
time)*, **2007**
Chromogenic print
Edition of 7
14 × 11 in. (35.6 × 27.9 cm)
Courtesy of Stephen Wirtz Gallery,
San Francisco

122. *similar to a baptism*, **2007**
Chromogenic print
Edition of 5
30 × 40 in. (76.2 × 101.6 cm)
Courtesy of Stephen Wirtz Gallery,
San Francisco

123. *a single perfect moment*, **2007**
Chromogenic print
Edition of 7
14 × 11 in. (35.6 × 27.9 cm)
Courtesy of Stephen Wirtz Gallery,
San Francisco

124. Untitled, 2010
Ceramic statue on painted pallet
15 ¼ × 35 ¼ × 17 in. (38.7 × 89.5 ×
43.2 cm)
Courtesy of Stephen Wirtz Gallery,
San Francisco

Taravat Talepasand

125. *Angel of Iran (Dirty 50cc)*, **1982–2010**
Enamel on MB5 motorcycle
45 × 66 × 22 in. (114.3 × 167.6 × 55.9 cm)
Courtesy of the artist and Marx &
Zavattero, San Francisco

126. *The Censored Garden*, **2008**
Egg tempera and gold leaf on linen
44 × 30 in. (111.8 × 76.2 cm)
Collection of Michael Frank Black,
Scottsdale, Arizona

127. *Hey Haji*, **2010**
Graphite on paper
40 × 30 in. (101.6 × 76.2 cm)
Courtesy of the artist and Marx &
Zavattero, San Francisco

Wu Tsang

128. *Damelo Todo (Give Me Everything)*,
2010
HD video, color, sound
20:07 min.
Courtesy of the artist

Zlatan Vukosavljevic

129. *DuckBunny Chamber*, **2010**
Aluminum, aluminum plate, foil, tape,
and slippers
96 × 204 × 96 in. (243.8 × 518.2 × 243.8 cm)
Courtesy of the artist

Nina Waisman

130. *Between Bodies/Tijuana*, **2008–10**
First showing 2008; new site-specific
iteration for OCMA (with new sound),
2010
Site-specific mixed media, computer,
software, electronics, audio equipment
With Pure Data programming by Marius
Schebella
Runs continuously, interaction times vary
Dimensions variable
Courtesy of the artist

Flora Wiegmann

131. *Wandering (Detail)*, **2010**
Thirteen site-specific dance
performances at the Orange County
Museum of Art
60 min. each
Courtesy of the artist

132. *Wandering (Still)*, **2010**
16mm film transferred to digital video,
color, sound
Sound design by Steve Roden
Edition of 3 with 2 AP
Infinite loop
Courtesy of the artist

Allison Wiese

133. *Untitled (Awning)*, **2010**
Aluminum and canvas
48 × 336 × 48 in. (121.9 × 853.4 × 121.9 cm)
Courtesy of the artist

Lisa Williamson

134. *As a Beer Mat and Cutting Board*, **2010**
Acrylic on linen
70 × 57 ½ in. (177.8 × 146.1 cm)
Courtesy of the artist and Shane
Campbell Gallery, Chicago

135. *Diagram*, **2010**
Photocopies
Unlimited edition
17 × 11 in. (43.2 × 27.9 cm)
Courtesy of the artist and Shane
Campbell Gallery, Chicago

136. *Double Lapel with a Visible Seam, 2010*
Acrylic on photograph
24 × 17 ¼ in. (61 × 43.8 cm)
Courtesy of the artist and Shane
Campbell Gallery, Chicago

137. *Peg Legs and Club Feet (Props)*, **2010**
Wood, acrylic, aluminum, and enamel
Feet: 5 ¼ × 3 ½ × 3 ½ in. (13.3 × 8.9 ×
8.9 cm) each
Legs: 60 × ½ in. (152.4 × 1.3 cm); 58 × ½
in. (147.3 × 1.3 cm)
Courtesy of the artist and Shane
Campbell Gallery, Chicago

138. *Shelf Painting/A Model Situation Has
Five Parts*, **2010**
Acrylic on linen, wood, and
miscellaneous objects
Painting: 24 × 18 × 1 ¾ in. (61 × 45.7 ×
4.4 cm)
Shelf: 4 × 54 × 9 in. (10.2 × 137.2 × 22.9 cm)
Model: 7 ½ × 13 × 7 in. (19.1 × 33 × 17.8 cm)
Courtesy of the artist and Shane
Campbell Gallery, Chicago

139. *There's Room for Your Head in the
Corner*, **2010**
Acrylic on linen
31 ¾ × 18 ½ in. (80.6 × 47 cm)
Courtesy of the artist and Shane
Campbell Gallery, Chicago

David Wilson

140. *Southern Mountain (Valverde)*, **2006**
Charcoal on board
10 × 12 in. (25.4 × 30.5 cm)
Courtesy of the artist

141. **Assorted ephemera, 2006–10**
Dimensions variable
Courtesy of the artist

142. *Day*, **2007**
Watercolor and pencil on found paper
8 ¼ × 39 in. (21 × 99.1 cm)
Courtesy of the artist

143. *Mount Diablo*, **2007**
Charcoal pencil on found paper
6 × 8 ¼ in. (15.2 × 21 cm)
Courtesy of the artist

144. *Ocean Beach Dune*, **2007**
Charcoal pencil on found paper
7 ¼ × 9 ¾ in. (18.4 × 24.8 cm)
Courtesy of the artist

145. *Sibley Canyon*, **2007**
Charcoal pencil on paper
6 × 7 ½ in. (15.2 × 19.1 cm)
Courtesy of the artist

146. *Eastern Mountains*, **2008**
Charcoal on board
10 × 20 ¼ in. (25.4 × 51.4 cm)
Courtesy of the artist

147. *December 7*, **2009**
Watercolor and pencil on found paper
9 × 6 in. (22.9 × 15.2 cm)
Courtesy of the artist

148. *December 8 Last Quarter*, **2009**
Watercolor and pencil on found paper
9 × 6 in. (22.9 × 15.2 cm)
Courtesy of the artist

149. *December 11 Rain*, **2009**
Watercolor on found paper
10 ½ × 7 ¼ in. (26.7 × 18.4 cm)
Courtesy of the artist

150. *December 17 No Moon*, **2009**
Watercolor on found paper
9 ¼ × 7 ¾ in. (23.5 × 19.7 cm)
Courtesy of the artist

151. *Fort Walking Instructions*, **2009**
Charcoal pencil on paper
10 panels, 8 ¼ × 4 in. (21 × 10.2 cm) each
Courtesy of the artist

152. *Shell*, **2009**
Sumi ink on found paper
1 ¾ × 1 ¾ in. (4.4 × 4.4 cm)
Courtesy of the artist

153. *Shell*, 2009
Sumi ink on found paper
1 ¾ × 1 ¾ in. (4.4 × 4.4 cm)
Courtesy of the artist

154. *Shell*, 2009
Sumi ink on found paper
3 ¾ × 3 in. (9.5 × 7.6 cm)
Courtesy of the artist

155. *Eucalyptus Grove Walking Directions*,
2010
Charcoal pencil on paper
10 panels, 8 ¼ × 4 in. (21 × 10.2 cm) each
Courtesy of the artist

156. *Walk to the Place (Takeaway Map)*,
2010
Photocopies
17 × 11 in. (43.2 × 27.9 cm)
Courtesy of the artist

Patrick Wilson

157. *Insomniac*, 2010
Acrylic on canvas
72 × 67 in. (182.9 × 170.2 cm)
Courtesy of the artist and Susanne
Vielmetter Los Angeles Projects

158. *Juliet*, 2010
Acrylic on canvas
17 × 17 in. (43.2 × 43.2 cm)
Courtesy of the artist and Marx &
Zavattero, San Francisco

159. *Romeo*, 2010
Acrylic on canvas
17 × 17 in. (43.2 × 43.2 cm)
Courtesy of the artist and Susanne
Vielmetter Los Angeles Projects

160. *Shape to the Unseen*, 2010
Acrylic on canvas
72 × 67 in. (182.9 × 170.2 cm)
Courtesy of the artist and Marx &
Zavattero, San Francisco

John Zurier

161. *Muuratsalo 3*, 2009
Oil on linen
84 × 58 in. (213.4 × 147.3 cm)
Courtesy of the artist and Gallery Paule
Anglim, San Francisco

162. *The Future of Ice*, 2010
Distemper on linen
108 × 75 in. (274.3 × 190.5 cm)
Courtesy of the artist and Peter Blum
Gallery, New York

163. *Night 46 (Kurashiki)*, 2010
Distemper on linen
30 × 20 in. (76.2 × 50.8 cm)
Courtesy of the artist and Peter Blum
Gallery, New York

164. *Night 49 (Ogata Kenzan)*, 2010
Distemper on linen
30 × 20 in. (76.2 × 50.8 cm)
Collection Goya Contemporary; courtesy
of Peter Blum Gallery, New York

Reproduction Credits

Unless otherwise noted, all photographs
are by Joshua White, J.W. Pictures Inc., Los
Angeles. Numbers refer to the page on which
an image appears.

Kelly Akashi: 129 (bottom)
Alissa Anderson: 189 (middle)
Kelly Barrie: 113 (bottom)
Charles Bergquist: 148 (bottom right), 149
©Gil Blank: 24, 26–27
Amanda Boyer: 64 (top right)
Marco Cisneros: 64 (top left, middle left)
Ian Cuevas: 180 (top)
Courtesy gallery@CALIT2: 173 (bottom)
©Katy Grannan: 78, 80, 81
Courtesy of Honor Fraser Gallery;
    photograph by William Nettles: 84
Calvin Lee: 142, 144 (bottom)
Terri Loewenthal: 189 (bottom)
Peter Macchia: 194, 196, 197
William Nettles: 82, 85
Robert Rooks: 109
Jessica Skloven: 32
Lee Thompson: 182, 184 (bottom)
Juan Thorp: 189 top
Devon Tsuno: 64 (bottom left), 64 (middle
    right)
Lindsay Upson Photography: 160
Chivan Wang: 38, 44, 47 (bottom right)
Robert Wedemeyer: 54
Colin Young-Wolff: 22 (top), 37, 47 (bottom
    left), 64 (bottom right), 176, 177 (top)

Contributors

Sarah C. Bancroft joined the Orange County Museum of Art as curator in May 2008. In addition to the 2010 California Biennial, Bancroft is organizing the much-anticipated exhibition *Richard Diebenkorn: The Ocean Park Series*, as well as *Two Schools of Cool*, both of which will open in fall 2011. In 2009 she curated *Video Work by Gao Shiquang and Chen Qiulin* at OCMA as part of the Ancient Paths, Modern Voices China Festival, organized by Carnegie Hall and the Segerstrom Center for the Arts, and she coordinated OCMA's presentation of the exhibition *Carlos Amorales: Discarded Spider*. Bancroft previously worked at the Solomon R. Guggenheim Museum in New York, where she cocurated *James Rosenquist: A Retrospective* (2003) with the late, great Walter Hopps and coordinated a masterpiece exhibition from the permanent collection that traveled to Rome and Tokyo. Bancroft received her MA in the history of art from the Courtauld Institute of Art in London in 2000. Just prior to moving to Orange County, she spent six months traveling from Stockholm to Rome conducting PhD research pertaining to the tour of James Rosenquist's monumental painting *F-111* through Europe in the mid-1960s. Her area of specialization is American art from the 1950s to the present.

Anna Brouwer, publications manager, joined the Orange County Museum of Art in 2007 to coordinate the exhibition *Birth of the Cool: California Art, Design, and Culture at Midcentury* and its catalog. Prior to moving to the West Coast, she was a specialist in twentieth-century design at Phillips de Pury & Company in New York. She received her BA from Swarthmore College and an MFA from the School of the Art Institute of Chicago.

Chloë Flores is a writer and curator based in Los Angeles. She is currently a candidate in the Master of Public Art Studies Program at the University of Southern California's Roski School of Fine Arts, investigating art and curatorial practices in the public sphere. She has contributed texts to numerous publications, including the catalog for the J. Paul Getty Museum's exhibition *California Video* and for Los Angeles Contemporary Exhibitions (LACE).

Katherine Lukacher is a graduate of Vassar College, where she majored in art history. She has studied archaeology with the Cornell University program in Torano di Borgorose, Italy, and art history at the Hermitage in Saint Petersburg, Russia, supplementing her education with internships at Christie's Auction House and the Robin Rice Gallery in New York City. At the Orange County Museum of Art, she provided research and administrative support for the 2010 California Biennial.

Stacie Martinez is a curatorial associate at the Orange County Museum of Art. A former marketing manager and a freelance graphic designer, she holds a BS in marketing and a BA in graphic design. She is currently a master's degree candidate in art history at California State University, Long Beach, and is writing her master's thesis on violence and the sacred in the works of French artist Annette Messager.

Karen Moss is adjunct curator at the Orange County Museum of Art, where she is currently working on *State of Mind: New California Art, c. 1970*, which opens at OCMA in fall 2011. As OCMA's former deputy director of exhibitions and programs, Moss organized numerous exhibitions, including *15 Minutes of Fame: Portraits from Ansel Adams to Andy Warhol* (2010); *Illumination: The Paintings of Georgia O'Keeffe, Agnes Pelton, Agnes Martin, and Florence Pierce* (2009); *Disorderly Conduct: Recent Art in Tumultuous Times* (2008); and *Art since the 1960s: California Experiments* (2007–8); she was also cocurator of the 2006 California Biennial. She teaches in the graduate programs at Otis College of Art and Design and the University of Southern California's Roski School of Fine Arts.

Grant Wahlquist (MA, theology and art, Fuller Theological Seminary; MA, religious studies, University of Nottingham, England; JD candidate, University of Southern California) is a lifelong Californian. Formerly a curatorial assistant at the Orange County Museum of Art, he has contributed to *Riviera*, *Art Ltd*, and *Aspect: The Chronicle of New Media Art*, as well as to the *Journal of Aesthetics and Protest* in conjunction with the 2008 California Biennial.